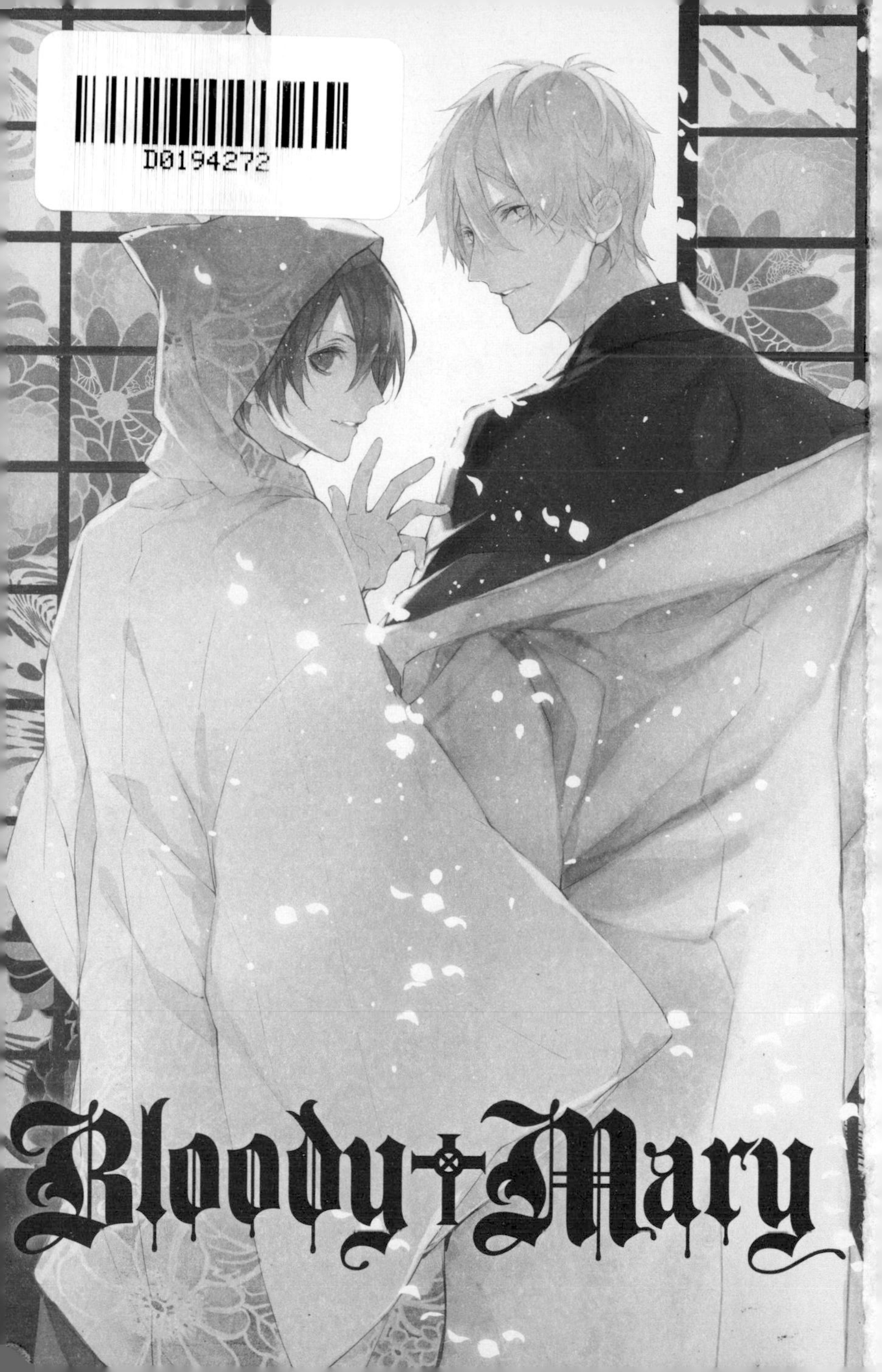
Bloody+Mary

# Bloody+Mary

## 10 contents

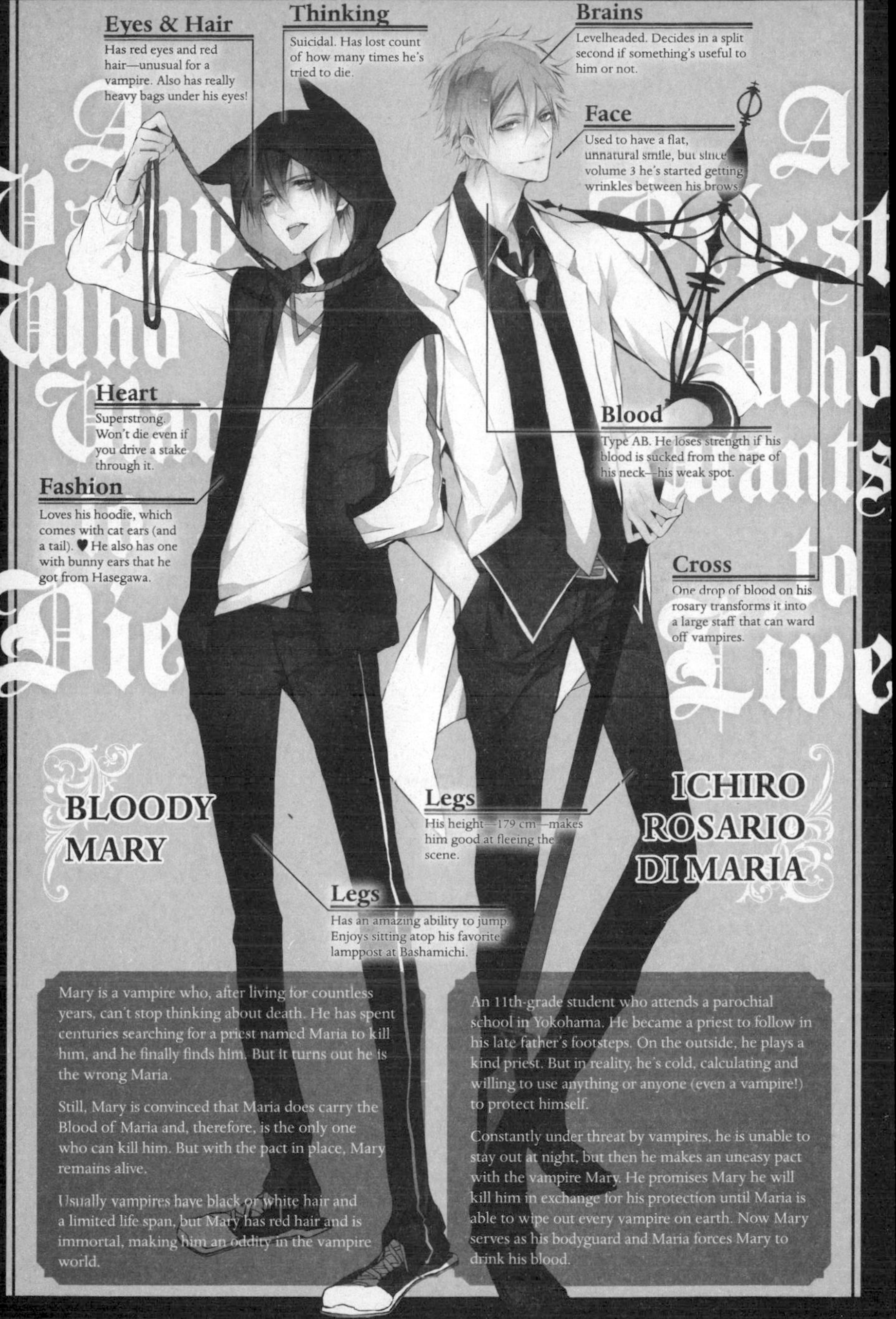
Eyes & Hair
Has red eyes and red hair—unusual for a vampire. Also has really heavy bags under his eyes!
Thinking
Suicidal. Has lost count of how many times he's tried to die.
Brains
Levelheaded. Decides in a split second if something's useful to him or not.
Face
Used to have a flat, unnatural smile, but since volume 3 he's started getting wrinkles between his brows.
Heart
Superstrong. Won't die even if you drive a stake through it.
Blood
Type AB. He loses strength if his blood is sucked from the nape of his neck—his weak spot.
Fashion
Loves his hoodie, which comes with cat ears (and a tail). ♥ He also has one with bunny ears that he got from Hasegawa.
Cross
One drop of blood on his rosary transforms it into a large staff that can ward off vampires.
BLOODY MARY
Legs
His height—179 cm—makes him good at fleeing the scene.
ICHIRO ROSARIO DI MARIA
Legs
Has an amazing ability to jump. Enjoys sitting atop his favorite lamppost at Bashamichi.

Mary is a vampire who, after living for countless years, can't stop thinking about death. He has spent centuries searching for a priest named Maria to kill him, and he finally finds him. But it turns out he is the wrong Maria.

Still, Mary is convinced that Maria does carry the Blood of Maria and, therefore, is the only one who can kill him. But with the pact in place, Mary remains alive.

Usually vampires have black or white hair and a limited life span, but Mary has red hair and is immortal, making him an oddity in the vampire world.

An 11th-grade student who attends a parochial school in Yokohama. He became a priest to follow in his late father's footsteps. On the outside, he plays a kind priest. But in reality, he's cold, calculating and willing to use anything or anyone (even a vampire!) to protect himself.

Constantly under threat by vampires, he is unable to stay out at night, but then he makes an uneasy pact with the vampire Mary. He promises Mary he will kill him in exchange for his protection until Maria is able to wipe out every vampire on earth. Now Mary serves as his bodyguard and Maria forces Mary to drink his blood.

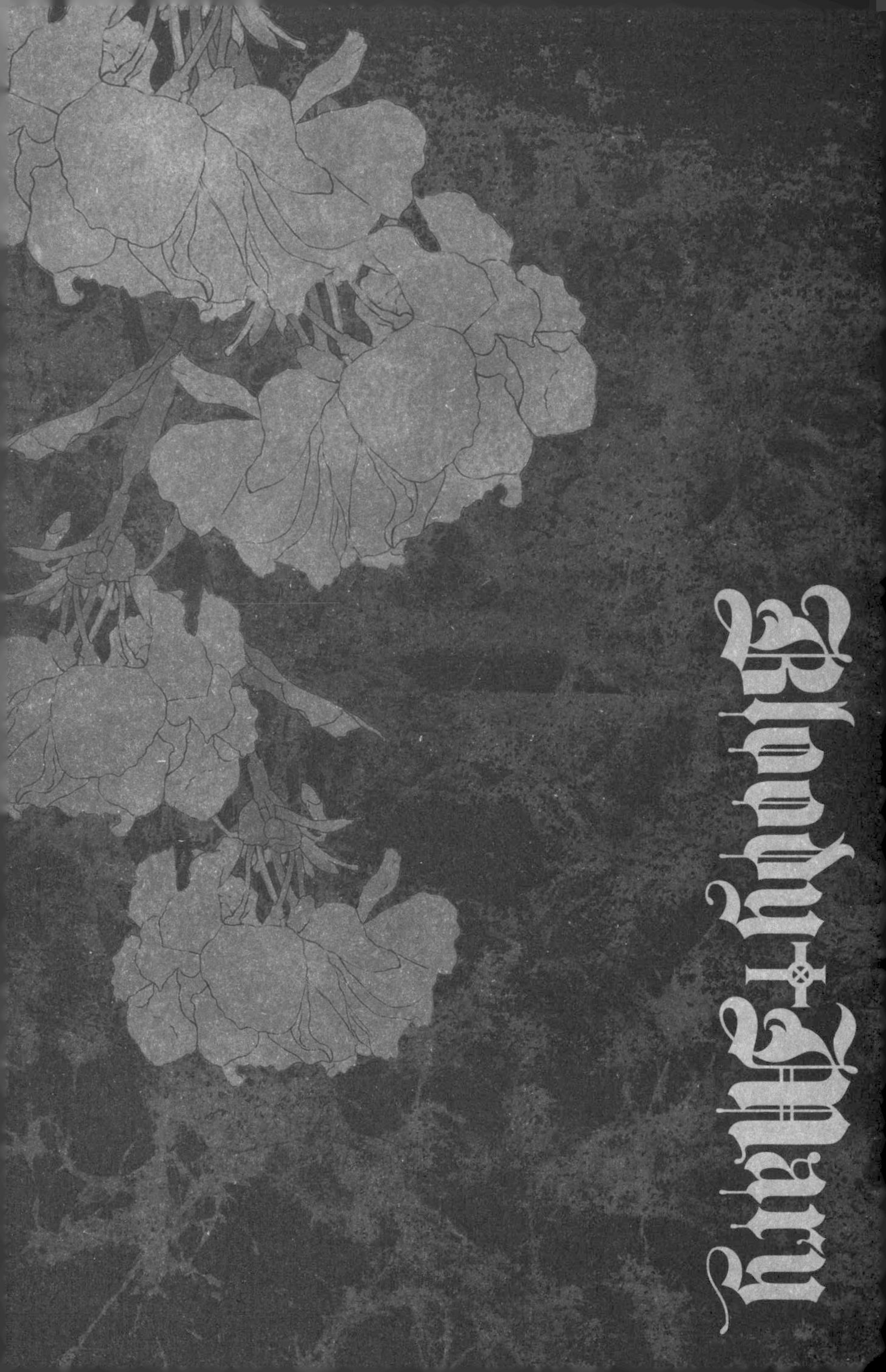
Black Butler

# BLOOD ✦ 37 The Whereabouts of Goodbye

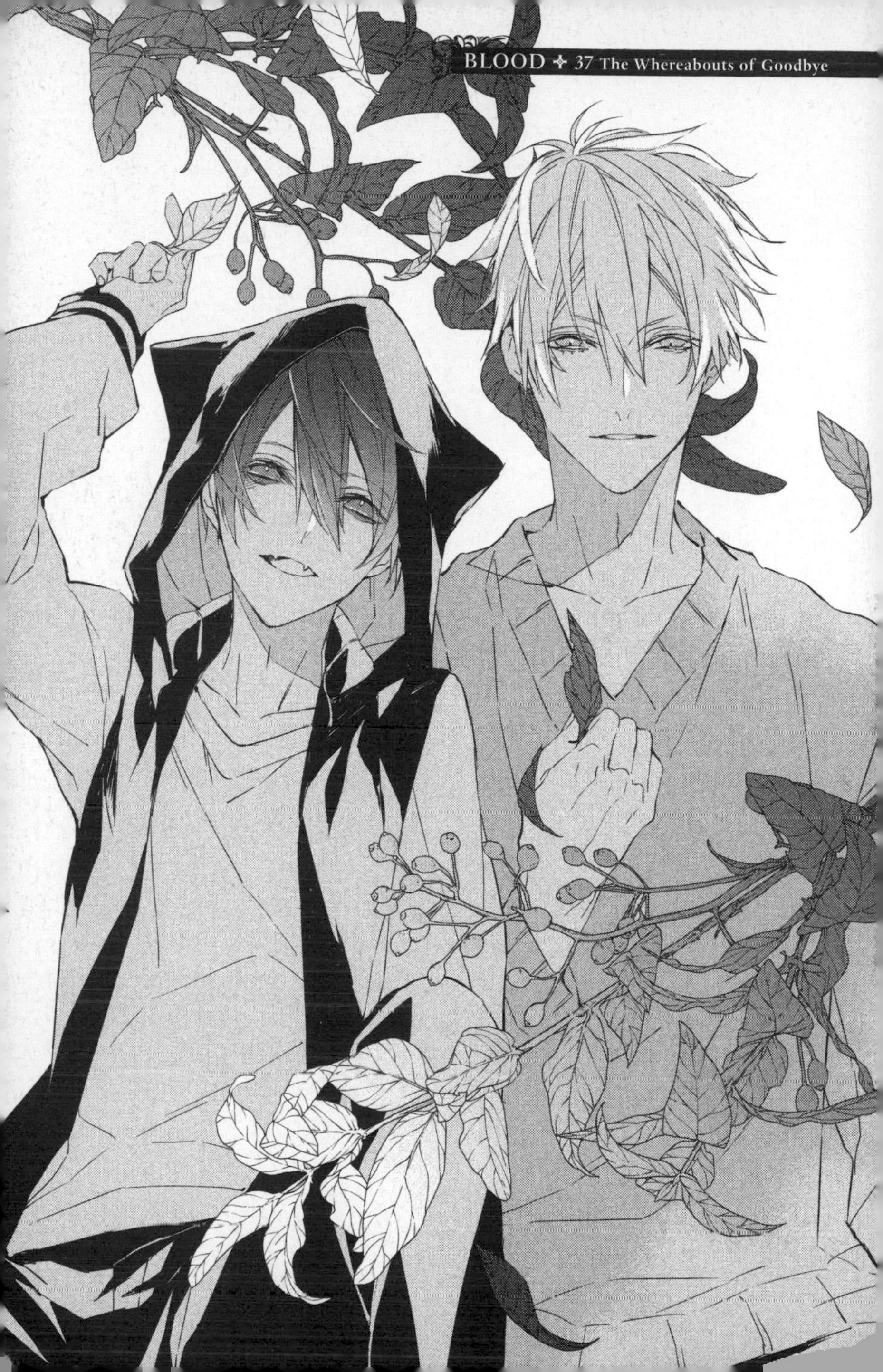

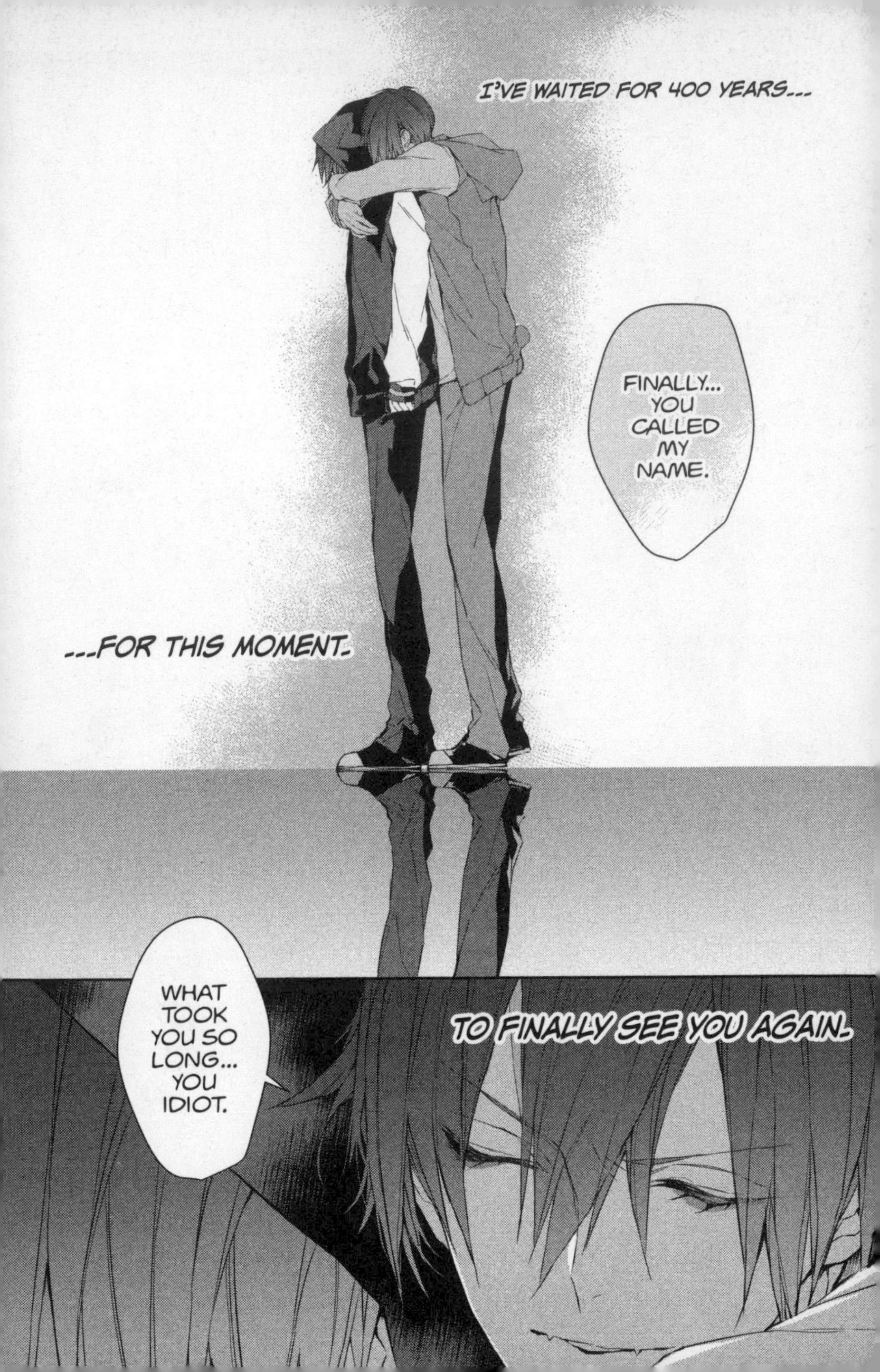
I'VE WAITED FOR 400 YEARS...
FINALLY... YOU CALLED MY NAME.
...FOR THIS MOMENT.
TO FINALLY SEE YOU AGAIN.
WHAT TOOK YOU SO LONG... YOU IDIOT.

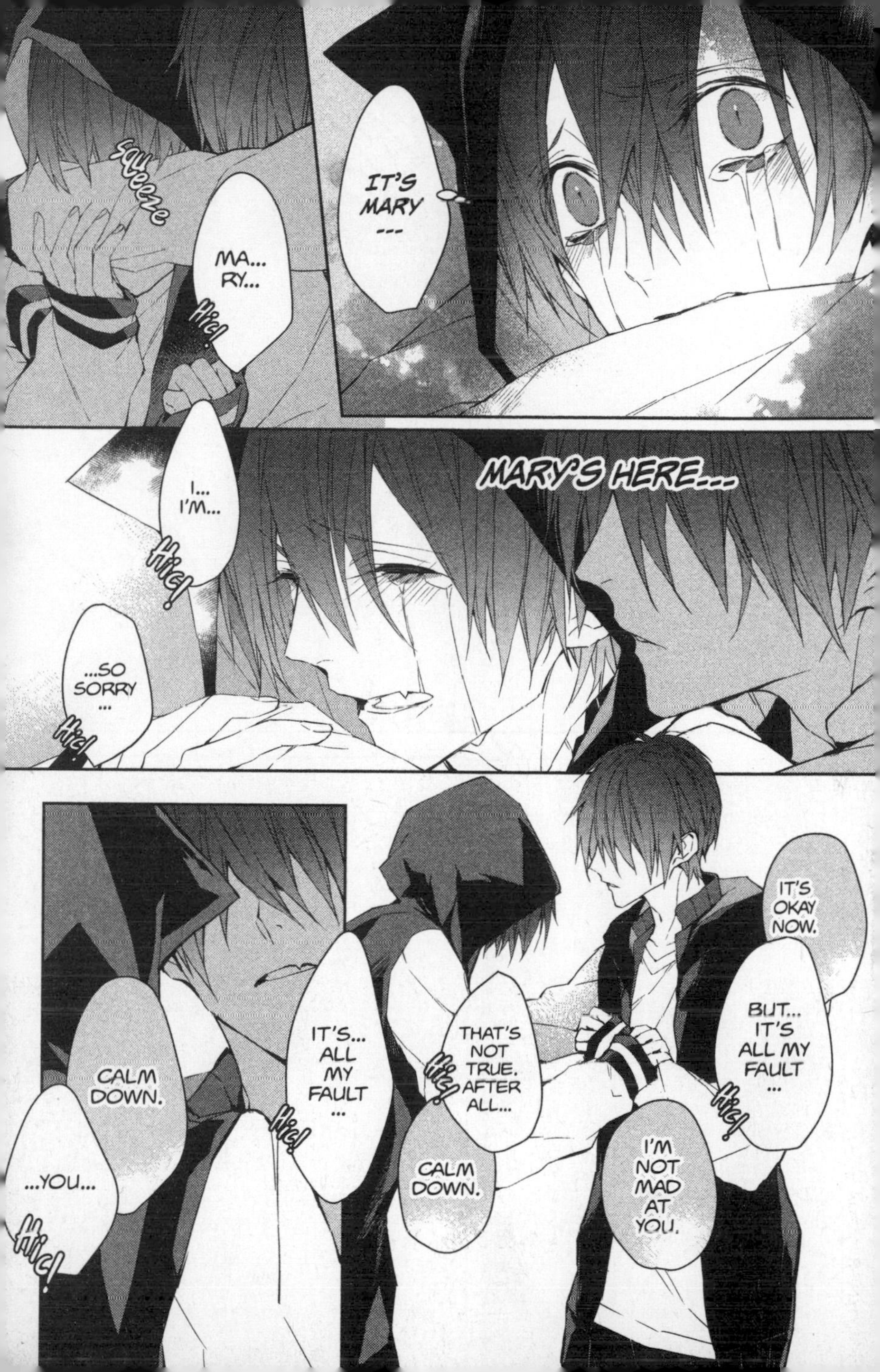
IT'S MARY ---
squeeze
MA... RY...
Hic!
MARY'S HERE...
I... I'M...
Hic!
...SO SORRY...
Hic!
IT'S OKAY NOW.
BUT... IT'S ALL MY FAULT...
Hic!
THAT'S NOT TRUE. AFTER ALL...
Hic!
I'M NOT MAD AT YOU.
CALM DOWN.
IT'S... ALL MY FAULT...
Hic!
CALM DOWN.
...YOU...
Hic!

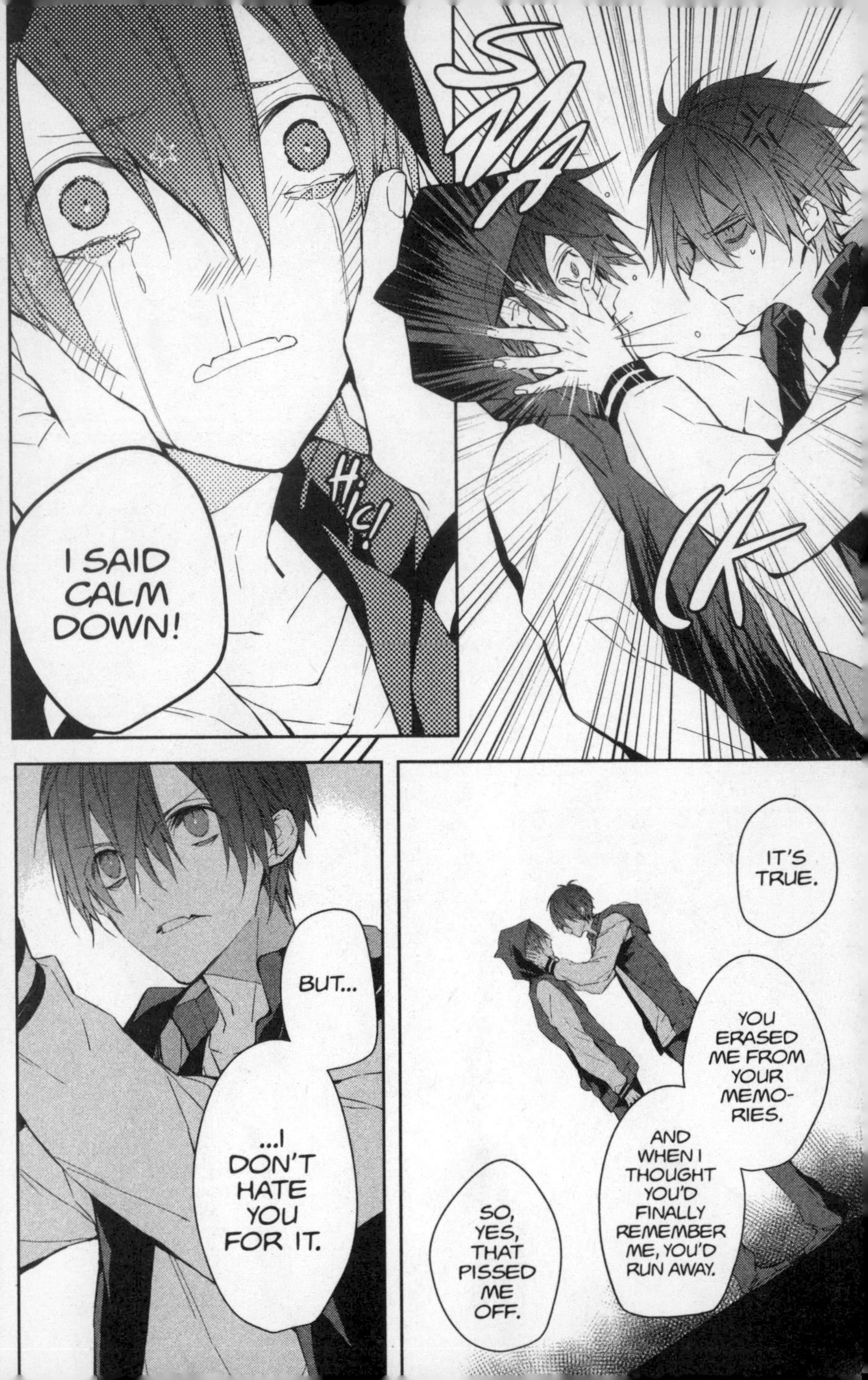
SMACK
Hic!
I SAID CALM DOWN!
IT'S TRUE.
YOU ERASED ME FROM YOUR MEMORIES.
AND WHEN I THOUGHT YOU'D FINALLY REMEMBER ME, YOU'D RUN AWAY.
SO, YES, THAT PISSED ME OFF.
BUT...
...I DON'T HATE YOU FOR IT.

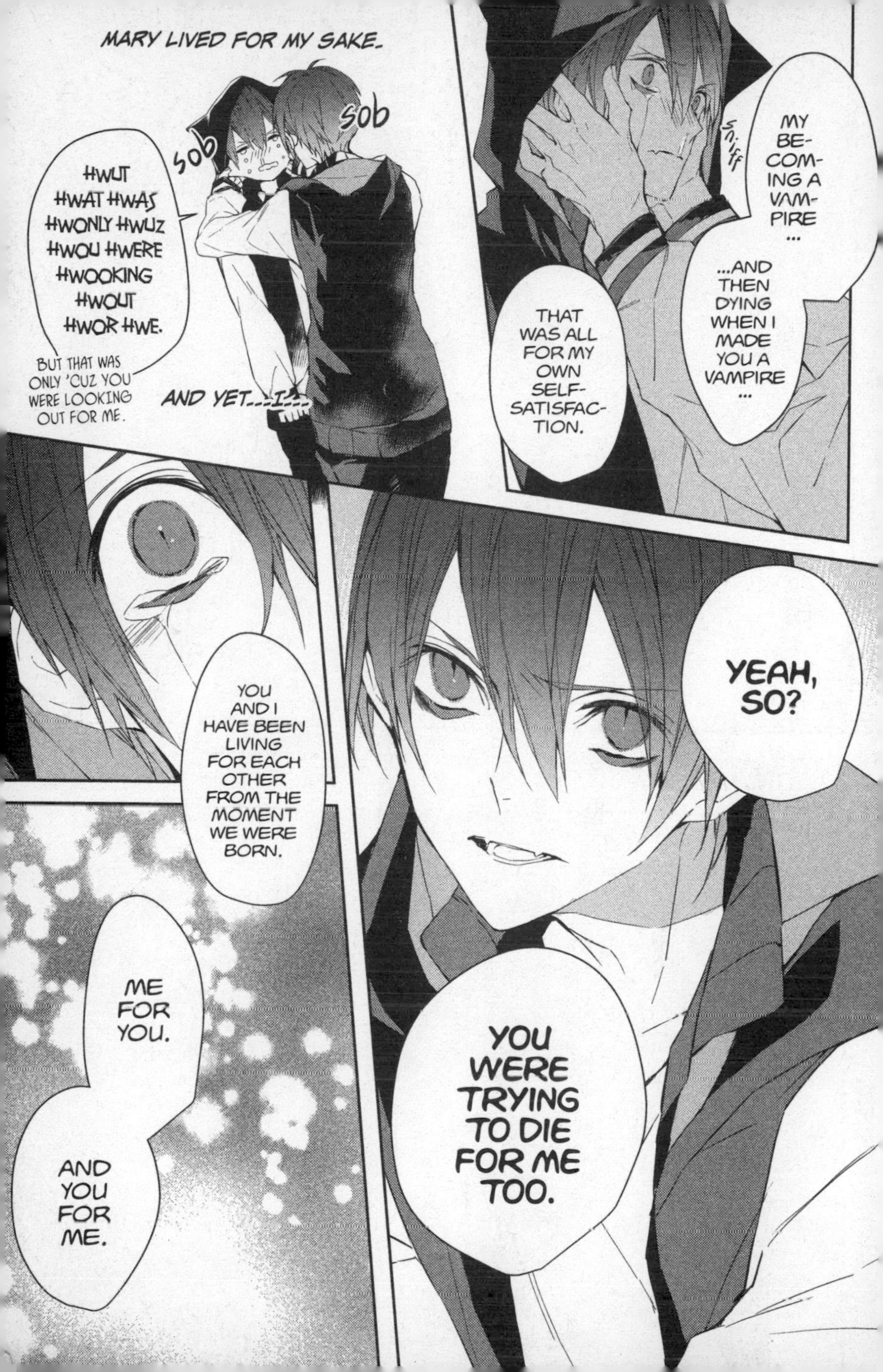
MY BE-COM-ING A VAM-PIRE...
sniff
...AND THEN DYING WHEN I MADE YOU A VAMPIRE...
THAT WAS ALL FOR MY OWN SELF-SATISFAC-TION.
MARY LIVED FOR MY SAKE.
sob
sob
HWUT HWAT HWAS HWONLY HWUZ HWOU HWERE HWOOKING HWOUT HWOR HWE.
BUT THAT WAS ONLY 'CUZ YOU WERE LOOKING OUT FOR ME.
AND YET...I...
YEAH, SO?
YOU WERE TRYING TO DIE FOR ME TOO.
YOU AND I HAVE BEEN LIVING FOR EACH OTHER FROM THE MOMENT WE WERE BORN.
ME FOR YOU.
AND YOU FOR ME.

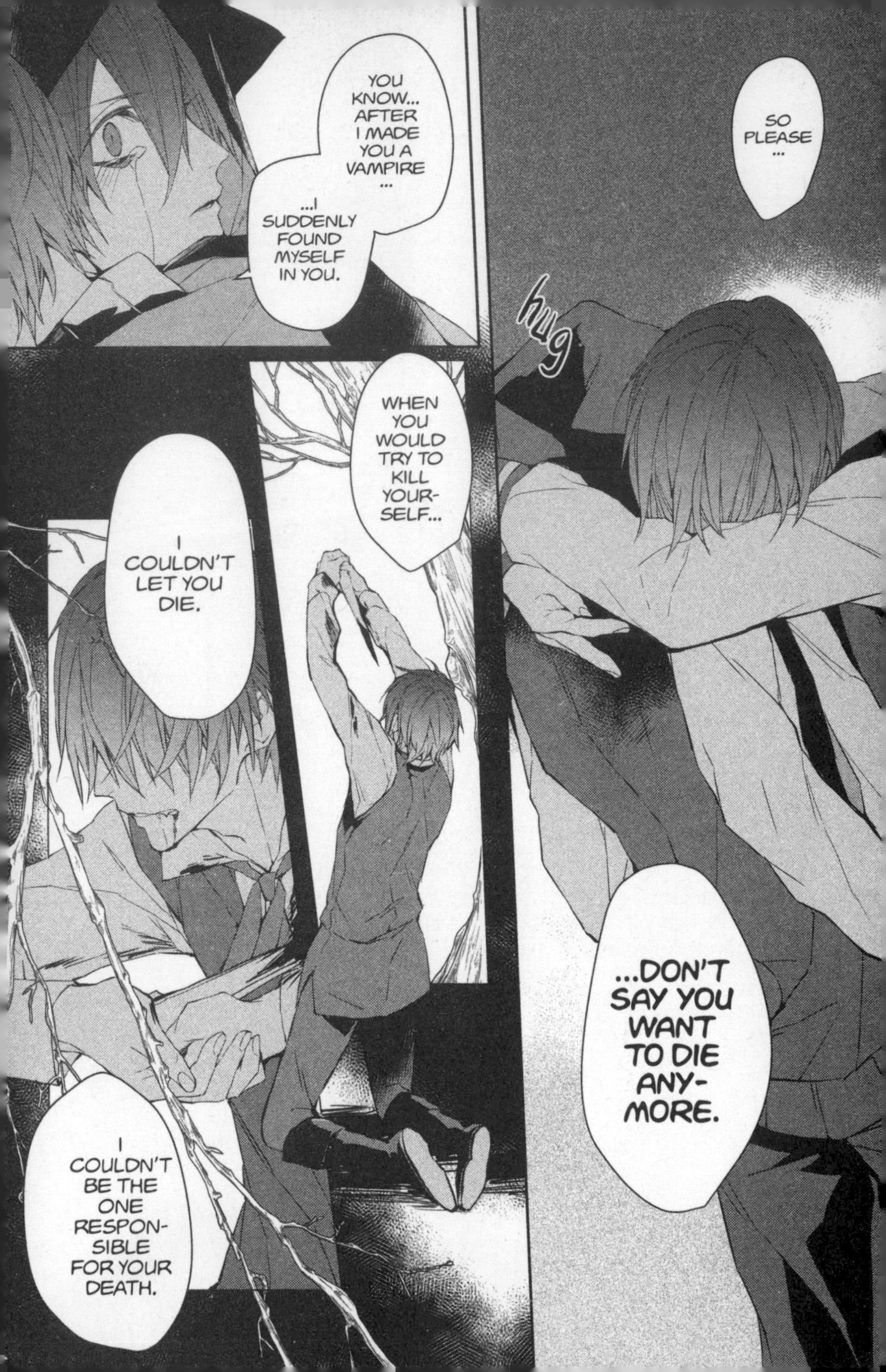
YOU KNOW... AFTER I MADE YOU A VAMPIRE ...
...I SUDDENLY FOUND MYSELF IN YOU.
WHEN YOU WOULD TRY TO KILL YOUR-SELF...
I COULDN'T LET YOU DIE.
I COULDN'T BE THE ONE RESPON-SIBLE FOR YOUR DEATH.
SO PLEASE ...
hug
...DON'T SAY YOU WANT TO DIE ANY-MORE.

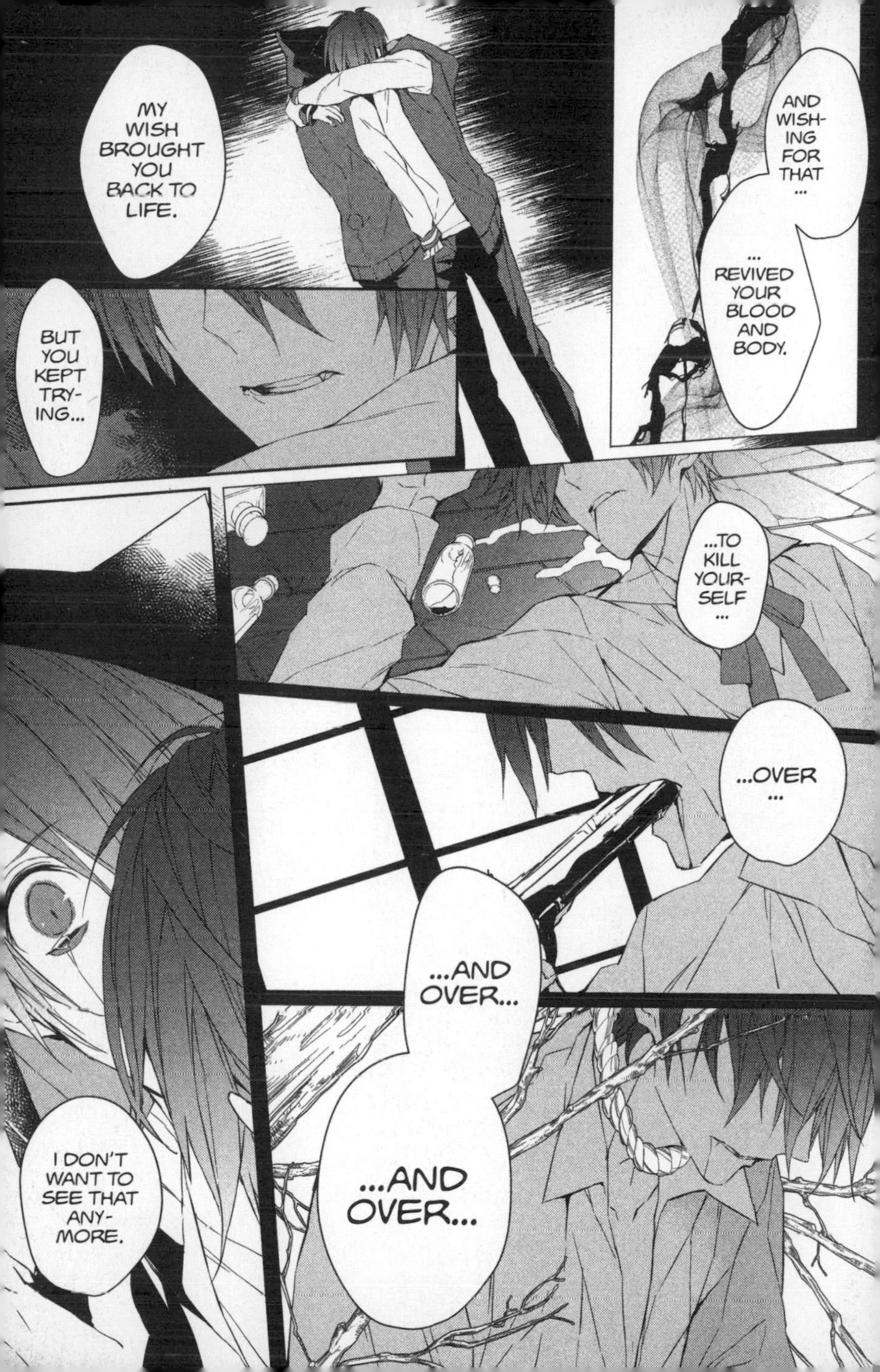
AND WISHING FOR THAT ...
... REVIVED YOUR BLOOD AND BODY.
MY WISH BROUGHT YOU BACK TO LIFE.
BUT YOU KEPT TRYING...
...TO KILL YOURSELF ...
...OVER ...
...AND OVER...
...AND OVER...
I DON'T WANT TO SEE THAT ANYMORE.

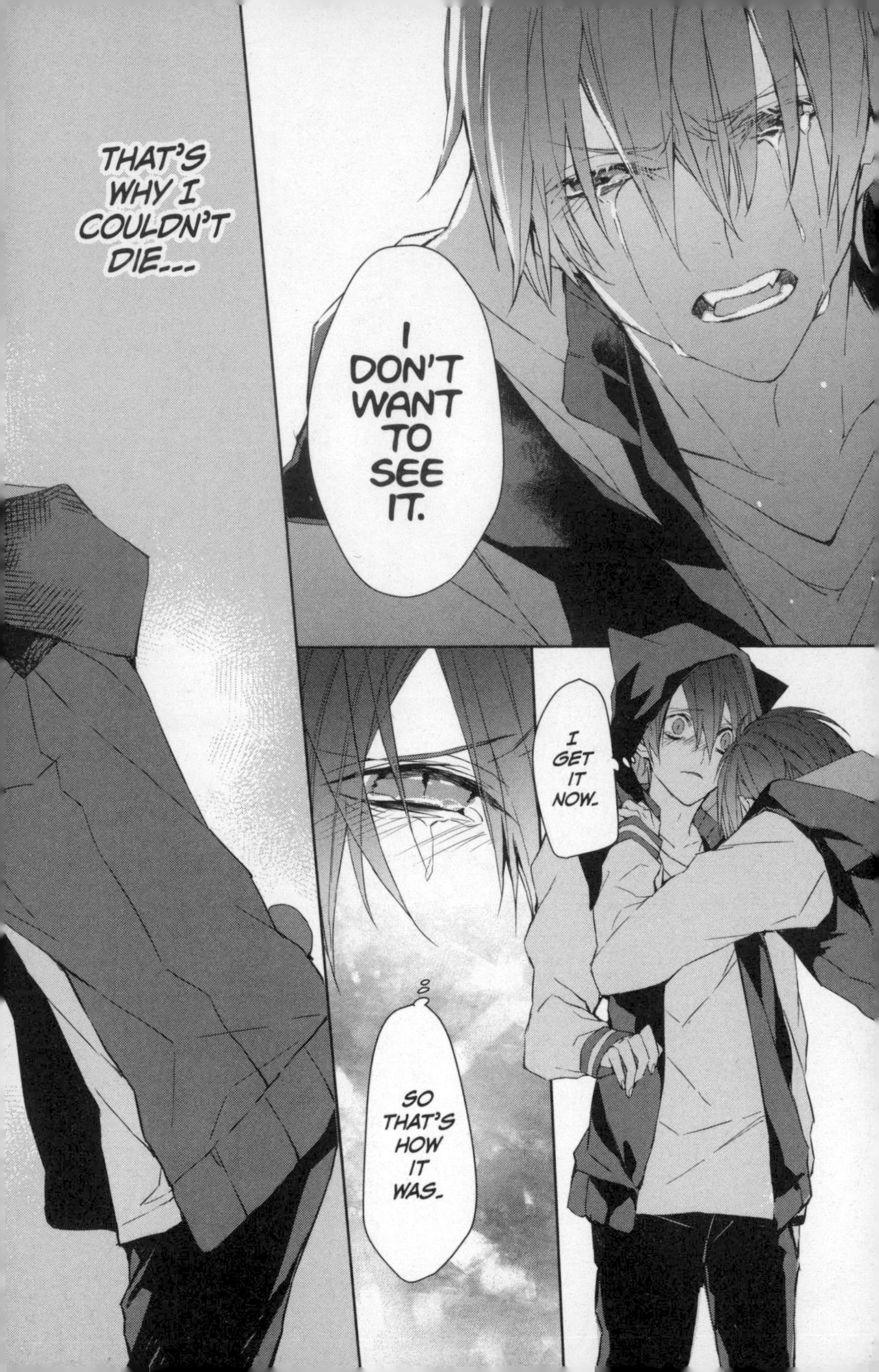
I DON'T WANT TO SEE IT.
I GET IT NOW...
SO THAT'S HOW IT WAS...
THAT'S WHY I COULDN'T DIE...

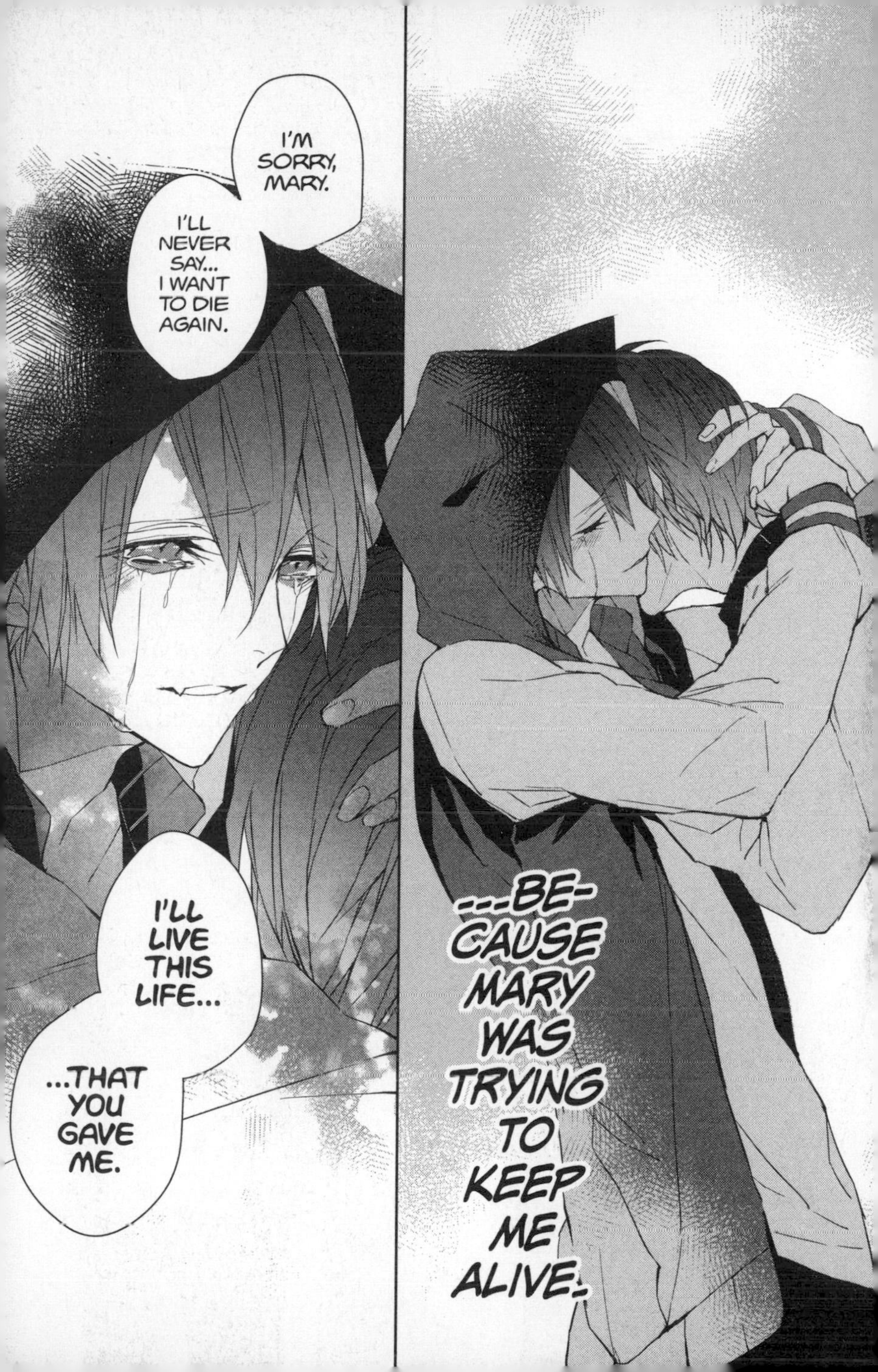

---BE-CAUSE MARY WAS TRYING TO KEEP ME ALIVE.
I'M SORRY, MARY.
I'LL NEVER SAY... I WANT TO DIE AGAIN.
I'LL LIVE THIS LIFE...
...THAT YOU GAVE ME.

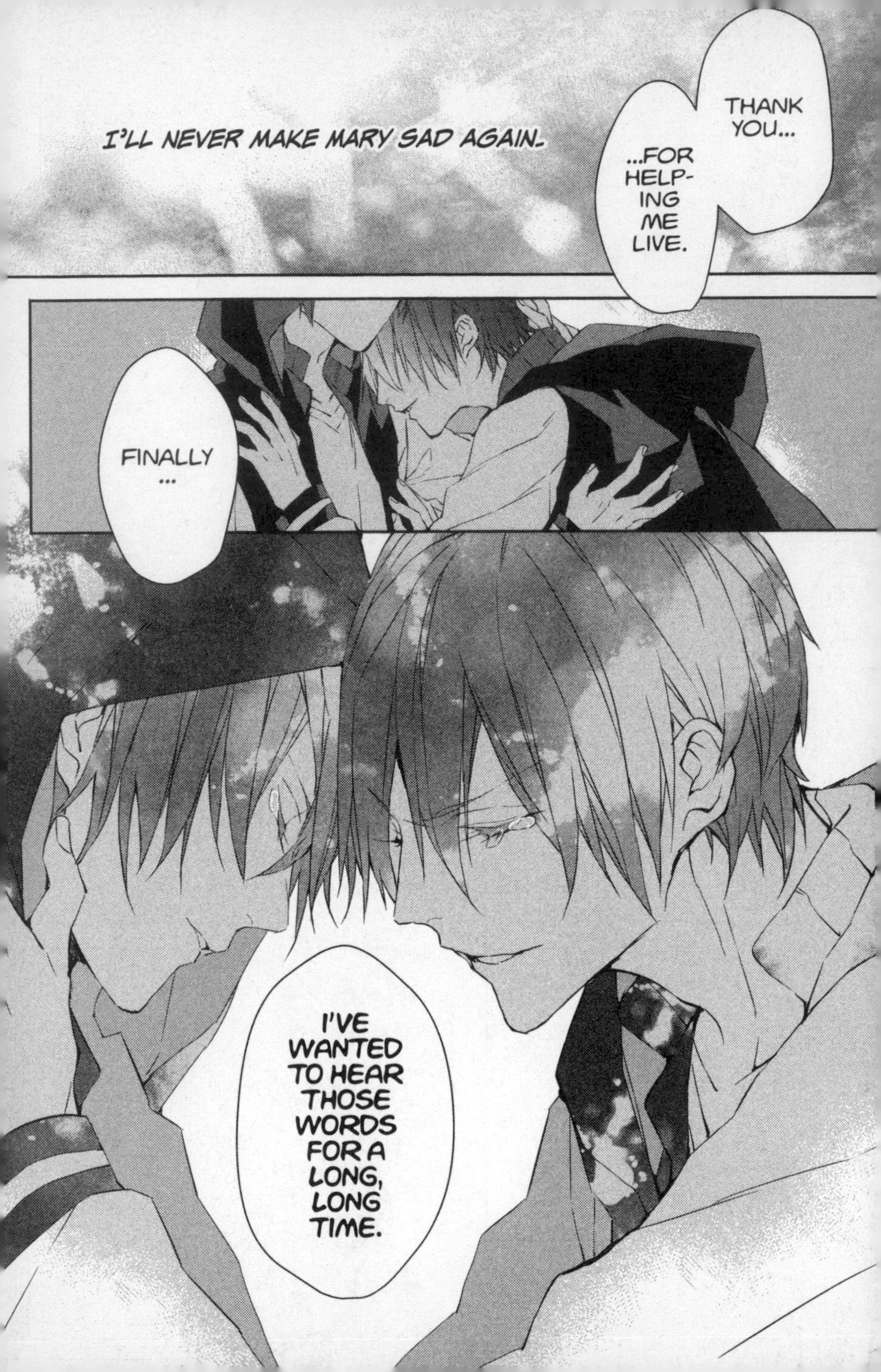
THANK YOU...
...FOR HELP-ING ME LIVE.
I'LL NEVER MAKE MARY SAD AGAIN.
FINALLY...
I'VE WANTED TO HEAR THOSE WORDS FOR A LONG, LONG TIME.

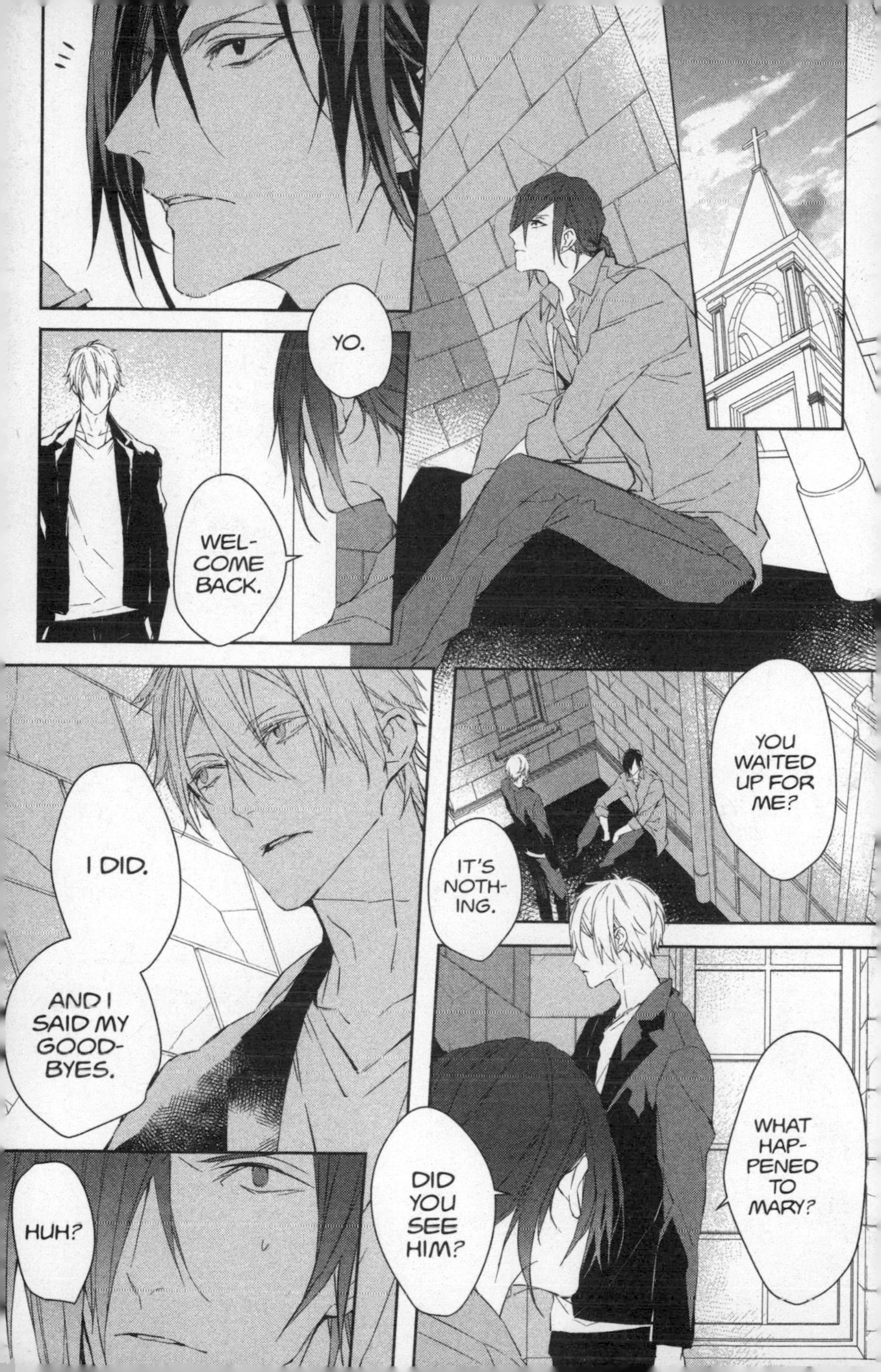
YO.
WEL-COME BACK.
YOU WAITED UP FOR ME?
IT'S NOTH-ING.
WHAT HAP-PENED TO MARY?
DID YOU SEE HIM?
I DID.
AND I SAID MY GOOD-BYES.
HUH?

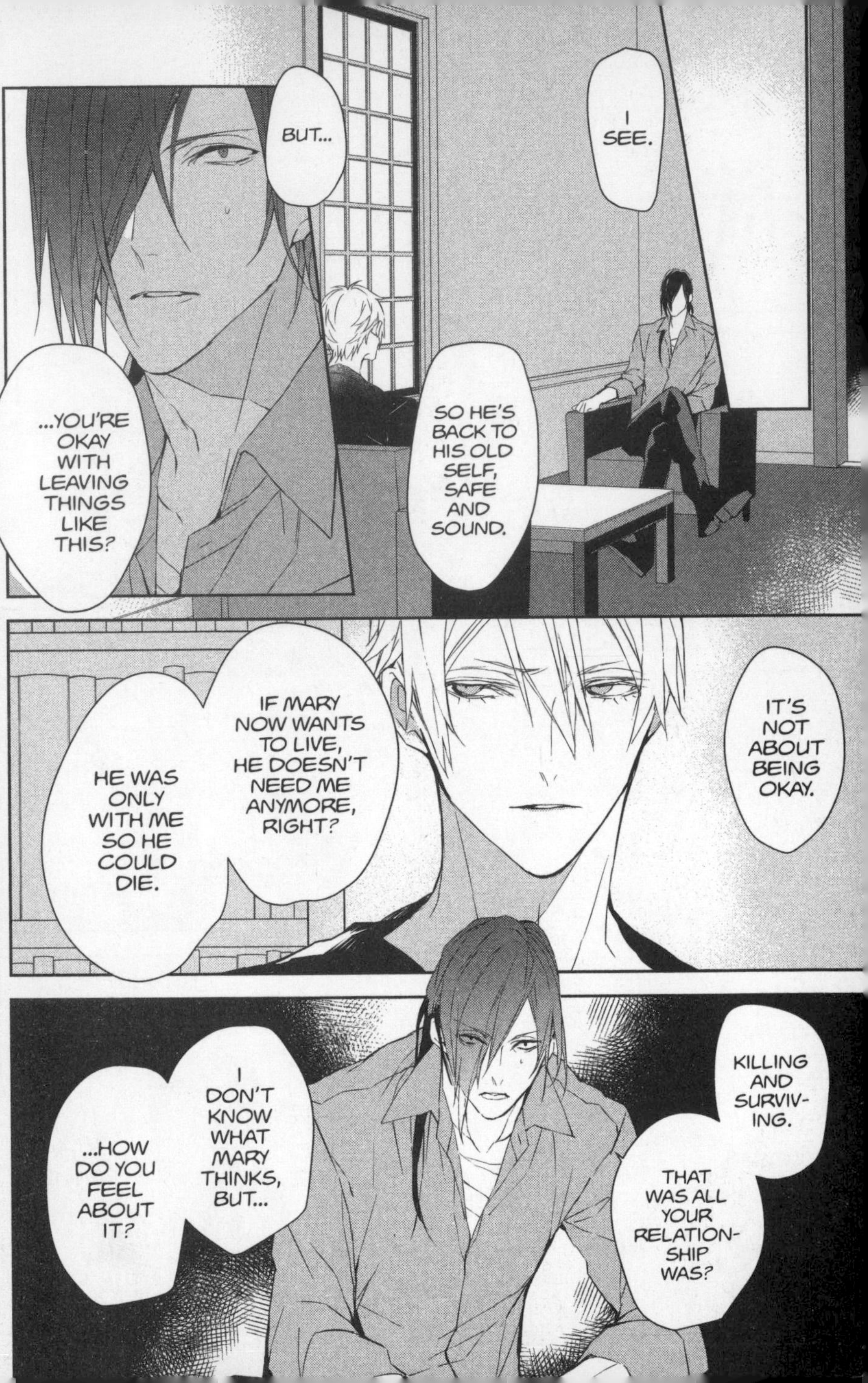
I SEE.
SO HE'S BACK TO HIS OLD SELF, SAFE AND SOUND.
BUT...
...YOU'RE OKAY WITH LEAVING THINGS LIKE THIS?
IT'S NOT ABOUT BEING OKAY.
IF MARY NOW WANTS TO LIVE, HE DOESN'T NEED ME ANYMORE, RIGHT?
HE WAS ONLY WITH ME SO HE COULD DIE.
KILLING AND SURVIV-ING.
THAT WAS ALL YOUR RELATION-SHIP WAS?
I DON'T KNOW WHAT MARY THINKS, BUT...
...HOW DO YOU FEEL ABOUT IT?

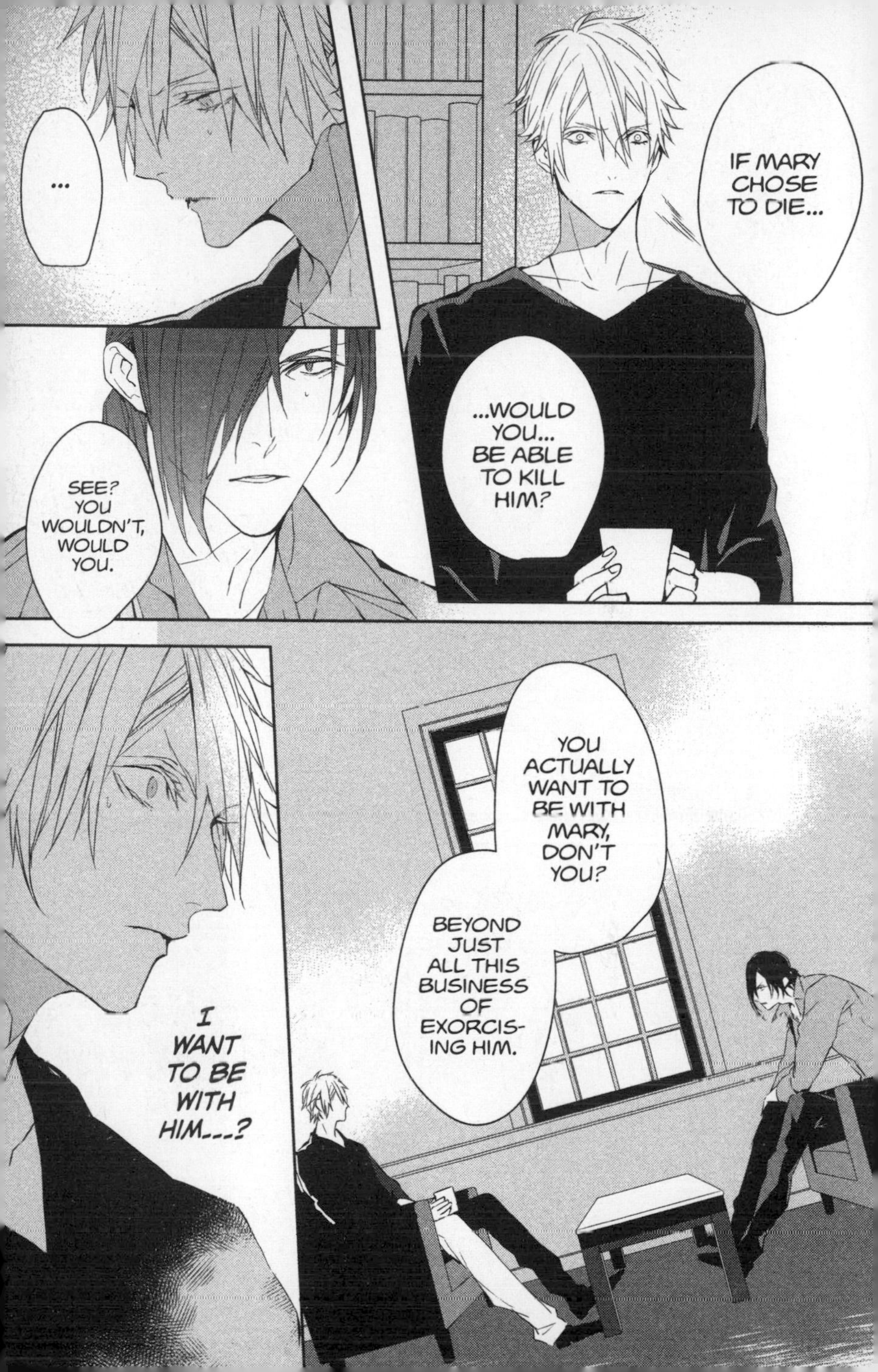
IF MARY CHOSE TO DIE...
...WOULD YOU... BE ABLE TO KILL HIM?
...
SEE? YOU WOULDN'T, WOULD YOU.
YOU ACTUALLY WANT TO BE WITH MARY, DON'T YOU?
BEYOND JUST ALL THIS BUSINESS OF EXORCIS-ING HIM.
I WANT TO BE WITH HIM...?

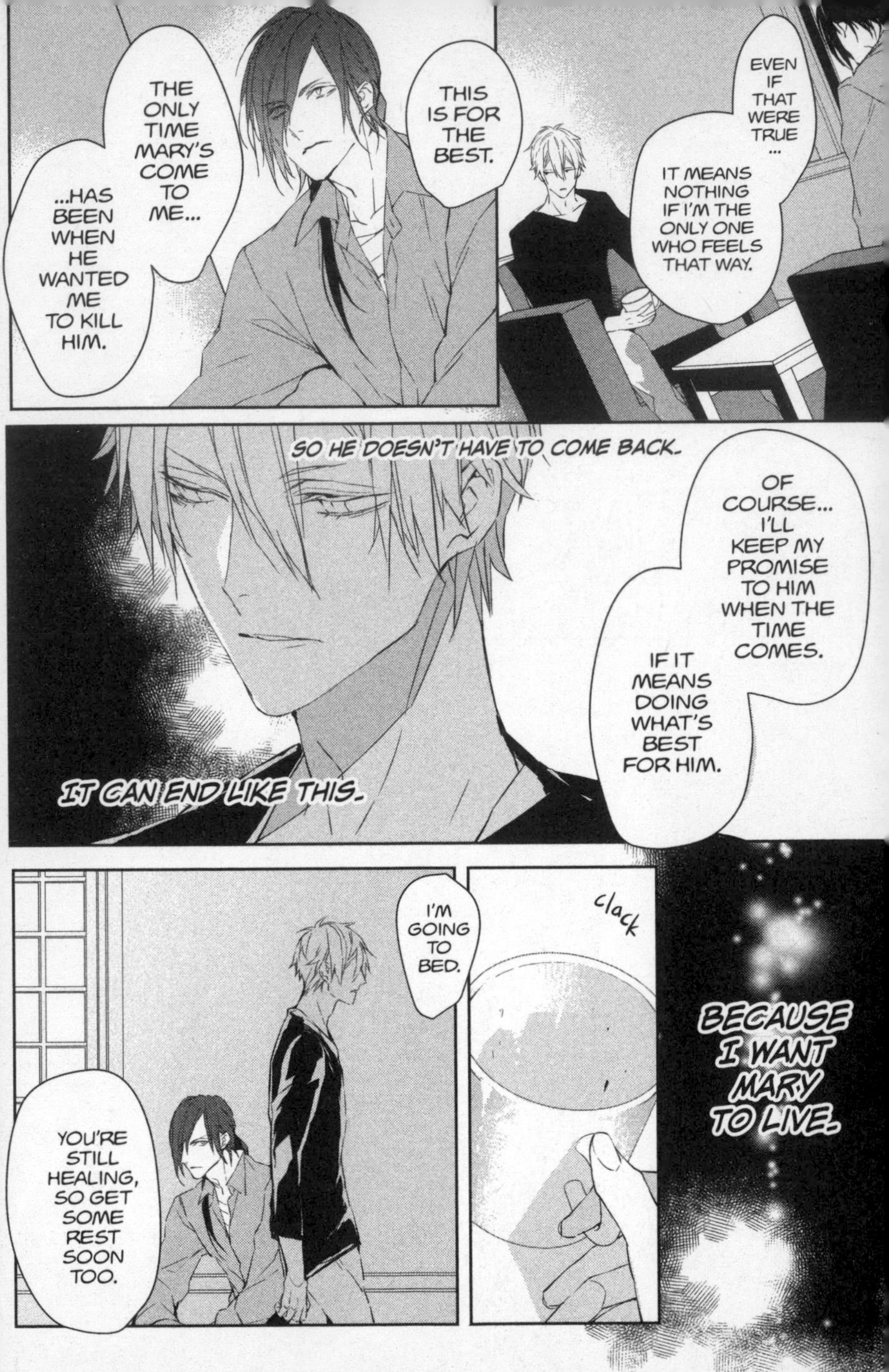
EVEN IF THAT WERE TRUE...
IT MEANS NOTHING IF I'M THE ONLY ONE WHO FEELS THAT WAY.
THIS IS FOR THE BEST.
THE ONLY TIME MARY'S COME TO ME...
...HAS BEEN WHEN HE WANTED ME TO KILL HIM.
OF COURSE... I'LL KEEP MY PROMISE TO HIM WHEN THE TIME COMES.
IF IT MEANS DOING WHAT'S BEST FOR HIM.
SO HE DOESN'T HAVE TO COME BACK.
IT CAN END LIKE THIS.
BECAUSE I WANT MARY TO LIVE.
clack
I'M GOING TO BED.
YOU'RE STILL HEALING, SO GET SOME REST SOON TOO.

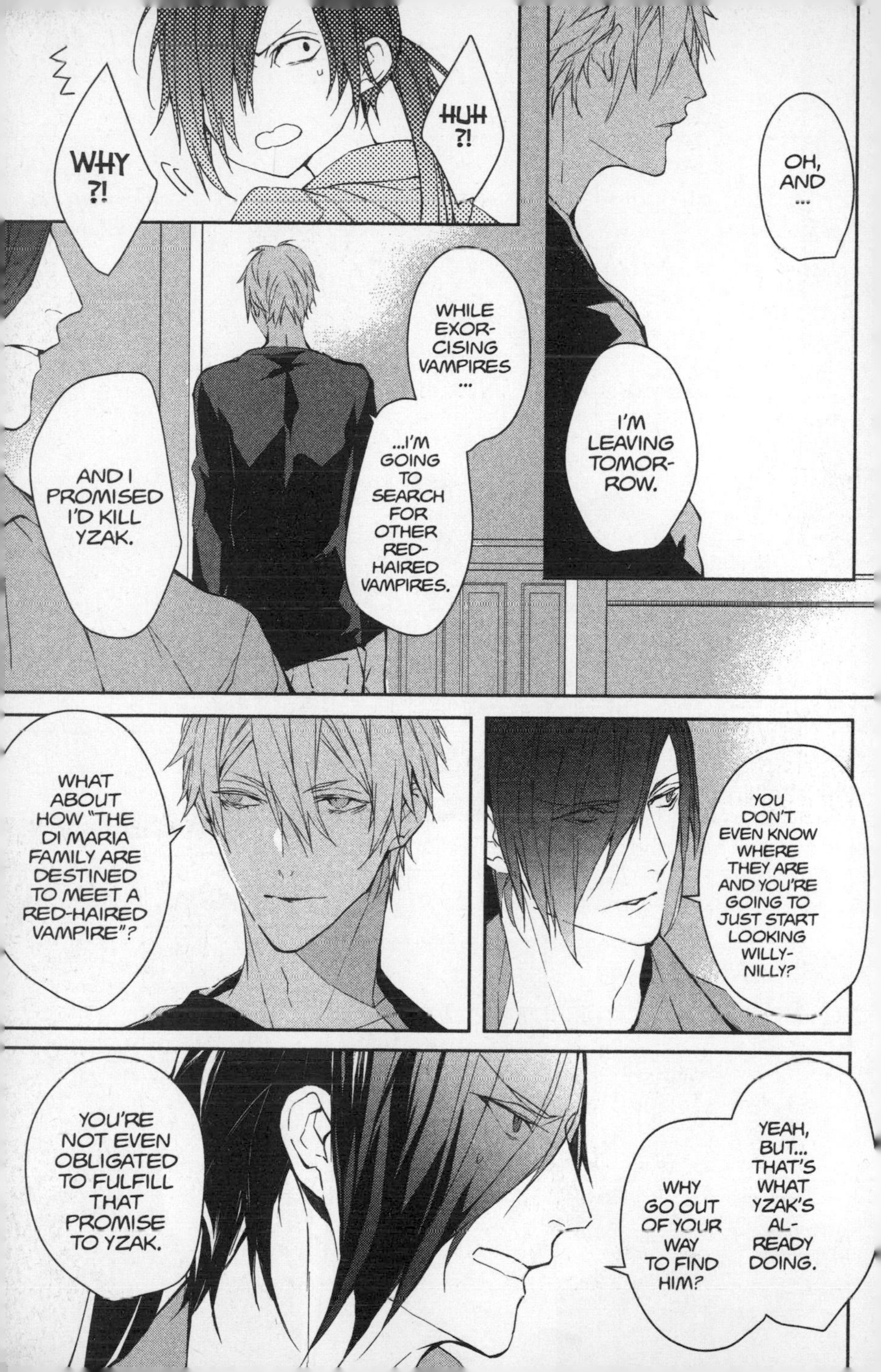
OH, AND ...
I'M LEAVING TOMORROW.
HUH ?!
WHY ?!
WHILE EXORCISING VAMPIRES ...
...I'M GOING TO SEARCH FOR OTHER RED-HAIRED VAMPIRES.
AND I PROMISED I'D KILL YZAK.
YOU DON'T EVEN KNOW WHERE THEY ARE AND YOU'RE GOING TO JUST START LOOKING WILLY-NILLY?
WHAT ABOUT HOW "THE DI MARIA FAMILY ARE DESTINED TO MEET A RED-HAIRED VAMPIRE"?
YEAH, BUT... THAT'S WHAT YZAK'S ALREADY DOING.
WHY GO OUT OF YOUR WAY TO FIND HIM?
YOU'RE NOT EVEN OBLIGATED TO FULFILL THAT PROMISE TO YZAK.

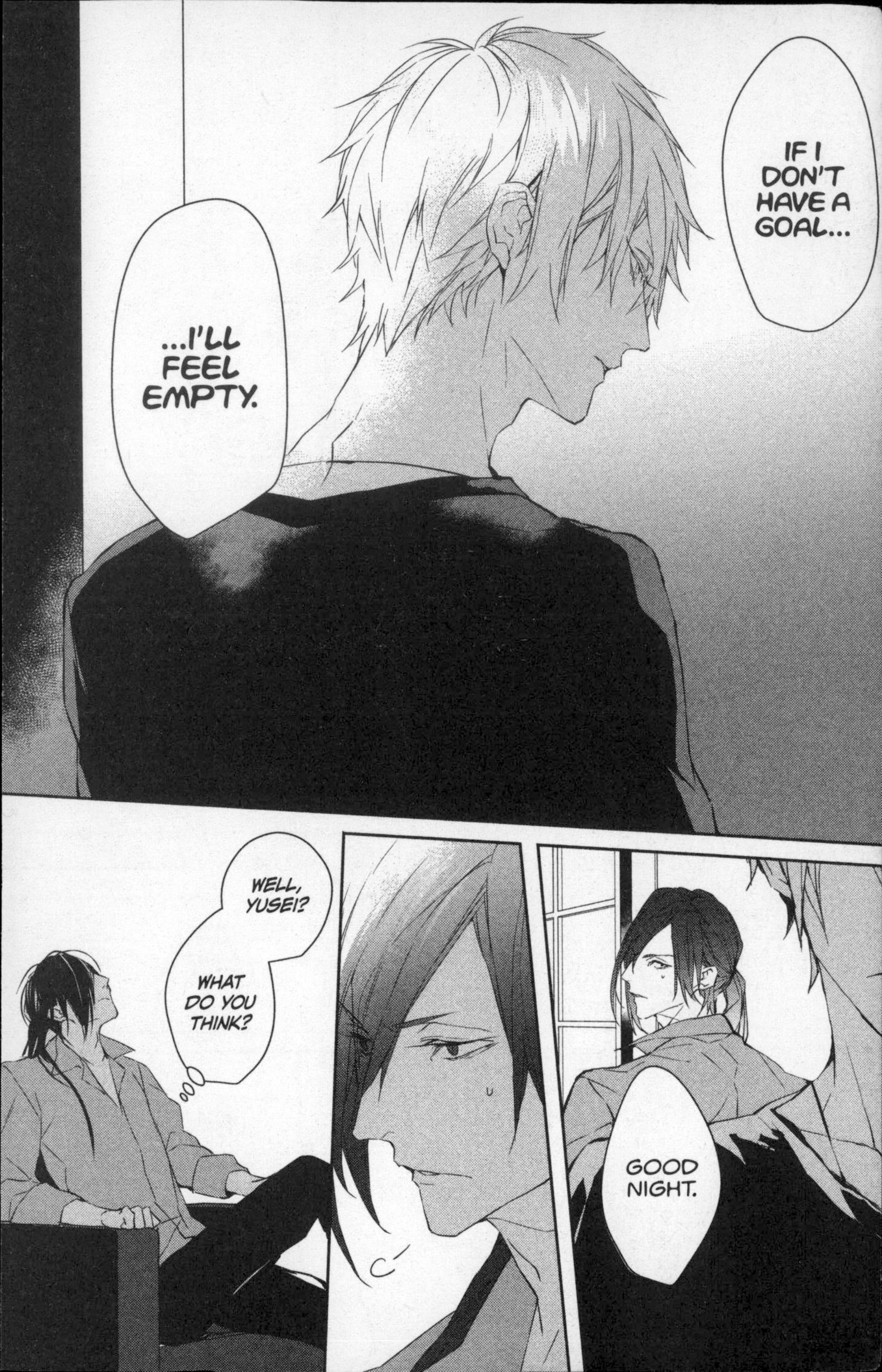
IF I DON'T HAVE A GOAL...
...I'LL FEEL EMPTY.
GOOD NIGHT.
WELL, YUSEI?
WHAT DO YOU THINK?

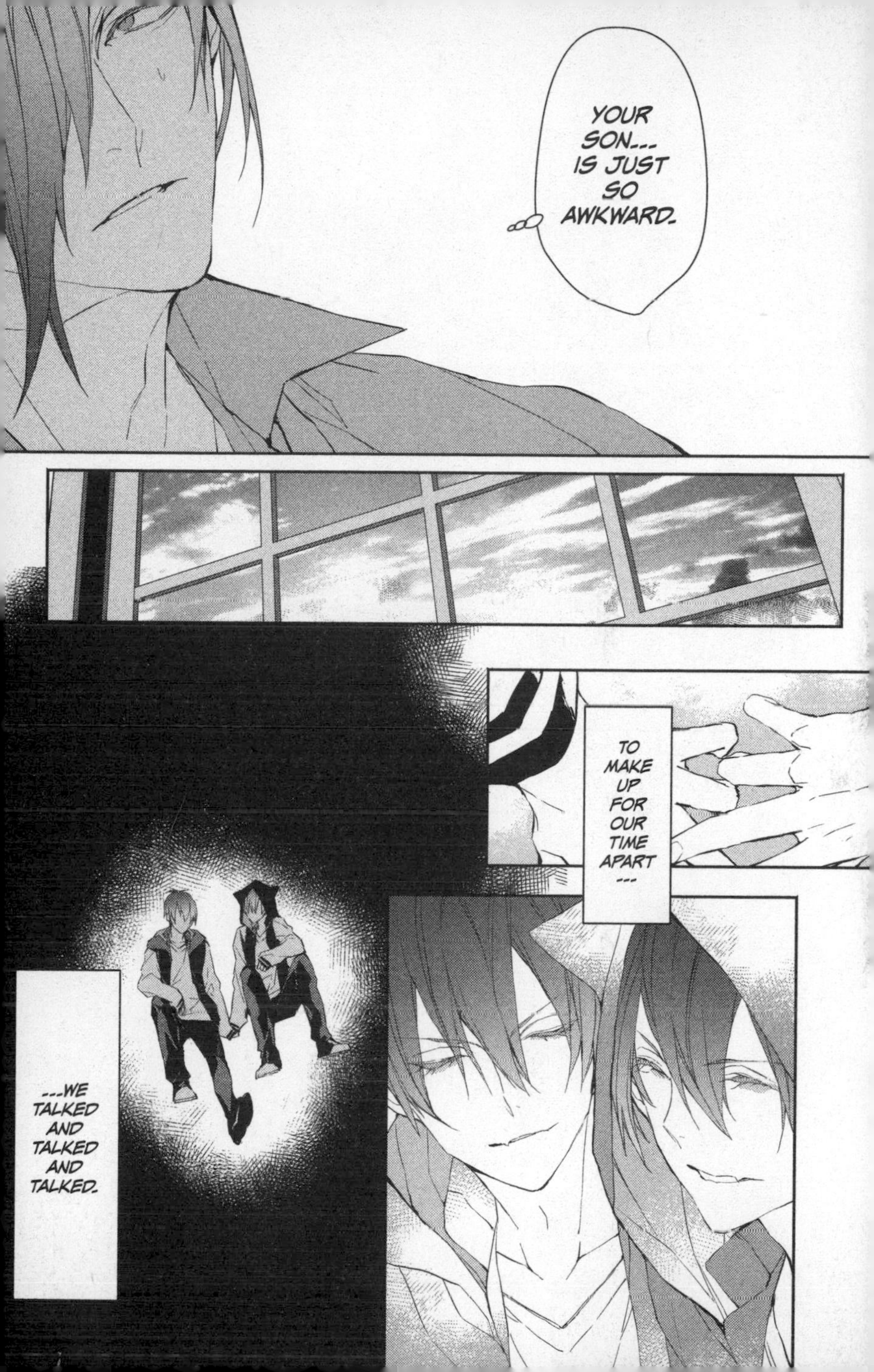
YOUR SON... IS JUST SO AWKWARD.
TO MAKE UP FOR OUR TIME APART ...
...WE TALKED AND TALKED AND TALKED.

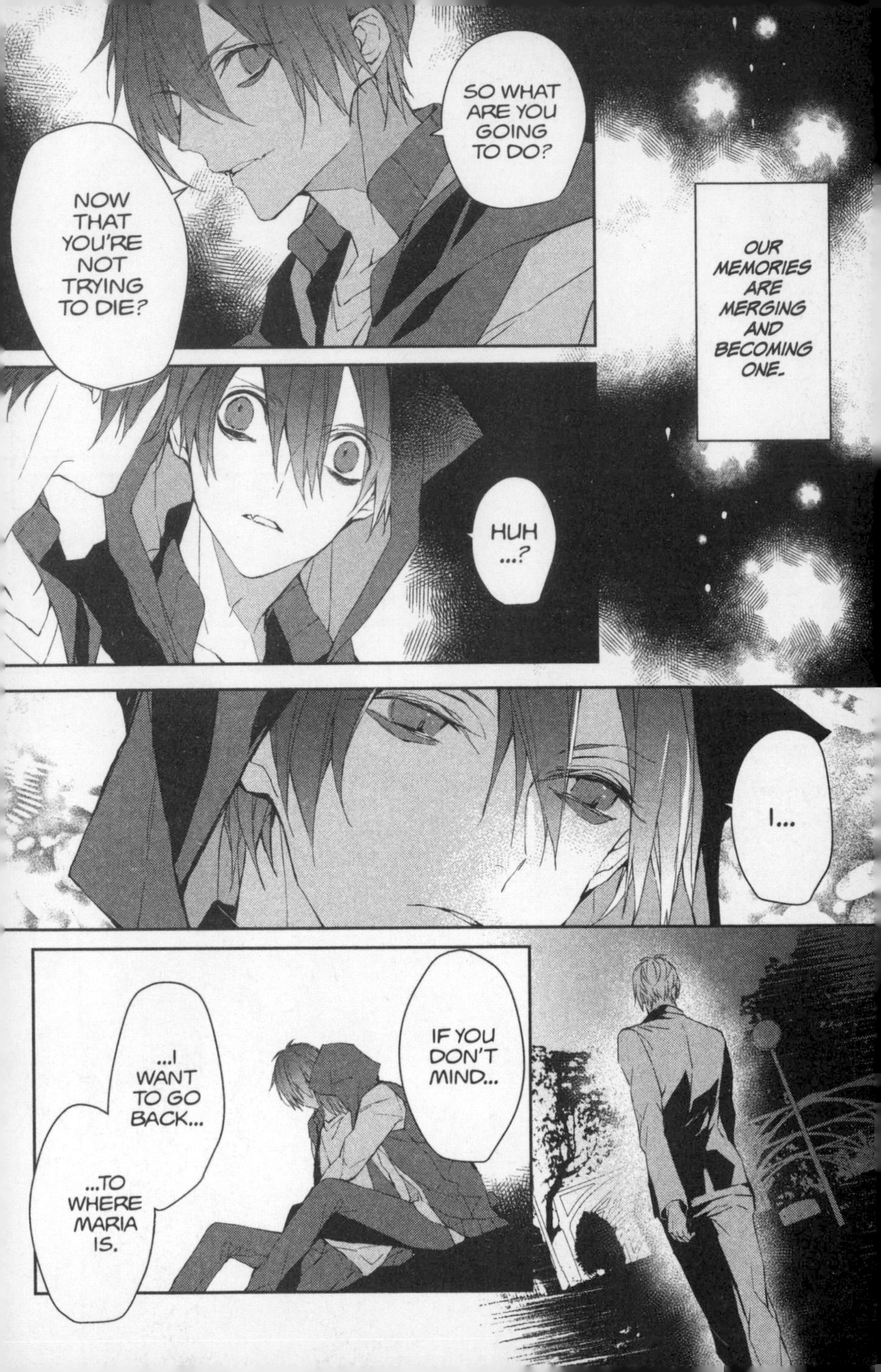
OUR MEMORIES ARE MERGING AND BECOMING ONE.
SO WHAT ARE YOU GOING TO DO?
NOW THAT YOU'RE NOT TRYING TO DIE?
HUH ...?
I...
IF YOU DON'T MIND...
...I WANT TO GO BACK...
...TO WHERE MARIA IS.

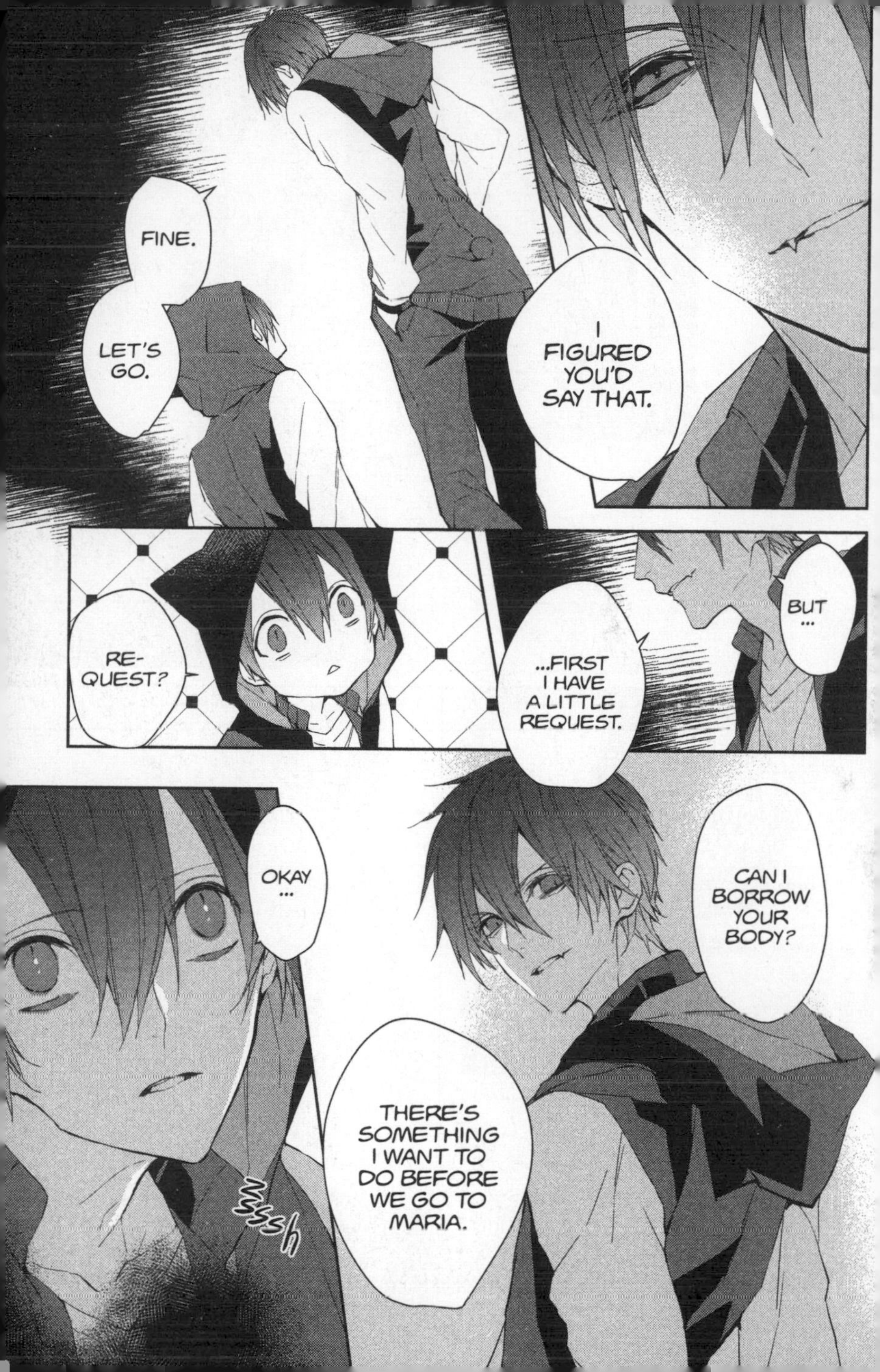
I FIGURED YOU'D SAY THAT.
FINE.
LET'S GO.
BUT ...
...FIRST I HAVE A LITTLE REQUEST.
RE-QUEST?
CAN I BORROW YOUR BODY?
THERE'S SOMETHING I WANT TO DO BEFORE WE GO TO MARIA.
OKAY ...
hsss

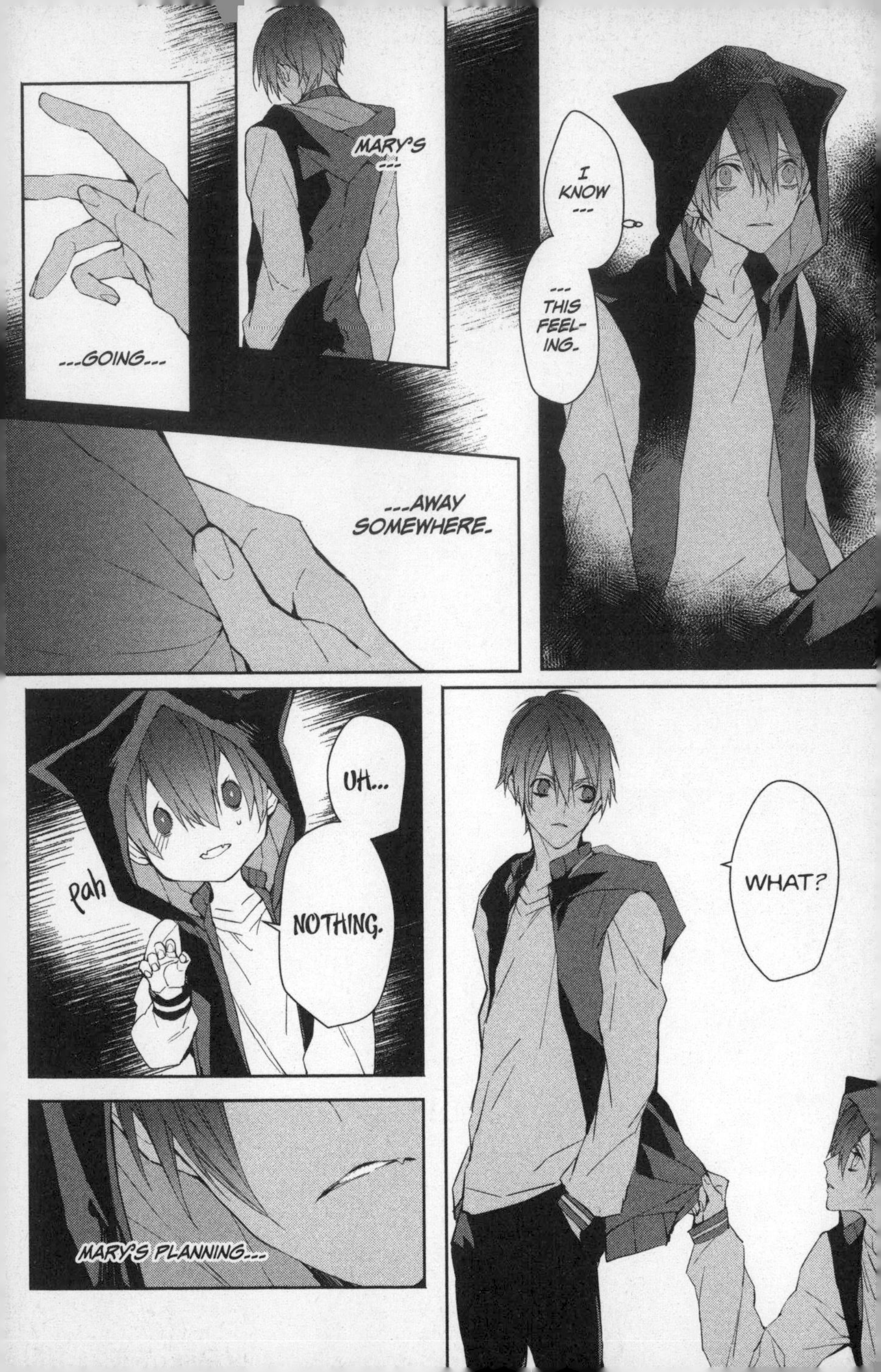
I KNOW ---
--- THIS FEEL-ING.
MARY'S ---
---GOING---
---AWAY SOMEWHERE.
WHAT?
UH...
NOTHING.
pah
MARY'S PLANNING...

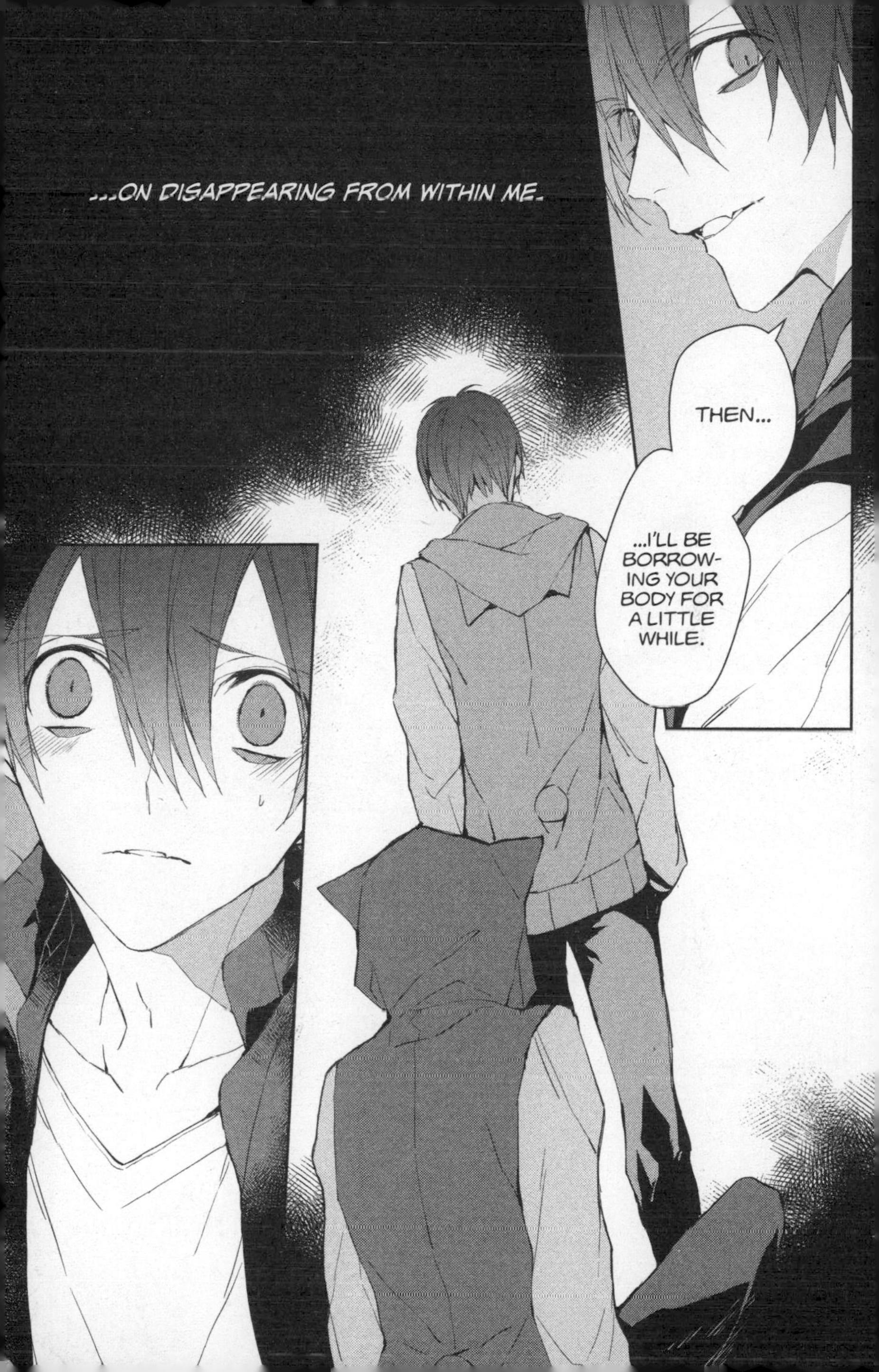
...ON DISAPPEARING FROM WITHIN ME.
THEN...
...I'LL BE BORROWING YOUR BODY FOR A LITTLE WHILE.

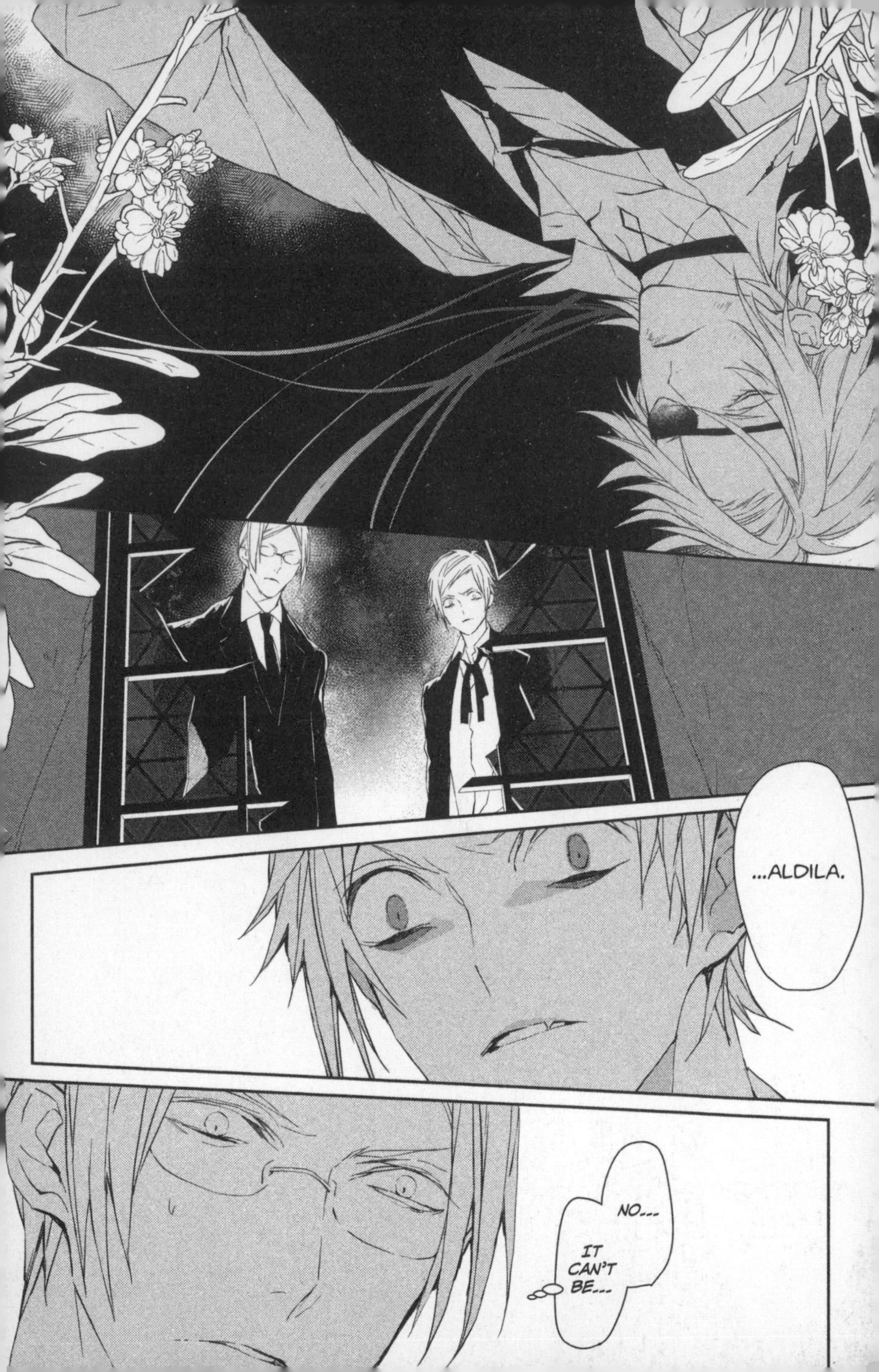
...ALDILA.
NO...
IT CAN'T BE...

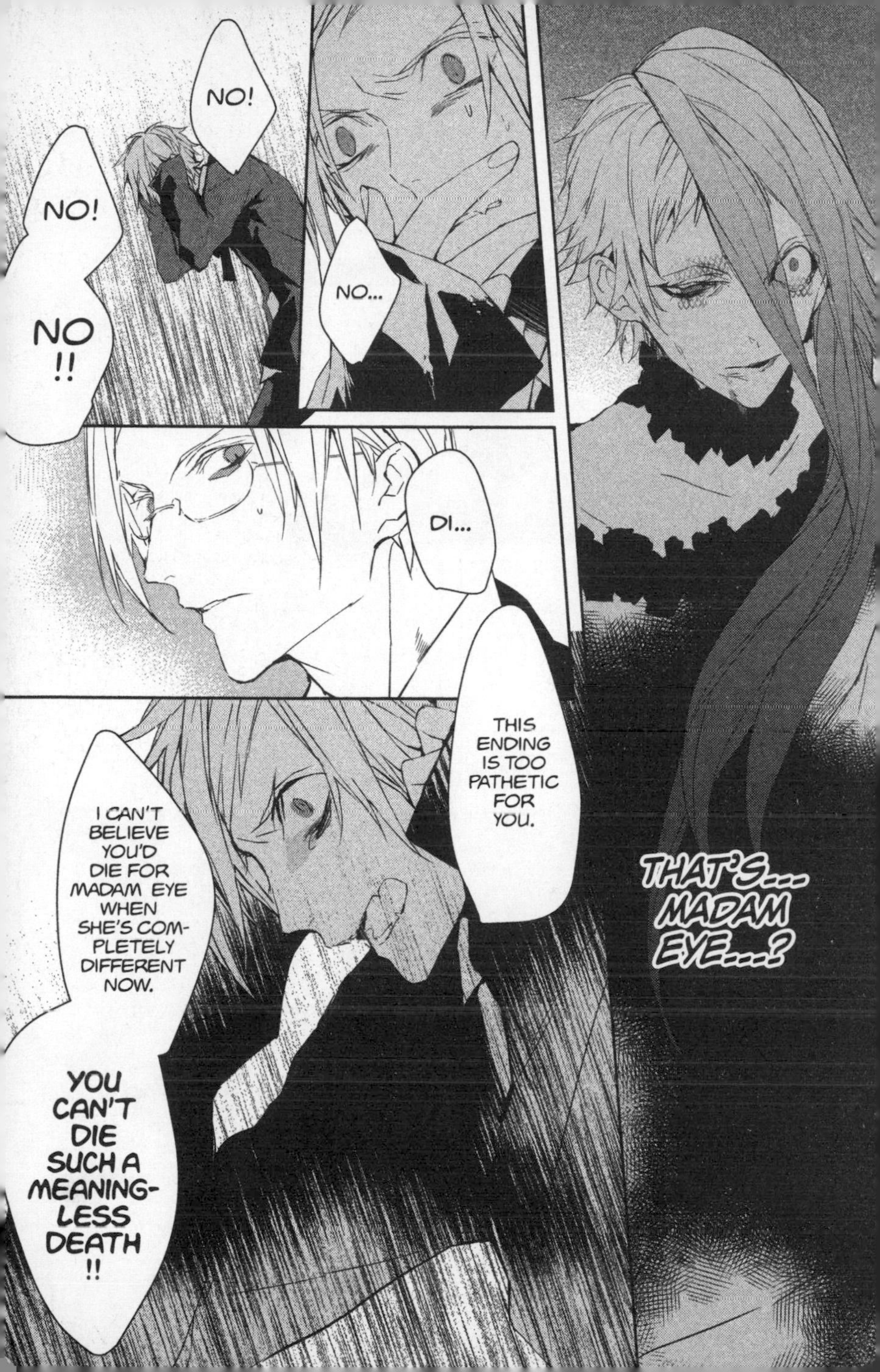
THAT'S... MADAM EYE...?
NO...
NO!
NO!
NO !!
DI...
THIS ENDING IS TOO PATHETIC FOR YOU.
I CAN'T BELIEVE YOU'D DIE FOR MADAM EYE WHEN SHE'S COMPLETELY DIFFERENT NOW.
YOU CAN'T DIE SUCH A MEANINGLESS DEATH !!

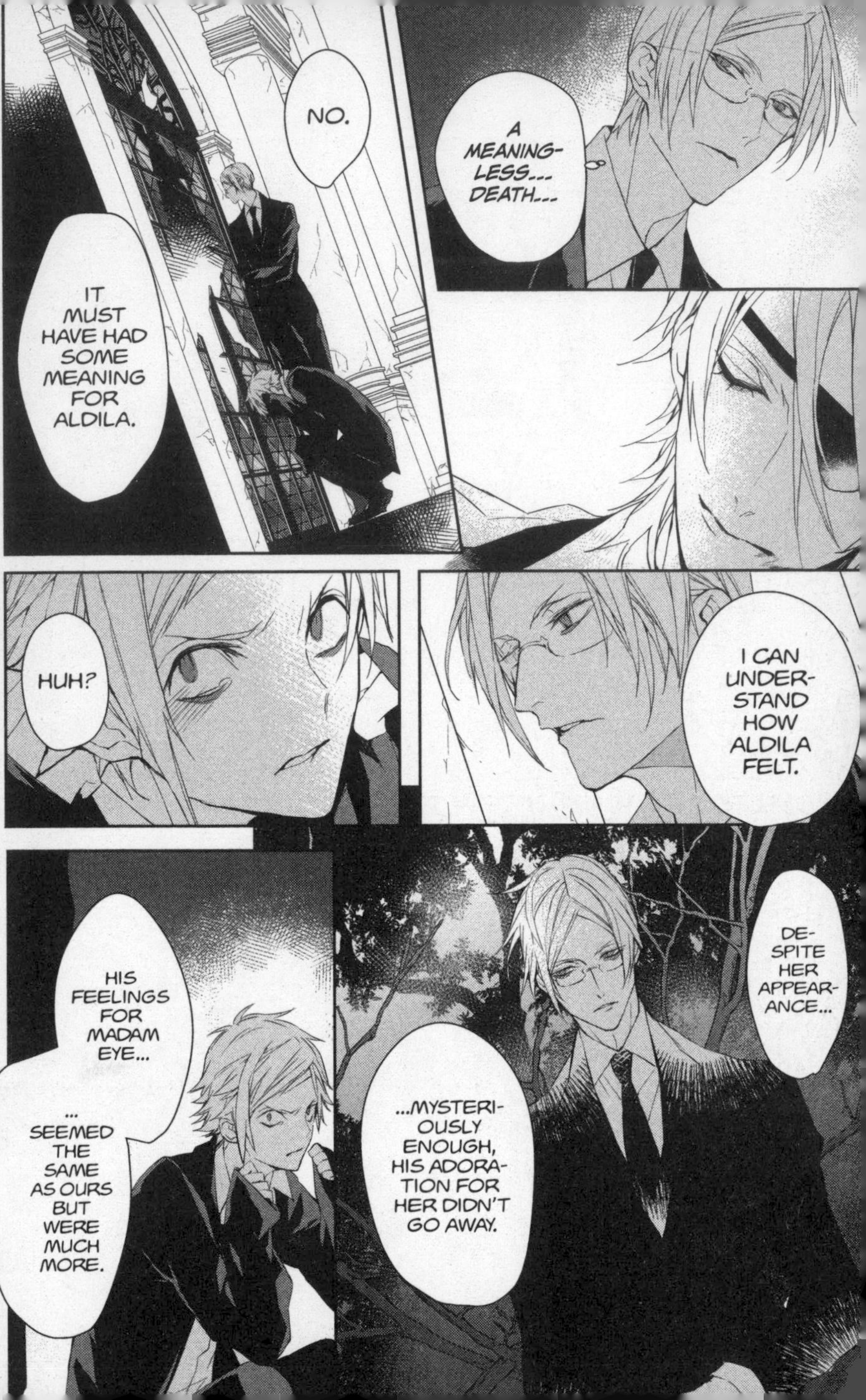
A MEANING-LESS... DEATH...
NO.
IT MUST HAVE HAD SOME MEANING FOR ALDILA.
I CAN UNDER-STAND HOW ALDILA FELT.
HUH?
DE-SPITE HER APPEAR-ANCE...
...MYSTERI-OUSLY ENOUGH, HIS ADORA-TION FOR HER DIDN'T GO AWAY.
HIS FEELINGS FOR MADAM EYE...
...SEEMED THE SAME AS OURS BUT WERE MUCH MORE.

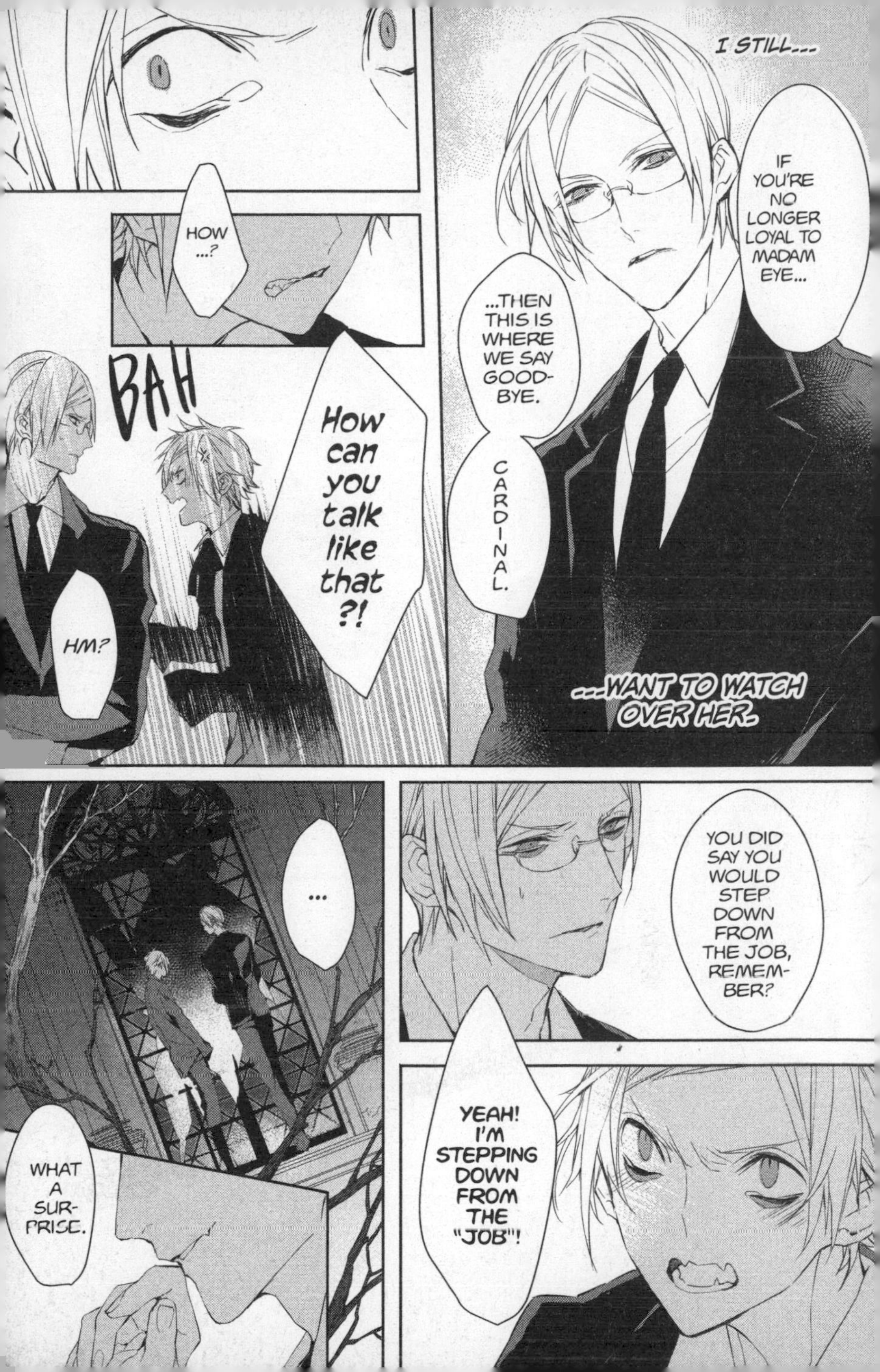
I STILL...
IF YOU'RE NO LONGER LOYAL TO MADAM EYE...
...THEN THIS IS WHERE WE SAY GOOD-BYE.
CARDINAL.
...WANT TO WATCH OVER HER.
HOW ...?
BAH
How can you talk like that?!
HM?
YOU DID SAY YOU WOULD STEP DOWN FROM THE JOB, REMEMBER?
YEAH! I'M STEPPING DOWN FROM THE "JOB"!
...
WHAT A SUR-PRISE.

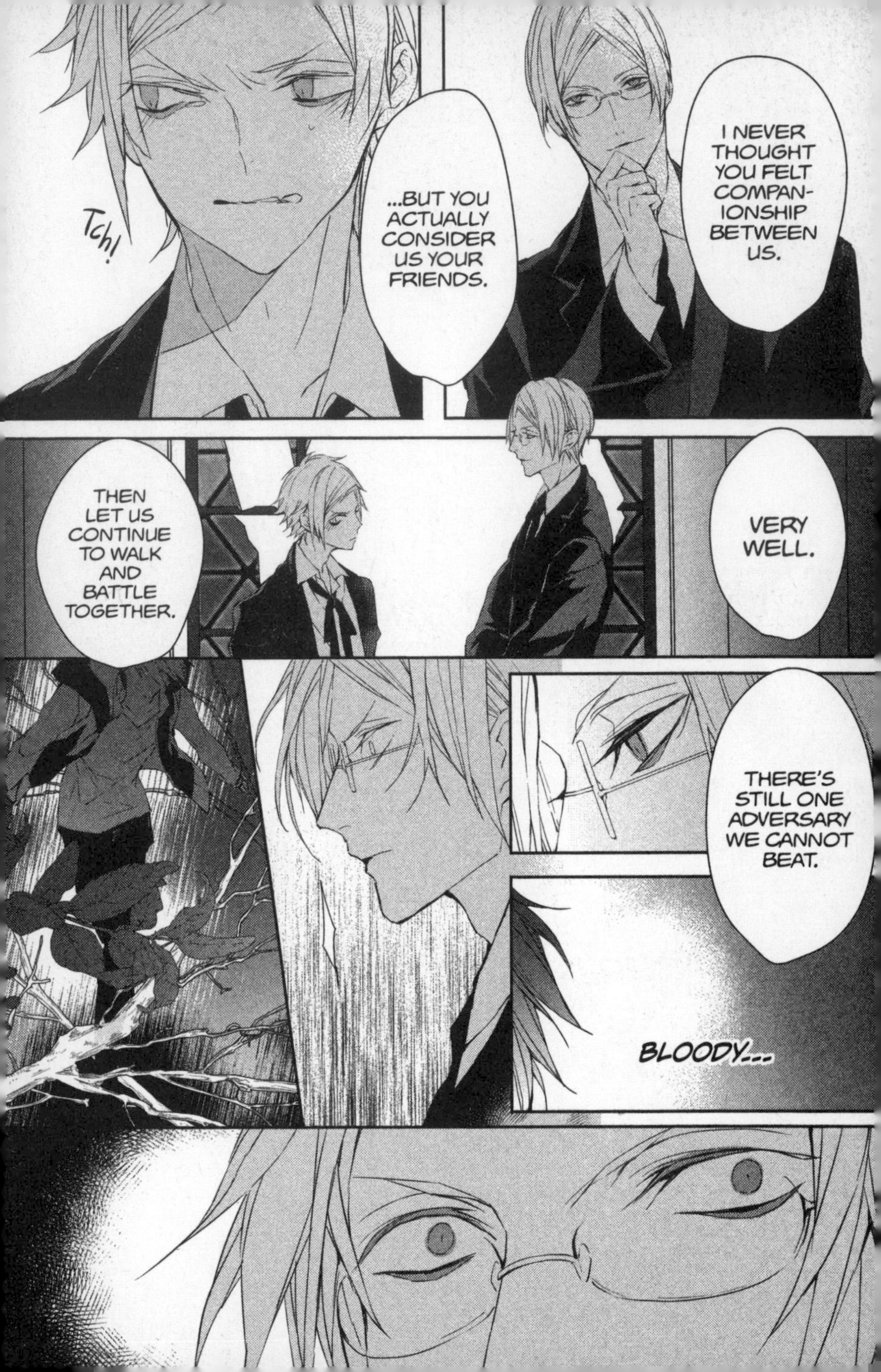
I NEVER THOUGHT YOU FELT COMPANIONSHIP BETWEEN US.
...BUT YOU ACTUALLY CONSIDER US YOUR FRIENDS.
Tch!
VERY WELL.
THEN LET US CONTINUE TO WALK AND BATTLE TOGETHER.
THERE'S STILL ONE ADVERSARY WE CANNOT BEAT.
BLOODY...

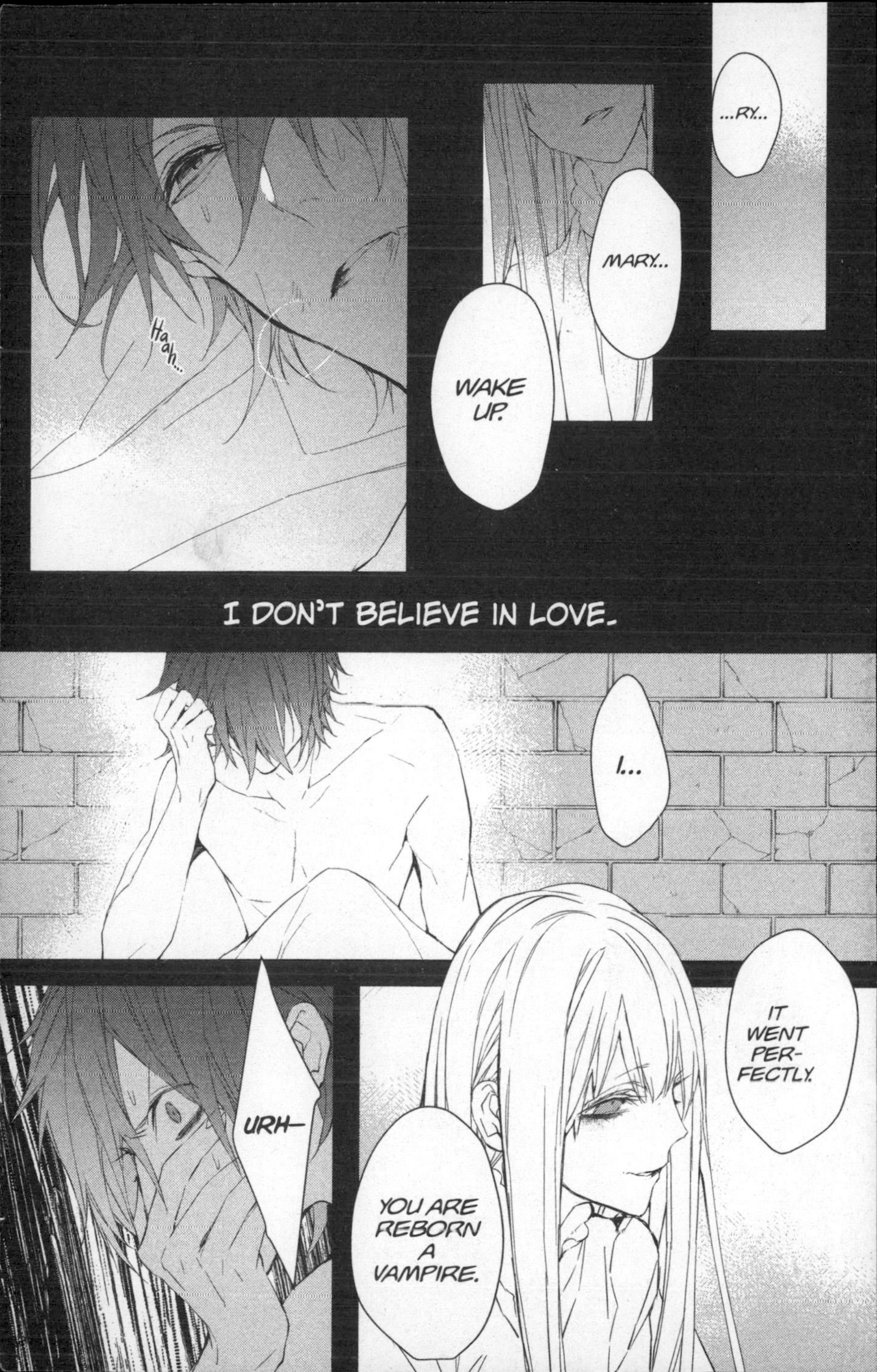
...RY...
MARY...
WAKE UP.
Haah...
I DON'T BELIEVE IN LOVE.
I...
IT WENT PER-FECTLY.
YOU ARE REBORN A VAMPIRE.
URH—

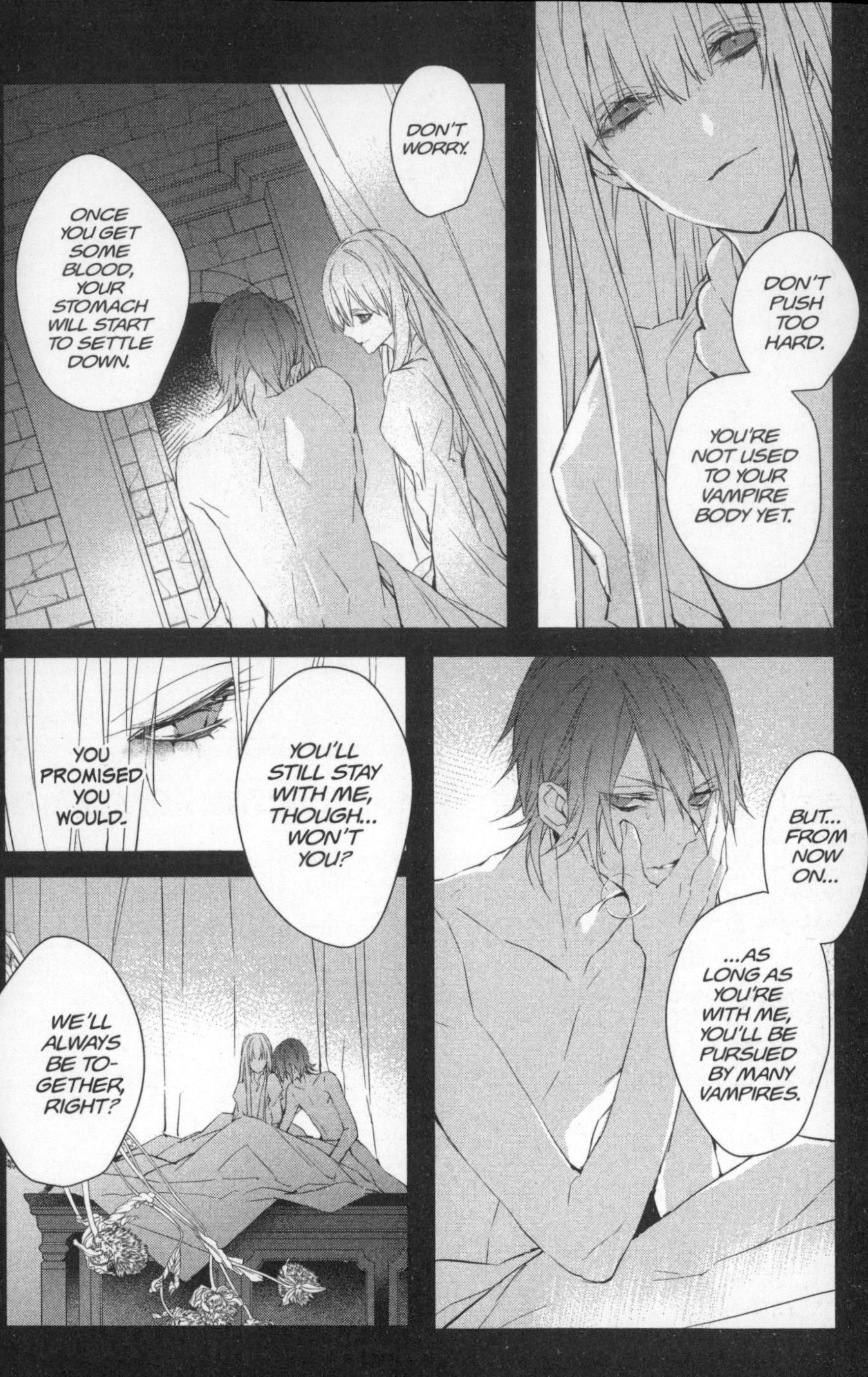
DON'T PUSH TOO HARD.
YOU'RE NOT USED TO YOUR VAMPIRE BODY YET.
DON'T WORRY.
ONCE YOU GET SOME BLOOD, YOUR STOMACH WILL START TO SETTLE DOWN.
BUT... FROM NOW ON...
...AS LONG AS YOU'RE WITH ME, YOU'LL BE PURSUED BY MANY VAMPIRES.
YOU'LL STILL STAY WITH ME, THOUGH... WON'T YOU?
YOU PROMISED YOU WOULD.
WE'LL ALWAYS BE TO-GETHER, RIGHT?

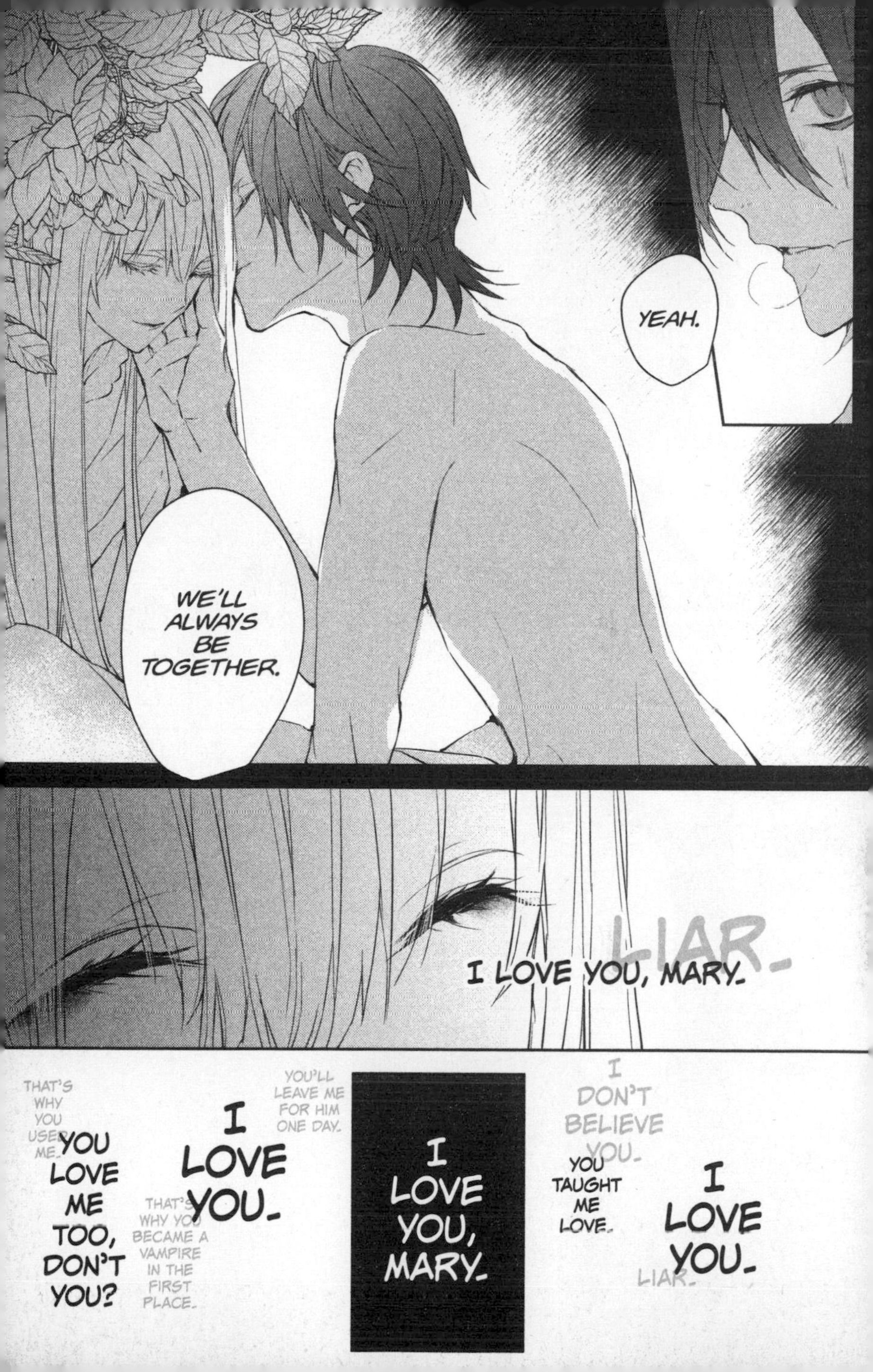
YEAH.
WE'LL ALWAYS BE TOGETHER.
LIAR.
I LOVE YOU, MARY.
I LOVE YOU.
LIAR.
I DON'T BELIEVE YOU.
YOU TAUGHT ME LOVE.
I LOVE YOU, MARY.
YOU'LL LEAVE ME FOR HIM ONE DAY.
I LOVE YOU.
THAT'S WHY YOU BECAME A VAMPIRE IN THE FIRST PLACE.
THAT'S WHY YOU USED ME.
YOU LOVE ME TOO, DON'T YOU?

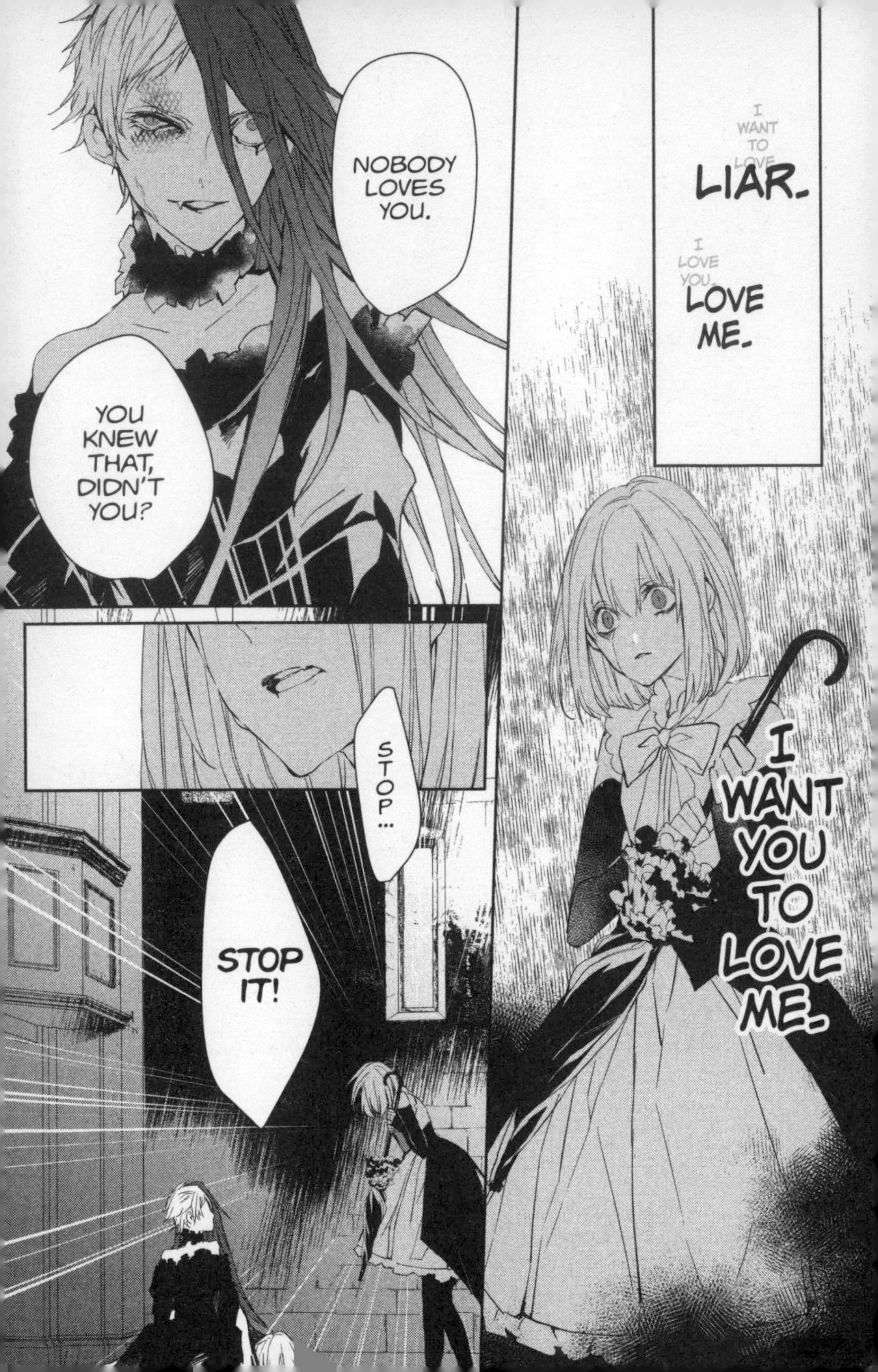
I WANT TO LOVE
LIAR.
I LOVE YOU.
LOVE ME.
I WANT YOU TO LOVE ME.
NOBODY LOVES YOU.
YOU KNEW THAT, DIDN'T YOU?
STOP...
STOP IT!

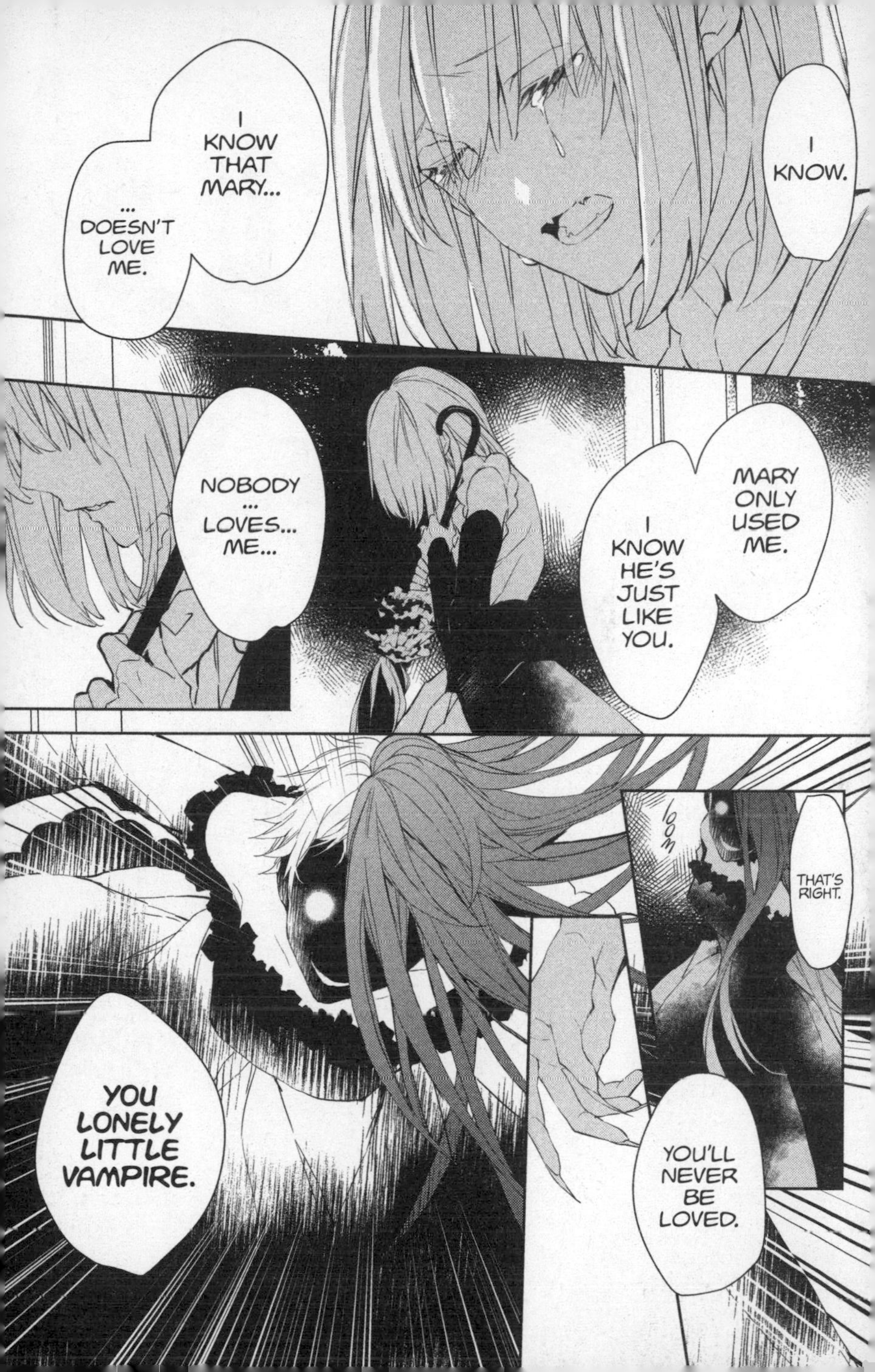
I KNOW.
I KNOW THAT MARY... ...DOESN'T LOVE ME.
MARY ONLY USED ME.
I KNOW HE'S JUST LIKE YOU.
NOBODY... LOVES... ME...
LOOM
THAT'S RIGHT.
YOU'LL NEVER BE LOVED.
YOU LONELY LITTLE VAMPIRE.

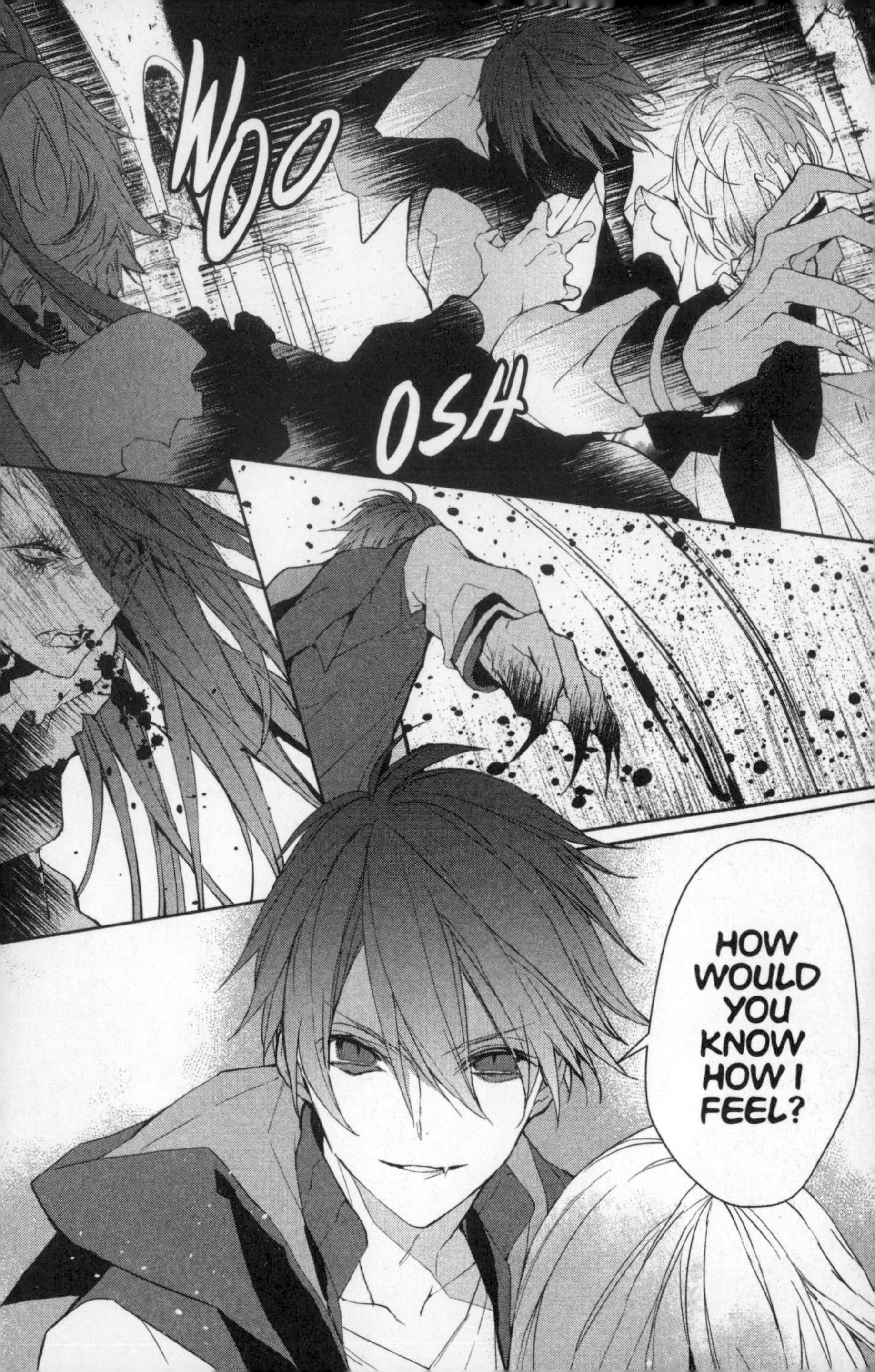
WOOOSH
HOW WOULD YOU KNOW HOW I FEEL?

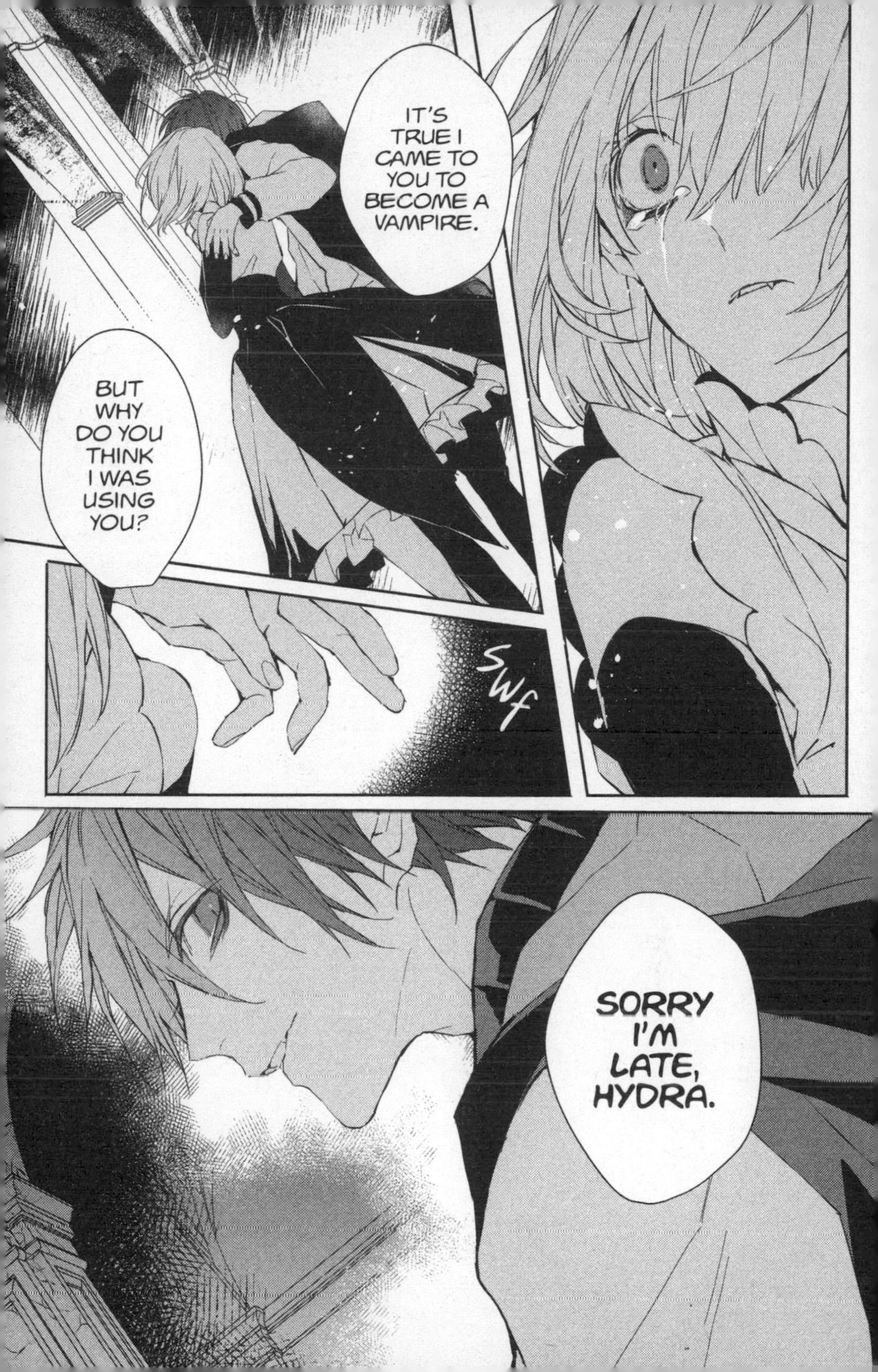
IT'S TRUE I CAME TO YOU TO BECOME A VAMPIRE.
BUT WHY DO YOU THINK I WAS USING YOU?
SWF
SORRY I'M LATE, HYDRA.

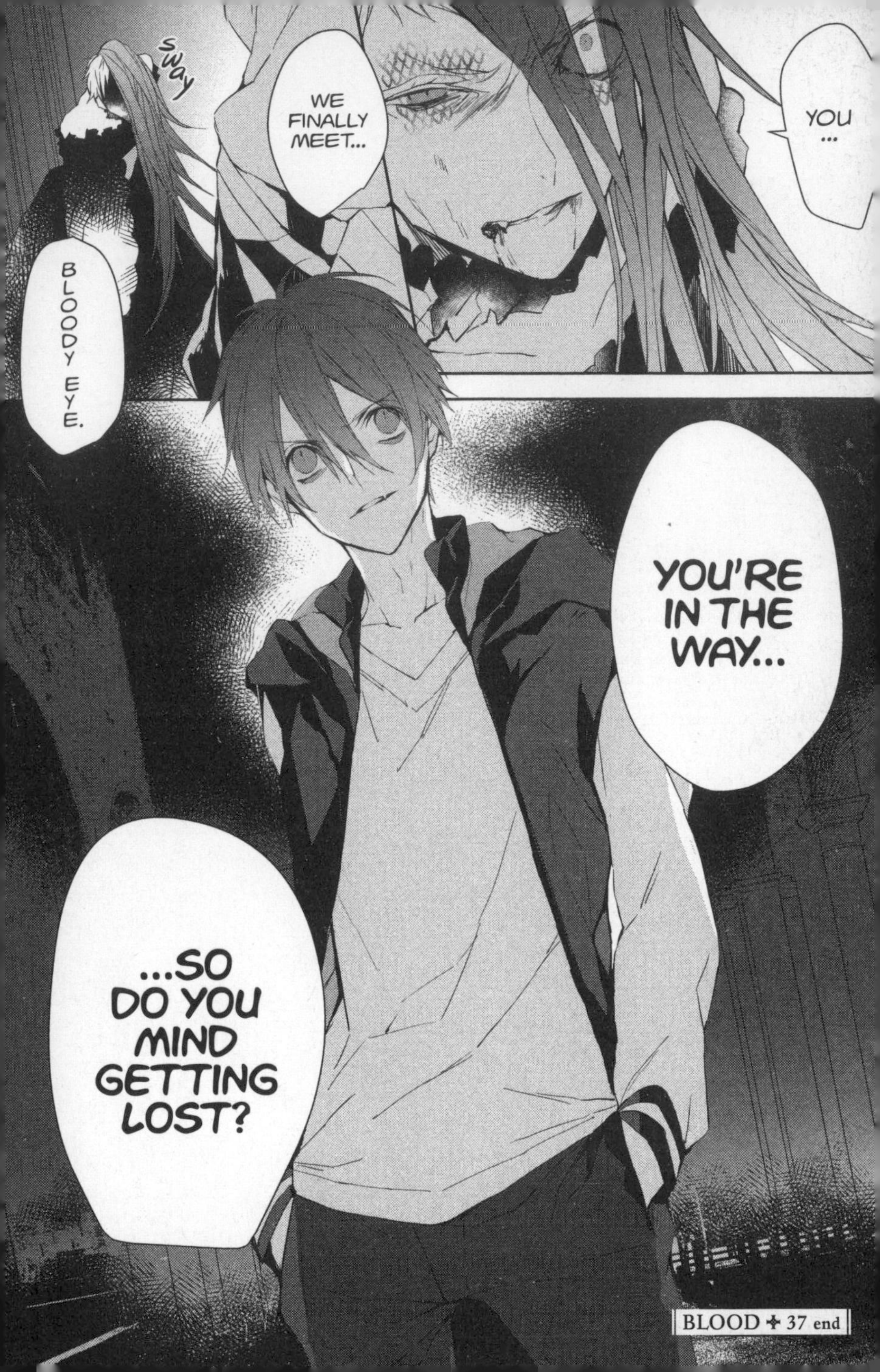
YOU ...
WE FINALLY MEET...
SWAY
BLOODY EYE.
YOU'RE IN THE WAY...
...SO DO YOU MIND GETTING LOST?

BLOOD ✦ 37 end

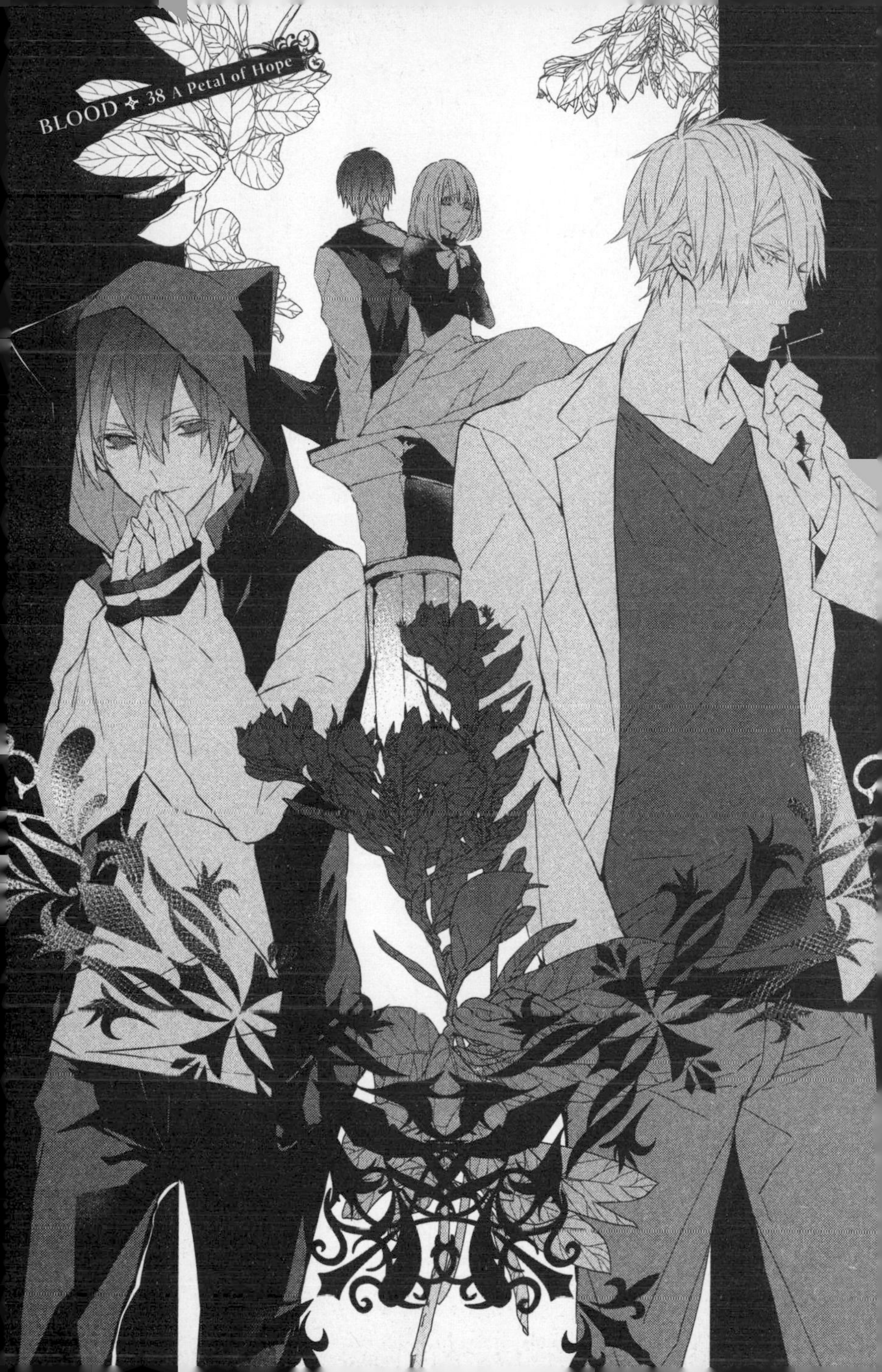
BLOOD ✣ 38 A Petal of Hope

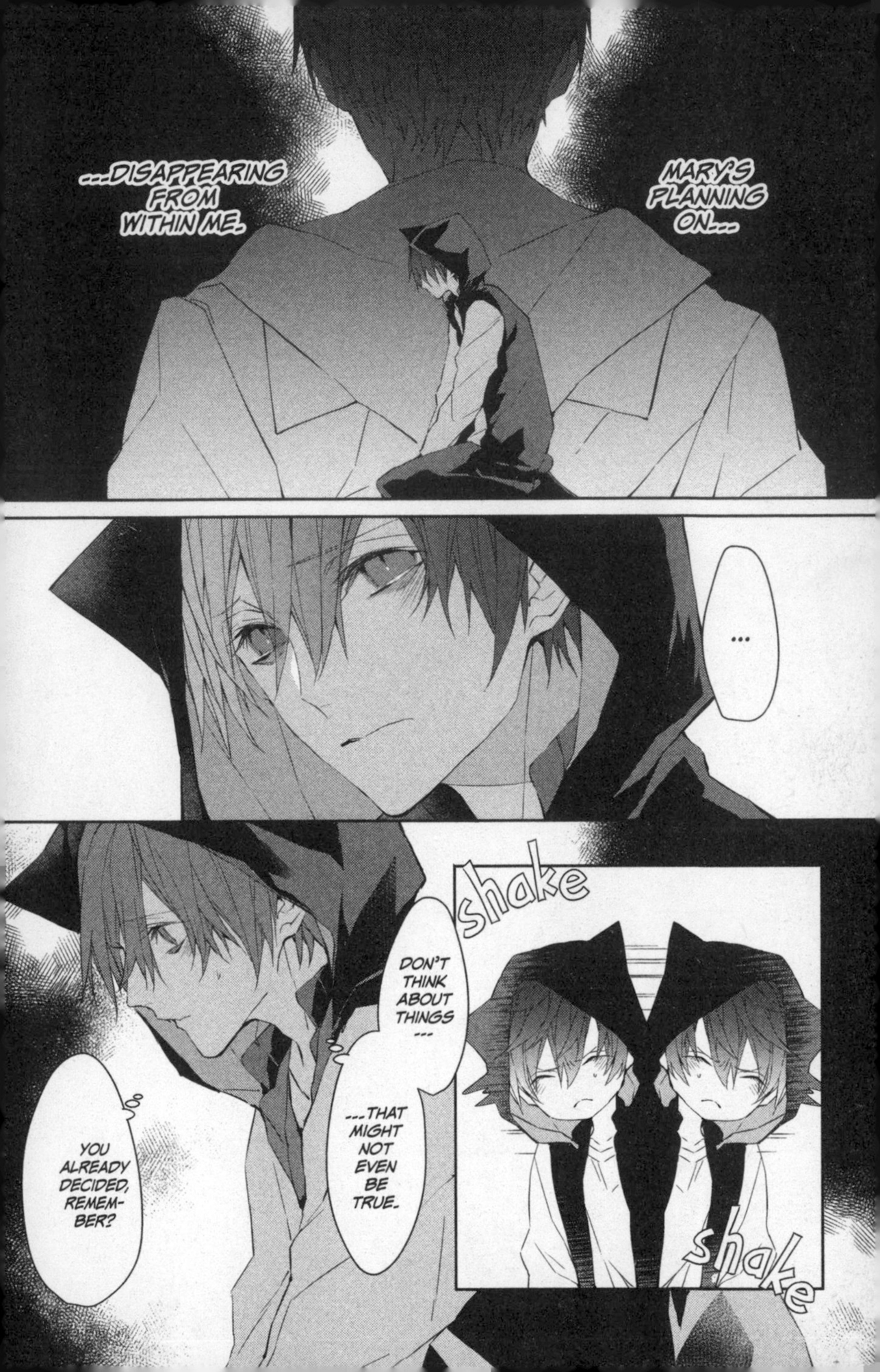
MARY'S PLANNING ON...
...DISAPPEARING FROM WITHIN ME.
...
shake
shake
DON'T THINK ABOUT THINGS---
---THAT MIGHT NOT EVEN BE TRUE.
YOU ALREADY DECIDED, REMEM-BER?

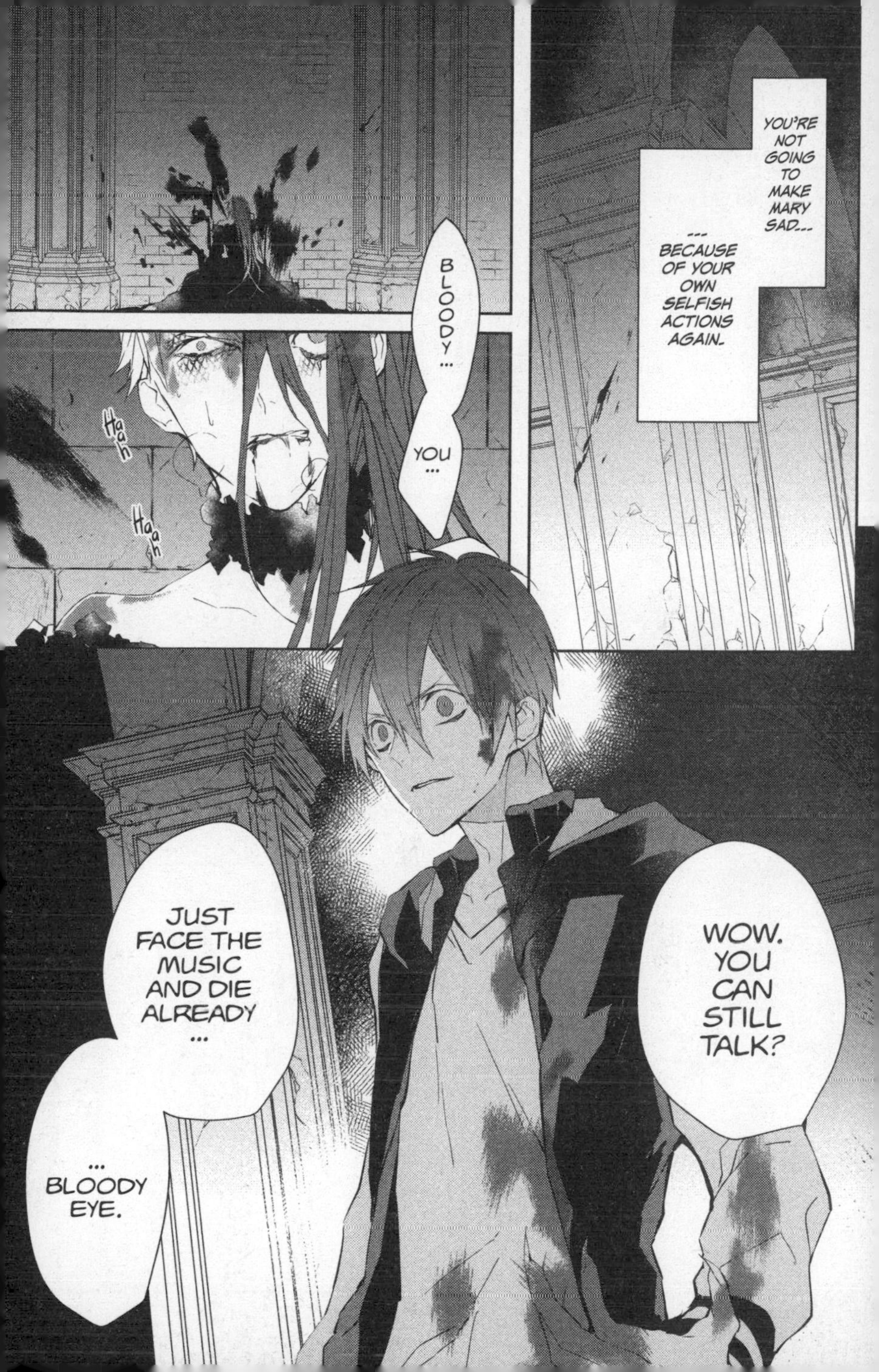
YOU'RE NOT GOING TO MAKE MARY SAD...
...BECAUSE OF YOUR OWN SELFISH ACTIONS AGAIN.
BLOODY...
YOU...
Haah
Haah
WOW. YOU CAN STILL TALK?
JUST FACE THE MUSIC AND DIE ALREADY...
...BLOODY EYE.

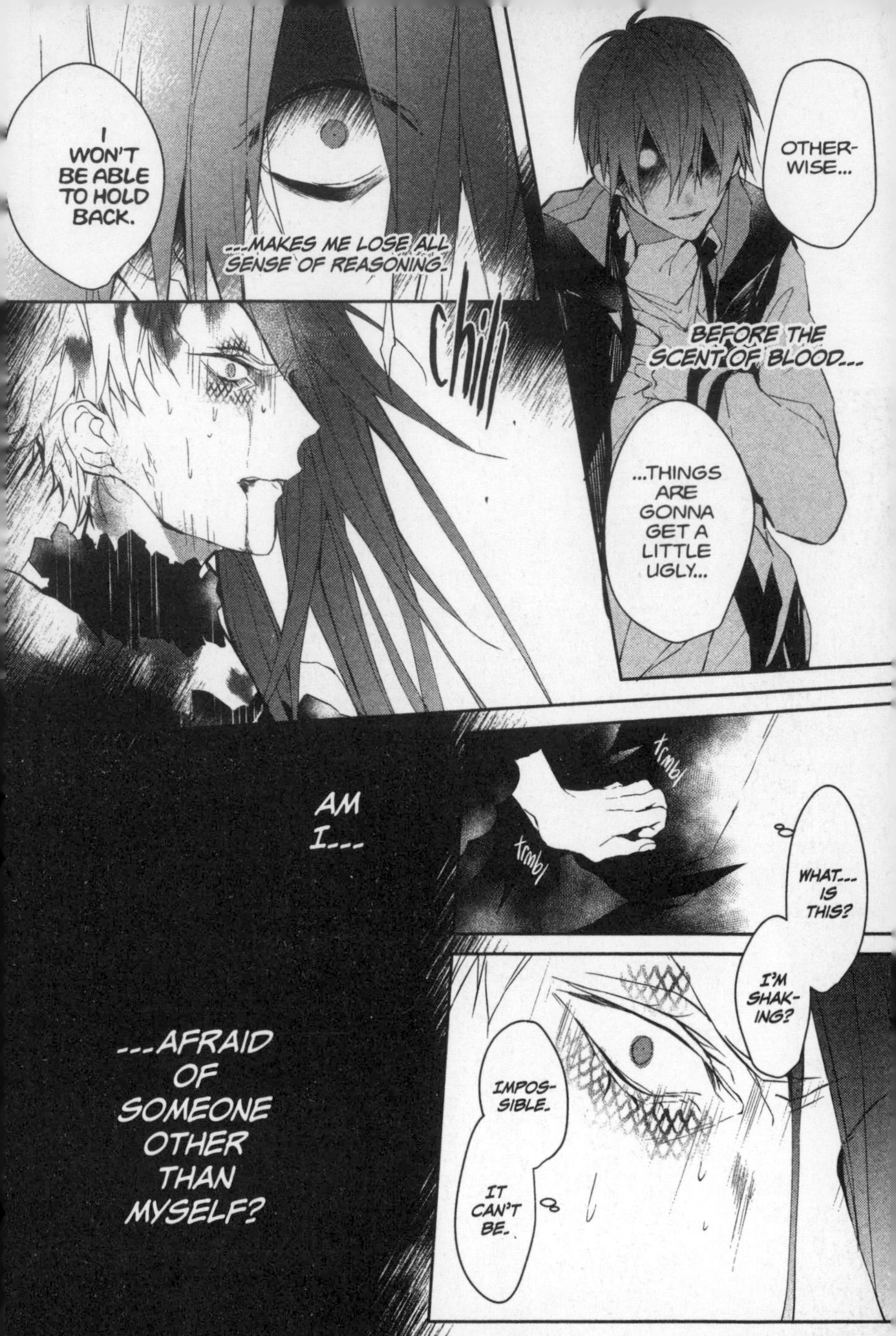
OTHER-WISE...
BEFORE THE SCENT OF BLOOD...
...THINGS ARE GONNA GET A LITTLE UGLY...
I WON'T BE ABLE TO HOLD BACK.
...MAKES ME LOSE ALL SENSE OF REASONING.
chill
trmbl
trmbl
WHAT... IS THIS?
I'M SHAK-ING?
IMPOS-SIBLE.
IT CAN'T BE.
AM I...
...AFRAID OF SOMEONE OTHER THAN MYSELF?

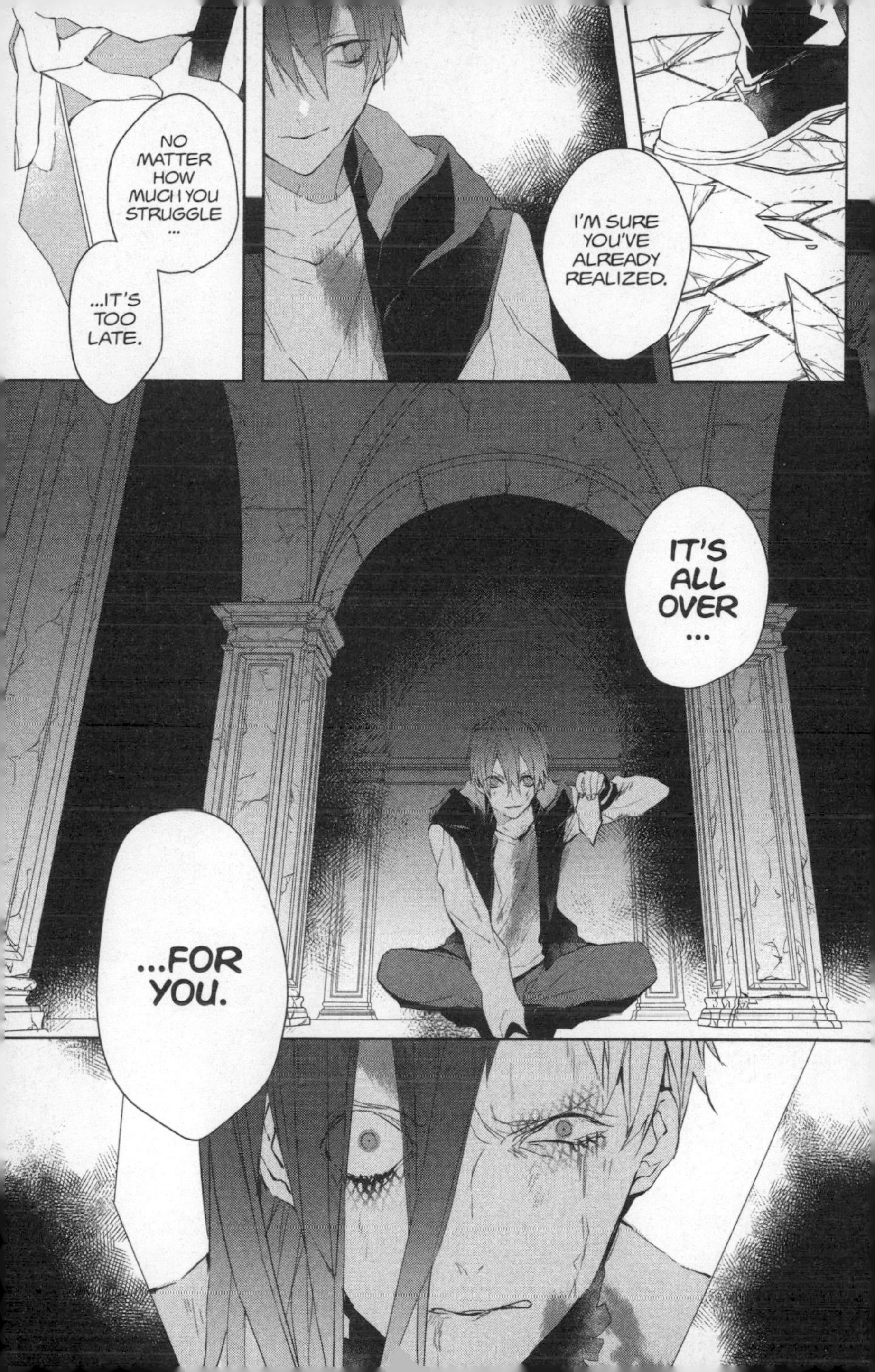
I'M SURE YOU'VE ALREADY REALIZED.
NO MATTER HOW MUCH YOU STRUGGLE...
...IT'S TOO LATE.
IT'S ALL OVER...
...FOR YOU.

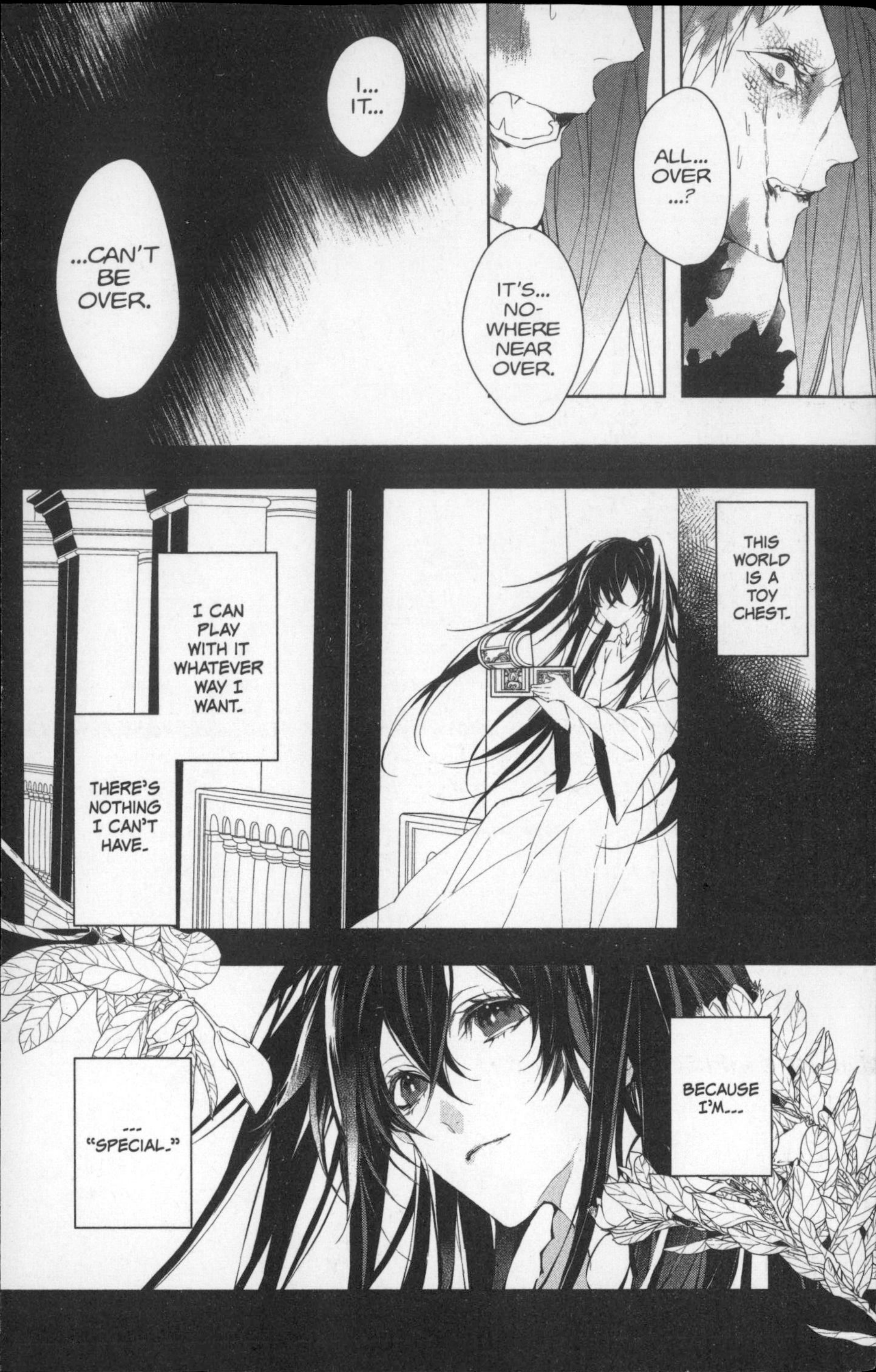
ALL... OVER ...?
IT'S... NO-WHERE NEAR OVER.
I... IT...
...CAN'T BE OVER.
THIS WORLD IS A TOY CHEST.
I CAN PLAY WITH IT WHATEVER WAY I WANT.
THERE'S NOTHING I CAN'T HAVE.
BECAUSE I'M...
... "SPECIAL."

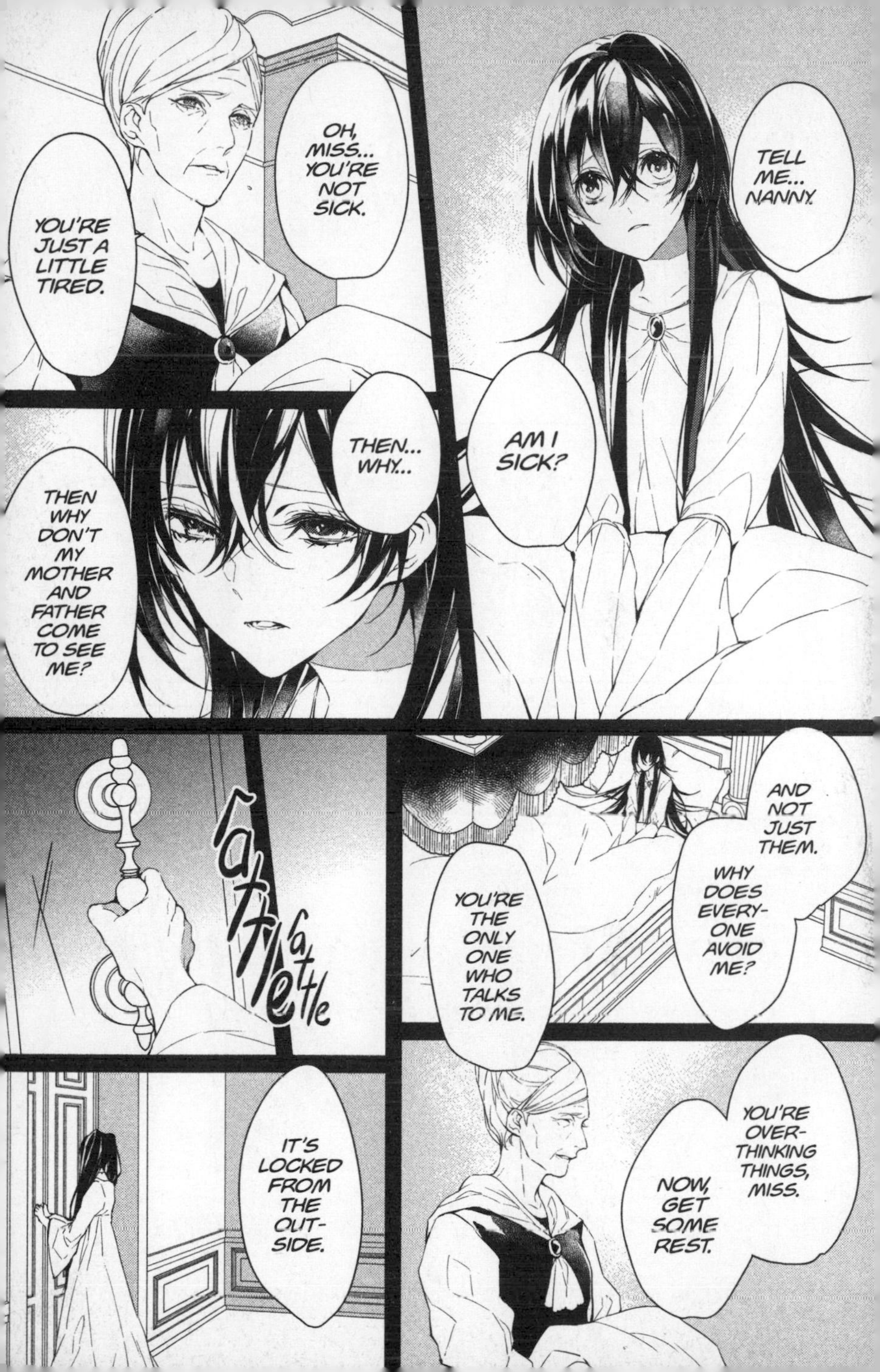
TELL ME... NANNY.
AM I SICK?
OH, MISS... YOU'RE NOT SICK.
YOU'RE JUST A LITTLE TIRED.
THEN... WHY...
THEN WHY DON'T MY MOTHER AND FATHER COME TO SEE ME?
AND NOT JUST THEM.
WHY DOES EVERY-ONE AVOID ME?
YOU'RE THE ONLY ONE WHO TALKS TO ME.
rattle rattle
IT'S LOCKED FROM THE OUT-SIDE.
YOU'RE OVER-THINKING THINGS, MISS.
NOW, GET SOME REST.

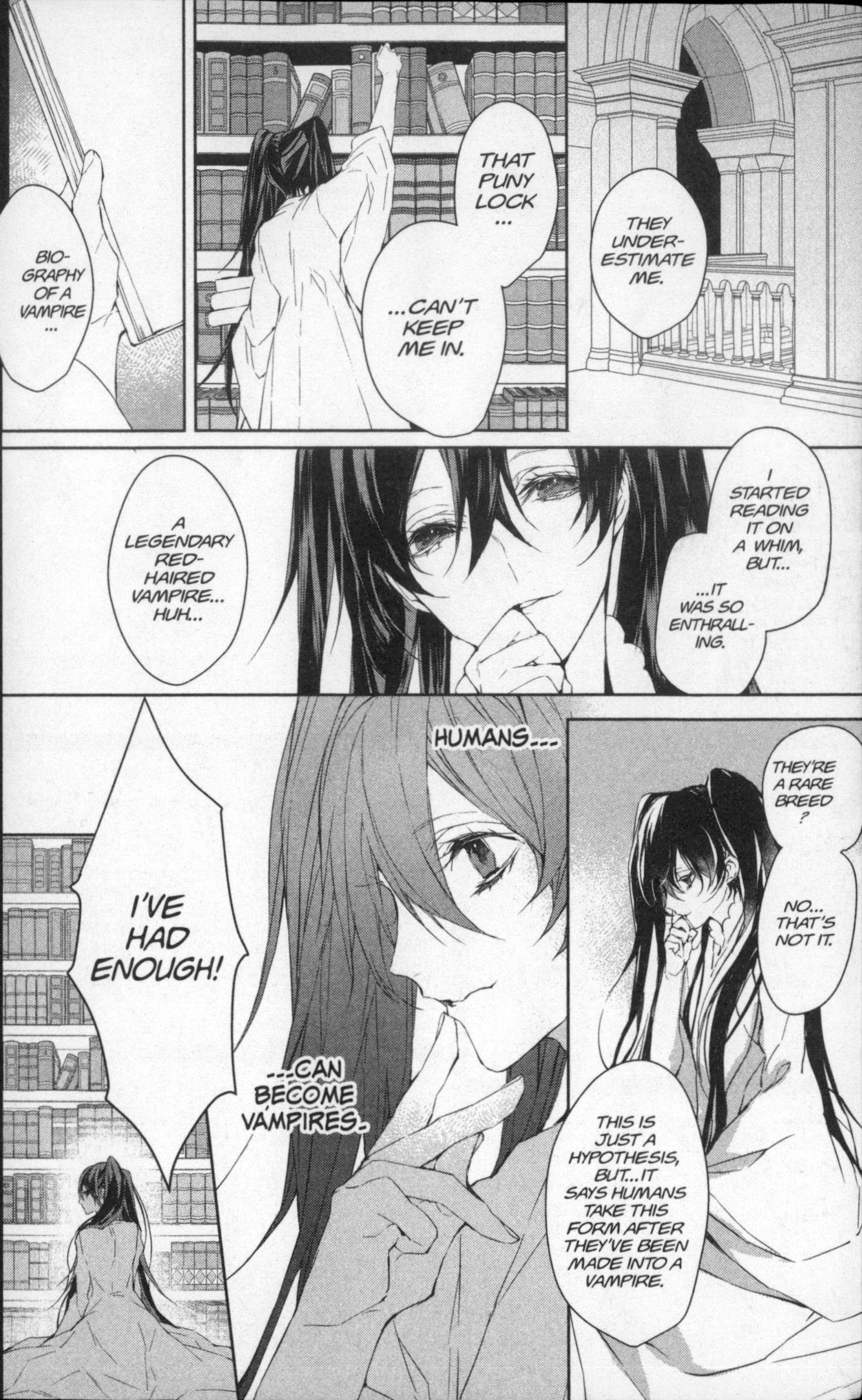
THEY UNDER-ESTIMATE ME.
THAT PUNY LOCK...
...CAN'T KEEP ME IN.
BIO-GRAPHY OF A VAMPIRE...
I STARTED READING IT ON A WHIM, BUT...
...IT WAS SO ENTHRALL-ING.
A LEGENDARY RED-HAIRED VAMPIRE... HUH...
THEY'RE A RARE BREED?
NO... THAT'S NOT IT.
THIS IS JUST A HYPOTHESIS, BUT...IT SAYS HUMANS TAKE THIS FORM AFTER THEY'VE BEEN MADE INTO A VAMPIRE.
HUMANS...
...CAN BECOME VAMPIRES.
I'VE HAD ENOUGH!

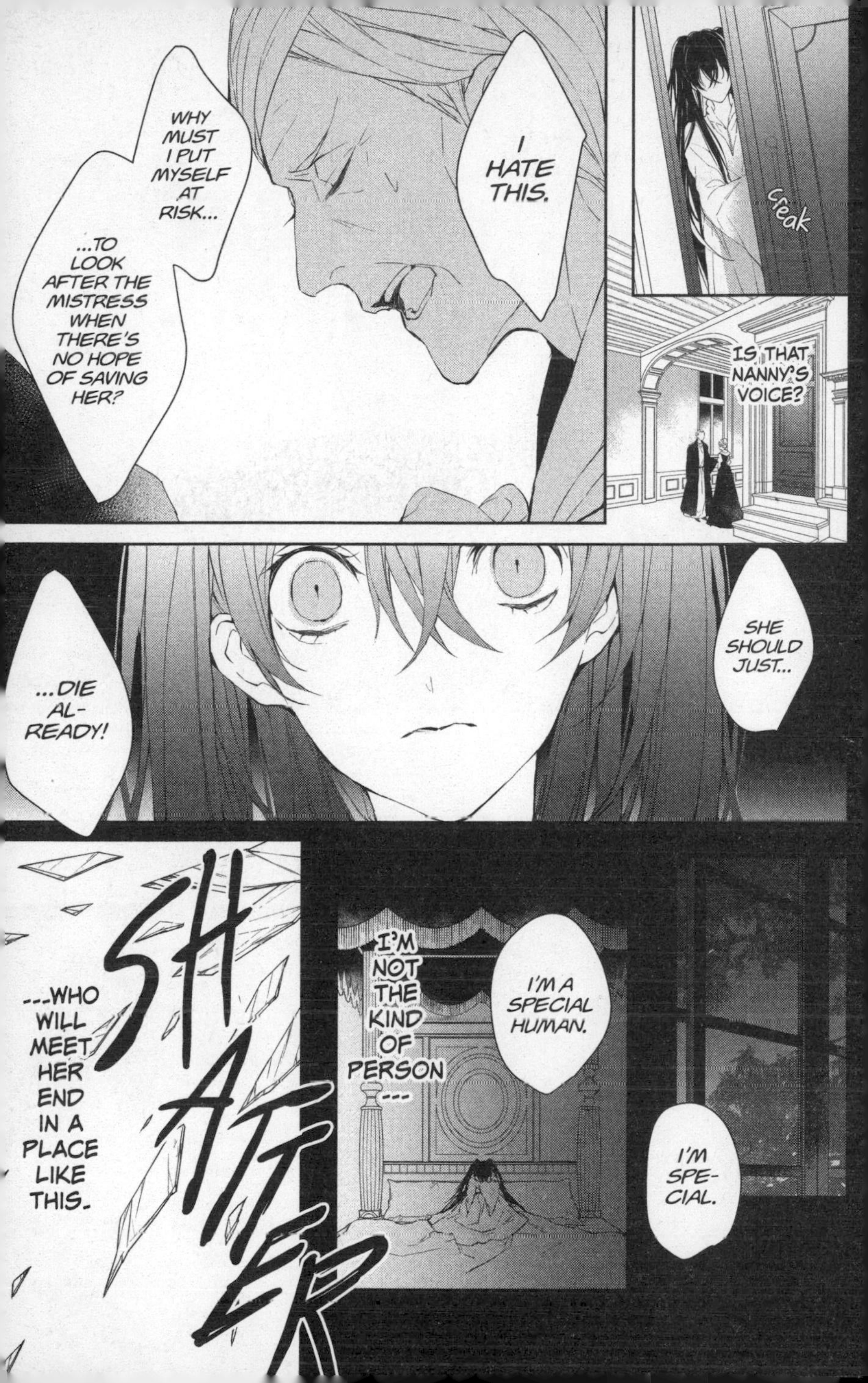
creak
IS THAT NANNY'S VOICE?
I HATE THIS.
WHY MUST I PUT MYSELF AT RISK...
...TO LOOK AFTER THE MISTRESS WHEN THERE'S NO HOPE OF SAVING HER?
SHE SHOULD JUST...
...DIE AL-READY!
I'M A SPECIAL HUMAN.
I'M SPE-CIAL.
I'M NOT THE KIND OF PERSON---
---WHO WILL MEET HER END IN A PLACE LIKE THIS.
SHATTER

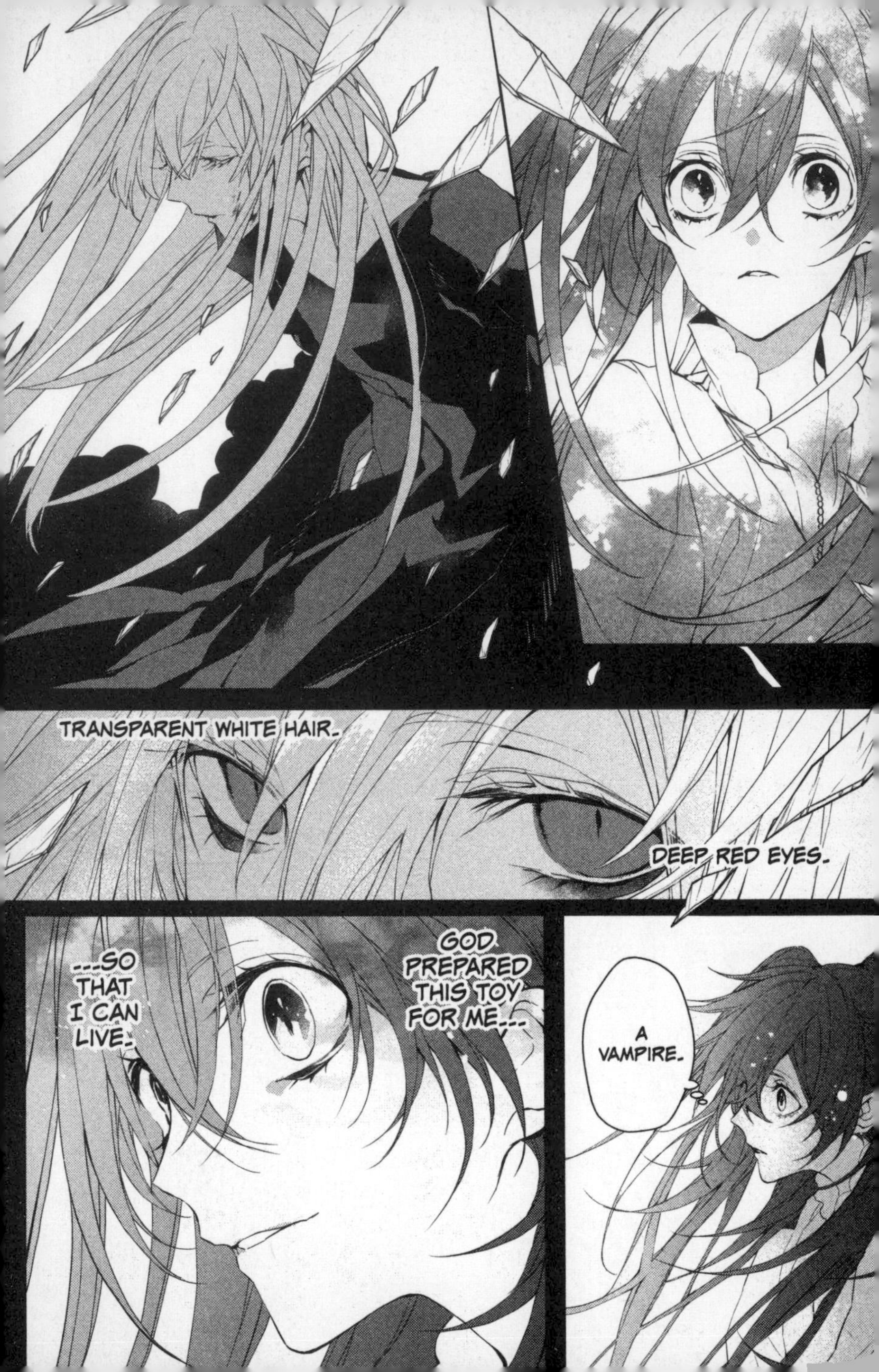
TRANSPARENT WHITE HAIR.
DEEP RED EYES.
A VAMPIRE.
GOD PREPARED THIS TOY FOR ME...
...SO THAT I CAN LIVE.

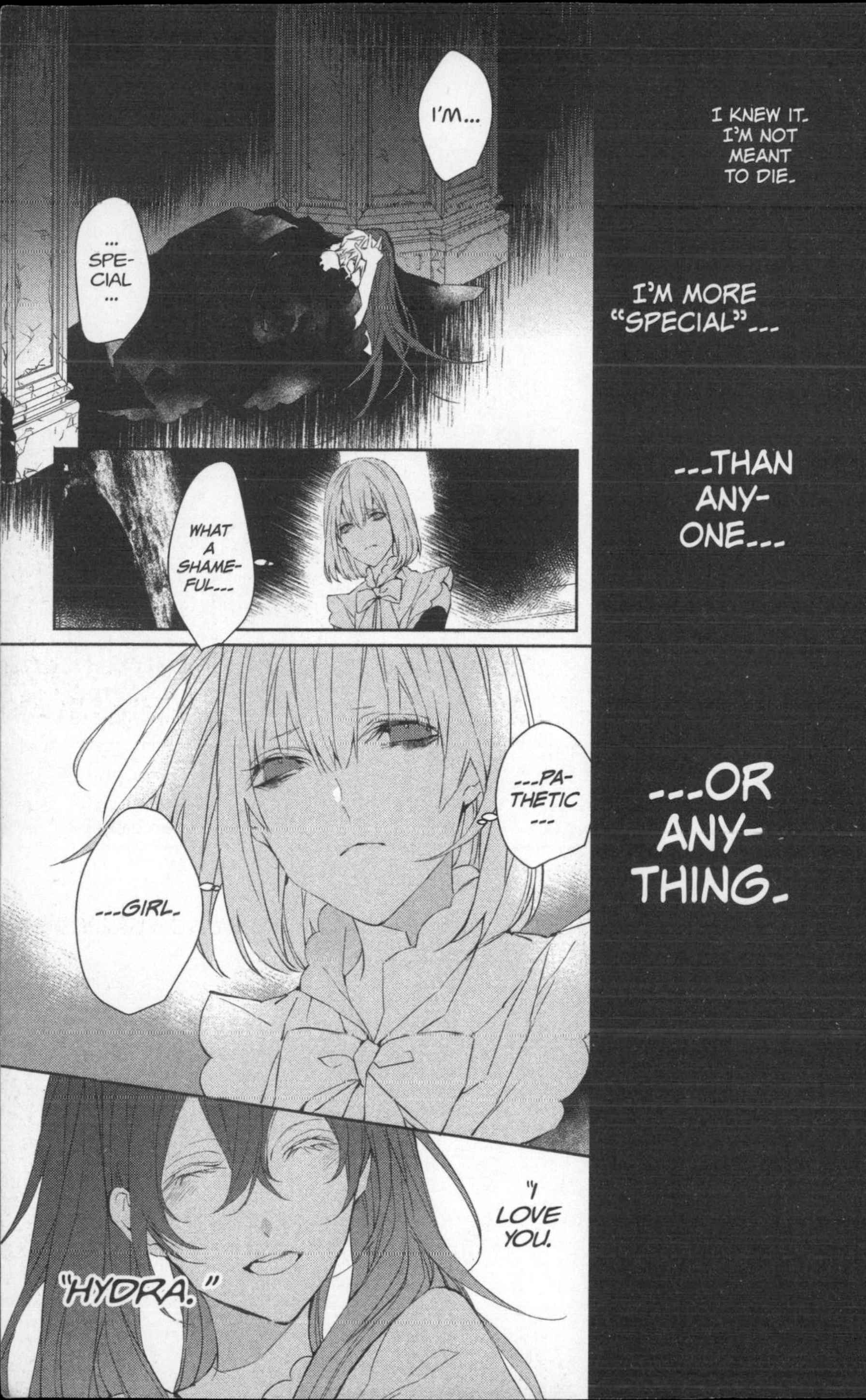
I KNEW IT. I'M NOT MEANT TO DIE.
I'M MORE "SPECIAL"...
...THAN ANYONE...
...OR ANYTHING.
I'M...
...SPECIAL...
WHAT A SHAMEFUL...
...PATHETIC...
...GIRL.
"I LOVE YOU.
"HYDRA."

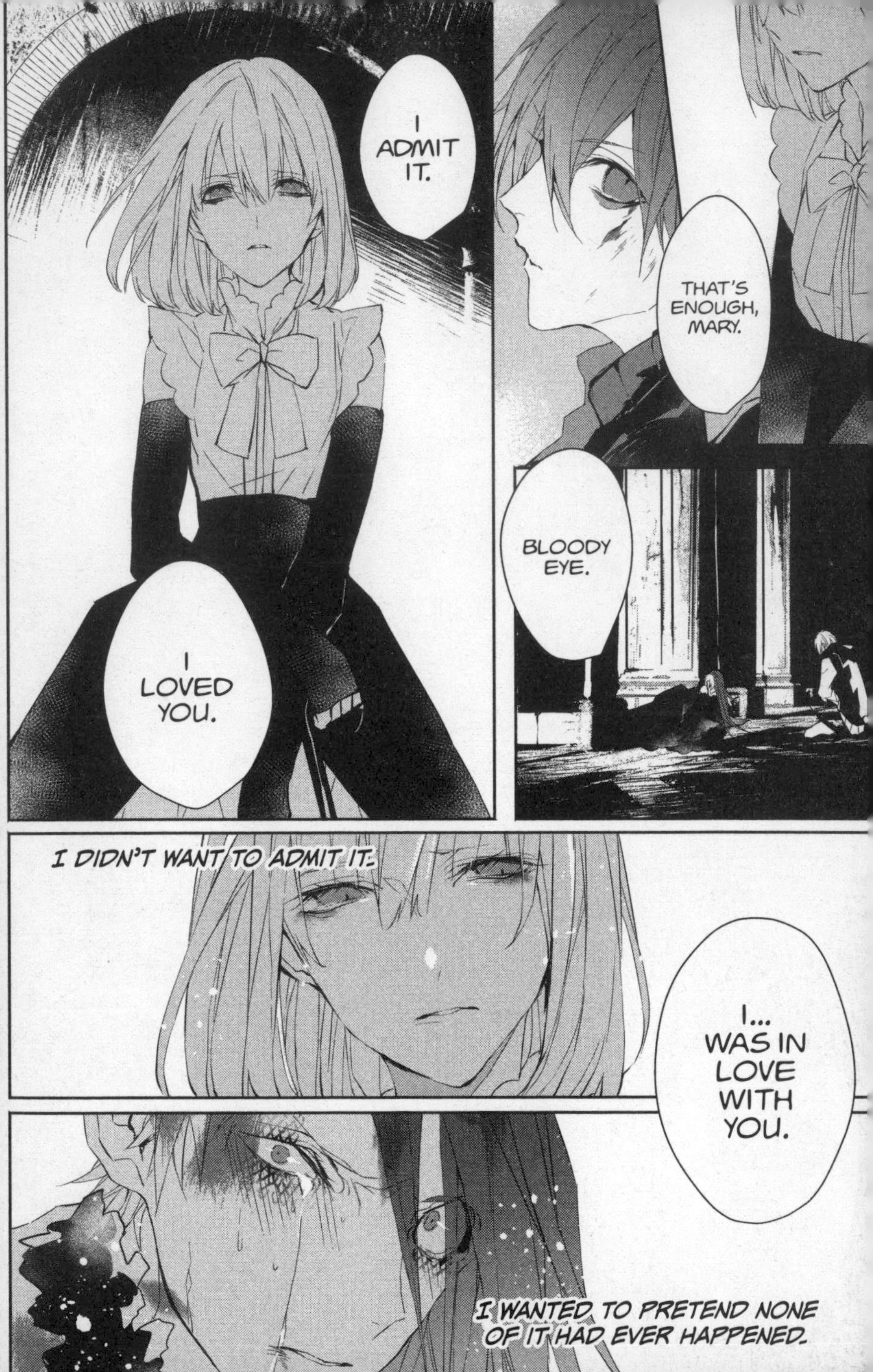
THAT'S ENOUGH, MARY.
BLOODY EYE.
I ADMIT IT.
I LOVED YOU.
I DIDN'T WANT TO ADMIT IT.
I... WAS IN LOVE WITH YOU.
I WANTED TO PRETEND NONE OF IT HAD EVER HAPPENED.

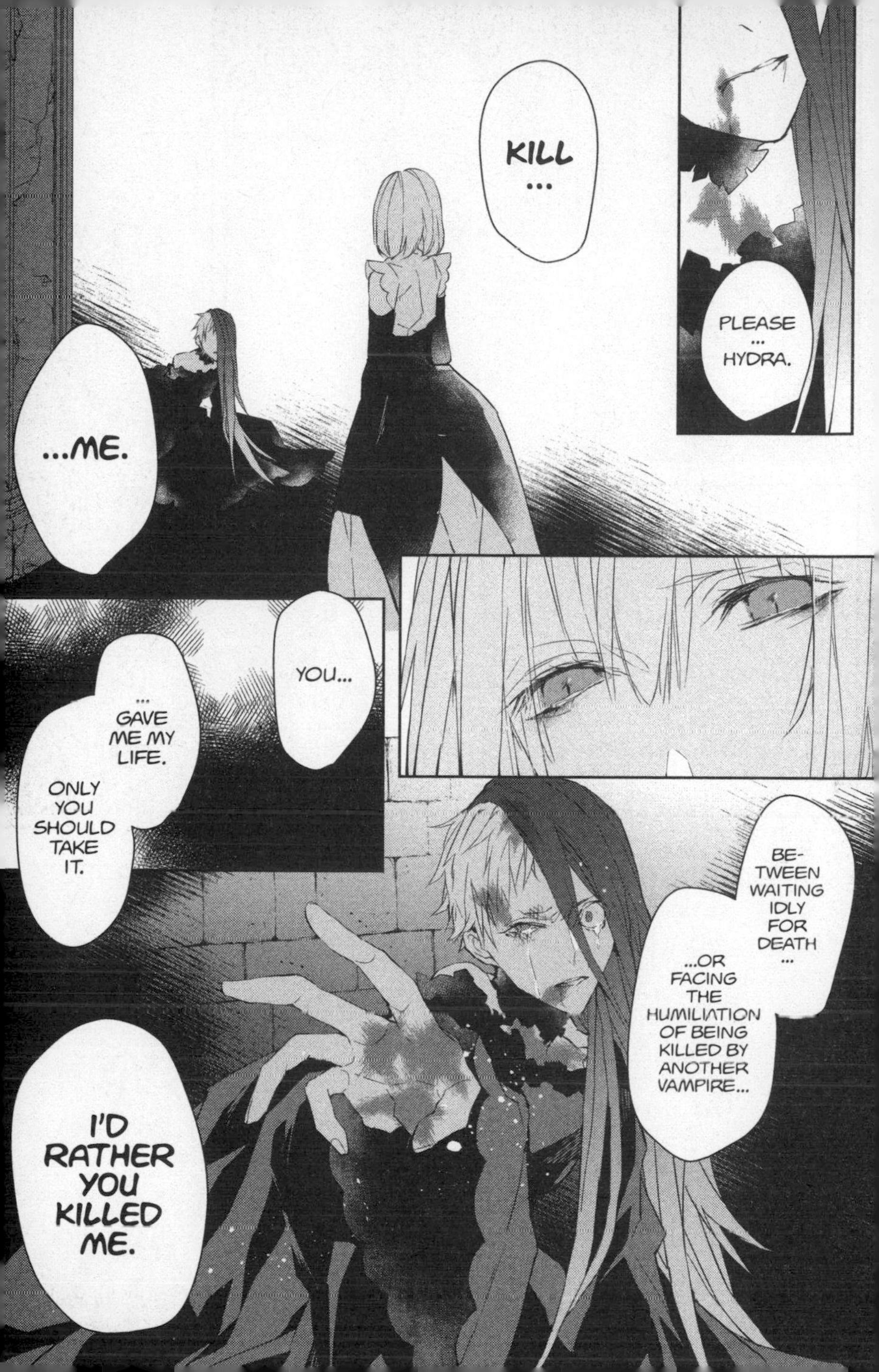
PLEASE ... HYDRA.
KILL ...
...ME.
YOU...
... GAVE ME MY LIFE.
ONLY YOU SHOULD TAKE IT.
BE-TWEEN WAITING IDLY FOR DEATH ...
...OR FACING THE HUMILIATION OF BEING KILLED BY ANOTHER VAMPIRE...
I'D RATHER YOU KILLED ME.

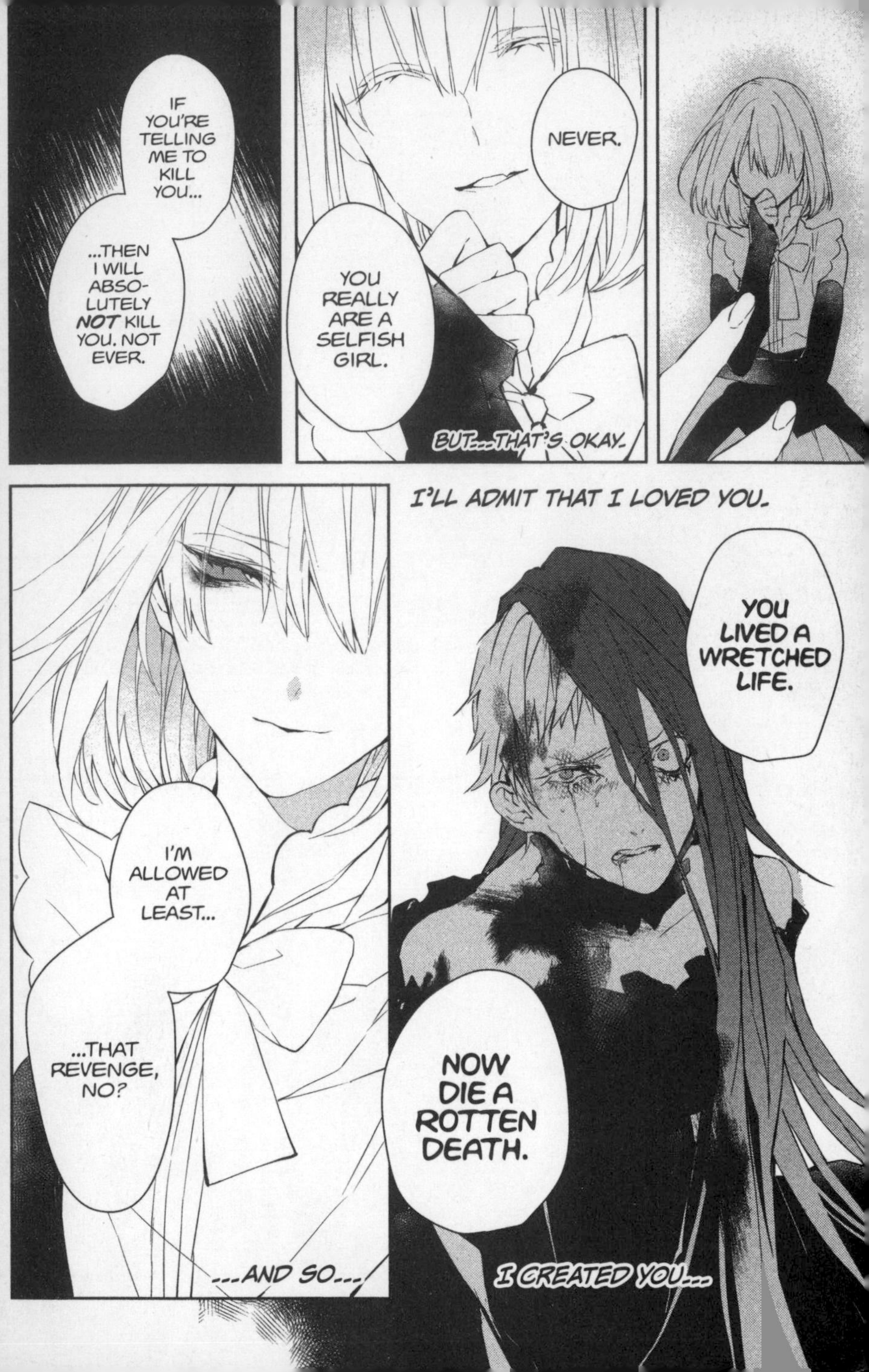
NEVER.
YOU REALLY ARE A SELFISH GIRL.
BUT...THAT'S OKAY.
IF YOU'RE TELLING ME TO KILL YOU...
...THEN I WILL ABSOLUTELY NOT KILL YOU. NOT EVER.
I'LL ADMIT THAT I LOVED YOU.
YOU LIVED A WRETCHED LIFE.
NOW DIE A ROTTEN DEATH.
I CREATED YOU...
I'M ALLOWED AT LEAST...
...THAT REVENGE, NO?
...AND SO...

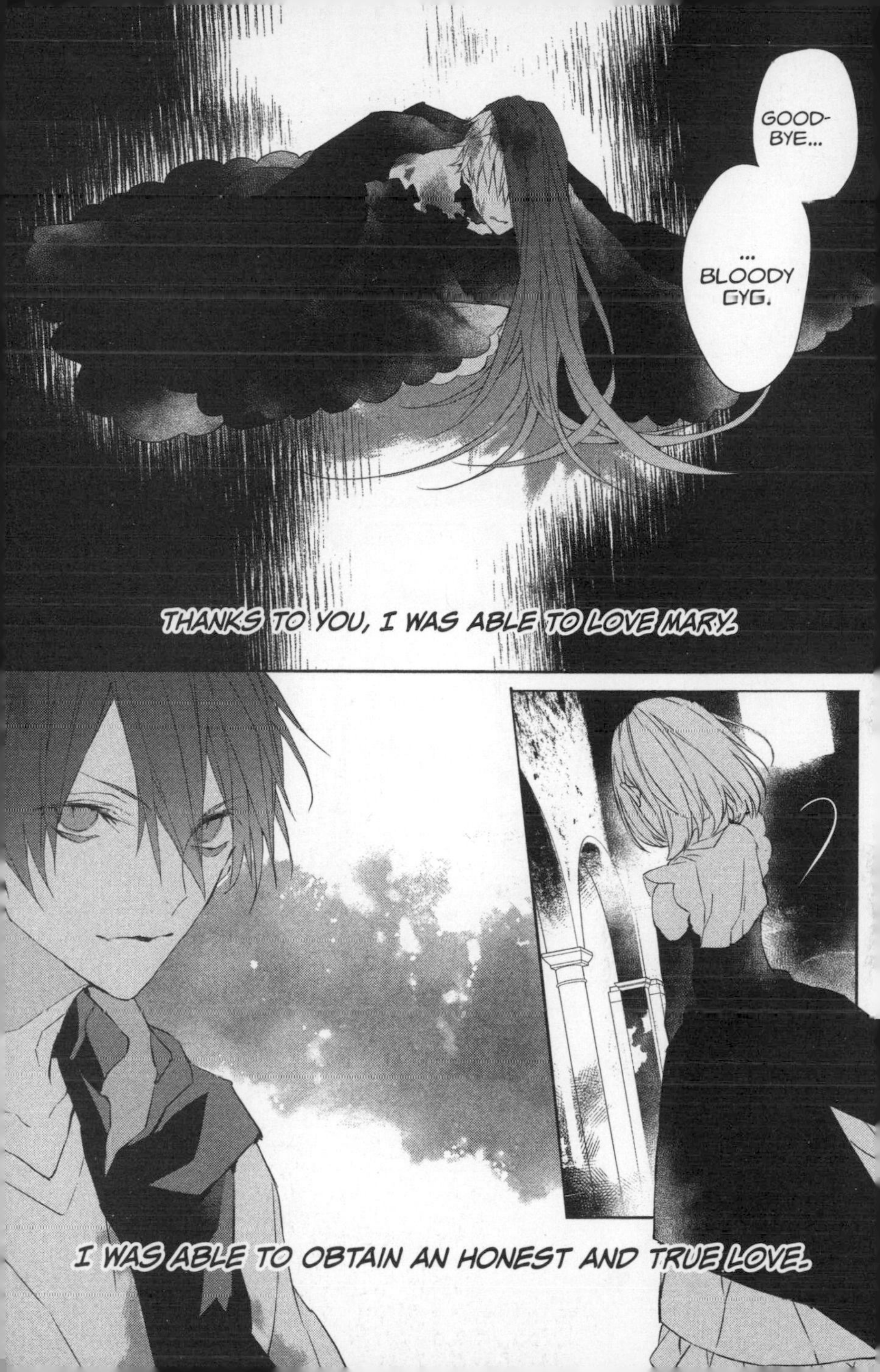
GOOD-BYE...
...BLOODY GYG.
THANKS TO YOU, I WAS ABLE TO LOVE MARY.
I WAS ABLE TO OBTAIN AN HONEST AND TRUE LOVE.

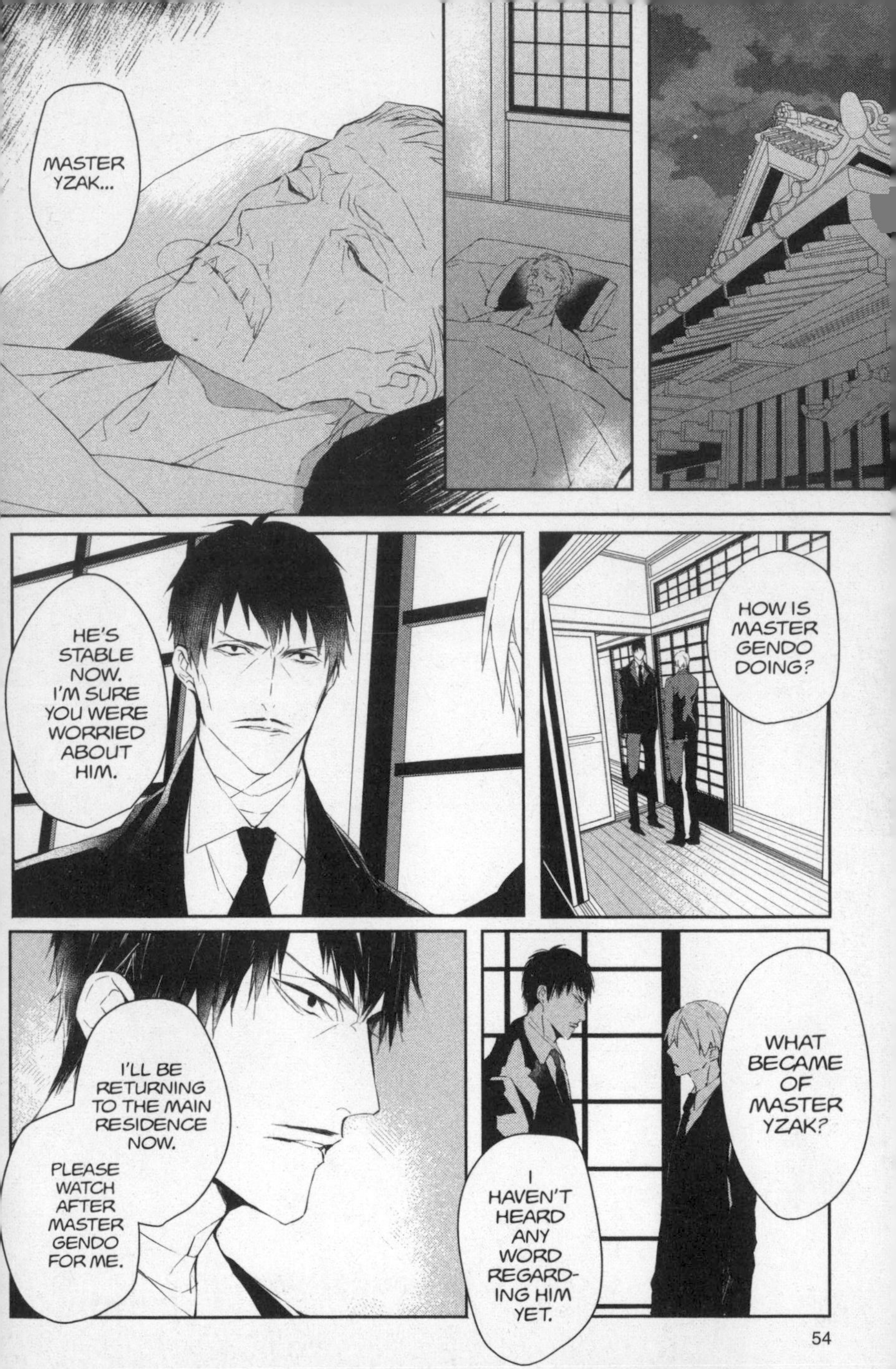
MASTER YZAK...
HOW IS MASTER GENDO DOING?
HE'S STABLE NOW. I'M SURE YOU WERE WORRIED ABOUT HIM.
WHAT BECAME OF MASTER YZAK?
I HAVEN'T HEARD ANY WORD REGARDING HIM YET.
I'LL BE RETURNING TO THE MAIN RESIDENCE NOW.
PLEASE WATCH AFTER MASTER GENDO FOR ME.

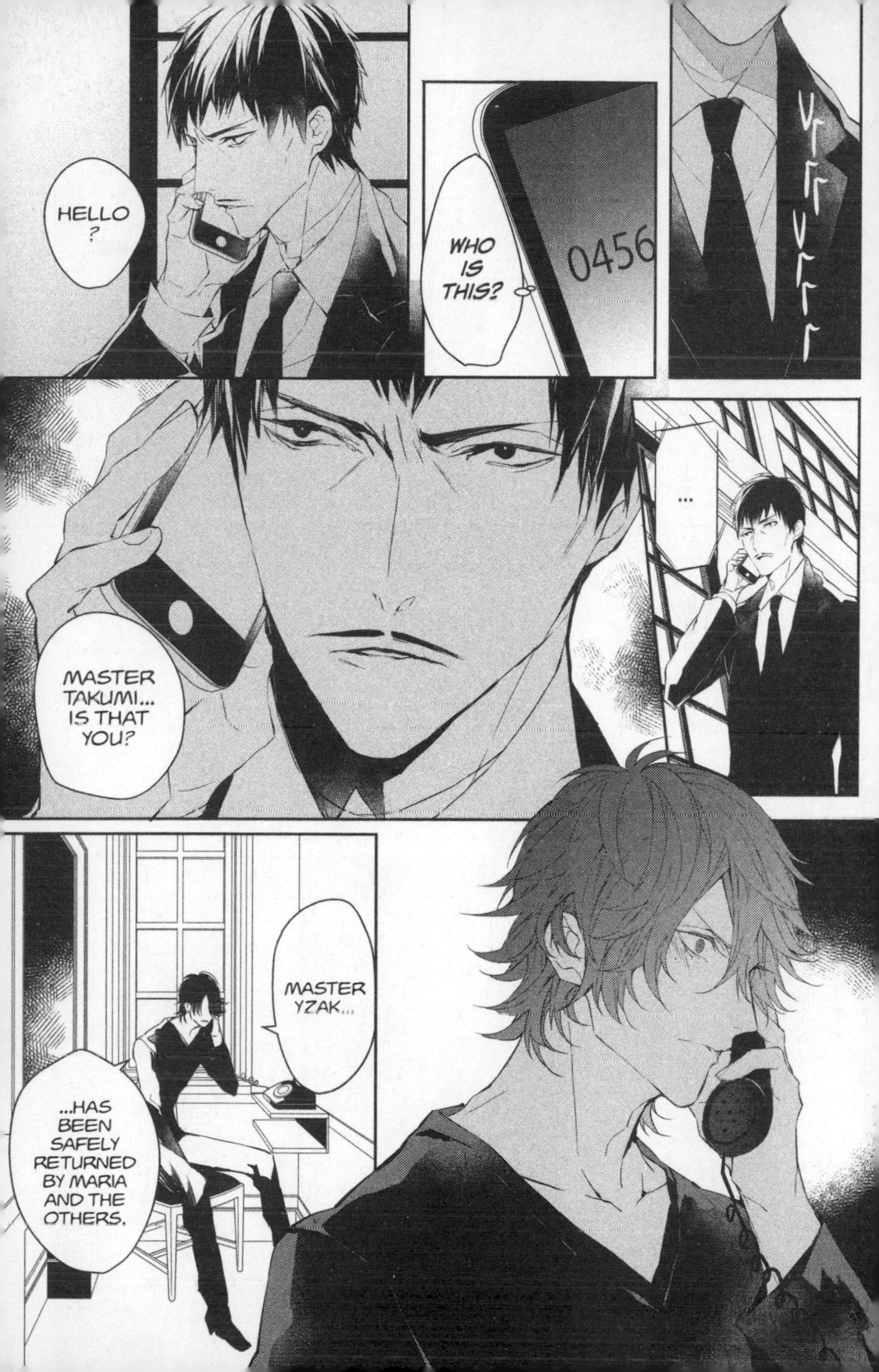
VRR VRRR
0456
WHO IS THIS?
HELLO ?
...
MASTER TAKUMI... IS THAT YOU?
MASTER YZAK...
...HAS BEEN SAFELY RETURNED BY MARIA AND THE OTHERS.

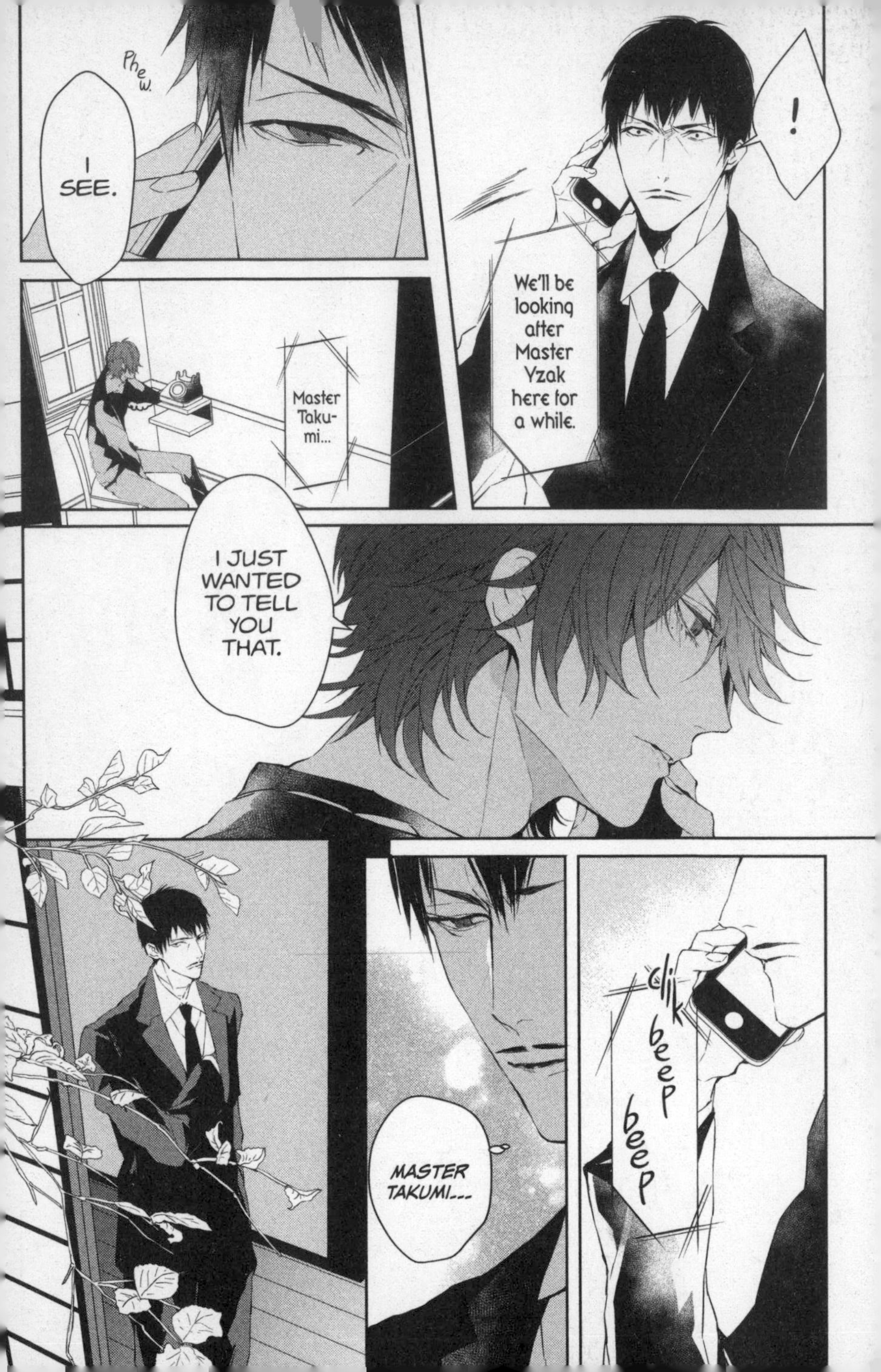
!
We'll be looking after Master Yzak here for a while.
Phew.
I SEE.
Master Taku-mi...
I JUST WANTED TO TELL YOU THAT.
clik
beep
beep
MASTER TAKUMI...

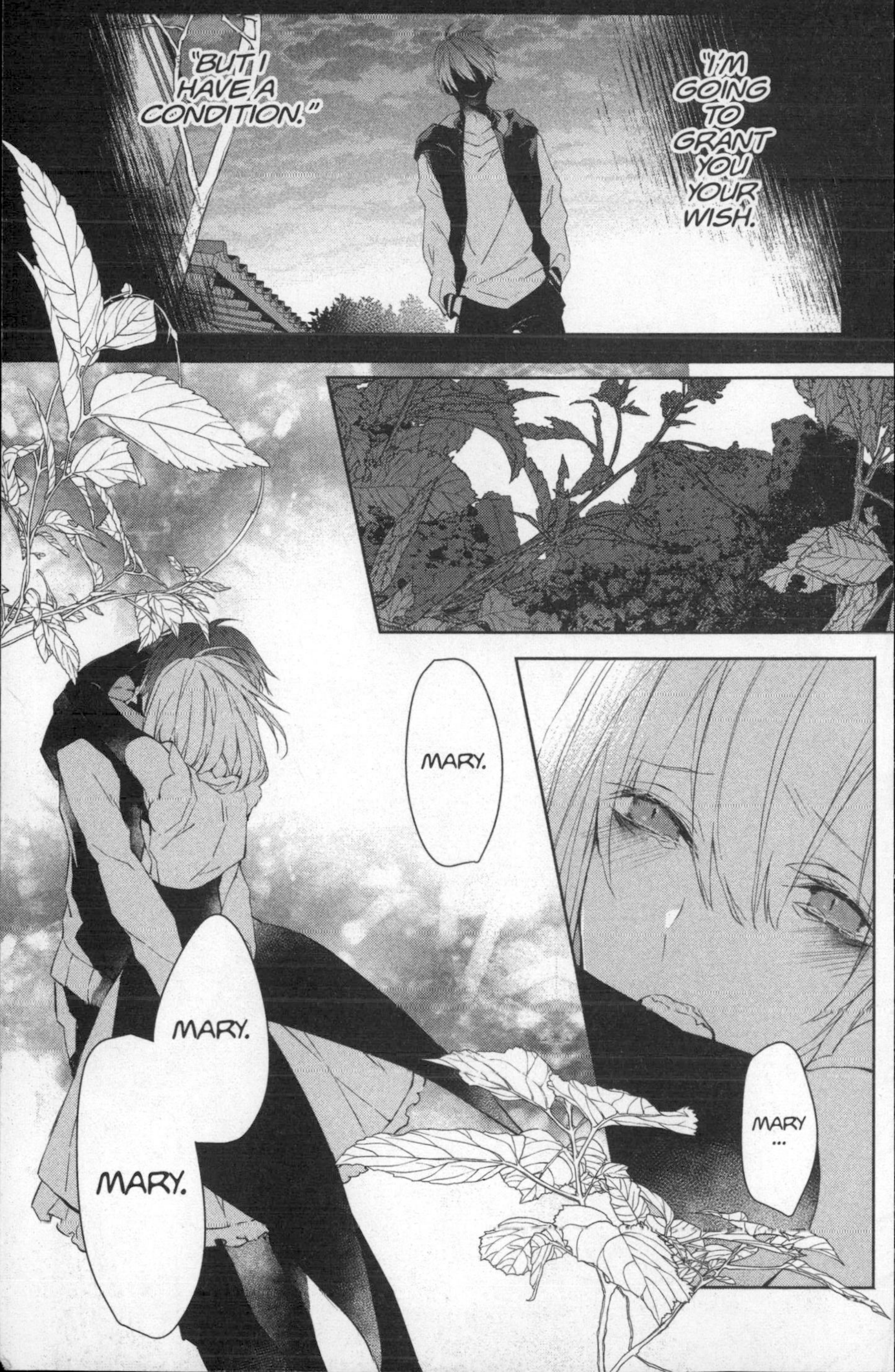
"I'M GOING TO GRANT YOU YOUR WISH.
"BUT I HAVE A CONDITION."
MARY ...
MARY.
MARY.
MARY.

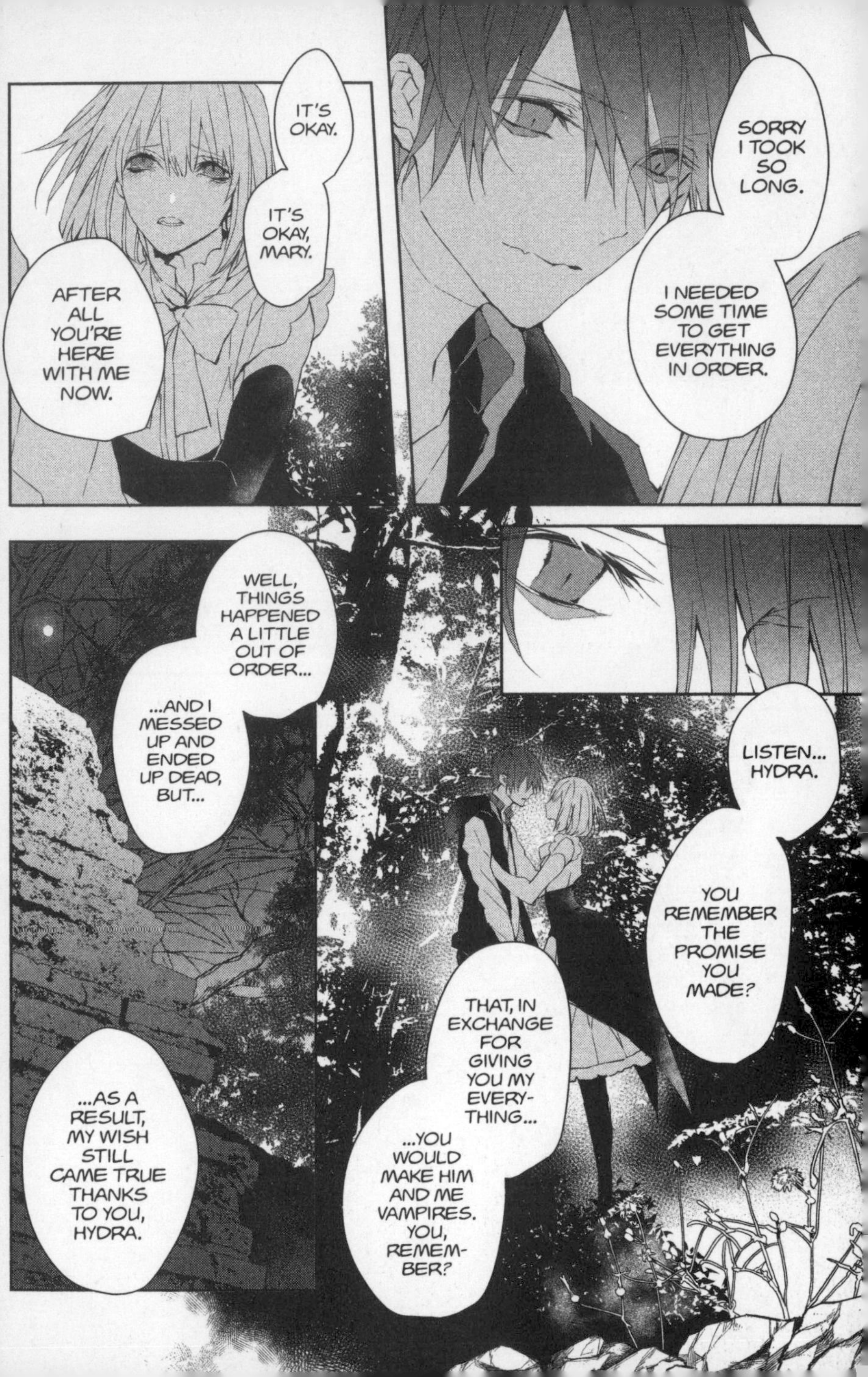
SORRY I TOOK SO LONG.
I NEEDED SOME TIME TO GET EVERYTHING IN ORDER.
IT'S OKAY.
IT'S OKAY, MARY.
AFTER ALL YOU'RE HERE WITH ME NOW.
LISTEN... HYDRA.
YOU REMEMBER THE PROMISE YOU MADE?
THAT, IN EXCHANGE FOR GIVING YOU MY EVERY-THING...
...YOU WOULD MAKE HIM AND ME VAMPIRES. YOU, REMEM-BER?
WELL, THINGS HAPPENED A LITTLE OUT OF ORDER...
...AND I MESSED UP AND ENDED UP DEAD, BUT...
...AS A RESULT, MY WISH STILL CAME TRUE THANKS TO YOU, HYDRA.

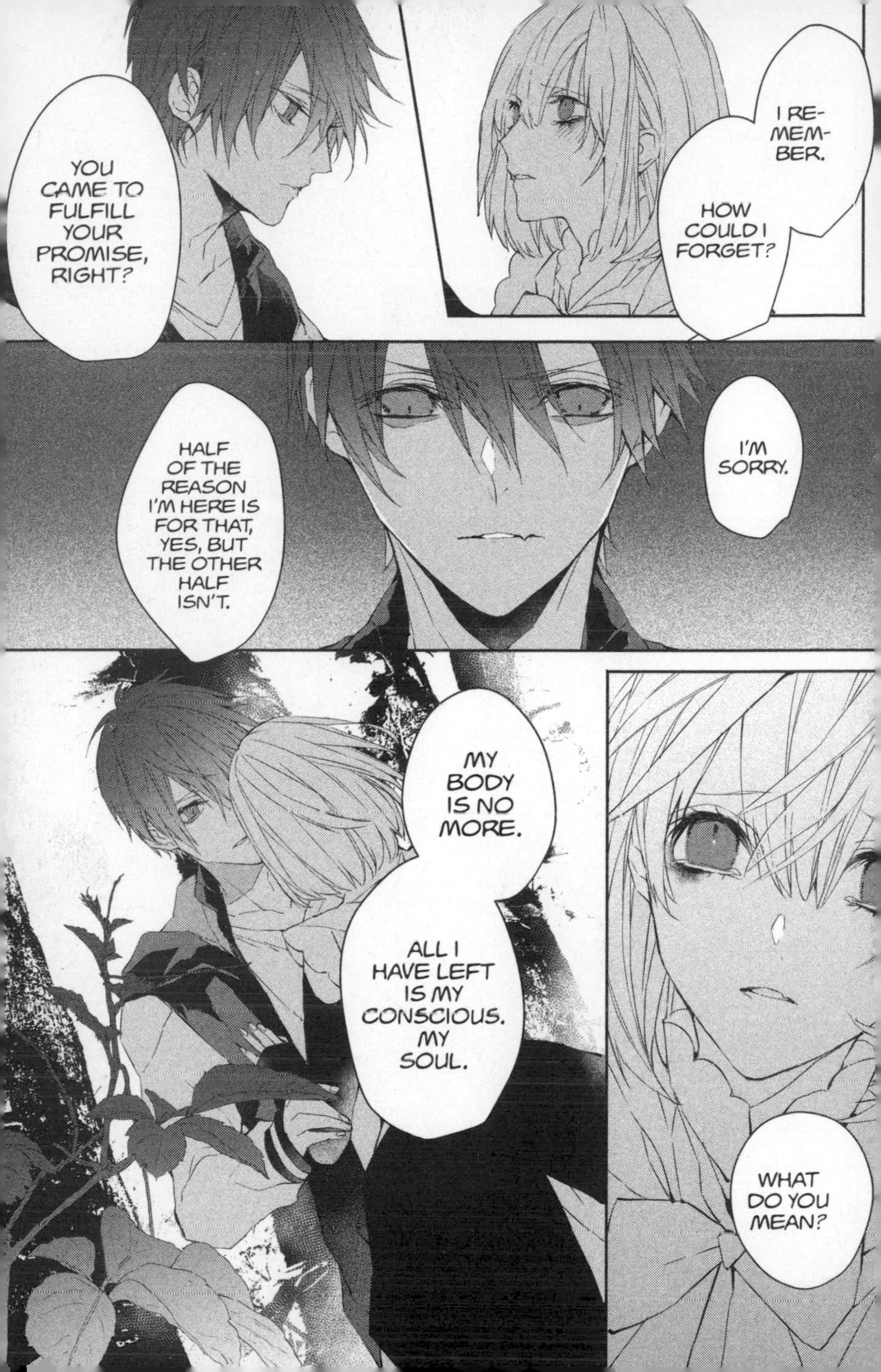
I RE-MEM-BER.
HOW COULD I FORGET?
YOU CAME TO FULFILL YOUR PROMISE, RIGHT?
I'M SORRY.
HALF OF THE REASON I'M HERE IS FOR THAT, YES, BUT THE OTHER HALF ISN'T.
WHAT DO YOU MEAN?
MY BODY IS NO MORE.
ALL I HAVE LEFT IS MY CONSCIOUS. MY SOUL.

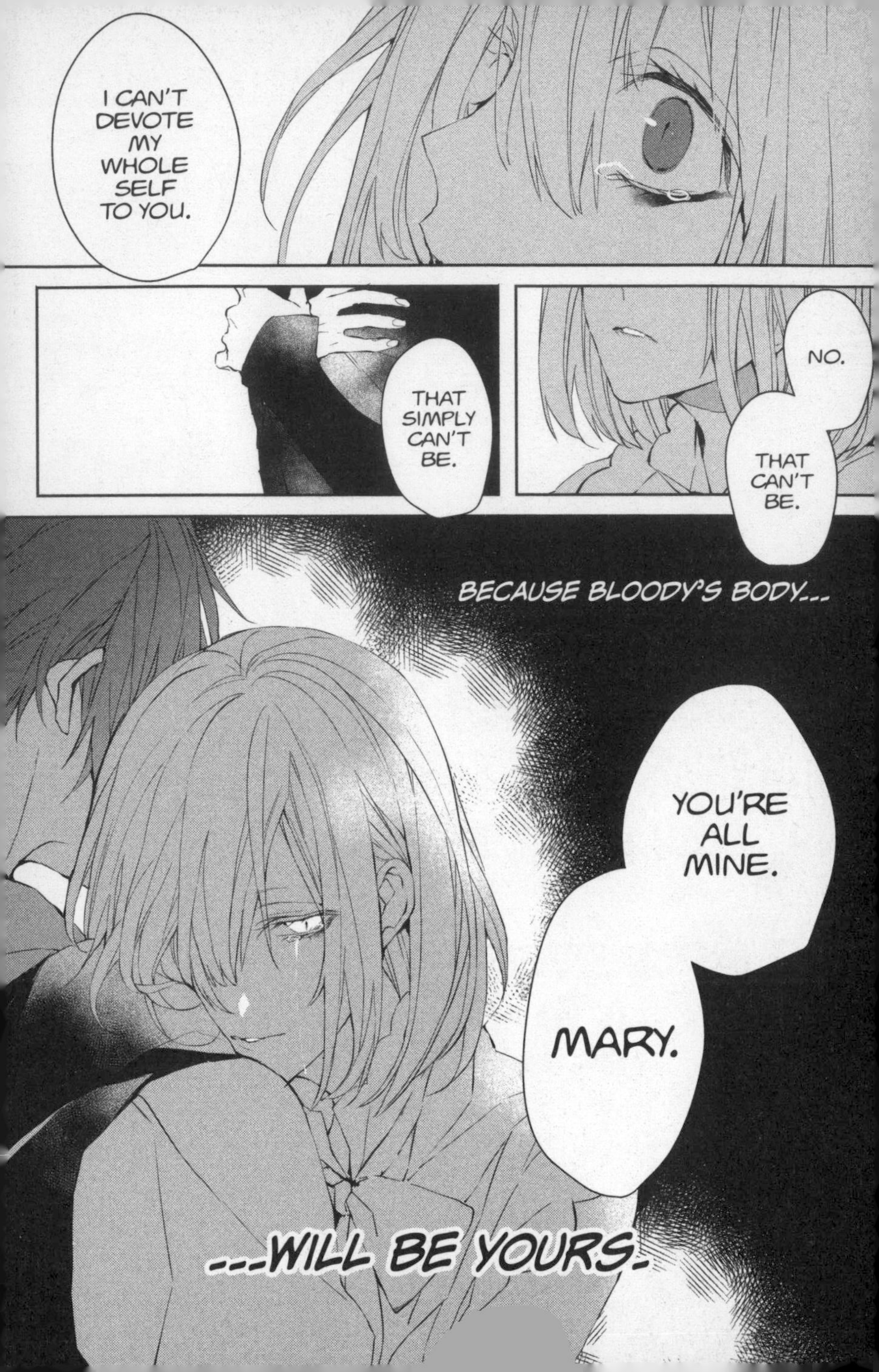
I CAN'T DEVOTE MY WHOLE SELF TO YOU.
NO.
THAT CAN'T BE.
THAT SIMPLY CAN'T BE.
BECAUSE BLOODY'S BODY...
YOU'RE ALL MINE.
MARY.
...WILL BE YOURS.

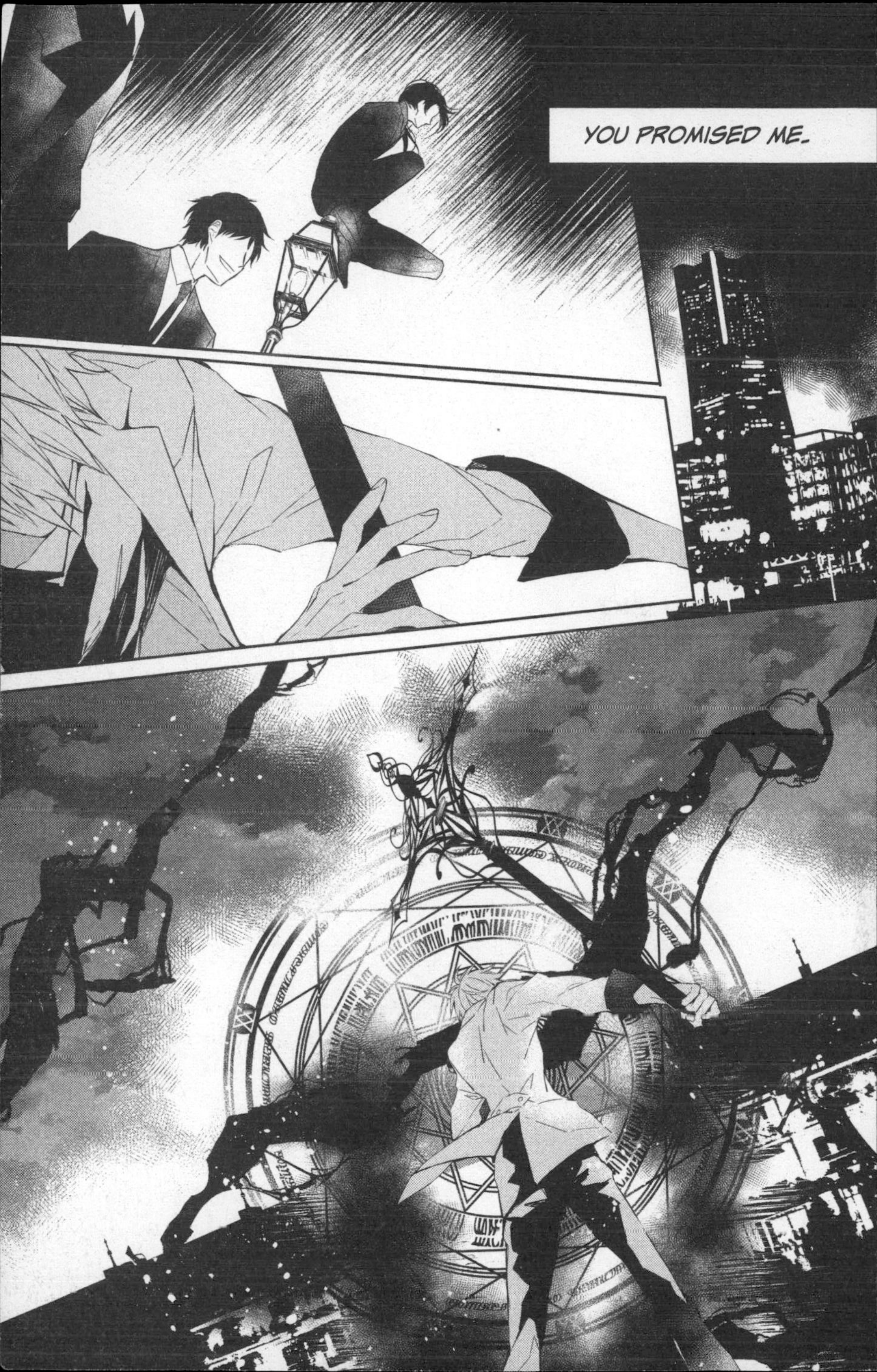
YOU PROMISED ME-

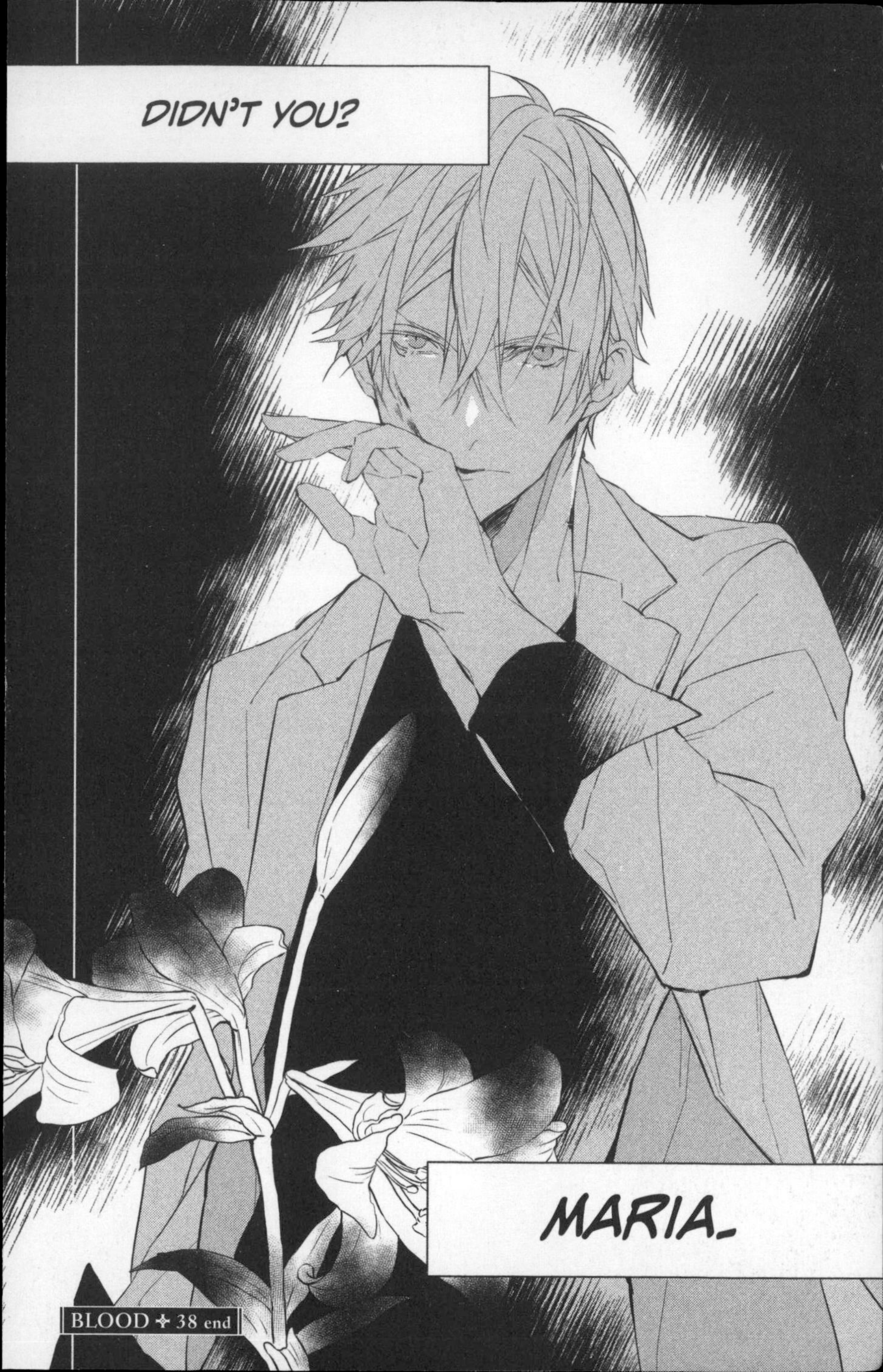
DIDN'T YOU?
MARIA_
BLOOD ✦ 38 end

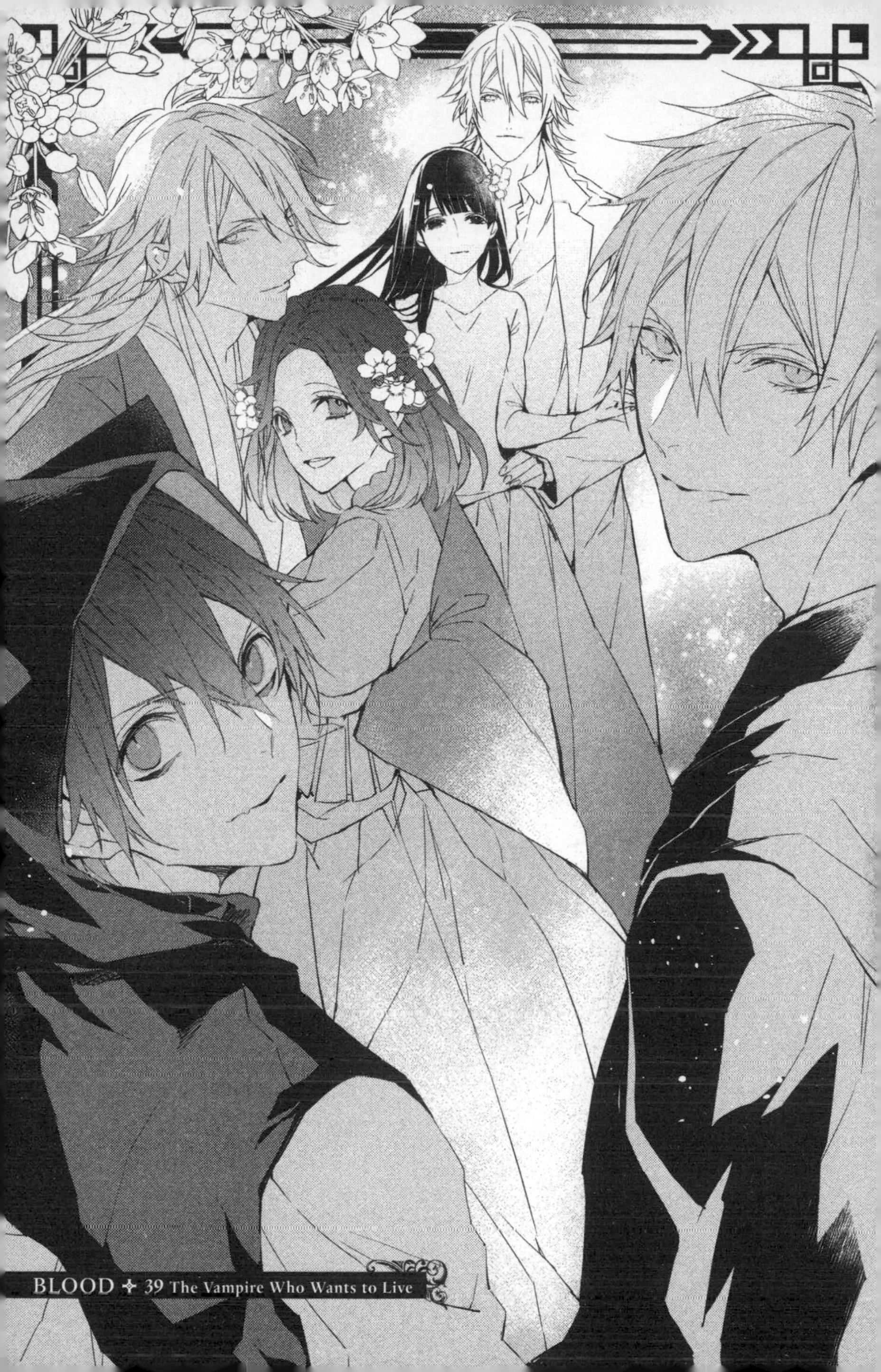

BLOOD ✣ 39 The Vampire Who Wants to Live

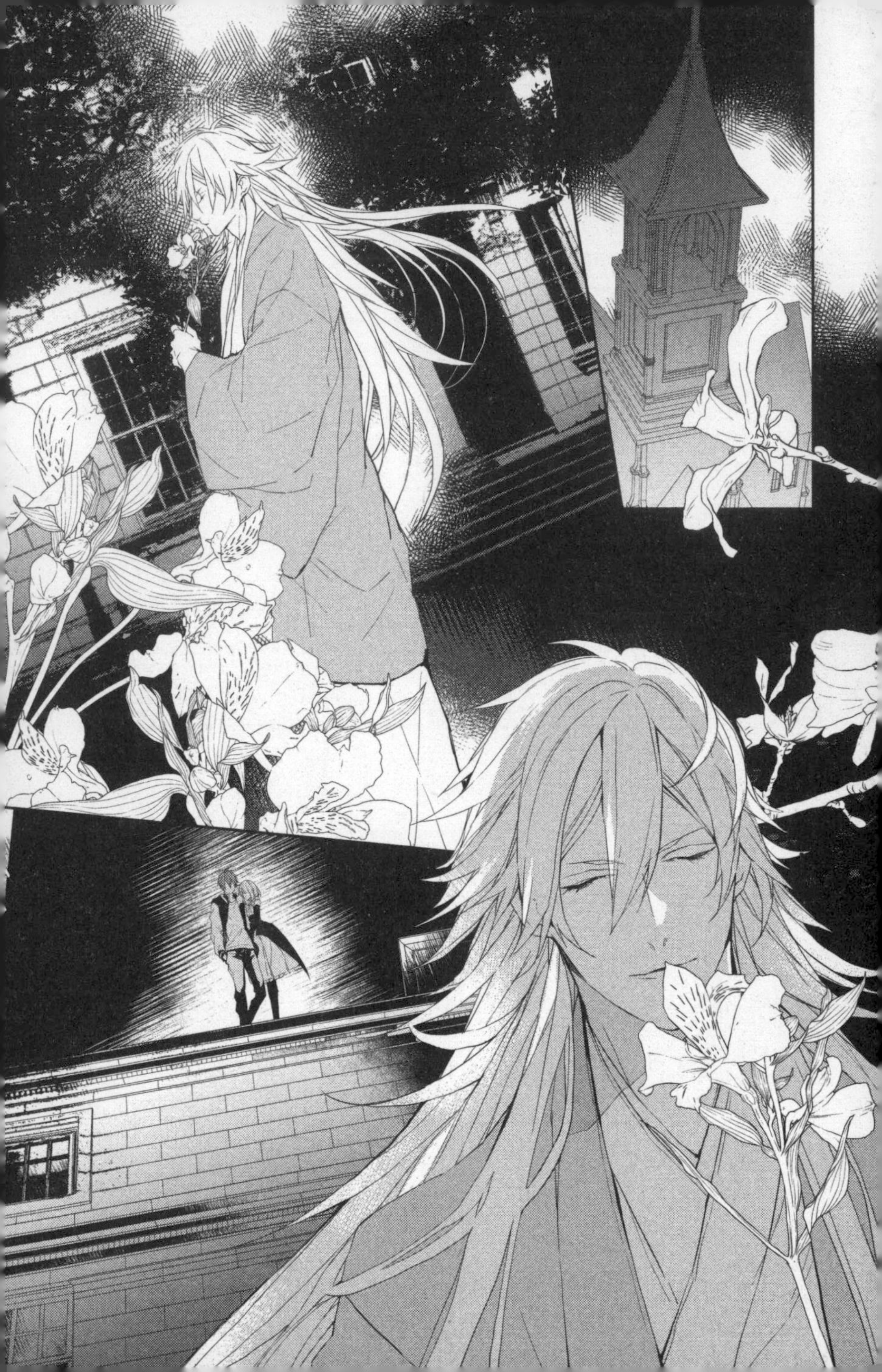

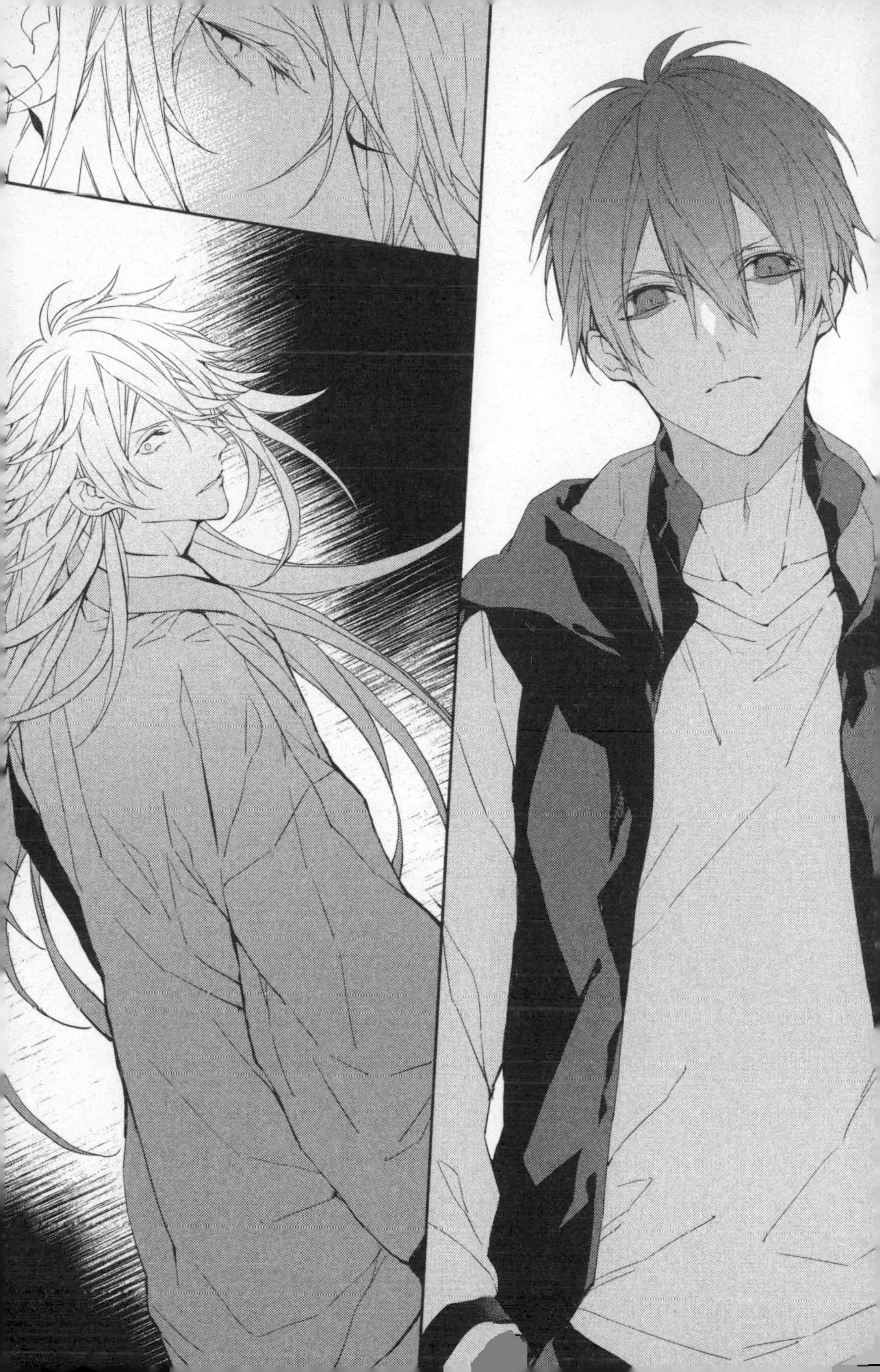

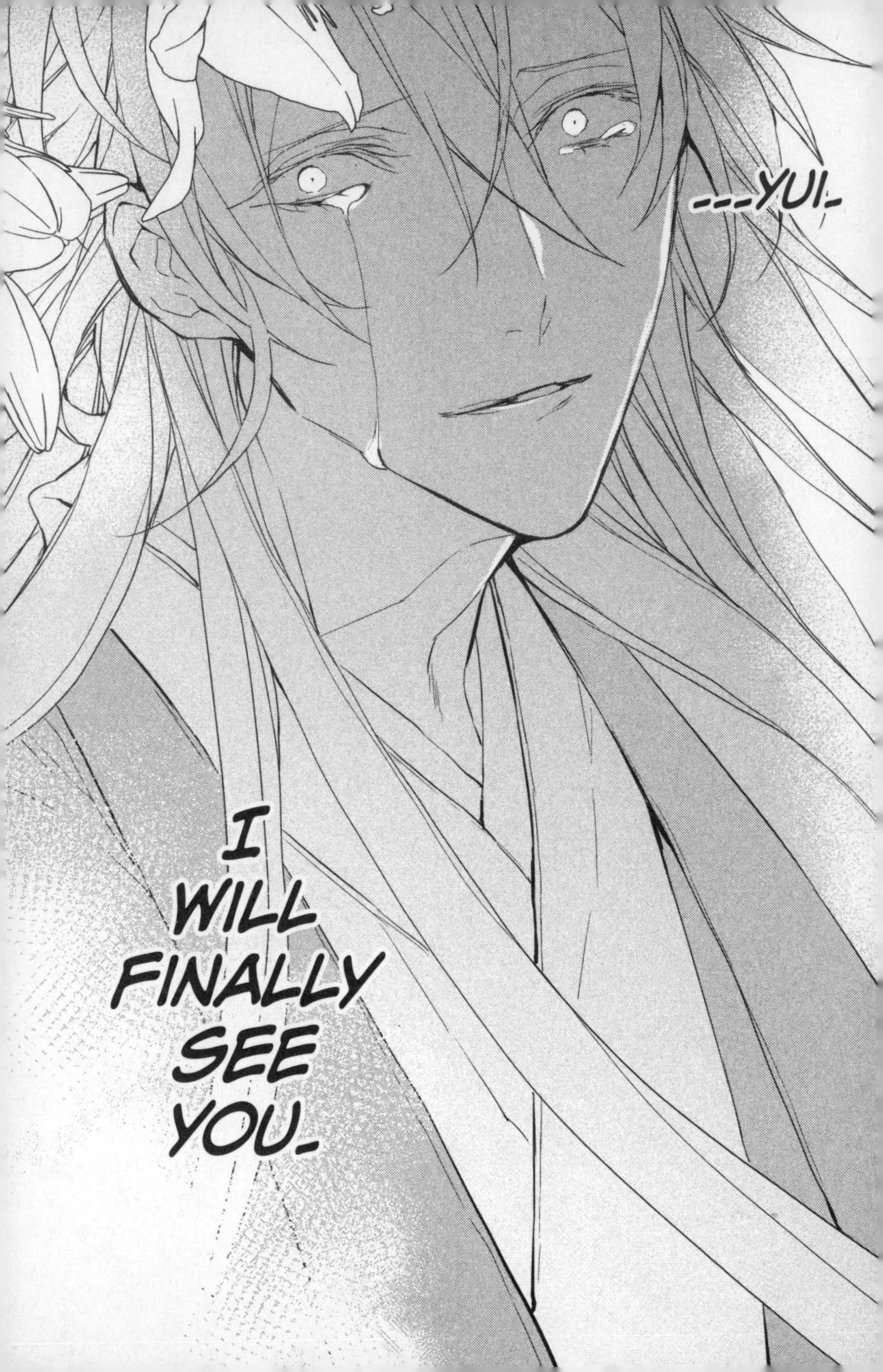
---YUI-
I WILL FINALLY SEE YOU-

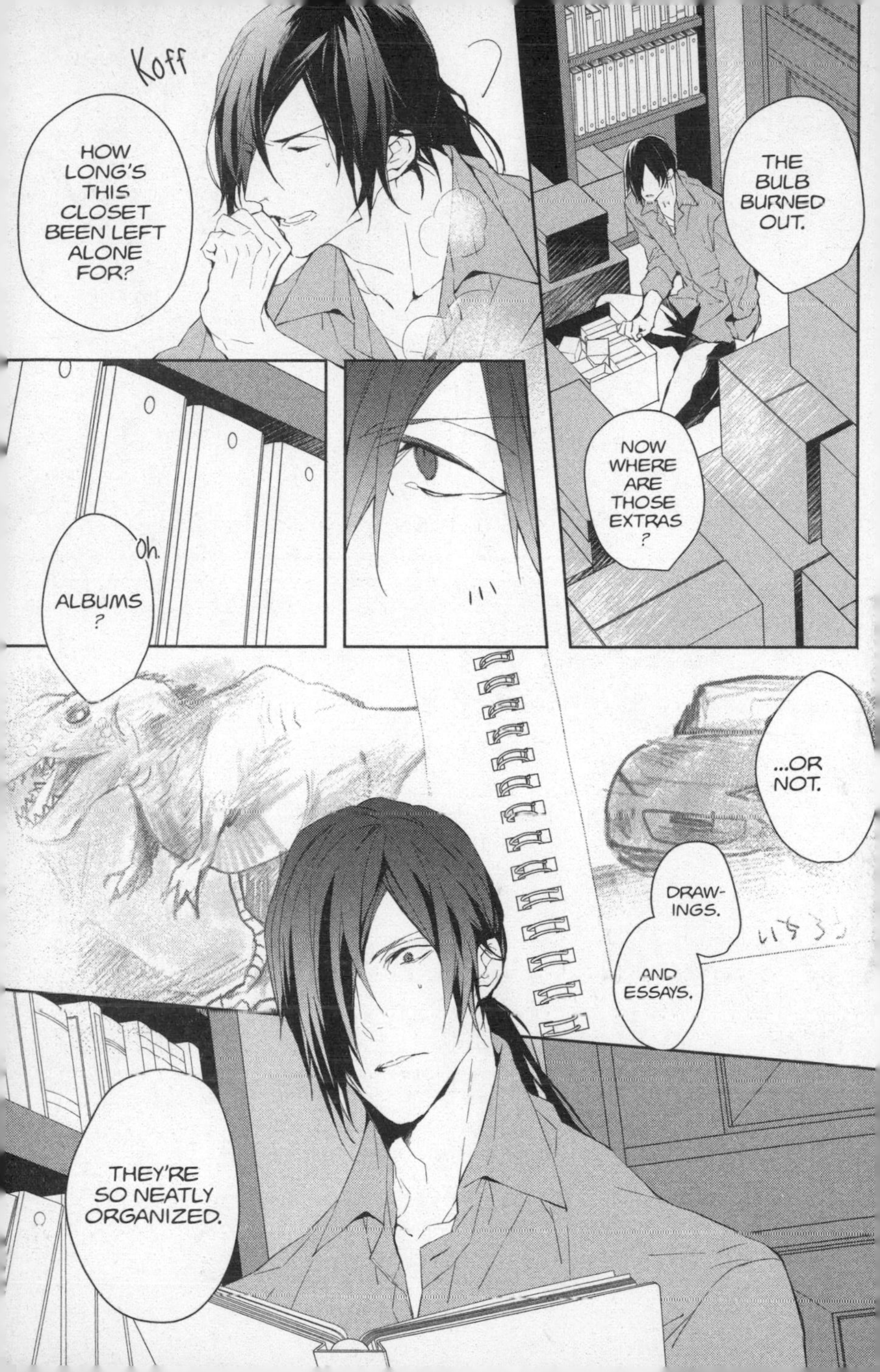
THE BULB BURNED OUT.
NOW WHERE ARE THOSE EXTRAS?
Koff
HOW LONG'S THIS CLOSET BEEN LEFT ALONE FOR?
Oh.
ALBUMS?
...OR NOT.
DRAWINGS.
AND ESSAYS.
THEY'RE SO NEATLY ORGANIZED.

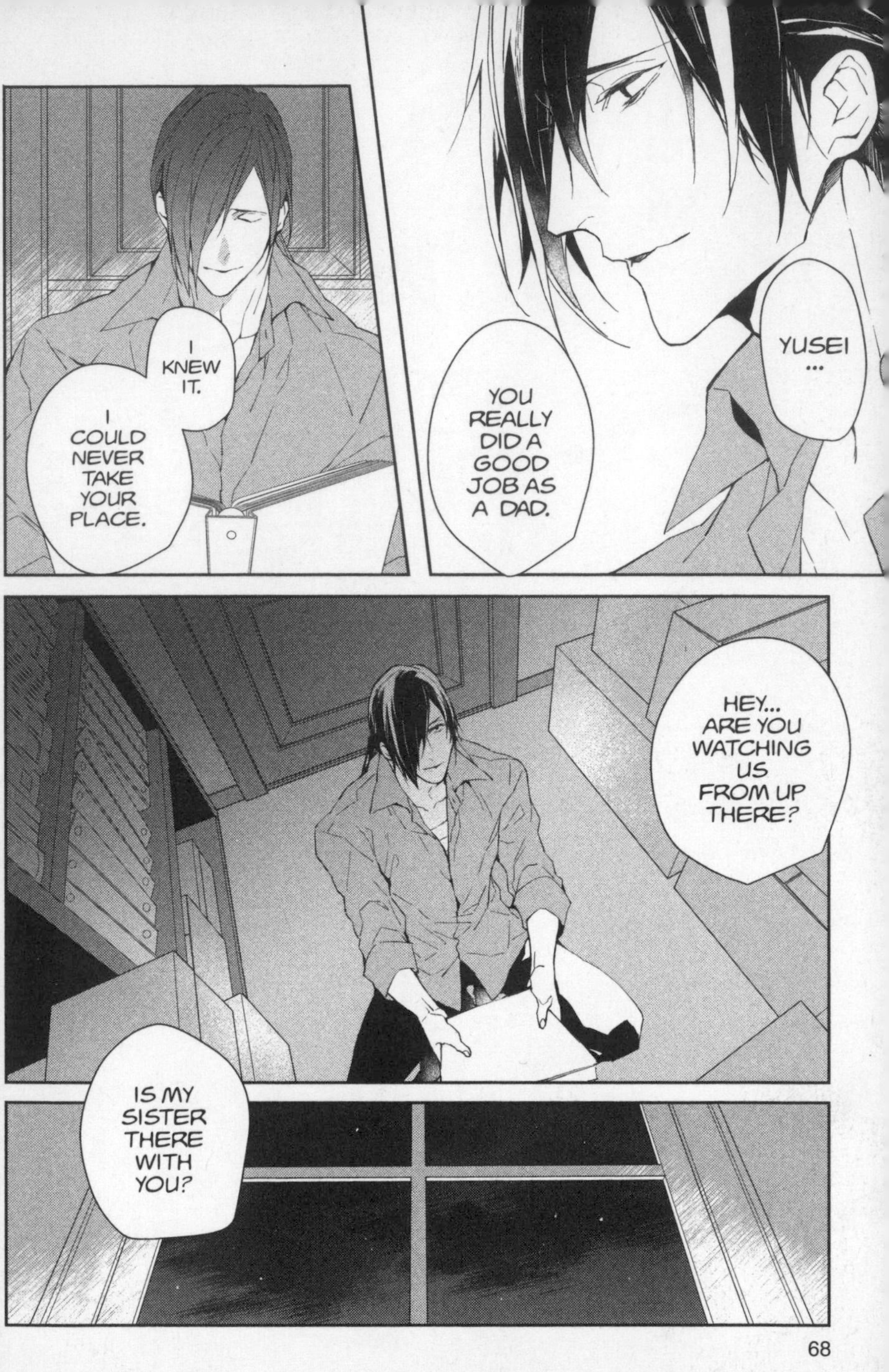
YUSEI ...
YOU REALLY DID A GOOD JOB AS A DAD.
I KNEW IT.
I COULD NEVER TAKE YOUR PLACE.
HEY... ARE YOU WATCHING US FROM UP THERE?
IS MY SISTER THERE WITH YOU?

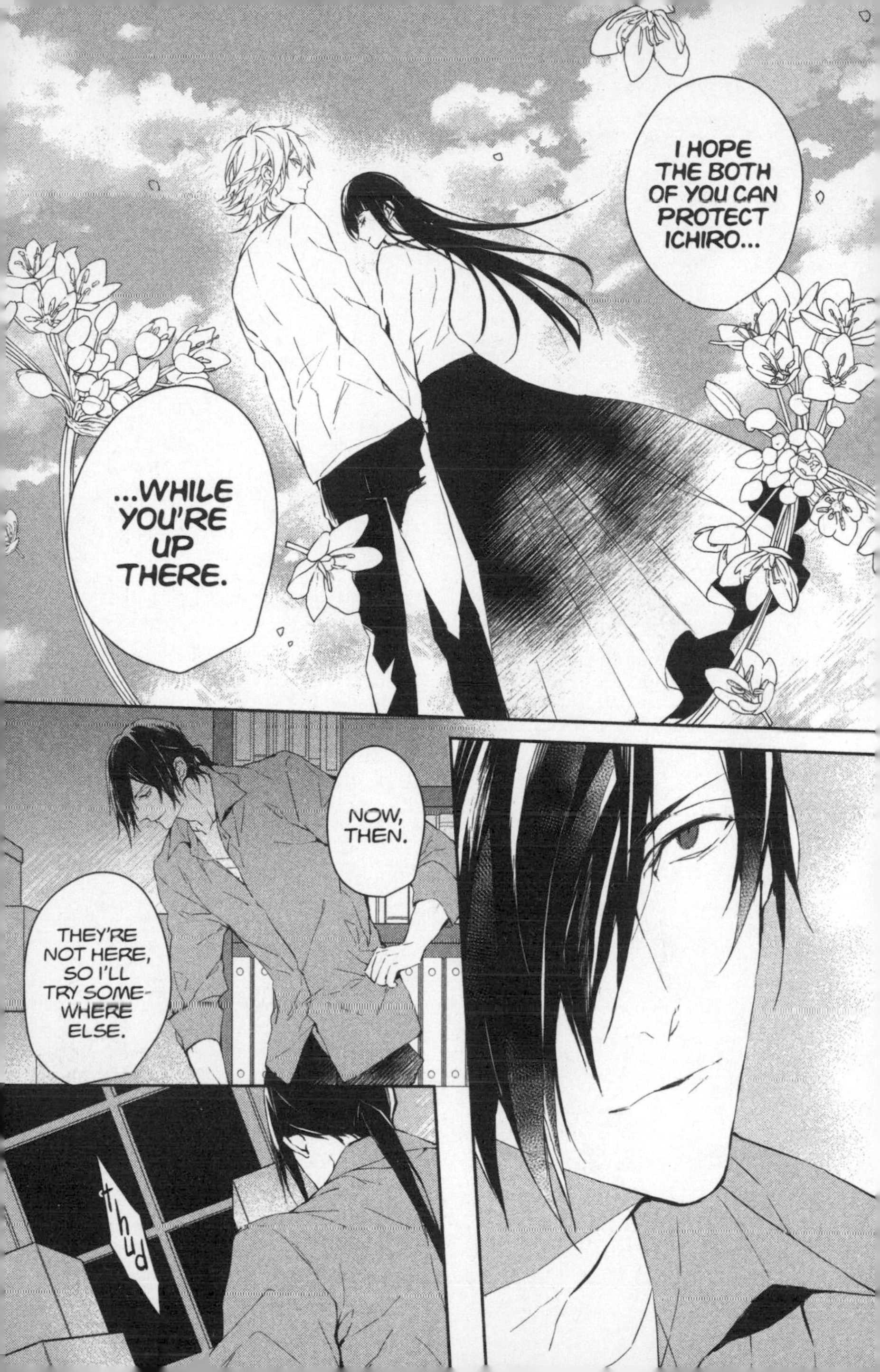
I HOPE THE BOTH OF YOU CAN PROTECT ICHIRO...
...WHILE YOU'RE UP THERE.
NOW, THEN.
THEY'RE NOT HERE, SO I'LL TRY SOME-WHERE ELSE.
thud

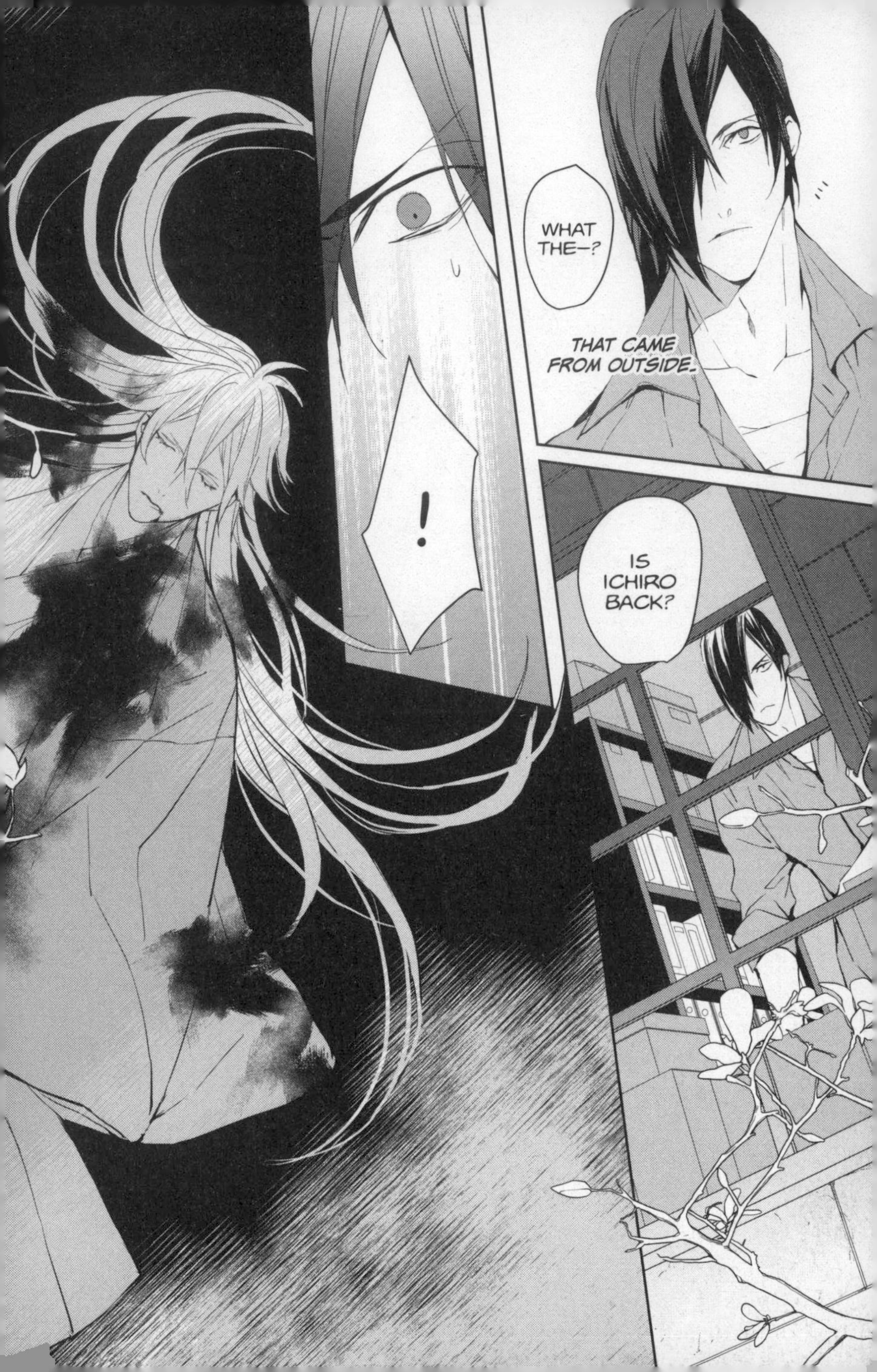
WHAT THE—?
THAT CAME FROM OUTSIDE.
!
IS ICHIRO BACK?

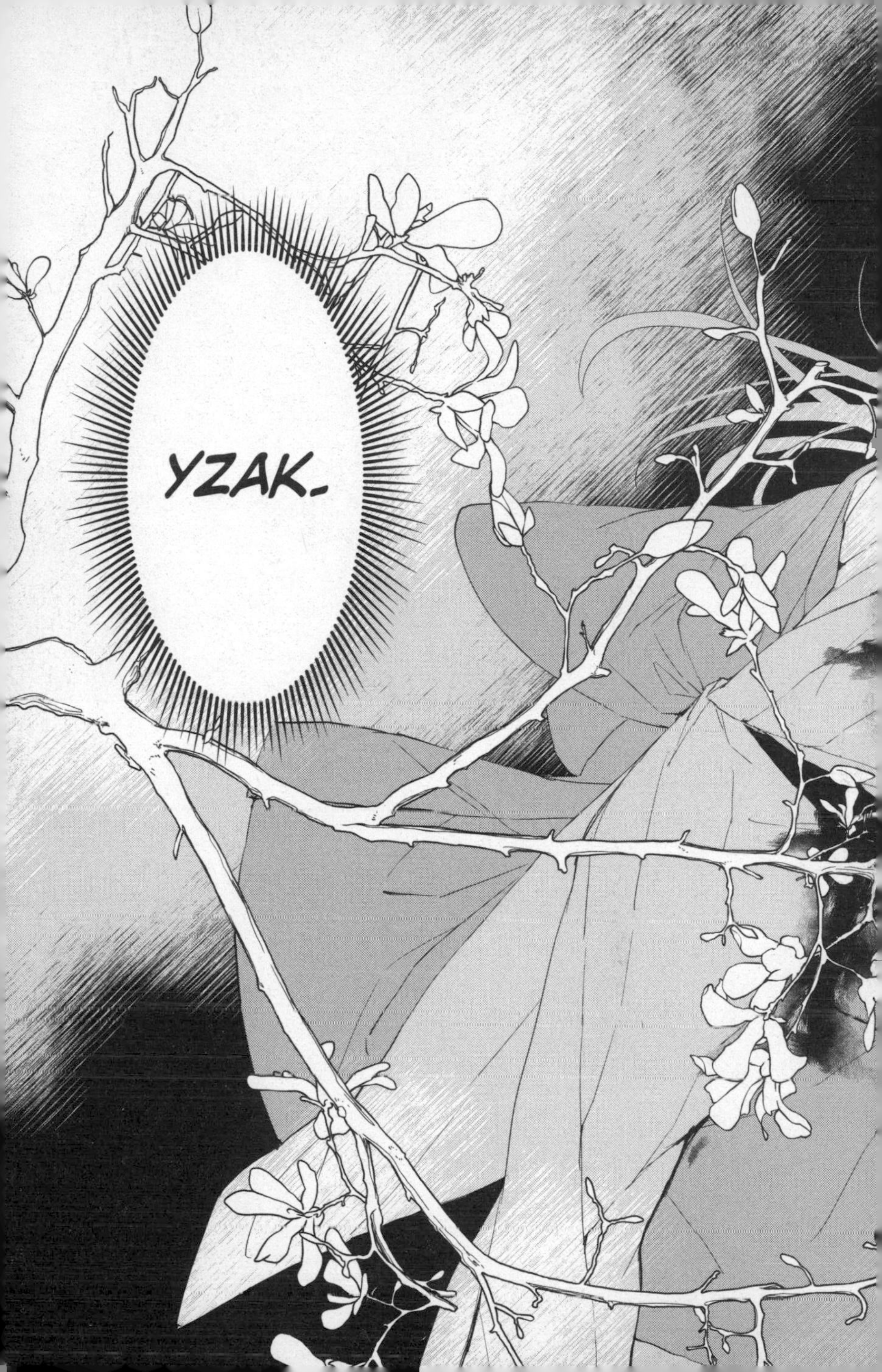
YZAK...

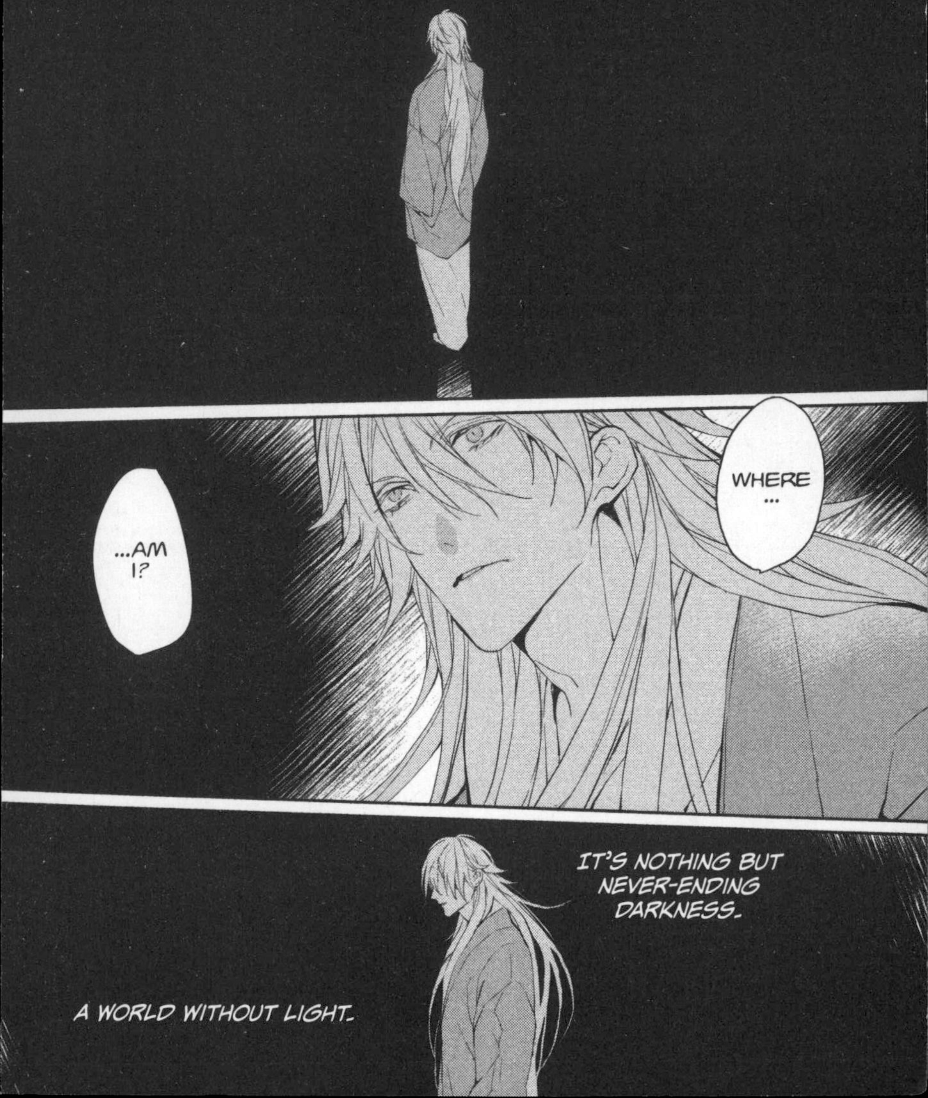
WHERE...
...AM I?
IT'S NOTHING BUT NEVER-ENDING DARKNESS.
A WORLD WITHOUT LIGHT.

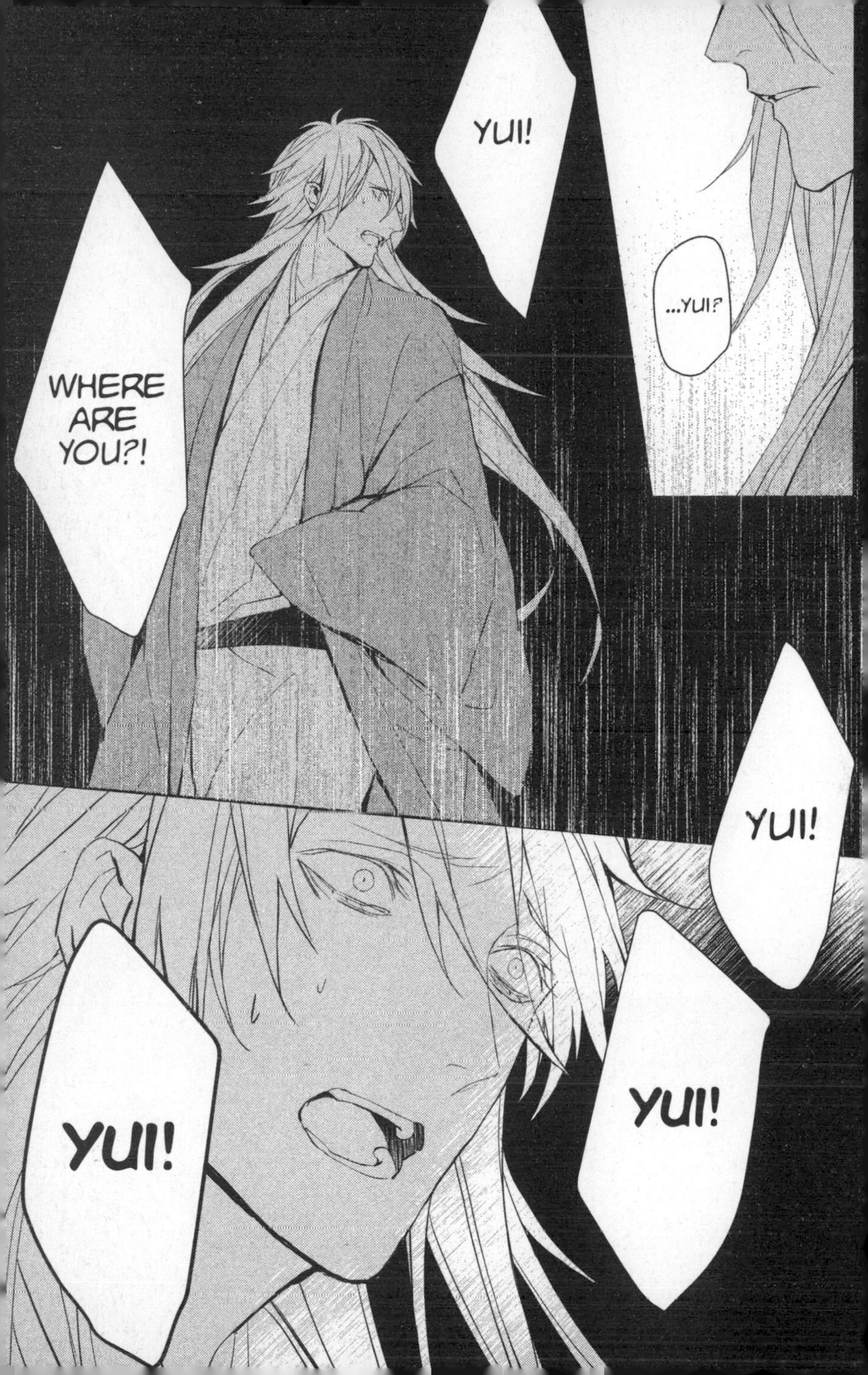
...YUI?
YUI!
WHERE ARE YOU?!
YUI!
YUI!
YUI!

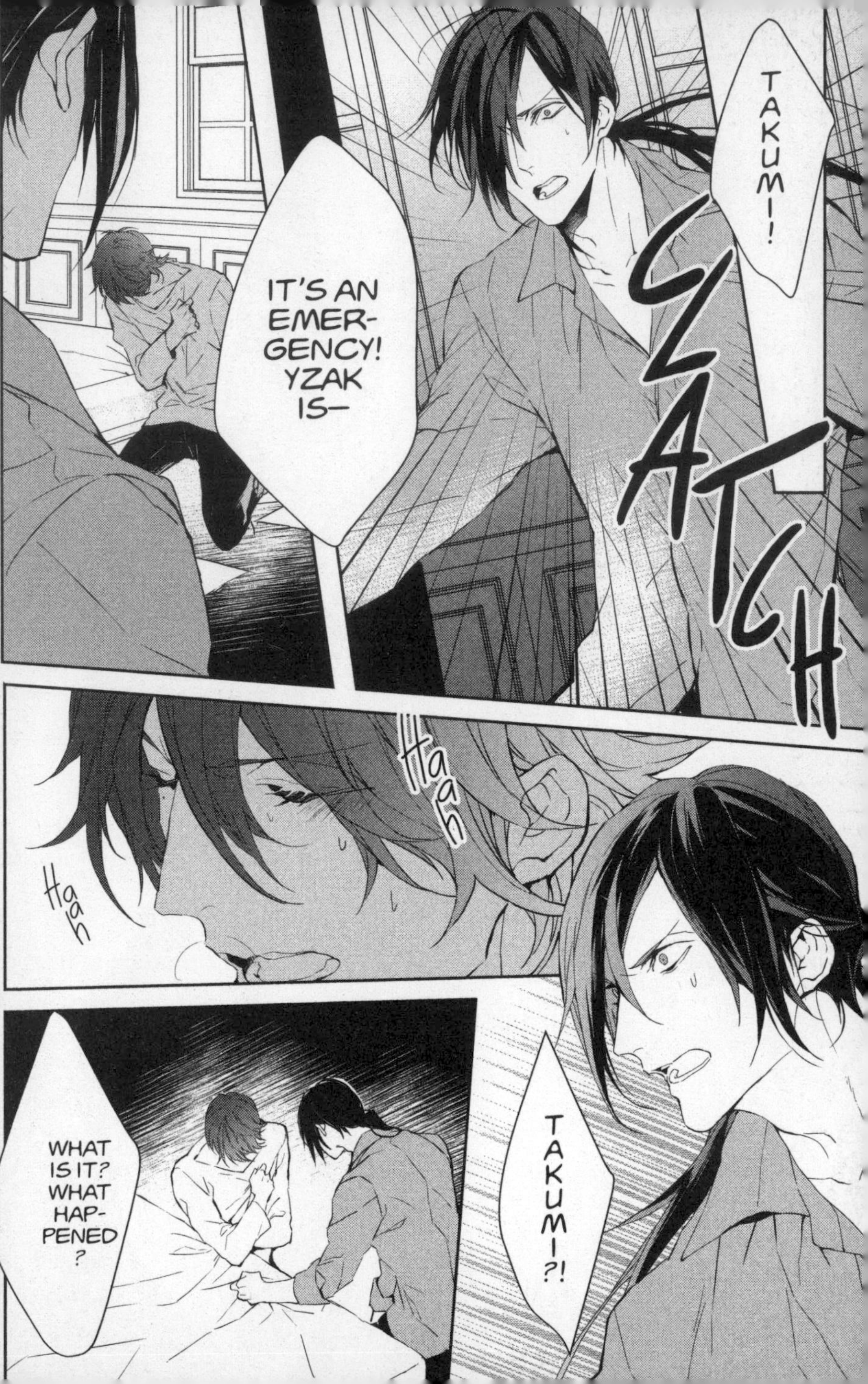
TAKUMI!
SLATCH
IT'S AN EMERGENCY! YZAK IS—
Haaah
Haaah
TAKUMI?!
WHAT IS IT? WHAT HAPPENED?

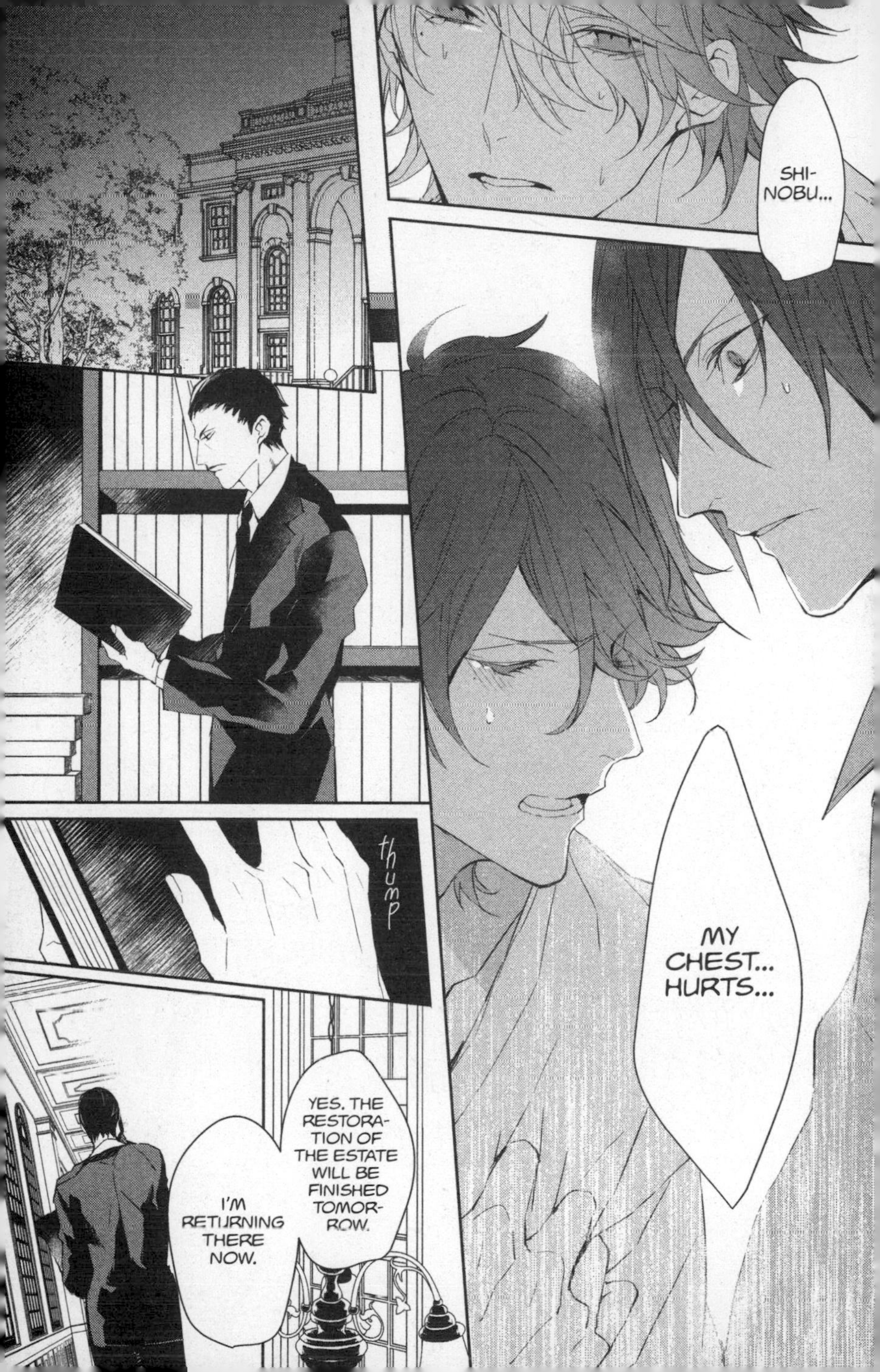
SHI-NOBU...
MY CHEST... HURTS...
thump
YES. THE RESTORATION OF THE ESTATE WILL BE FINISHED TOMORROW.
I'M RETURNING THERE NOW.

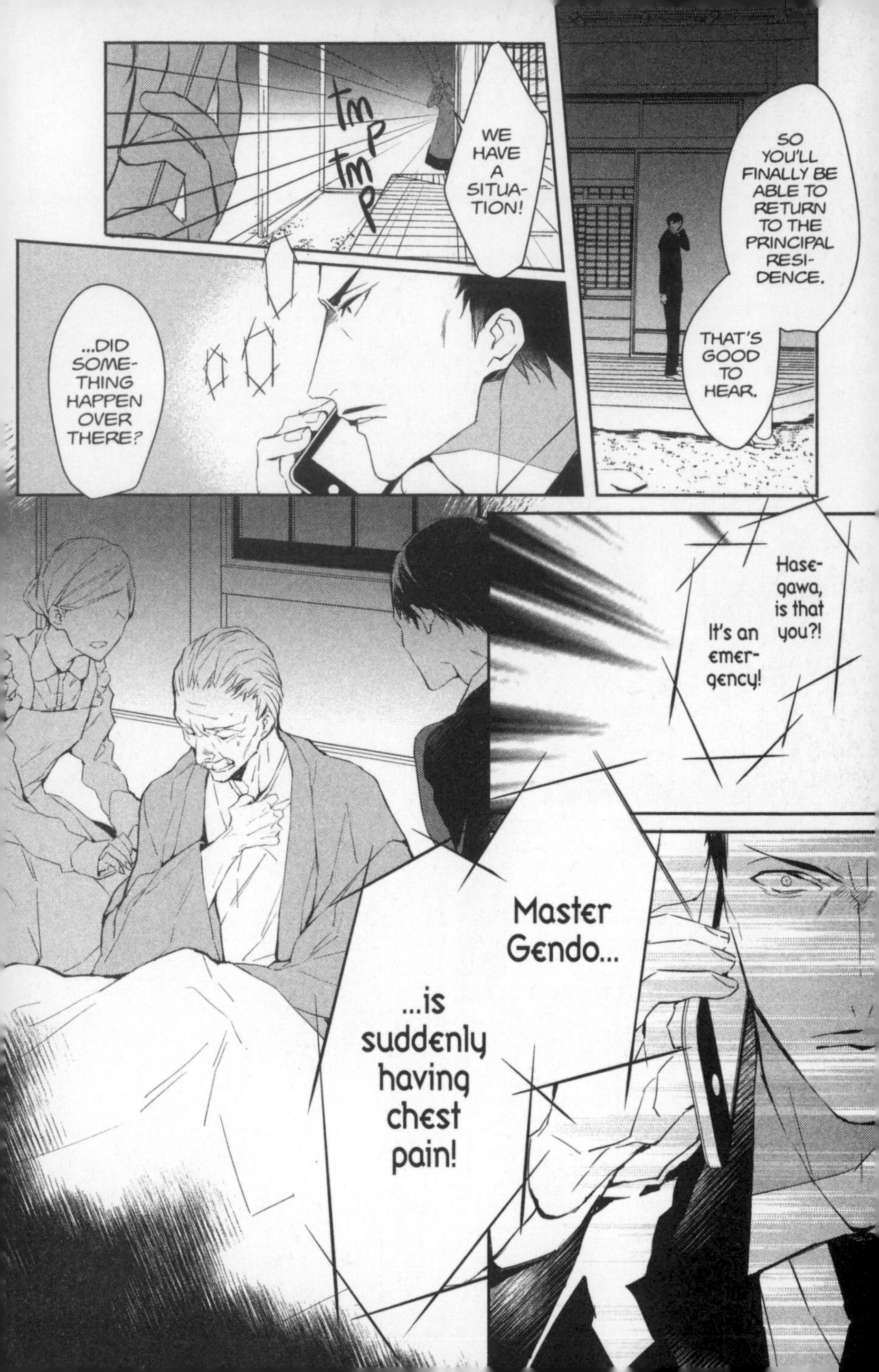
SO YOU'LL FINALLY BE ABLE TO RETURN TO THE PRINCIPAL RESIDENCE.
THAT'S GOOD TO HEAR.
WE HAVE A SITUATION!
tmp tmp
...DID SOMETHING HAPPEN OVER THERE?
Hasegawa, is that you?!
It's an emergency!
Master Gendo...
...is suddenly having chest pain!

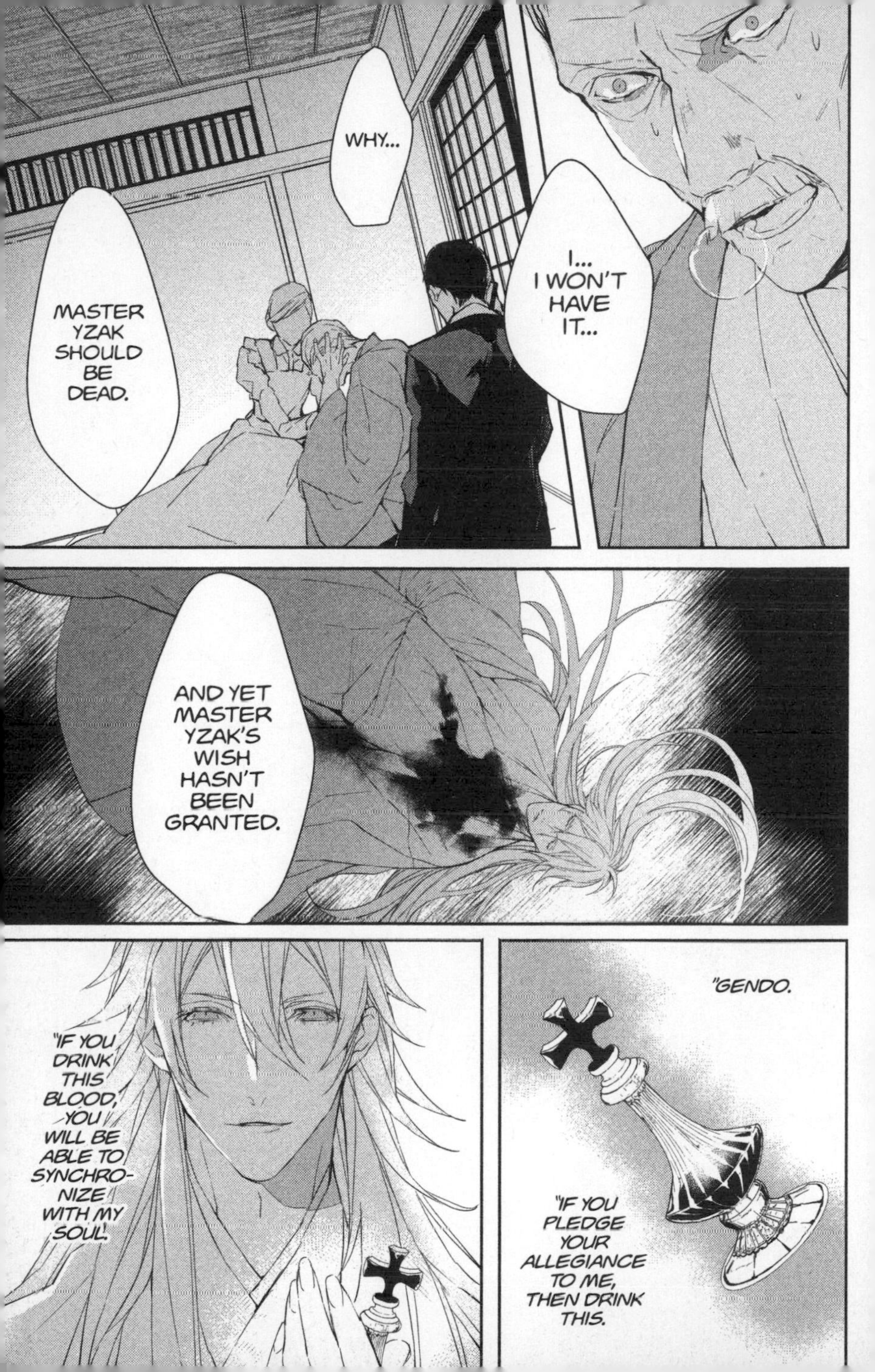
I... I WON'T HAVE IT...
WHY...
MASTER YZAK SHOULD BE DEAD.
AND YET MASTER YZAK'S WISH HASN'T BEEN GRANTED.
"GENDO.
"IF YOU PLEDGE YOUR ALLEGIANCE TO ME, THEN DRINK THIS.
"IF YOU DRINK THIS BLOOD, YOU WILL BE ABLE TO SYNCHRO-NIZE WITH MY SOUL.

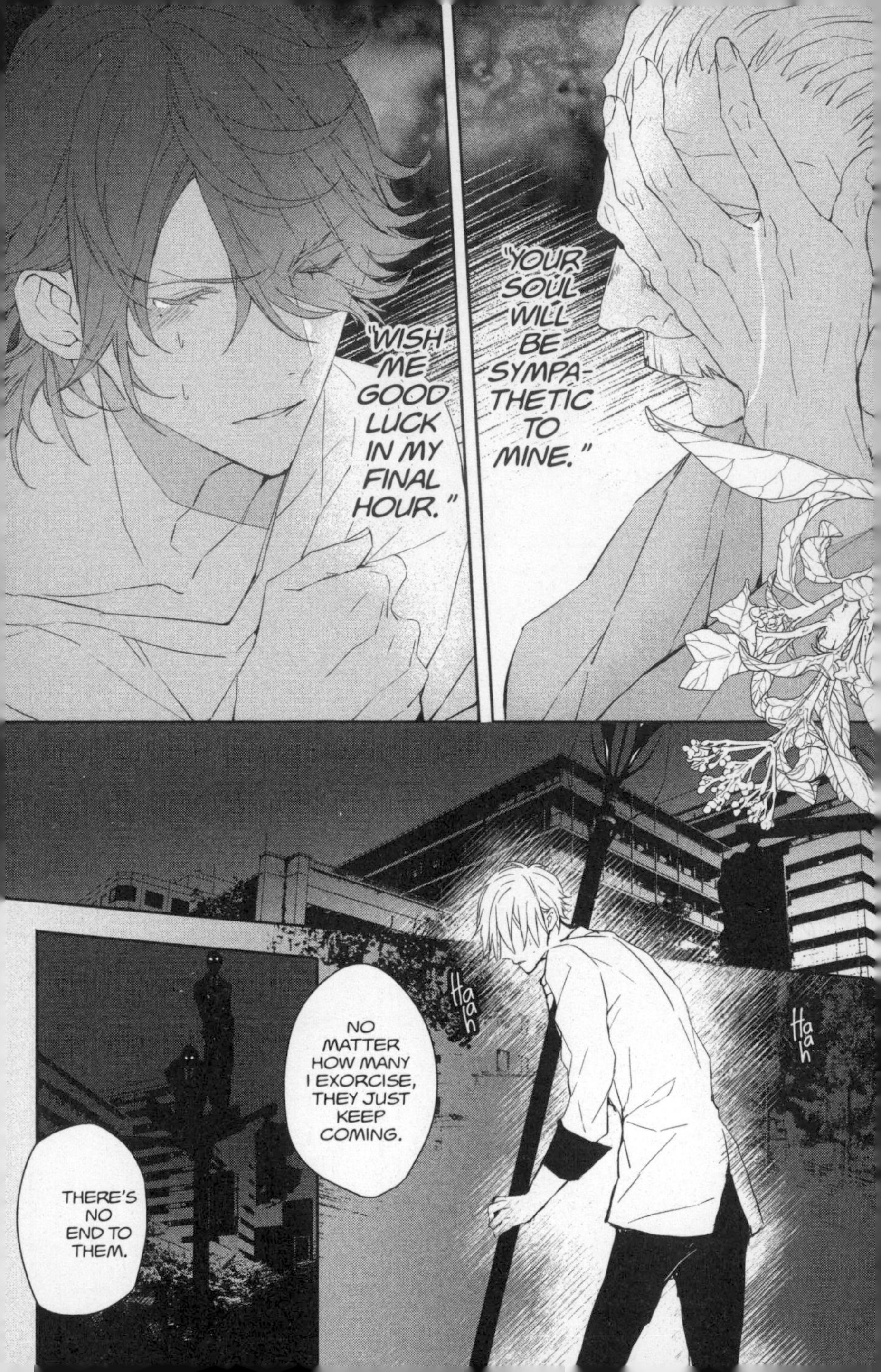
"YOUR SOUL WILL BE SYMPA-THETIC TO MINE."
"WISH ME GOOD LUCK IN MY FINAL HOUR."
Haah
Haah
NO MATTER HOW MANY I EXORCISE, THEY JUST KEEP COMING.
THERE'S NO END TO THEM.

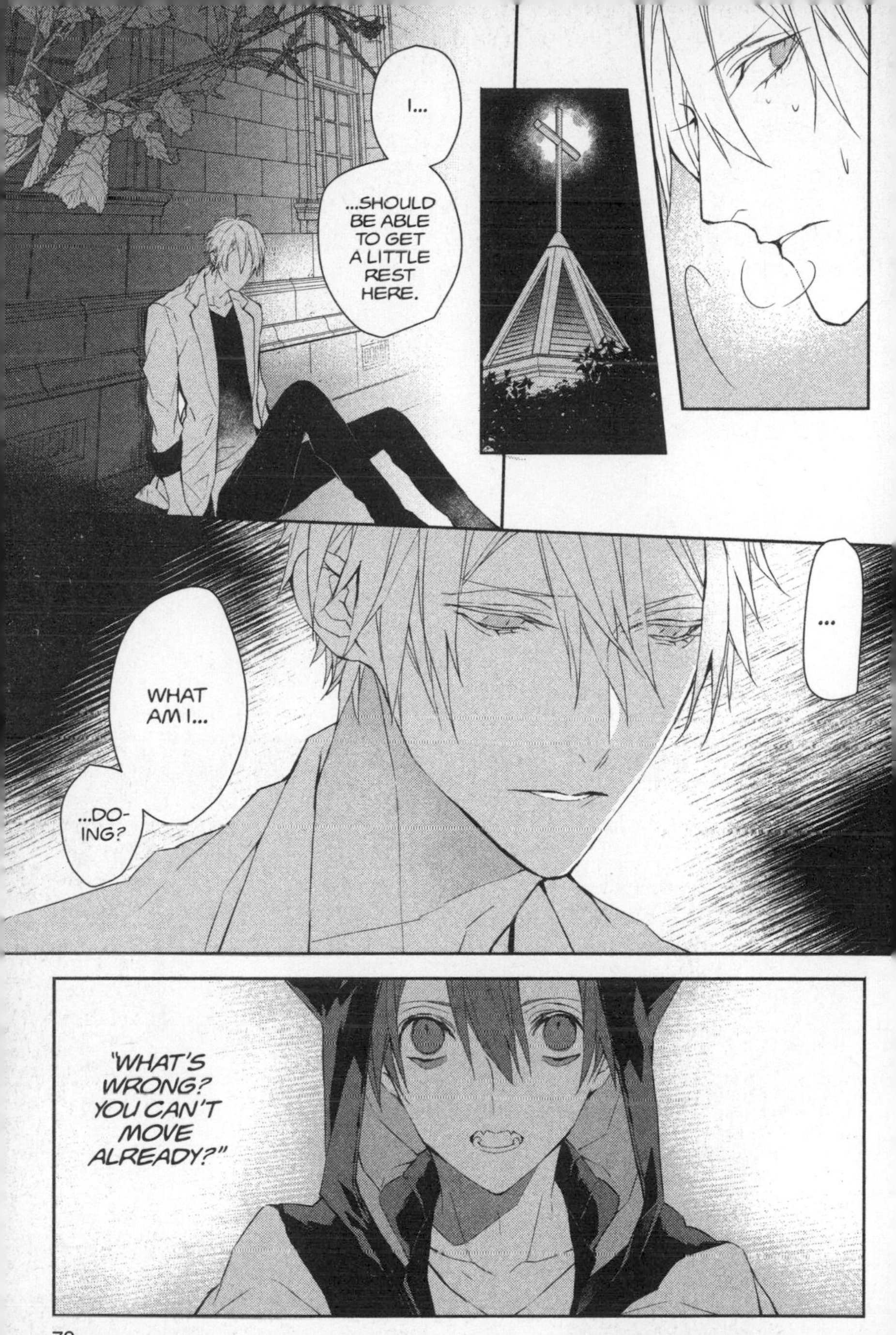
I...
...SHOULD BE ABLE TO GET A LITTLE REST HERE.
...
WHAT AM I...
...DO-ING?
"WHAT'S WRONG? YOU CAN'T MOVE ALREADY?"

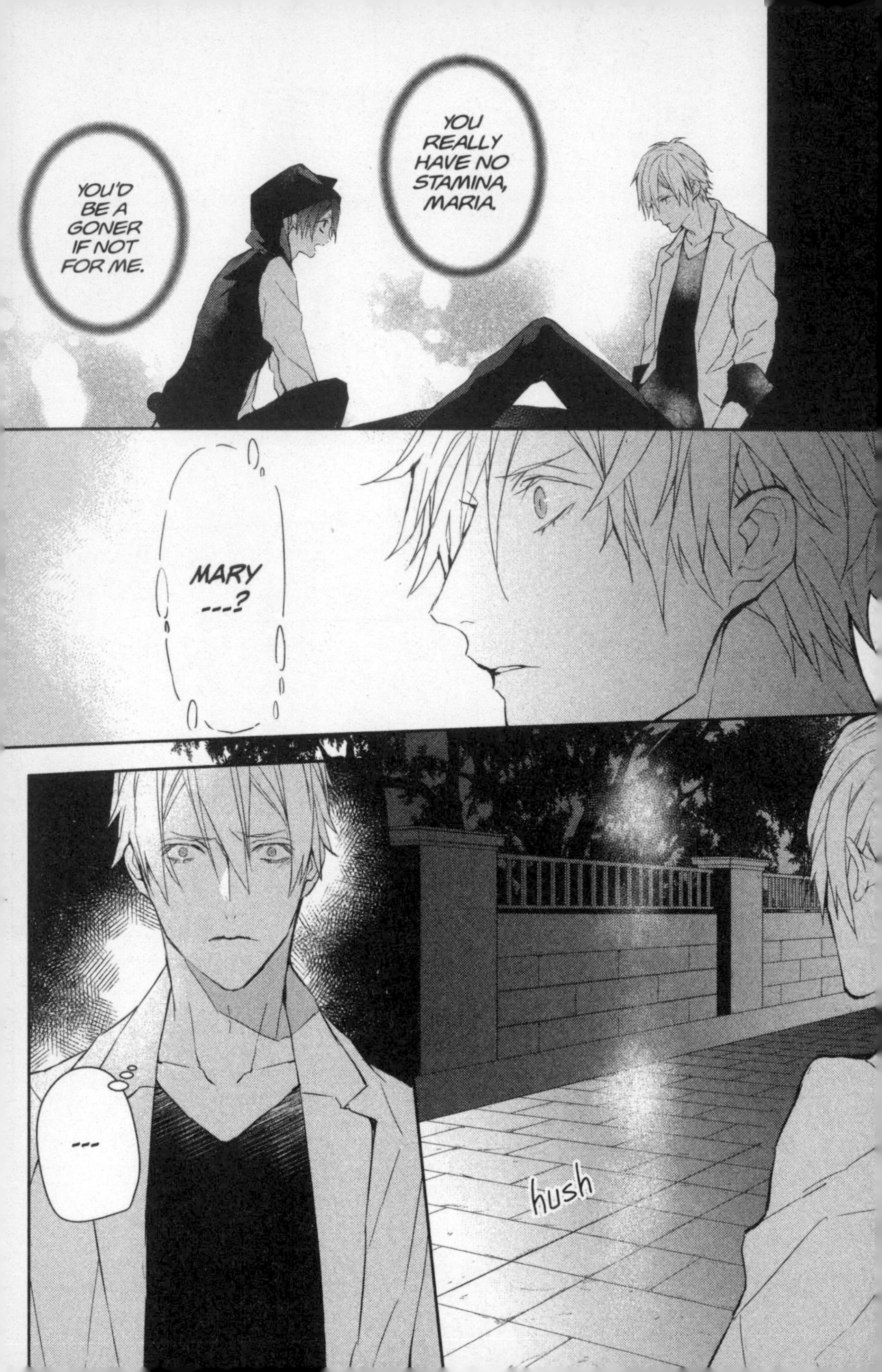
YOU REALLY HAVE NO STAMINA, MARIA.
YOU'D BE A GONER IF NOT FOR ME.
MARY---?
hush
---

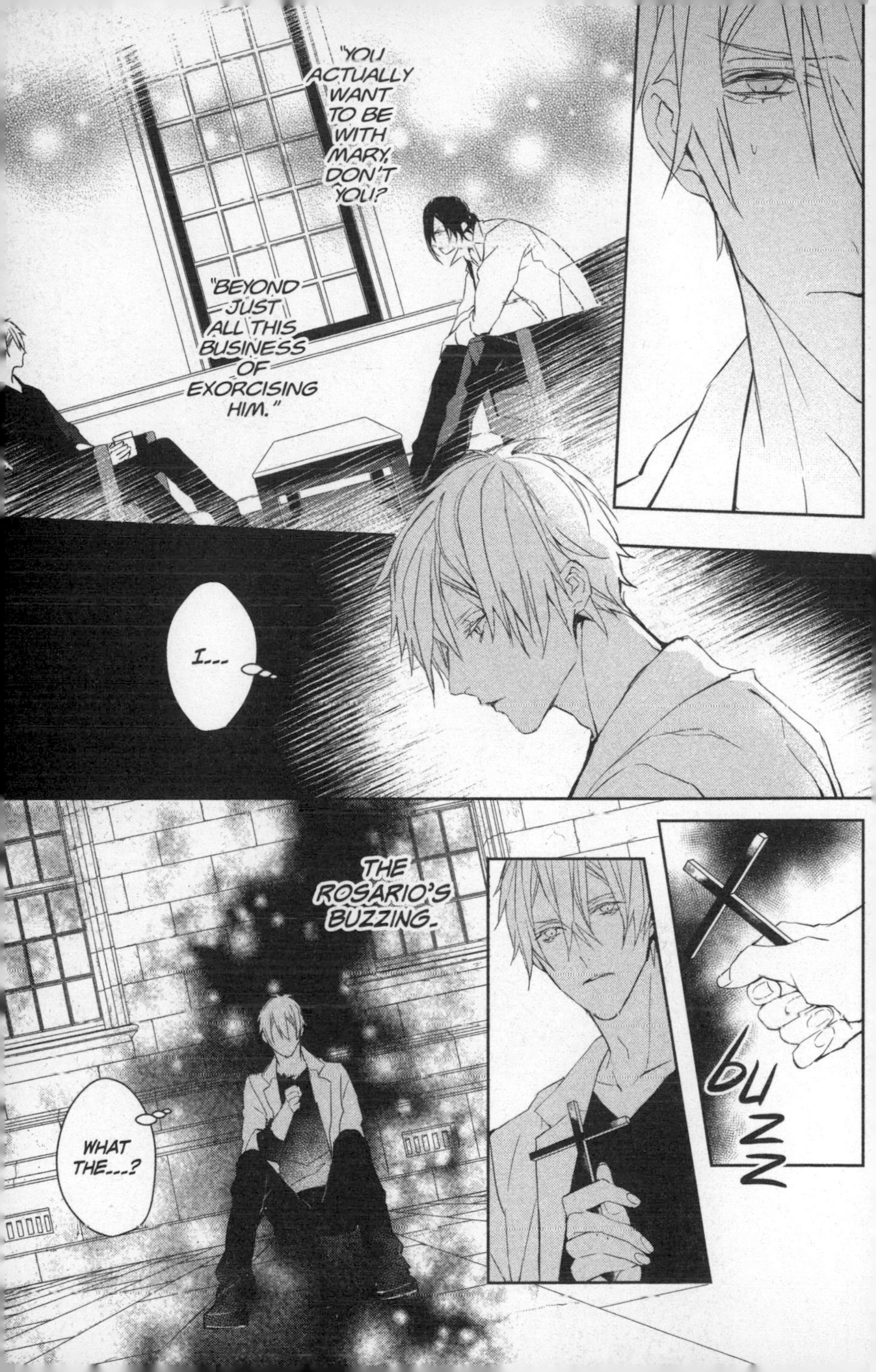
"YOU ACTUALLY WANT TO BE WITH MARY, DON'T YOU?
"BEYOND JUST ALL THIS BUSINESS OF EXORCISING HIM."
I...
buzz
THE ROSARIO'S BUZZING.
WHAT THE...?

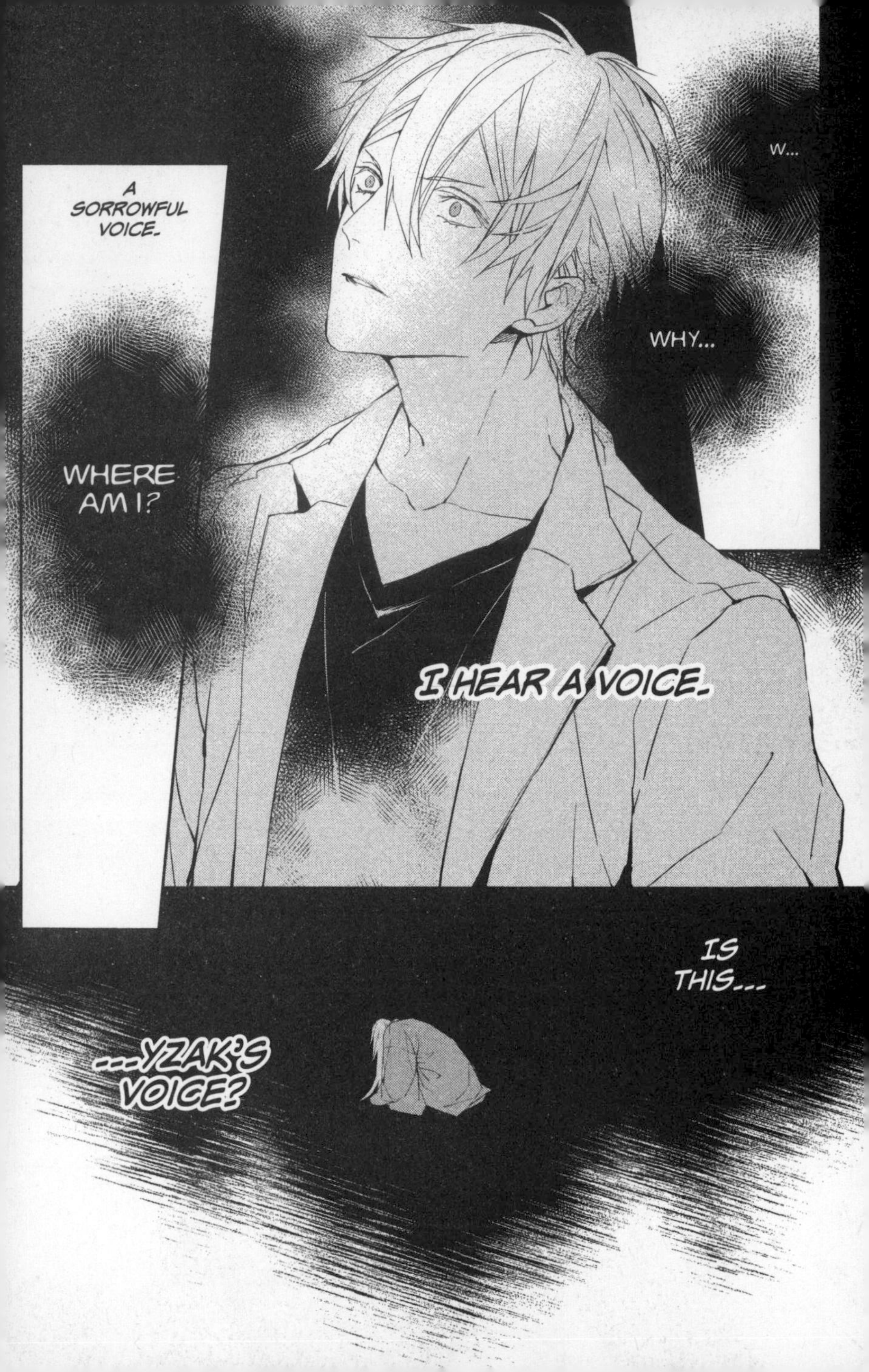
W...
WHY...
I HEAR A VOICE.
A SORROWFUL VOICE.
WHERE AM I?
IS THIS...
...YZAK'S VOICE?

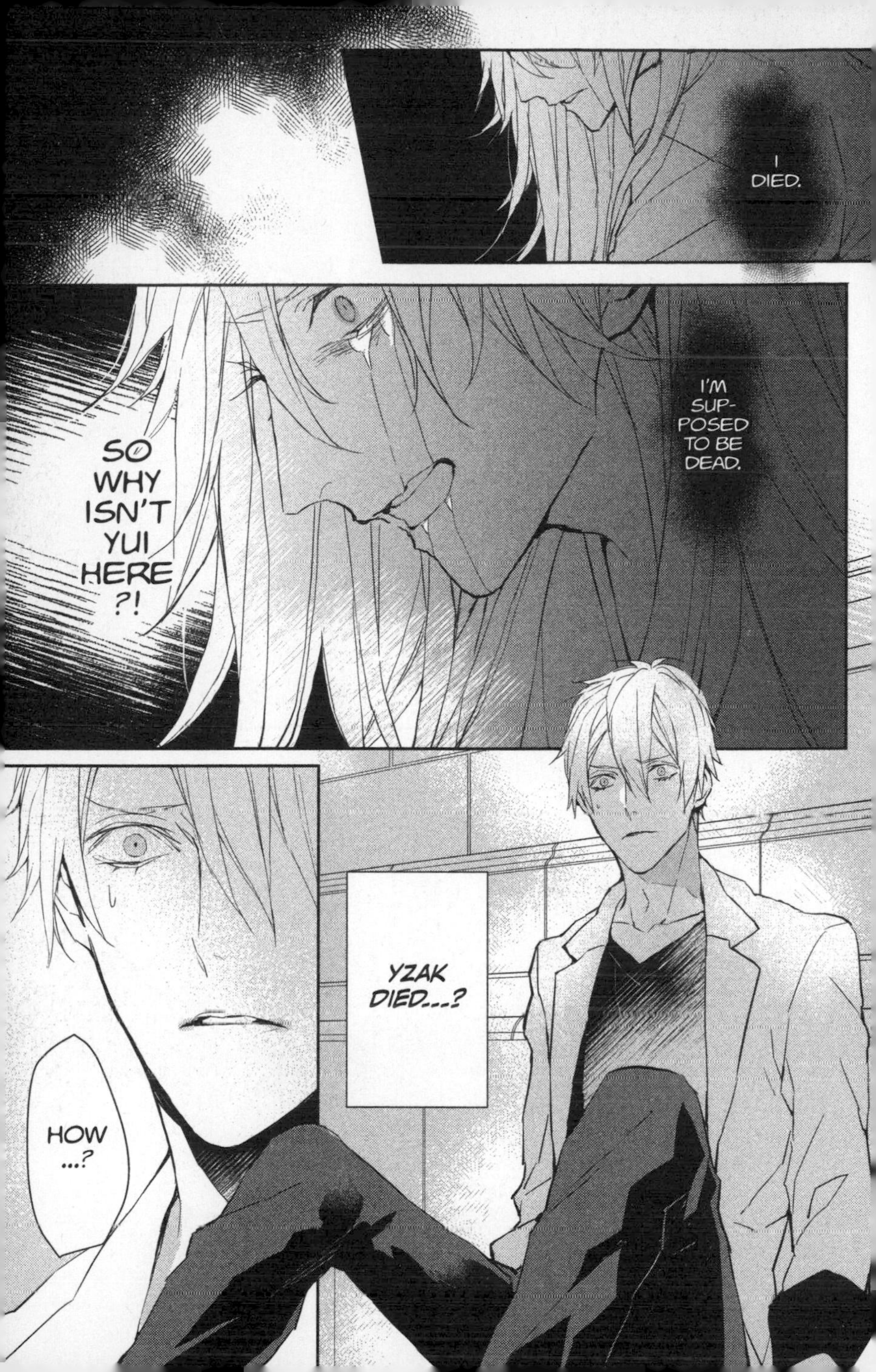
I DIED.
I'M SUP-POSED TO BE DEAD.
SO WHY ISN'T YUI HERE ?!
YZAK DIED...?
HOW ...?

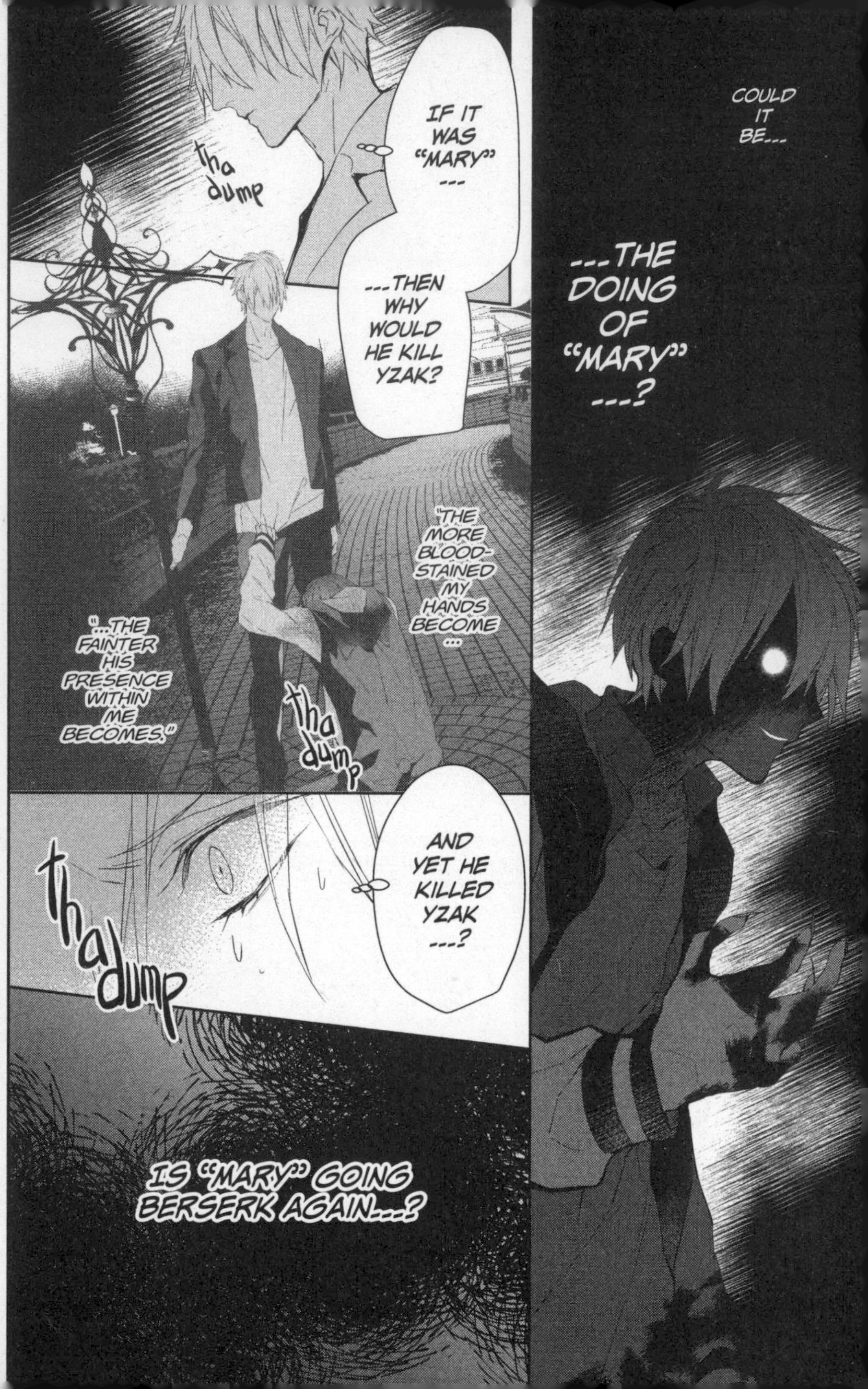
IF IT WAS "MARY" ---
tha dump
---THEN WHY WOULD HE KILL YZAK?
"THE MORE BLOOD-STAINED MY HANDS BECOME ...
"...THE FAINTER HIS PRESENCE WITHIN ME BECOMES."
tha dump
AND YET HE KILLED YZAK ---?
tha dump
IS "MARY" GOING BERSERK AGAIN...?
COULD IT BE...
---THE DOING OF "MARY" ---?

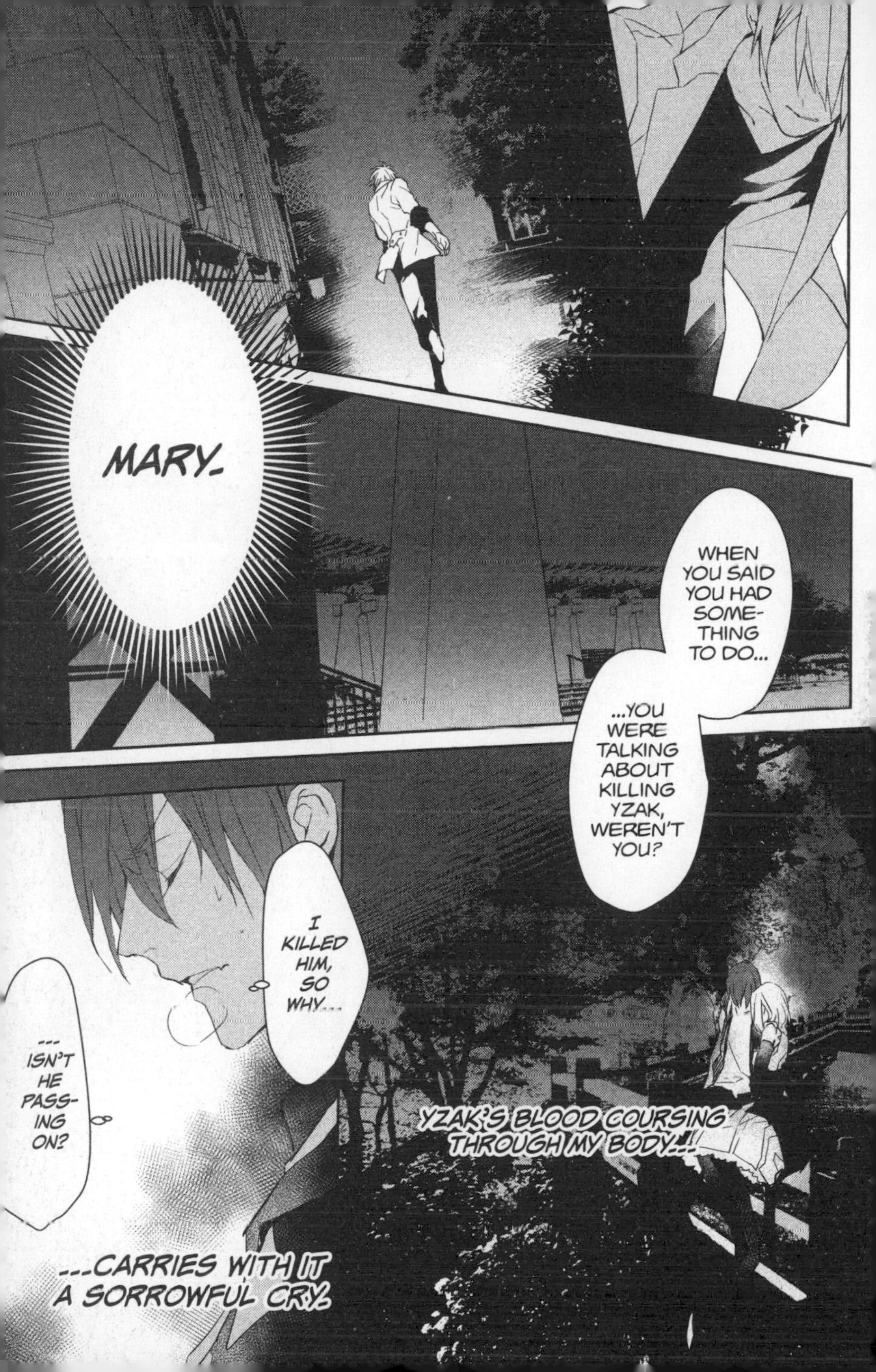
MARY_
WHEN YOU SAID YOU HAD SOME-THING TO DO...
...YOU WERE TALKING ABOUT KILLING YZAK, WEREN'T YOU?
I KILLED HIM, SO WHY...
...ISN'T HE PASSING ON?
YZAK'S BLOOD COURSING THROUGH MY BODY!!
...CARRIES WITH IT A SORROWFUL CRY.

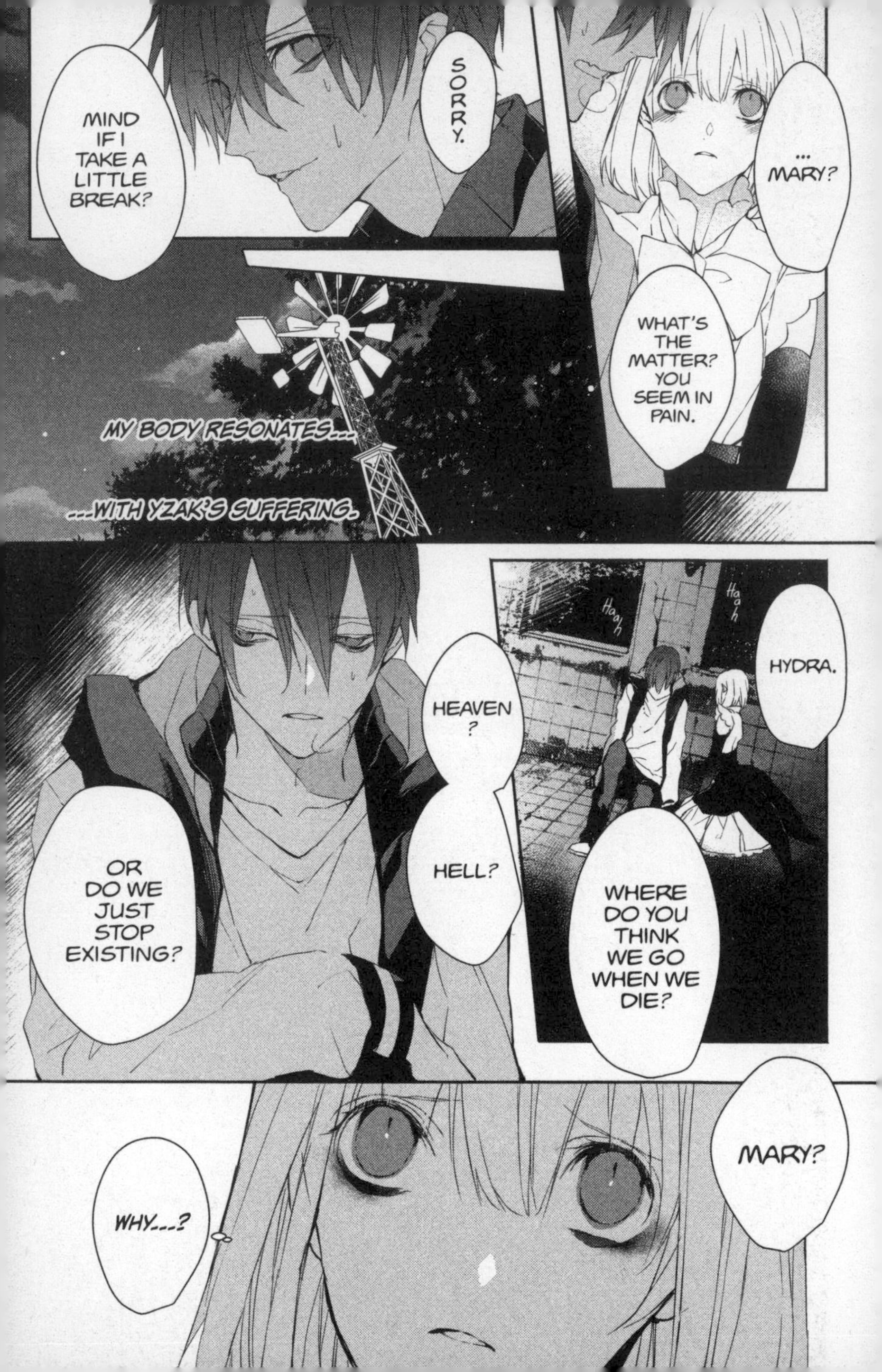
...MARY?
WHAT'S THE MATTER? YOU SEEM IN PAIN.
SORRY.
MIND IF I TAKE A LITTLE BREAK?
MY BODY RESONATES...
...WITH YZAK'S SUFFERING.
Haah
Haah
HYDRA.
WHERE DO YOU THINK WE GO WHEN WE DIE?
HEAVEN?
HELL?
OR DO WE JUST STOP EXISTING?
MARY?
WHY...?

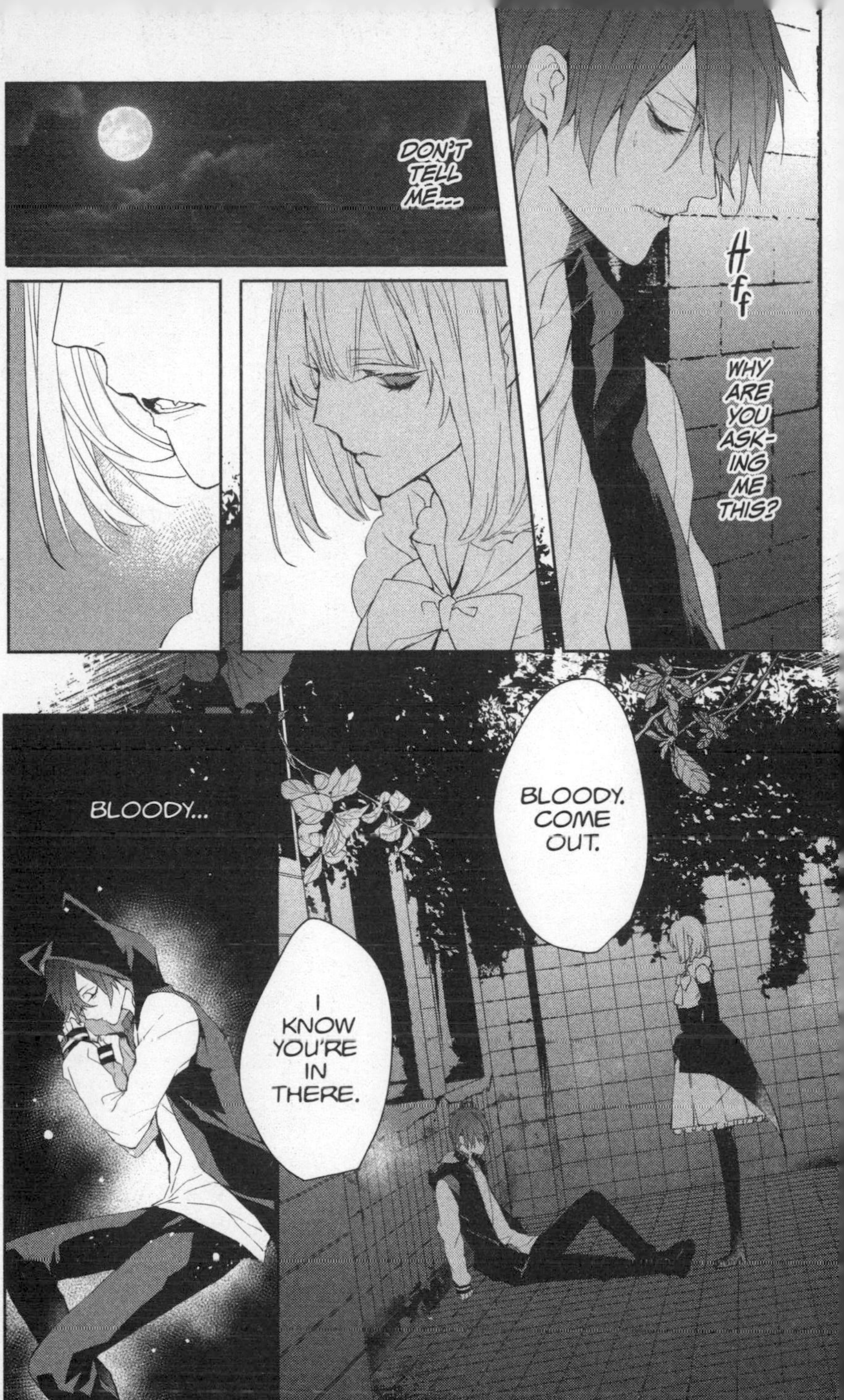
Hff
WHY ARE YOU ASK-ING ME THIS?
DON'T TELL ME...
BLOODY. COME OUT.
I KNOW YOU'RE IN THERE.
BLOODY...

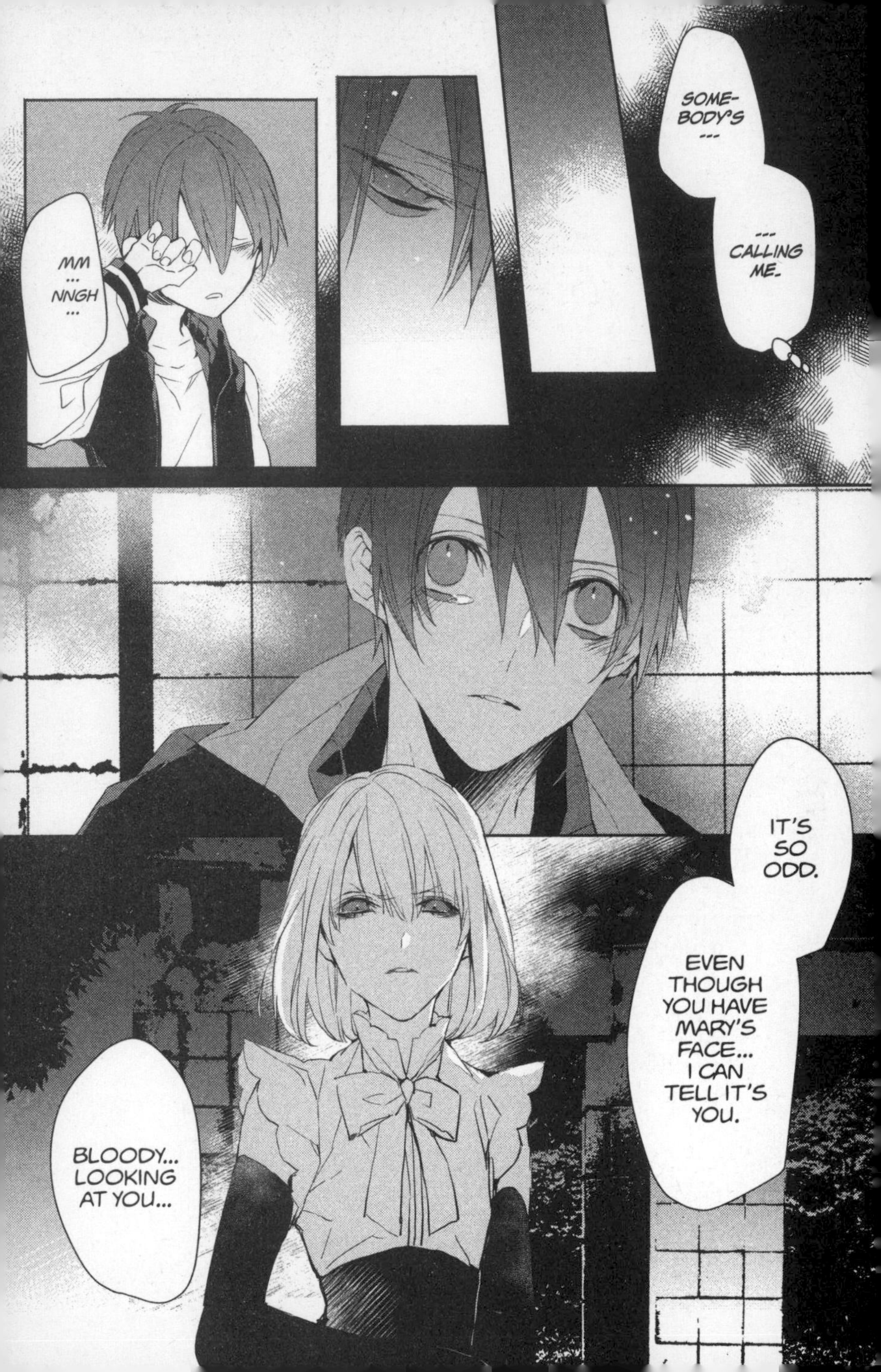
SOMEBODY'S --- --- CALLING ME.
MM... NNGH...
IT'S SO ODD.
EVEN THOUGH YOU HAVE MARY'S FACE... I CAN TELL IT'S YOU.
BLOODY... LOOKING AT YOU...

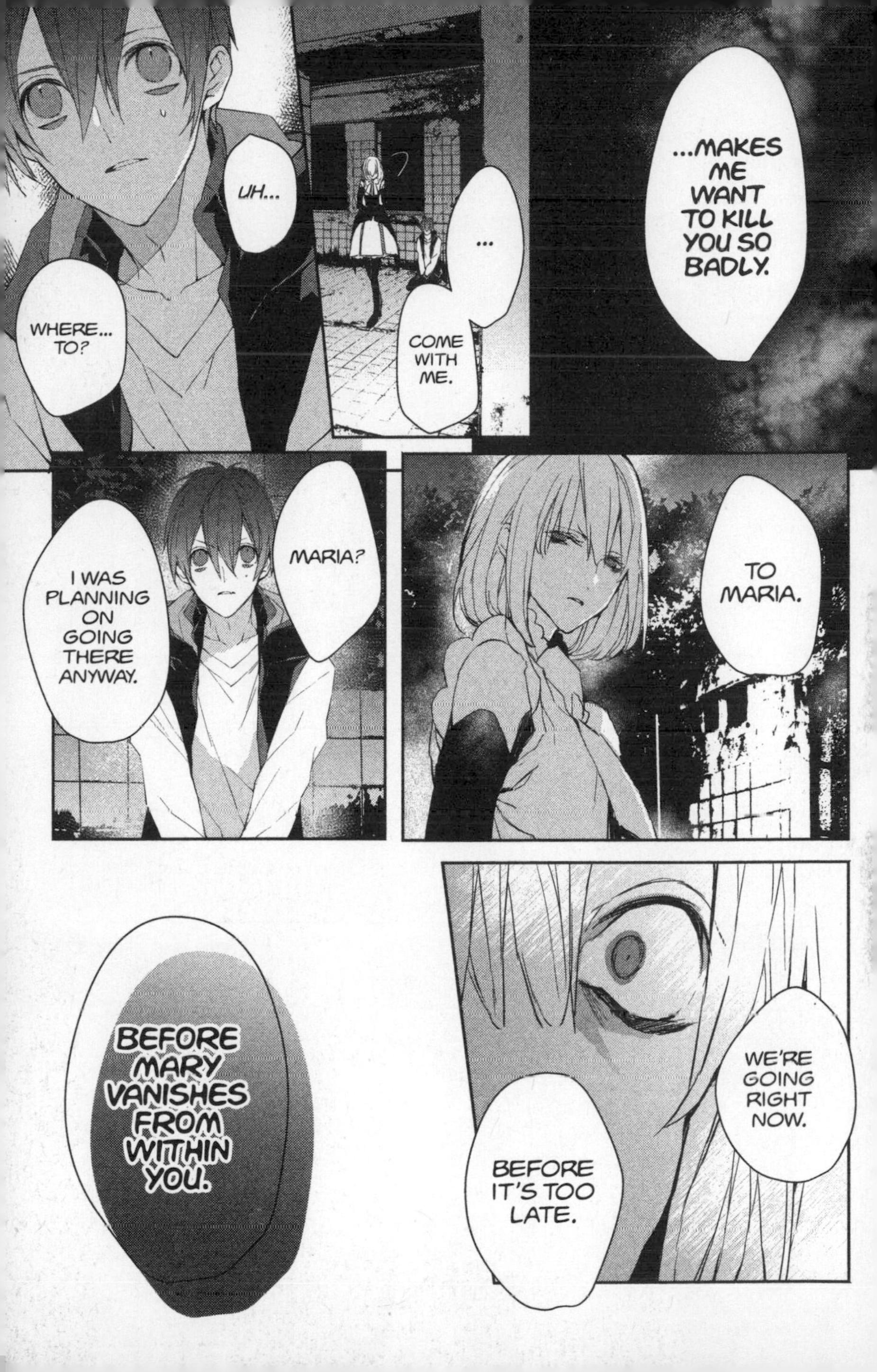
...MAKES ME WANT TO KILL YOU SO BADLY.
...
COME WITH ME.
UH...
WHERE... TO?
TO MARIA.
MARIA?
I WAS PLANNING ON GOING THERE ANYWAY.
WE'RE GOING RIGHT NOW.
BEFORE IT'S TOO LATE.
BEFORE MARY VANISHES FROM WITHIN YOU.

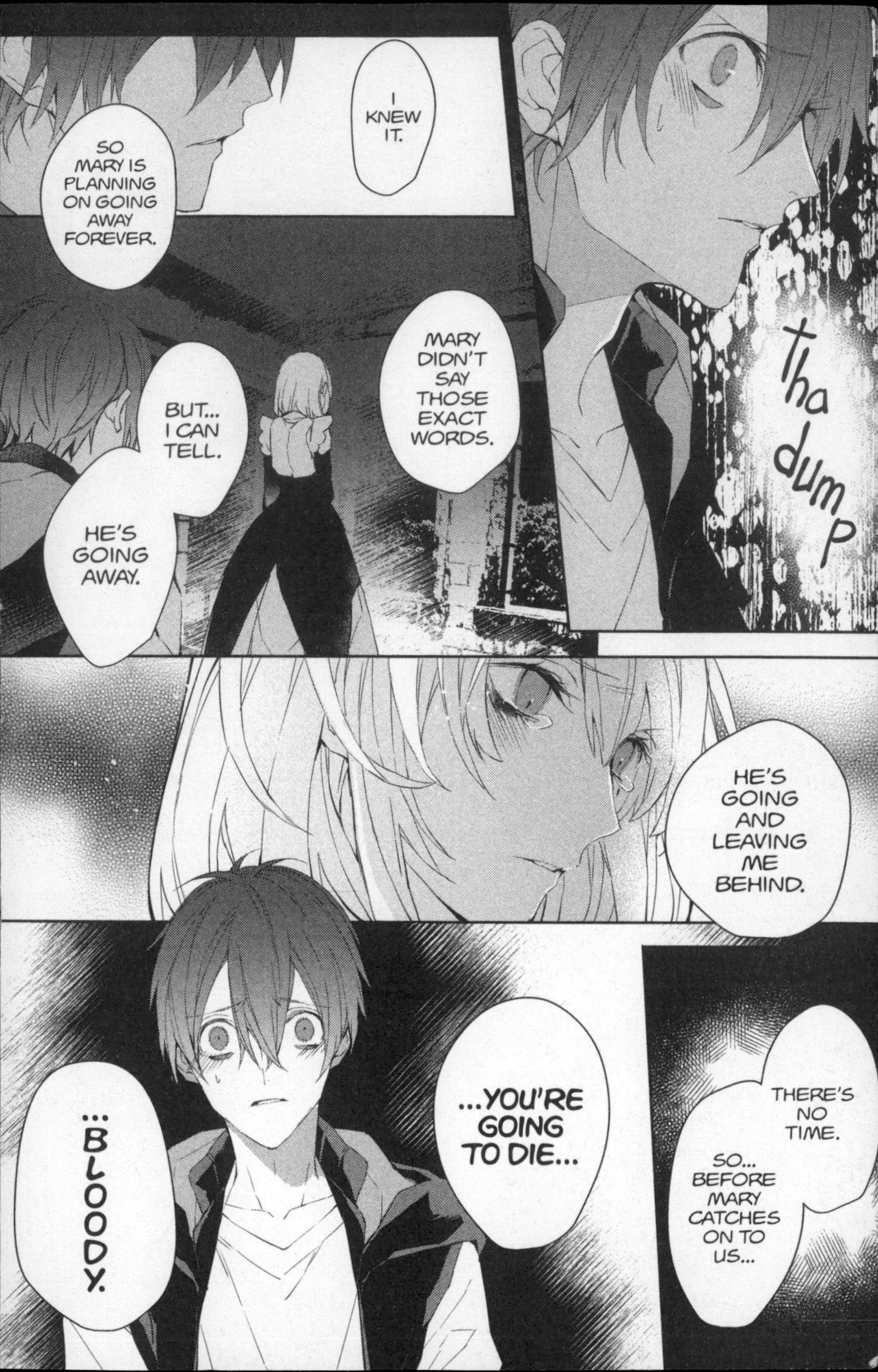
tha dump
I KNEW IT.
SO MARY IS PLANNING ON GOING AWAY FOREVER.
MARY DIDN'T SAY THOSE EXACT WORDS.
BUT... I CAN TELL.
HE'S GOING AWAY.
HE'S GOING AND LEAVING ME BEHIND.
THERE'S NO TIME.
SO... BEFORE MARY CATCHES ON TO US...
...YOU'RE GOING TO DIE...
...BLOODY.

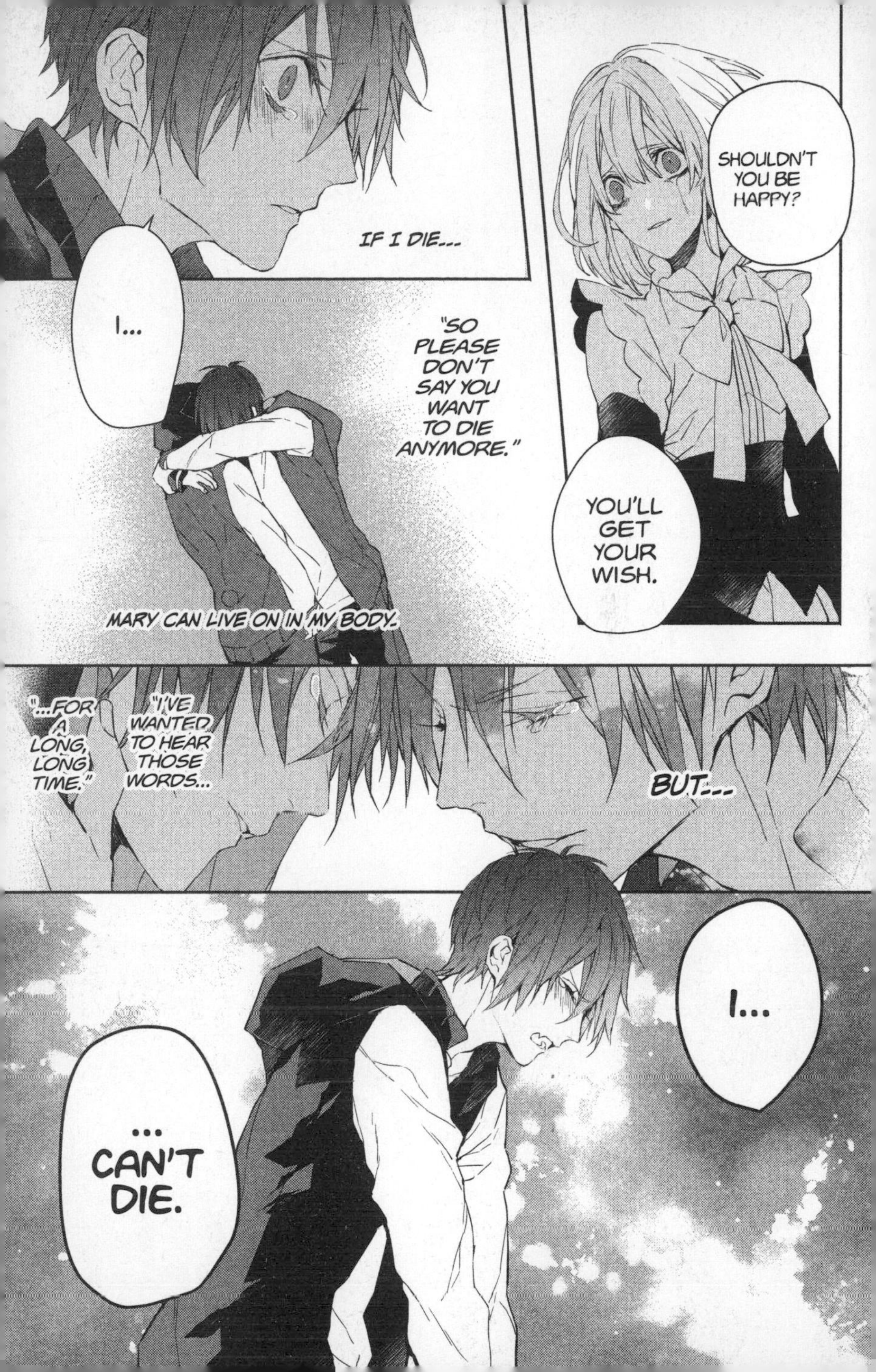
SHOULDN'T YOU BE HAPPY?
YOU'LL GET YOUR WISH.
IF I DIE...
"SO PLEASE DON'T SAY YOU WANT TO DIE ANYMORE."
I...
MARY CAN LIVE ON IN MY BODY.
BUT...
"I'VE WANTED TO HEAR THOSE WORDS...
"...FOR A LONG, LONG TIME."
I...
...CAN'T DIE.

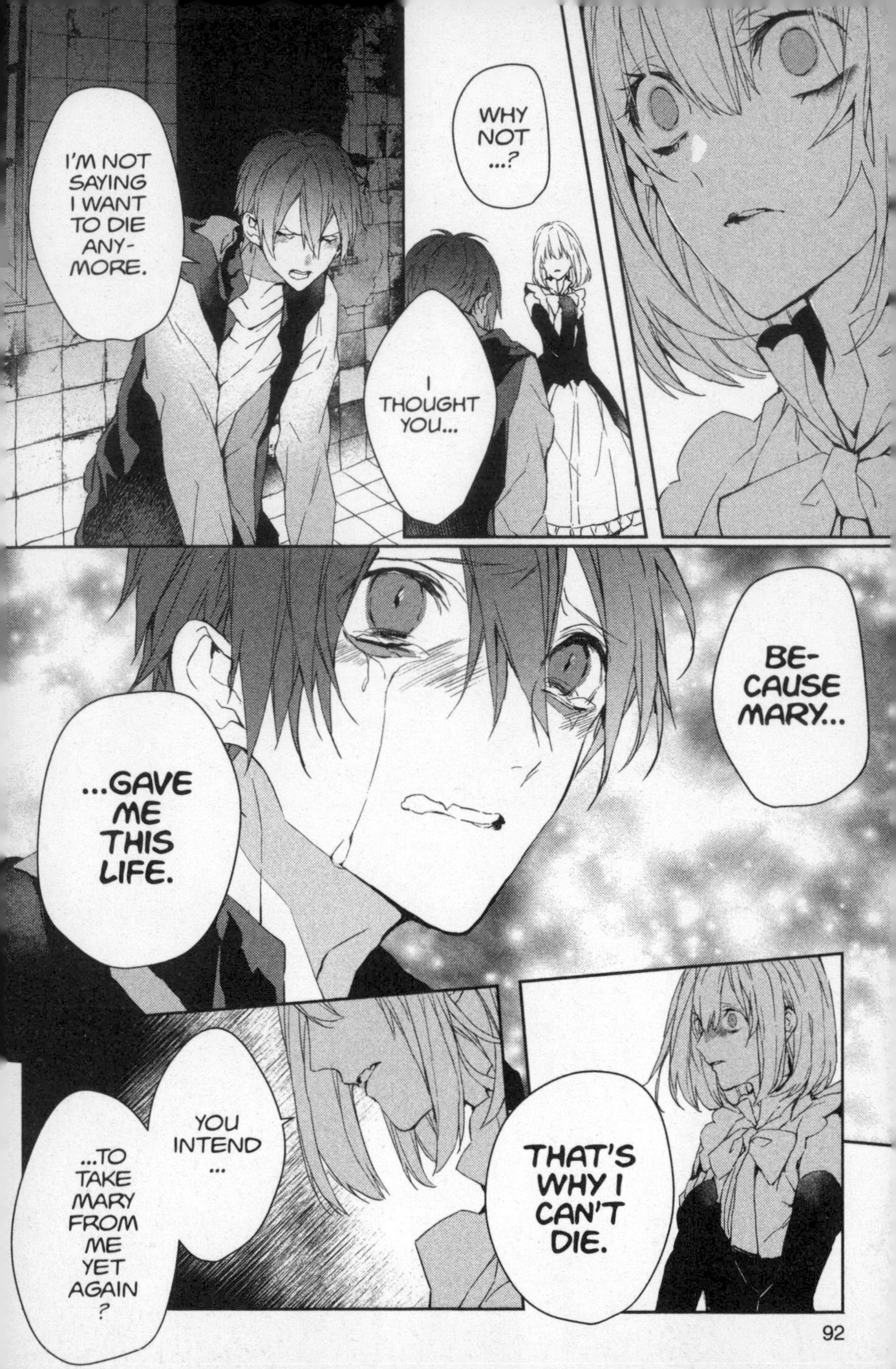
WHY NOT ...?
I THOUGHT YOU...
I'M NOT SAYING I WANT TO DIE ANY-MORE.
BE-CAUSE MARY...
...GAVE ME THIS LIFE.
THAT'S WHY I CAN'T DIE.
YOU INTEND ...
...TO TAKE MARY FROM ME YET AGAIN ?

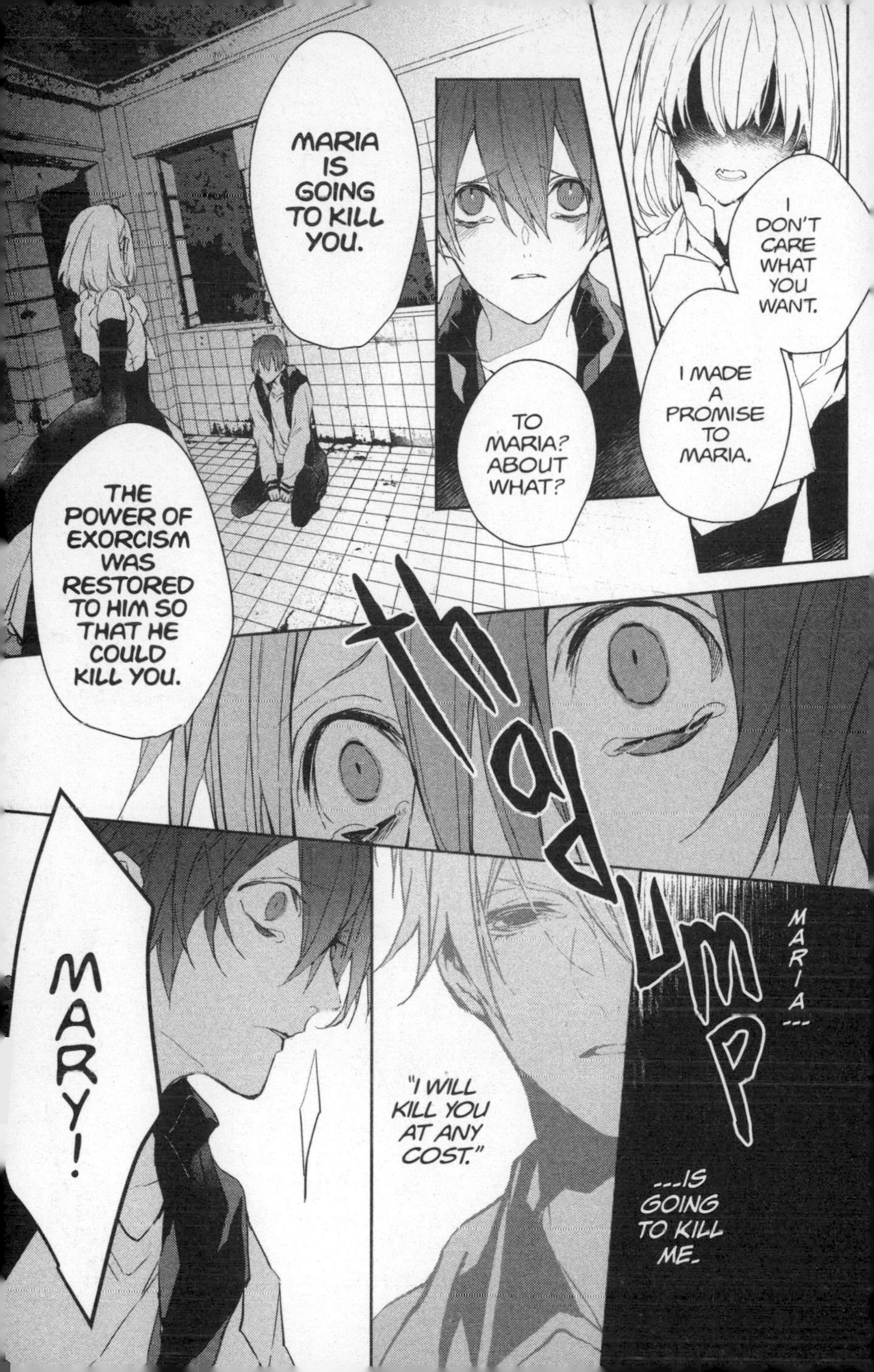
I DON'T CARE WHAT YOU WANT.
I MADE A PROMISE TO MARIA.
TO MARIA? ABOUT WHAT?
MARIA IS GOING TO KILL YOU.
THE POWER OF EXORCISM WAS RESTORED TO HIM SO THAT HE COULD KILL YOU.
thadump
MARIA---
---IS GOING TO KILL ME.
"I WILL KILL YOU AT ANY COST."
MARY!

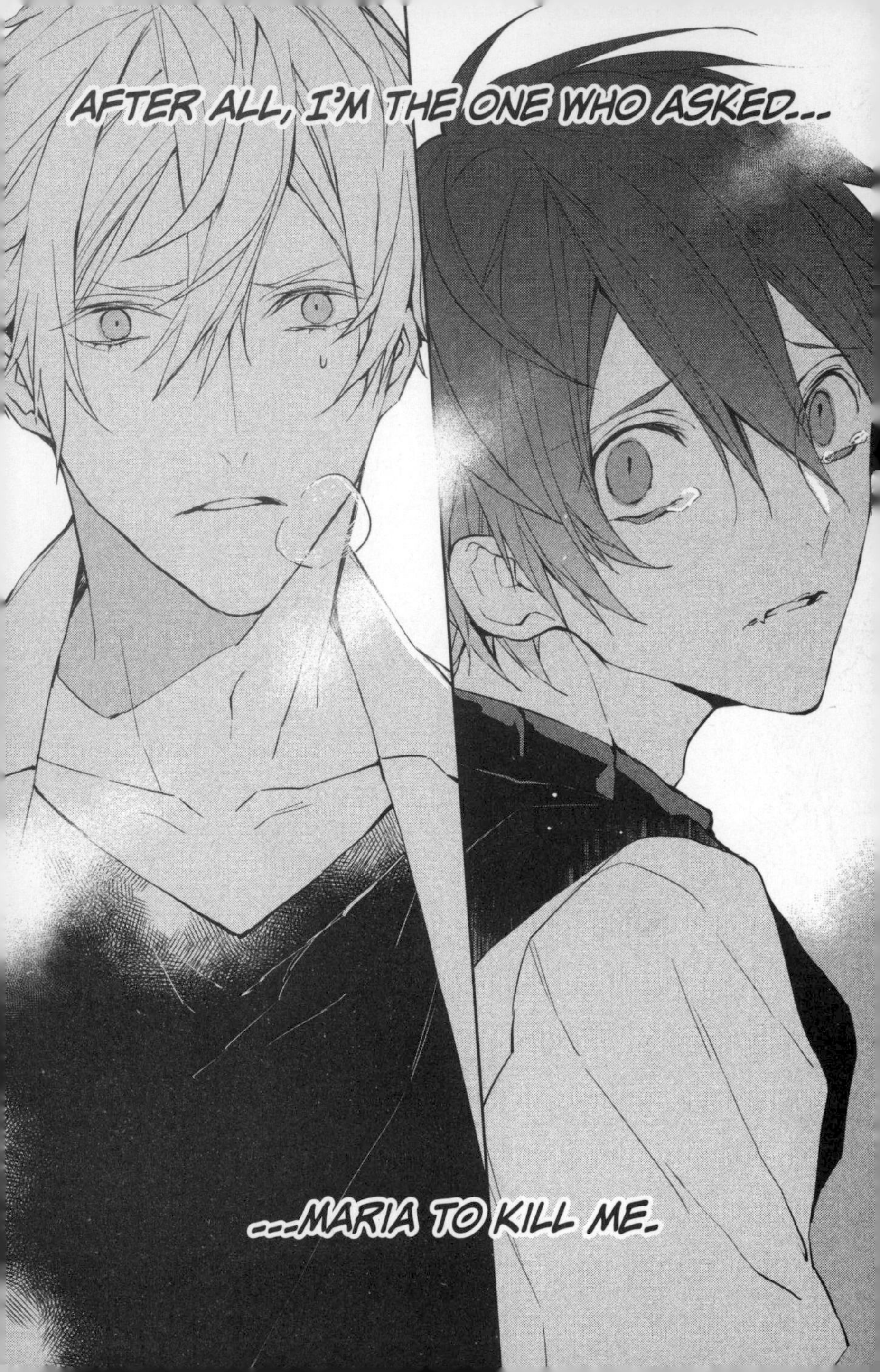
AFTER ALL, I'M THE ONE WHO ASKED...
...MARIA TO KILL ME.

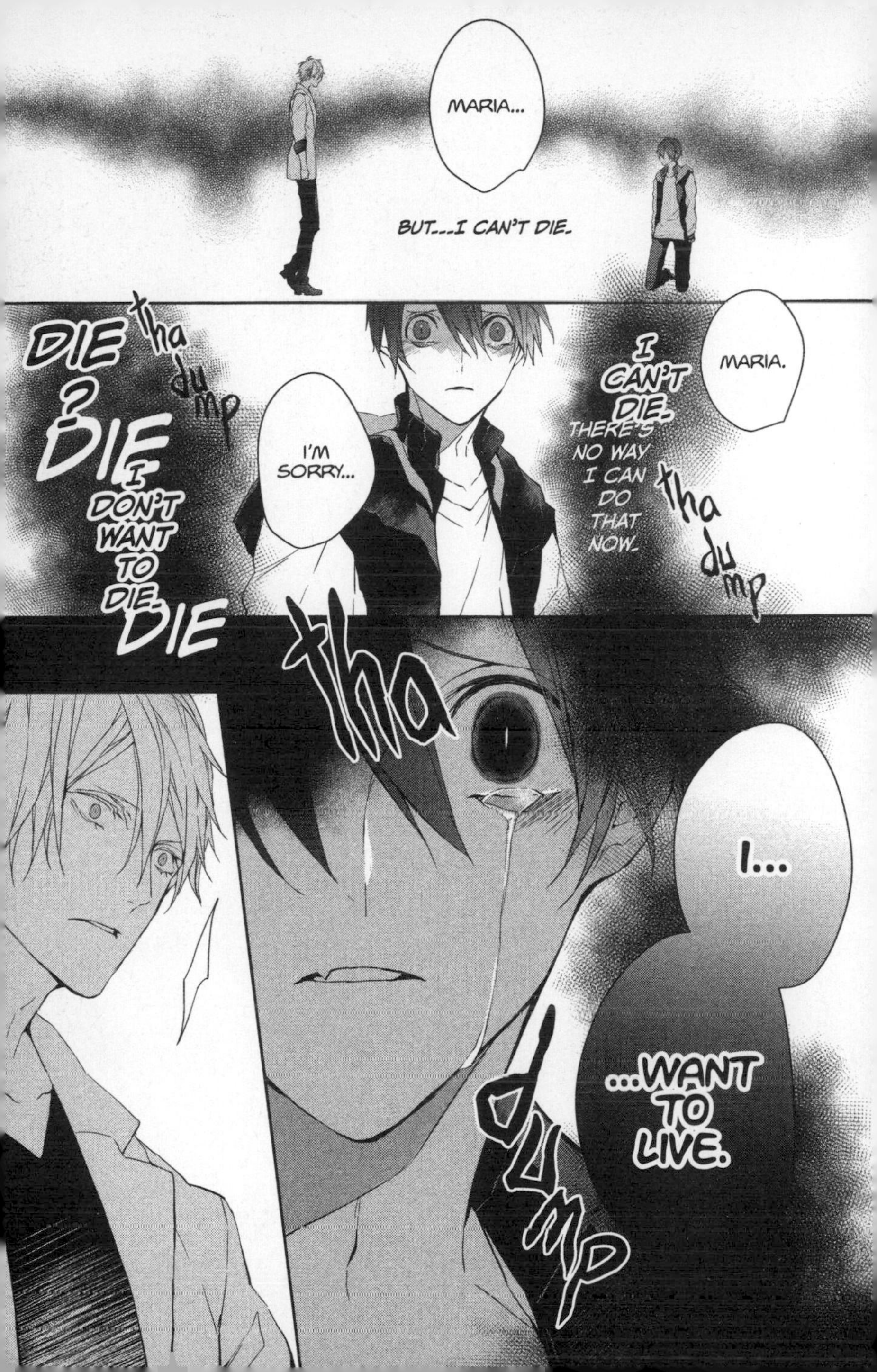
MARIA...
BUT...I CAN'T DIE.
MARIA.
I CAN'T DIE.
THERE'S NO WAY I CAN DO THAT NOW.
tha dump
I'M SORRY...
tha dump
DIE? DIE
I DON'T WANT TO DIE
DIE
I...
...WANT TO LIVE.
tha dump

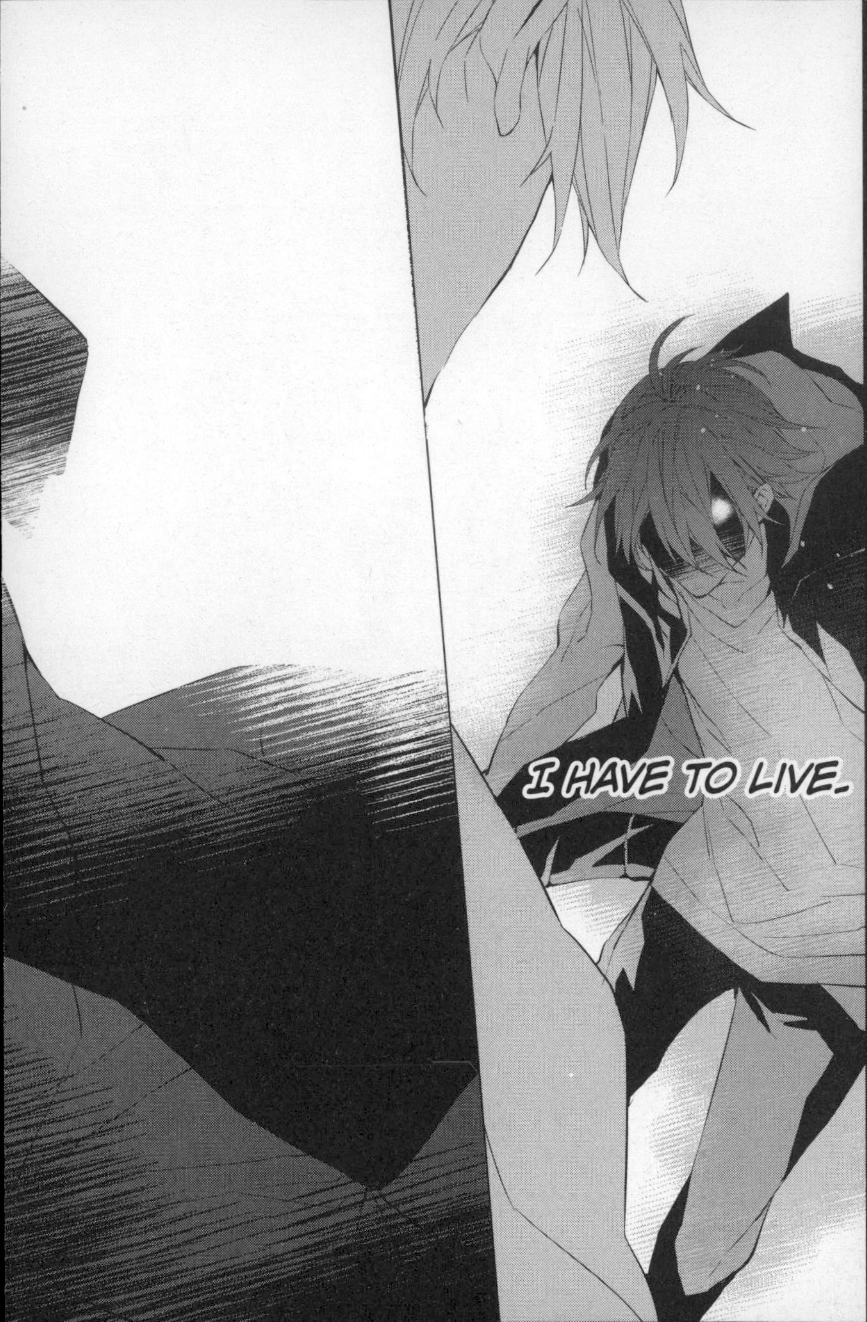
I HAVE TO LIVE.

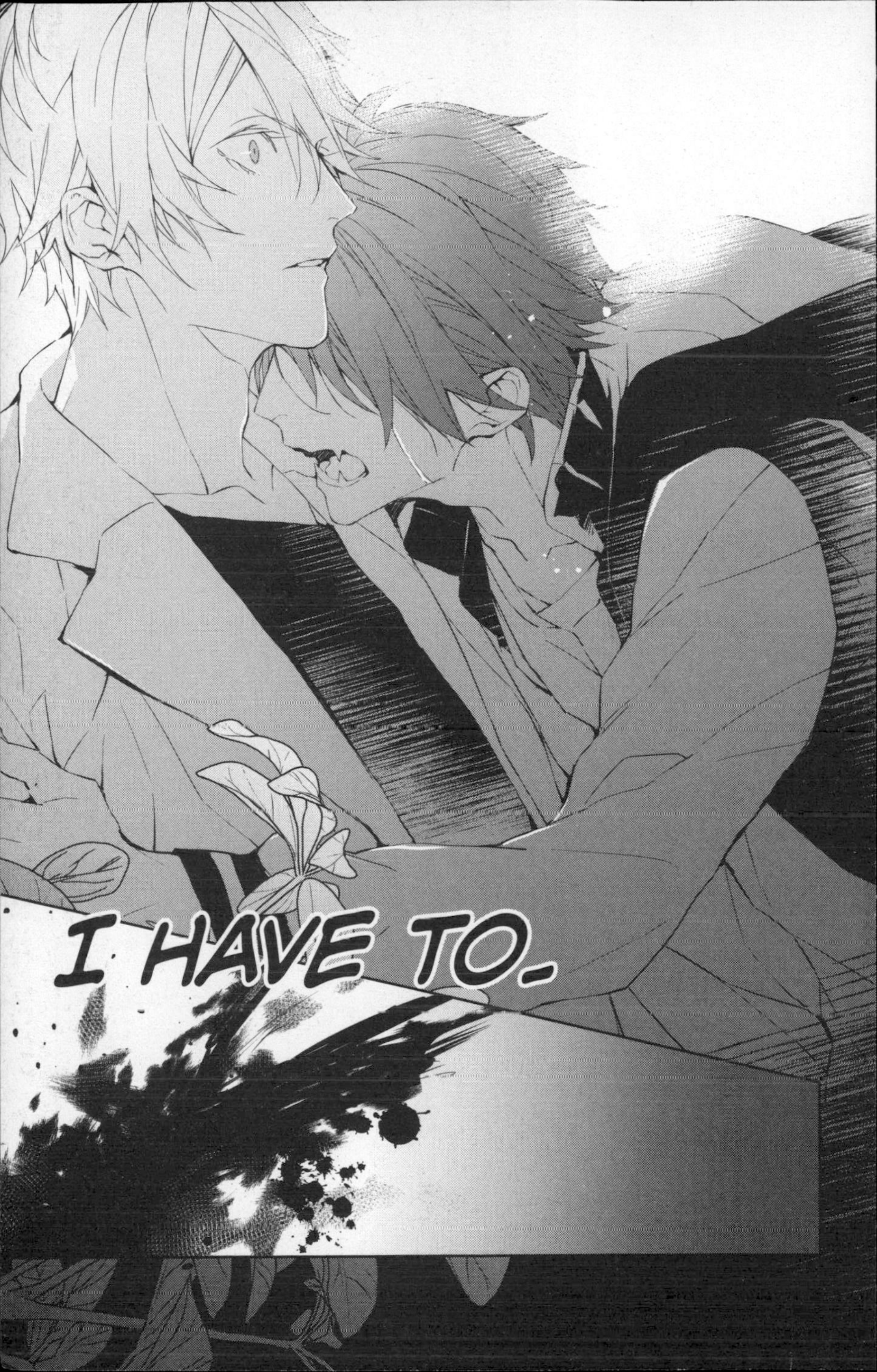
I HAVE TO...

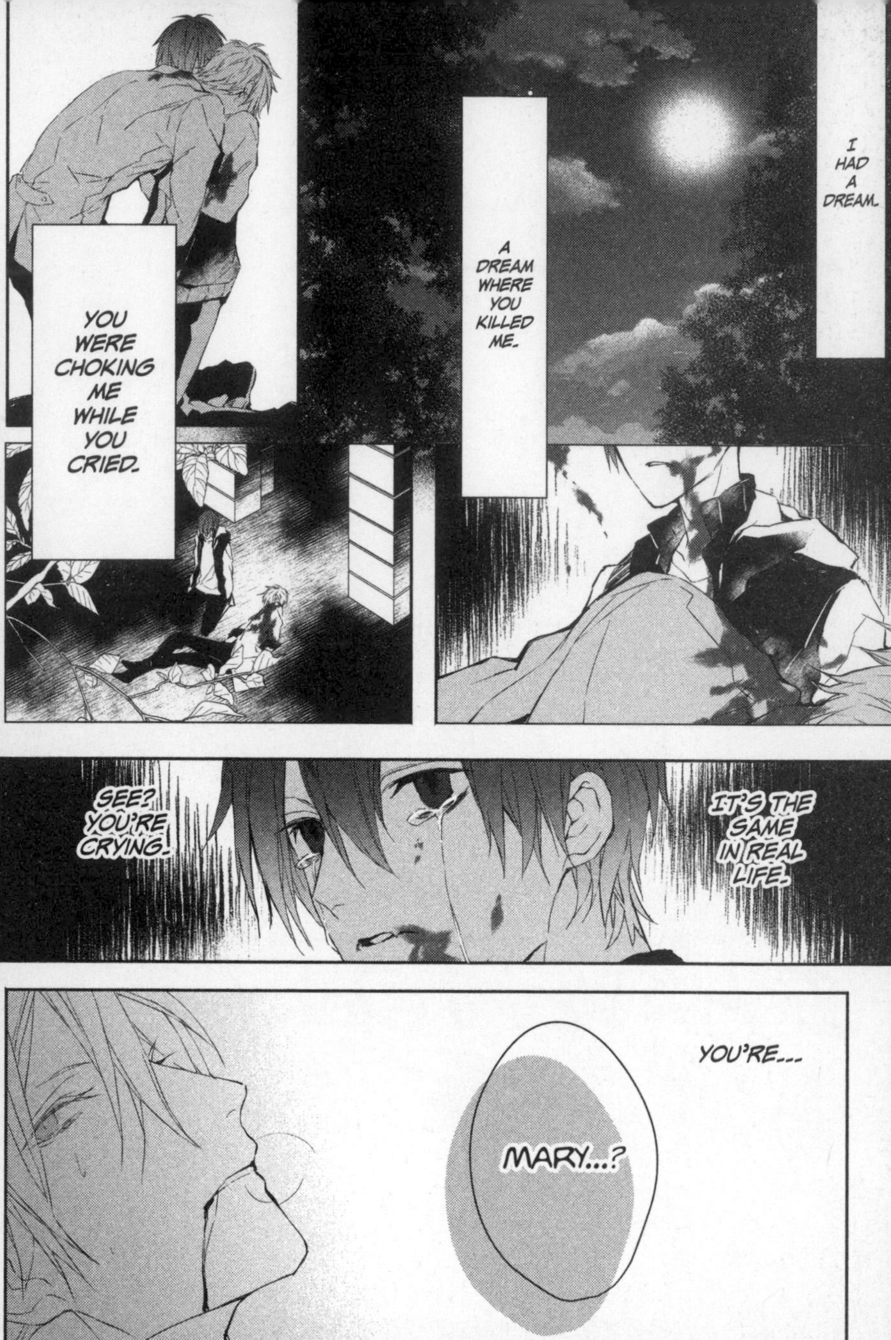
I HAD A DREAM.
A DREAM WHERE YOU KILLED ME.
YOU WERE CHOKING ME WHILE YOU CRIED.
IT'S THE SAME IN REAL LIFE.
SEE? YOU'RE CRYING.
YOU'RE...
MARY...?

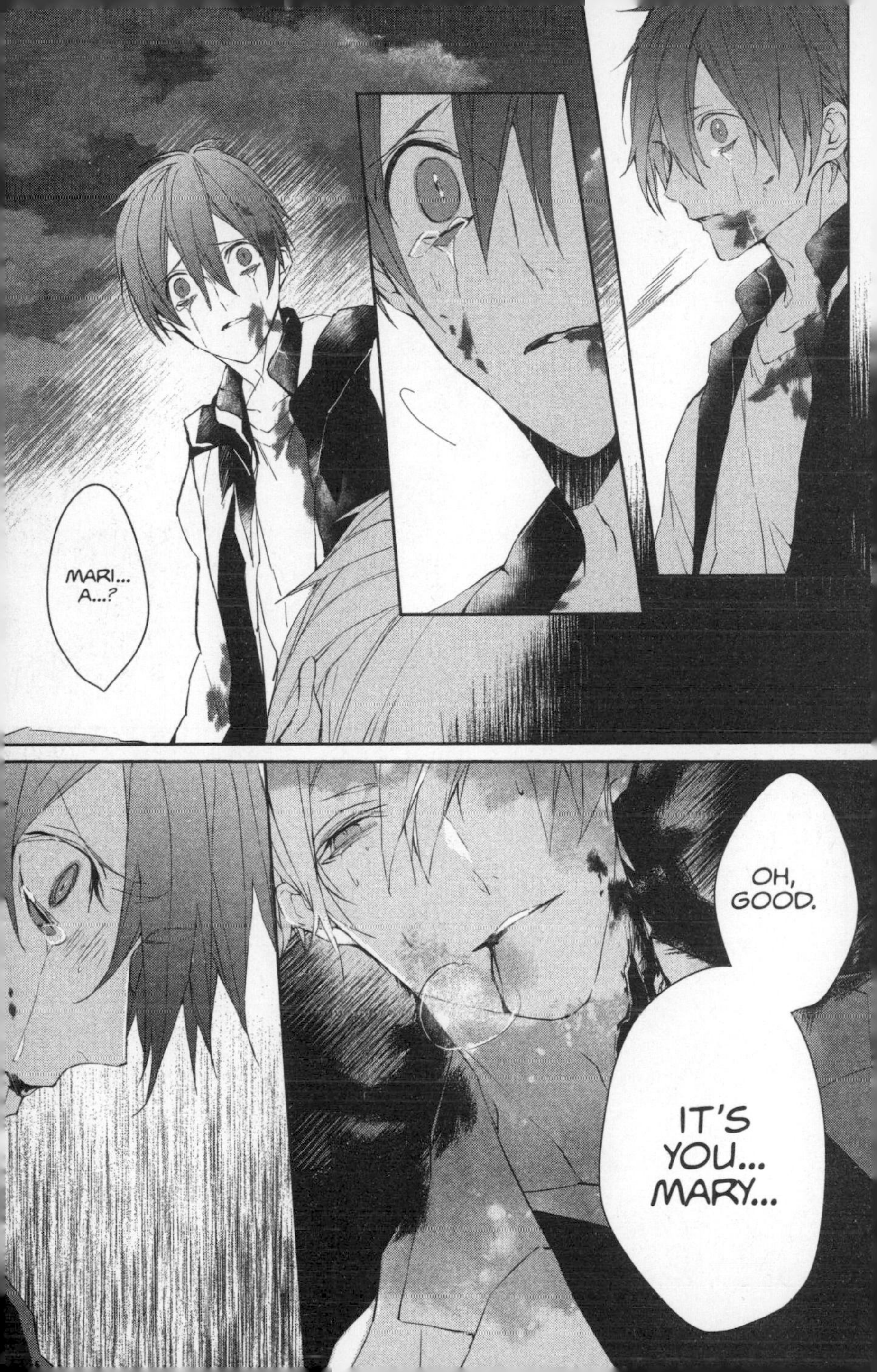
MARI... A...?
OH, GOOD.
IT'S YOU... MARY...

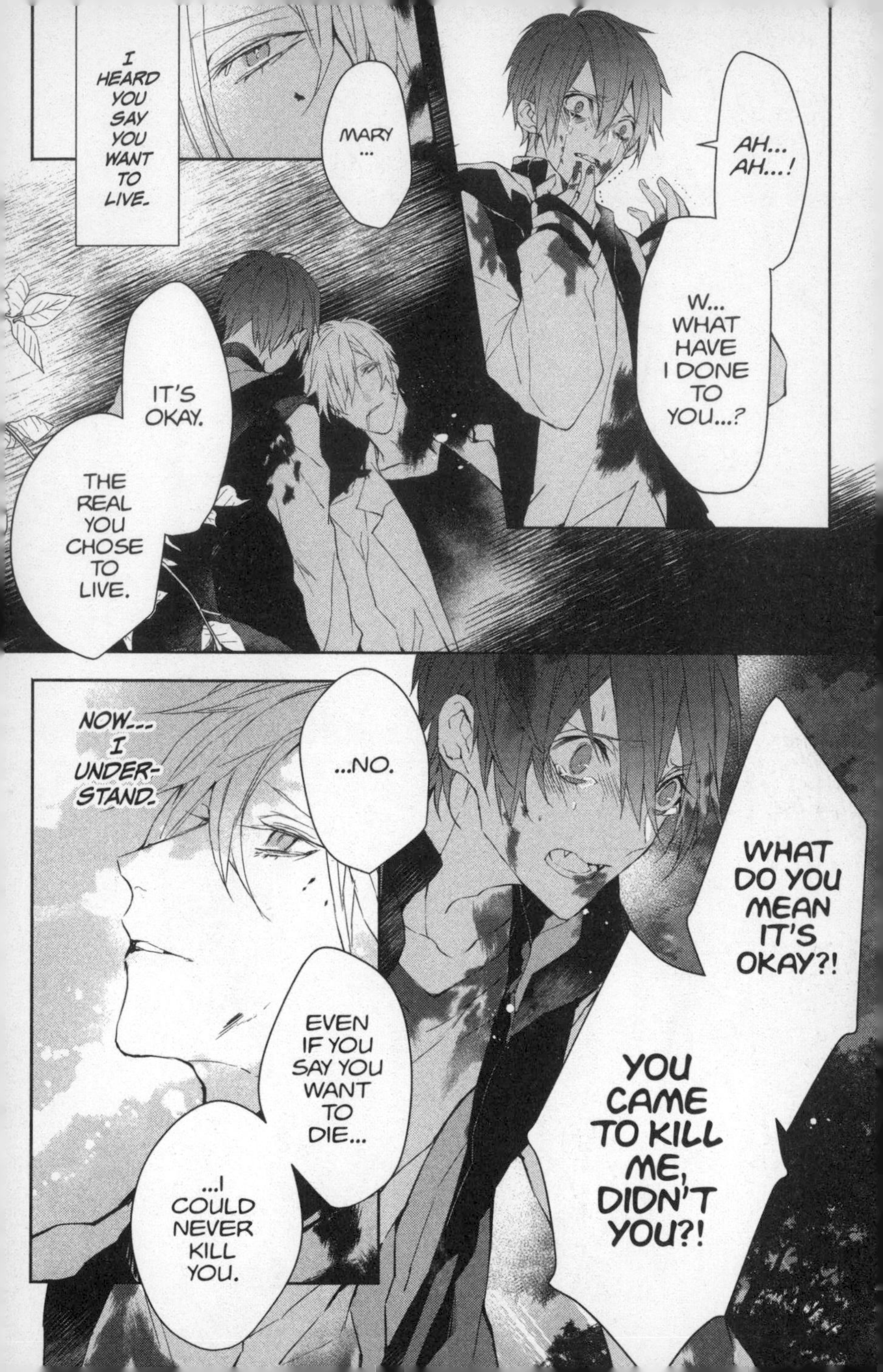
AH... AH...!
W... WHAT HAVE I DONE TO YOU...?
MARY ...
I HEARD YOU SAY YOU WANT TO LIVE.
IT'S OKAY.
THE REAL YOU CHOSE TO LIVE.
WHAT DO YOU MEAN IT'S OKAY?!
YOU CAME TO KILL ME, DIDN'T YOU?!
...NO.
NOW... I UNDERSTAND.
EVEN IF YOU SAY YOU WANT TO DIE...
...I COULD NEVER KILL YOU.

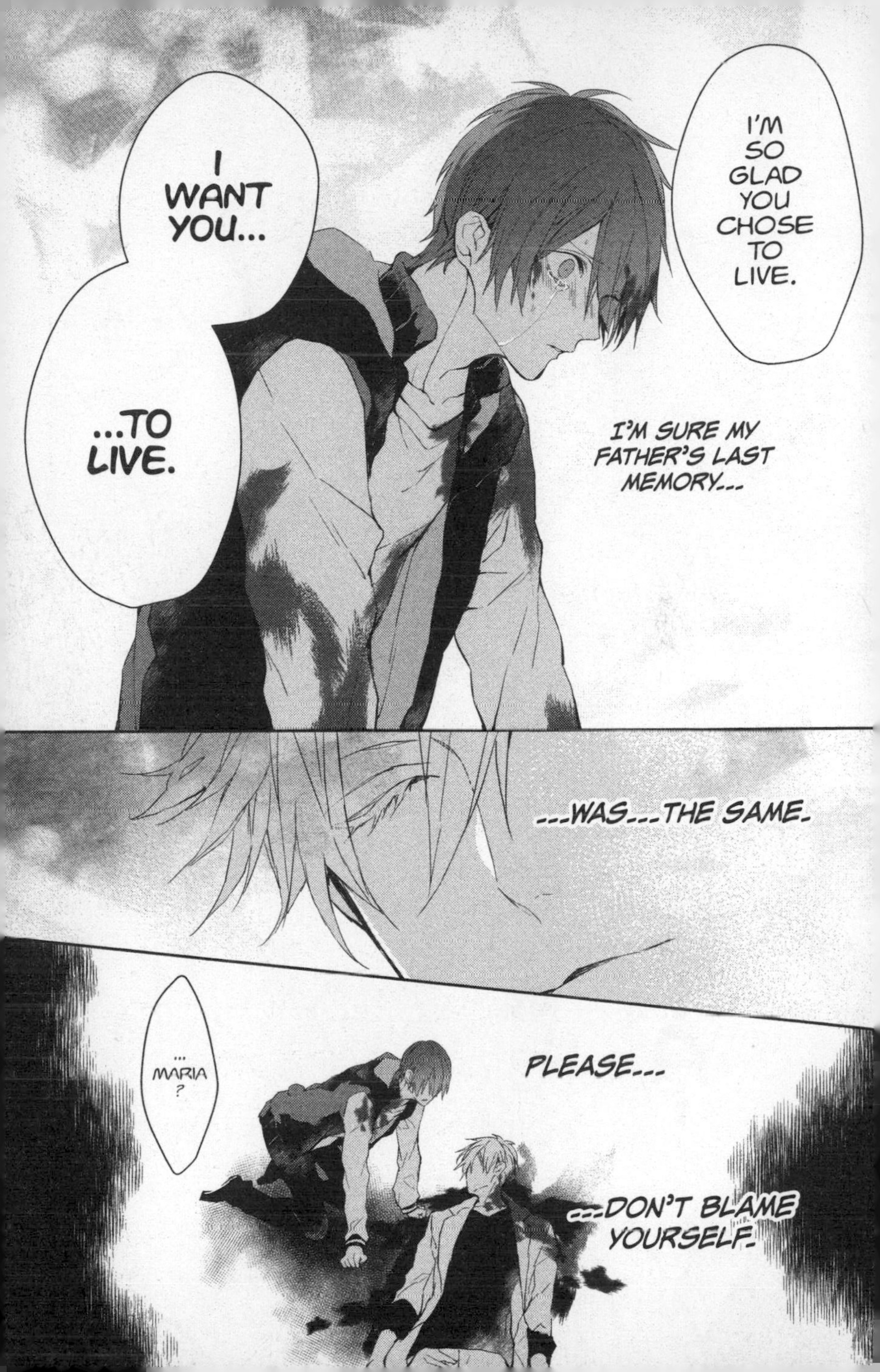
I'M SO GLAD YOU CHOSE TO LIVE.
I WANT YOU...
...TO LIVE.
I'M SURE MY FATHER'S LAST MEMORY...
...WAS...THE SAME.
PLEASE...
...MARIA?
...DON'T BLAME YOURSELF.

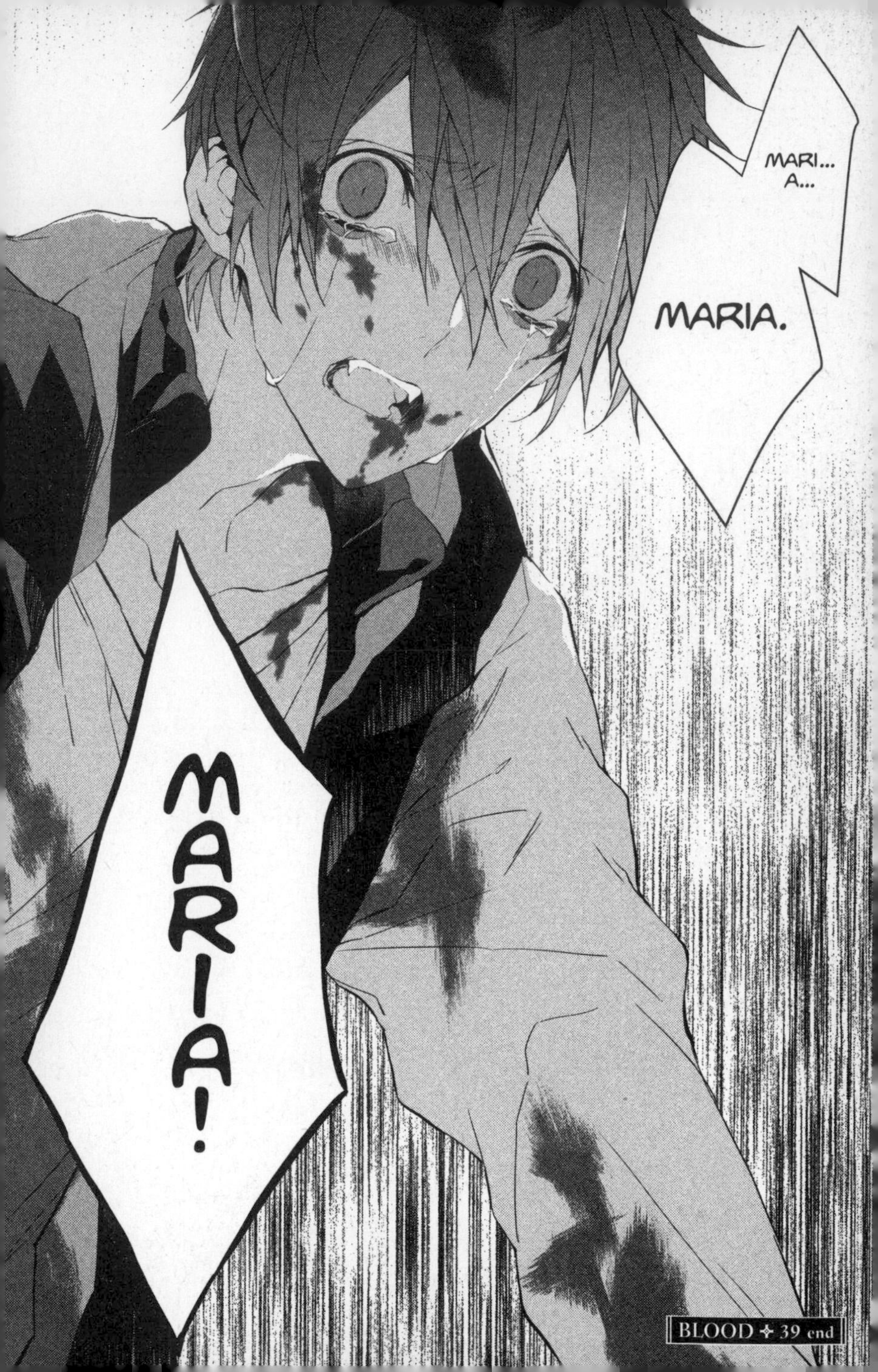
MARI... A...
MARIA.
MARIA!
BLOOD ✣ 39 end

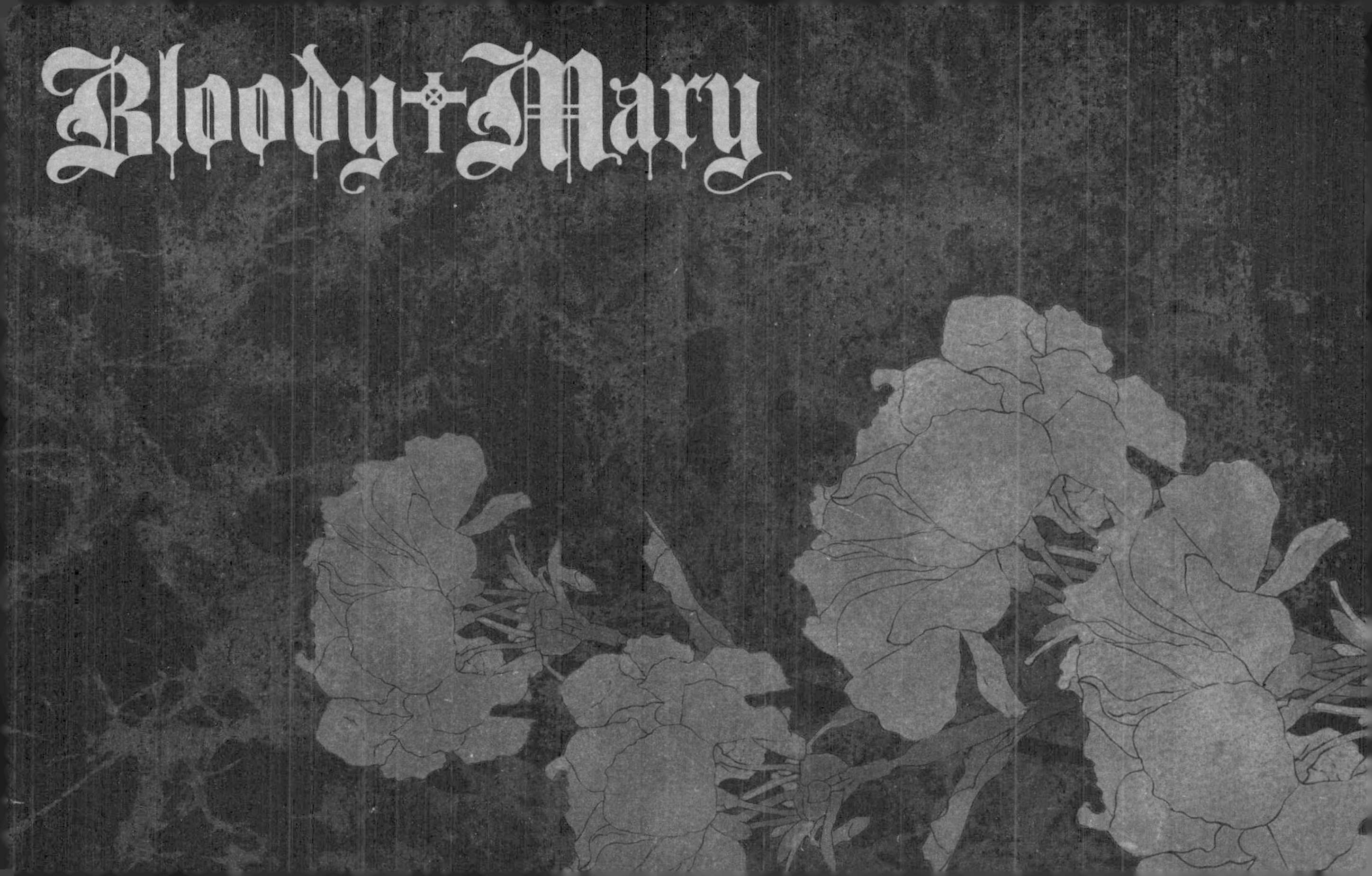
Bloody+Mary

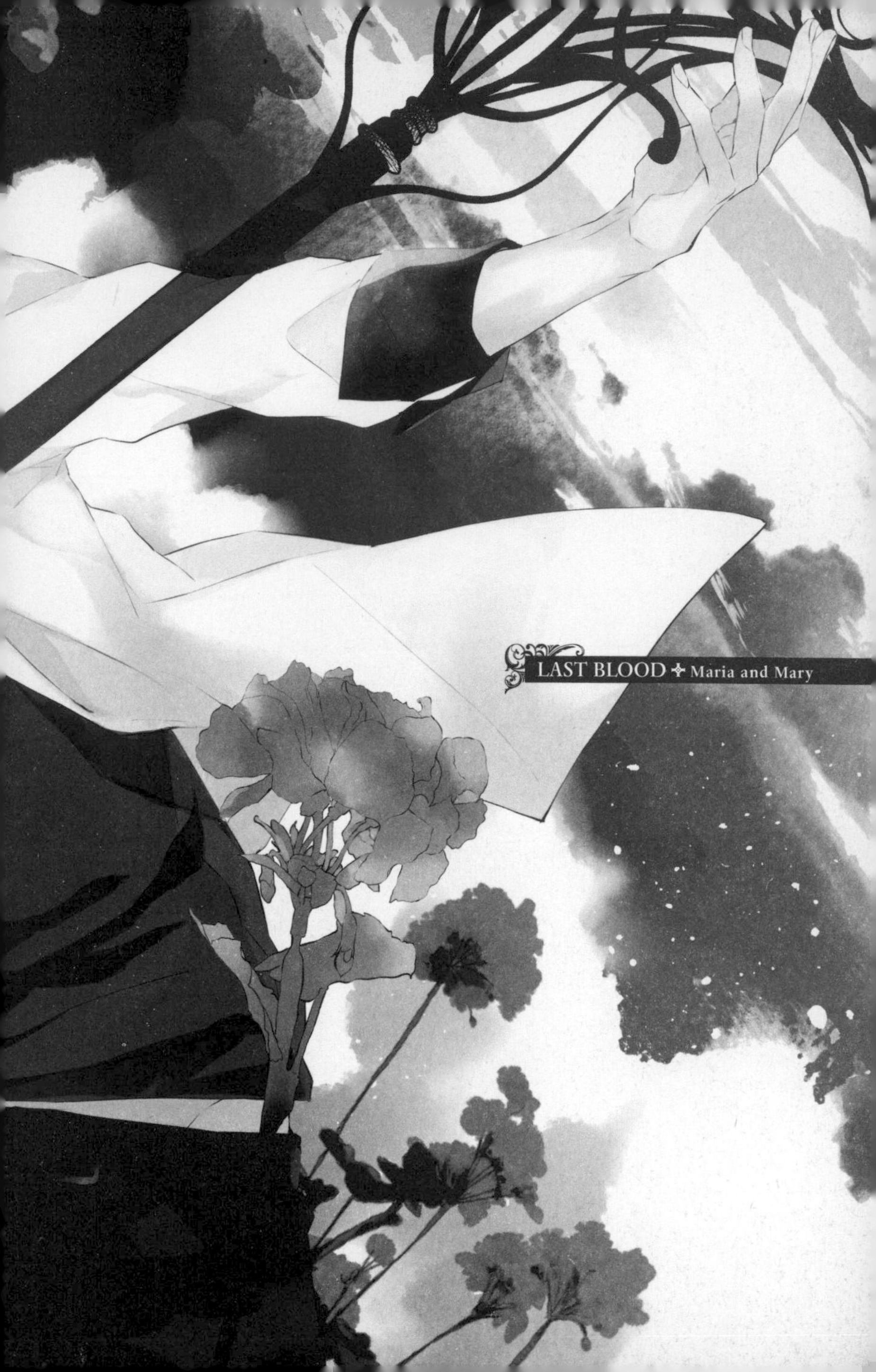
LAST BLOOD ✣ Maria and Mary

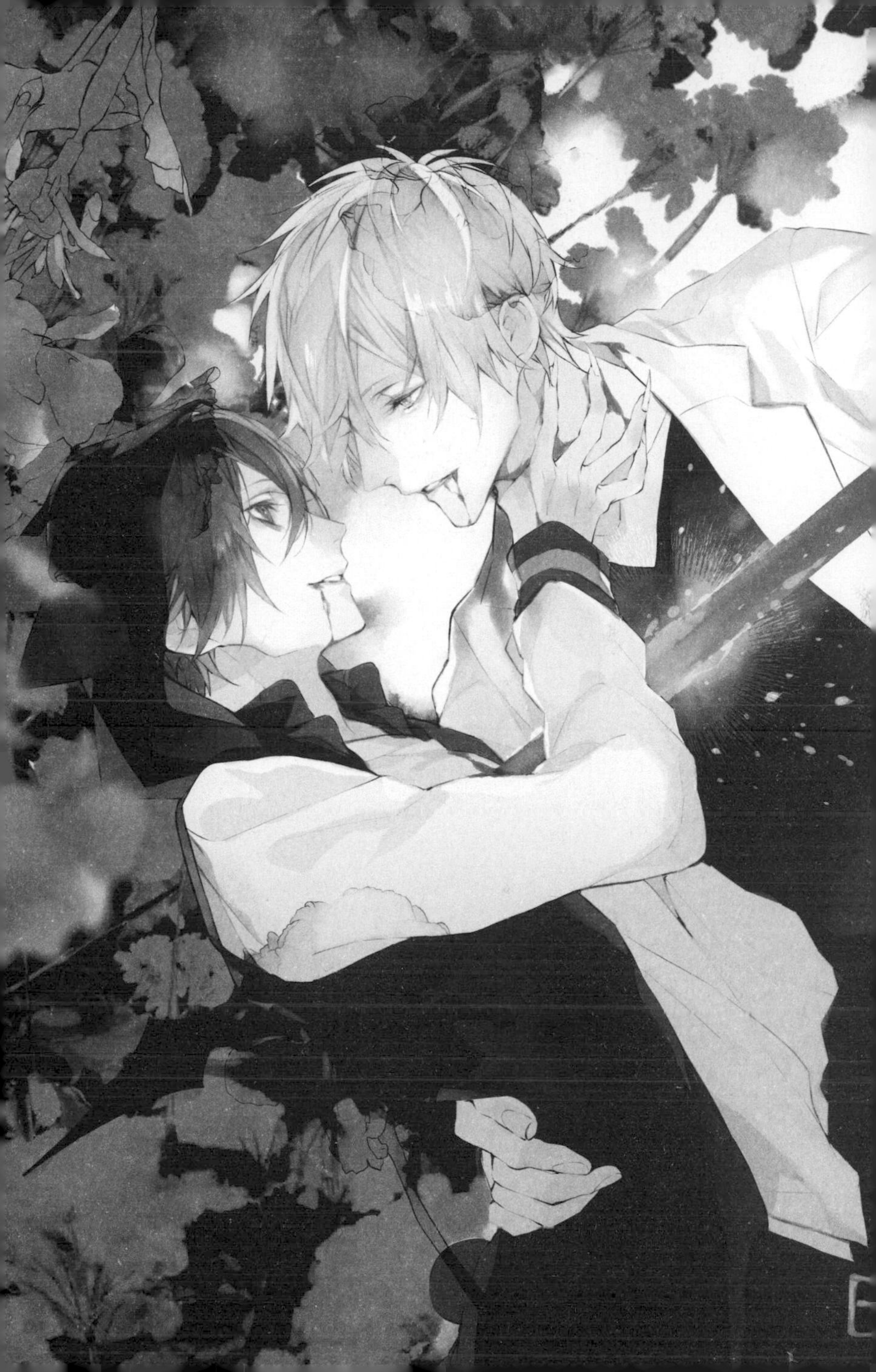

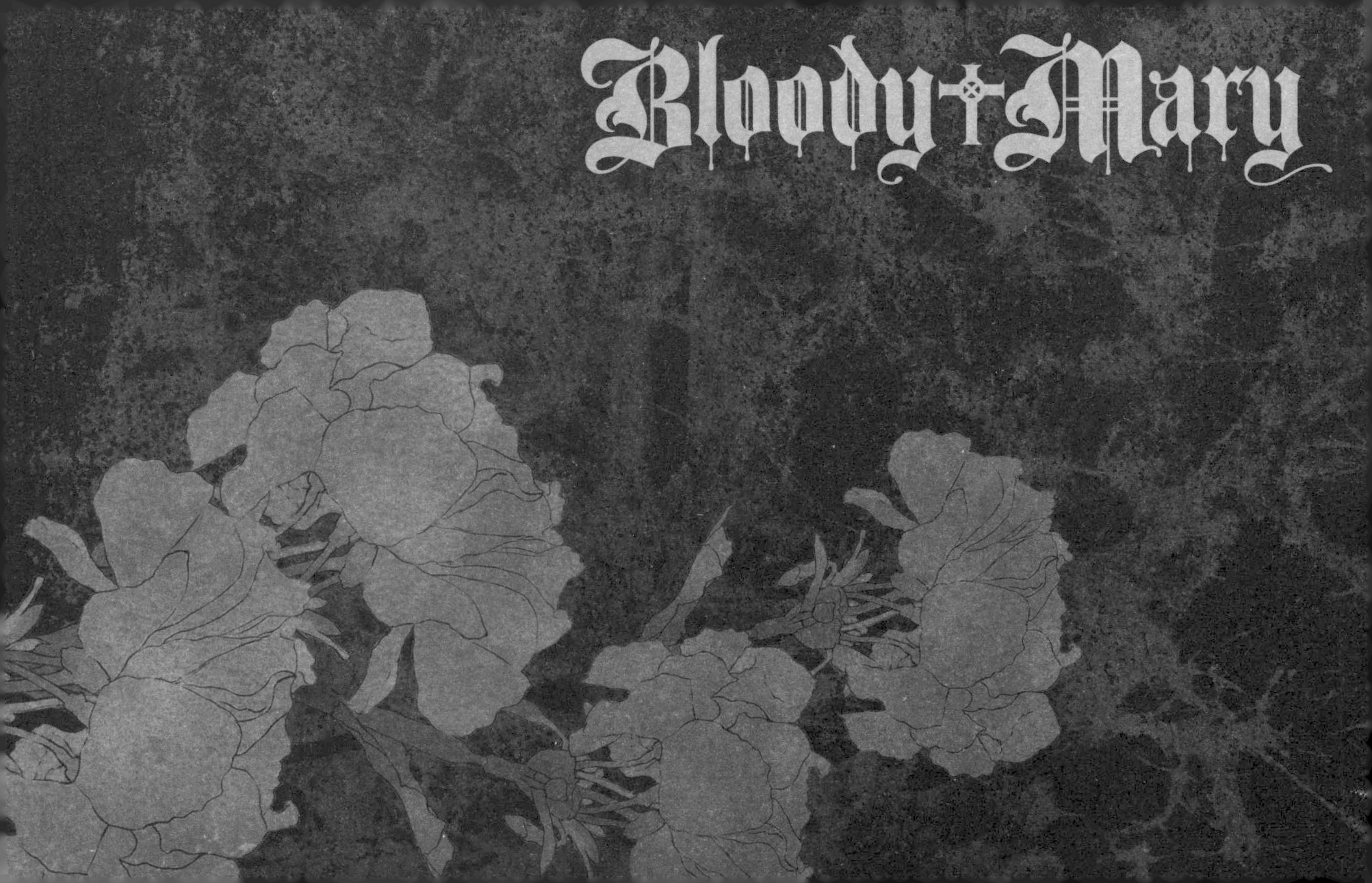
Bloody+Mary

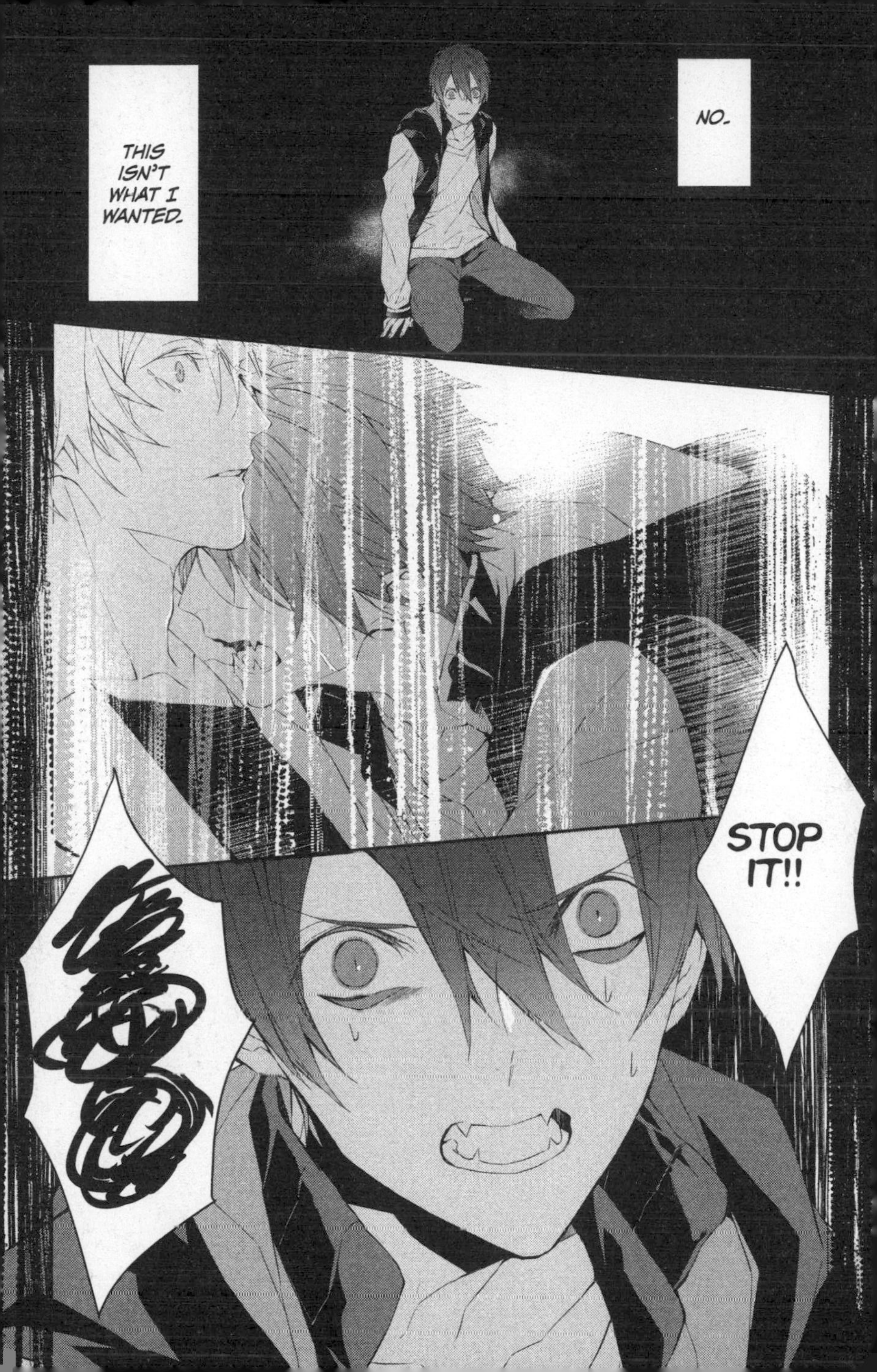
NO.
THIS ISN'T WHAT I WANTED.
STOP IT!!

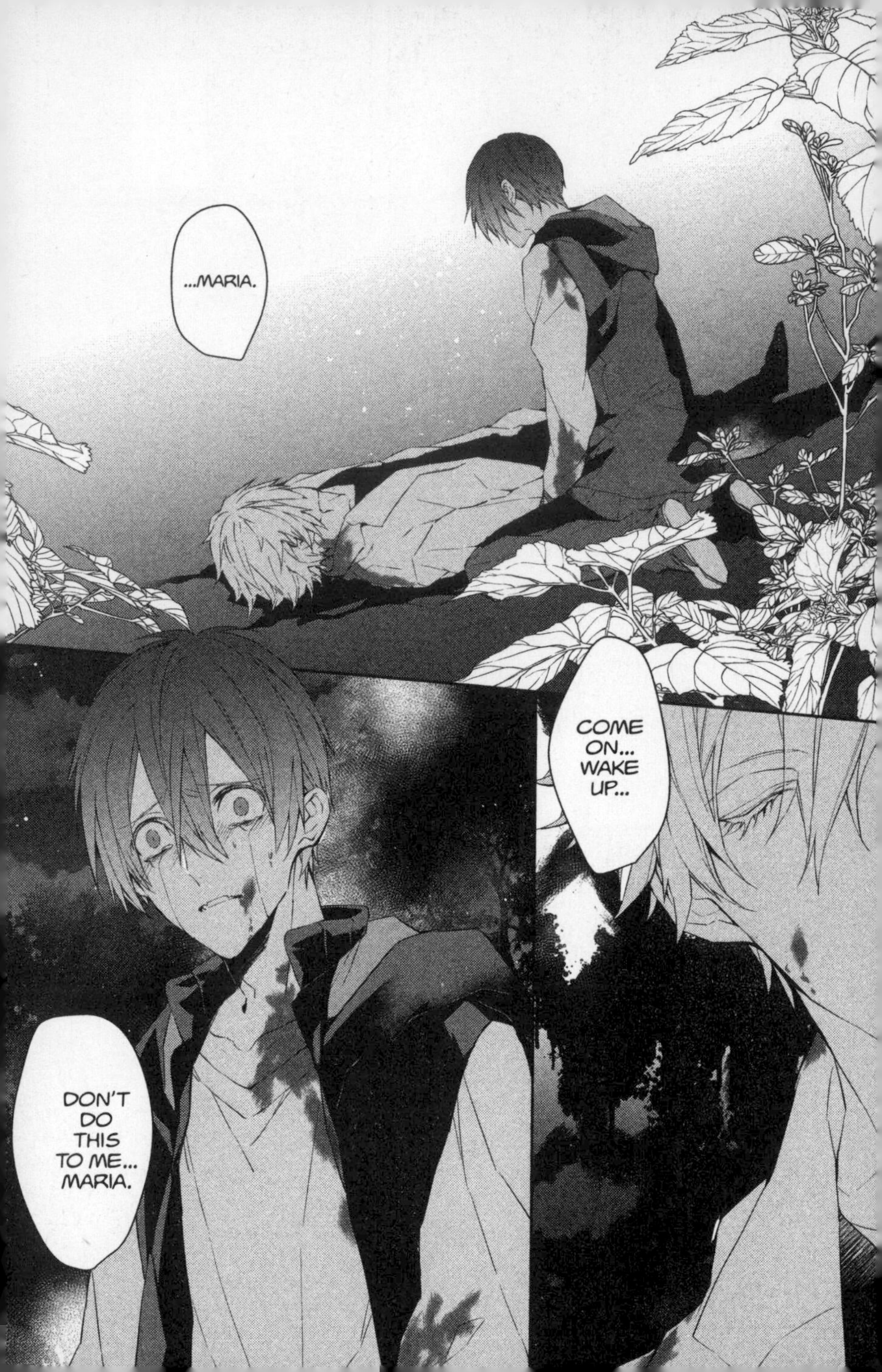
...MARIA.
COME ON... WAKE UP...
DON'T DO THIS TO ME... MARIA.

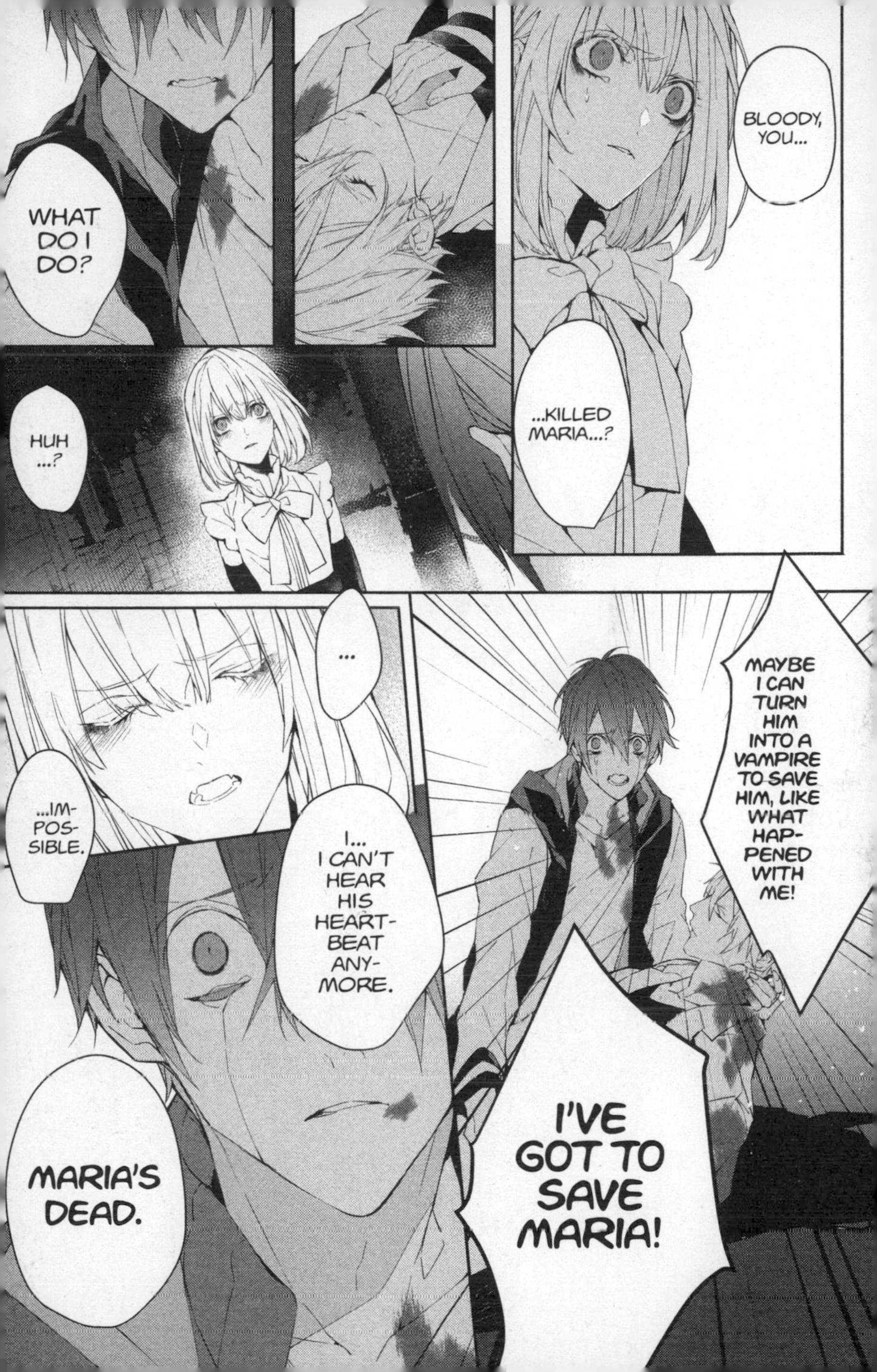
BLOODY, YOU...
...KILLED MARIA...?
WHAT DO I DO?
HUH ...?
MAYBE I CAN TURN HIM INTO A VAMPIRE TO SAVE HIM, LIKE WHAT HAP-PENED WITH ME!
I'VE GOT TO SAVE MARIA!
...
...IM-POS-SIBLE.
I... I CAN'T HEAR HIS HEART-BEAT ANY-MORE.
MARIA'S DEAD.

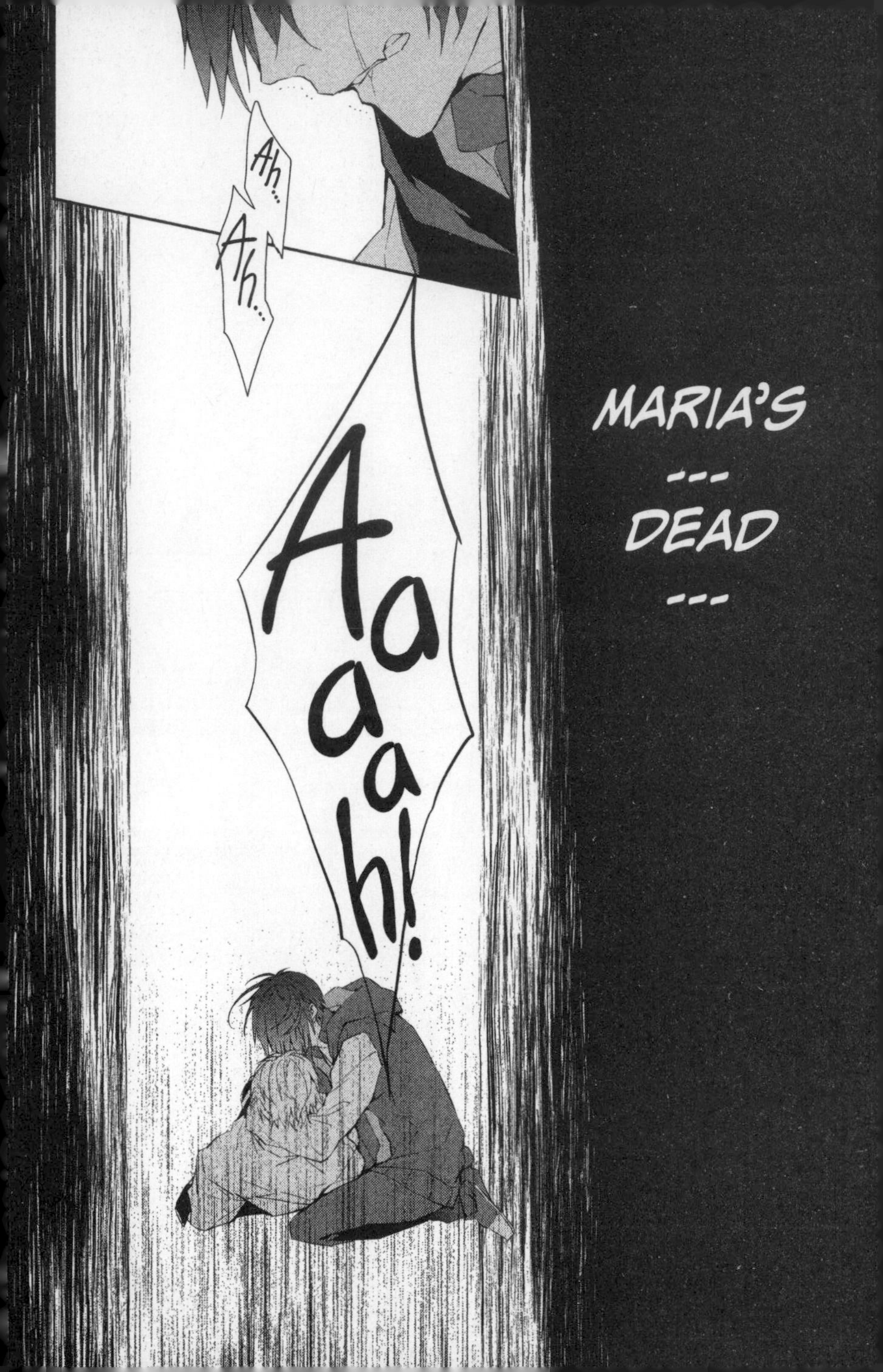
Ah...
Ah...
Aaaah!
MARIA'S
---
DEAD
---

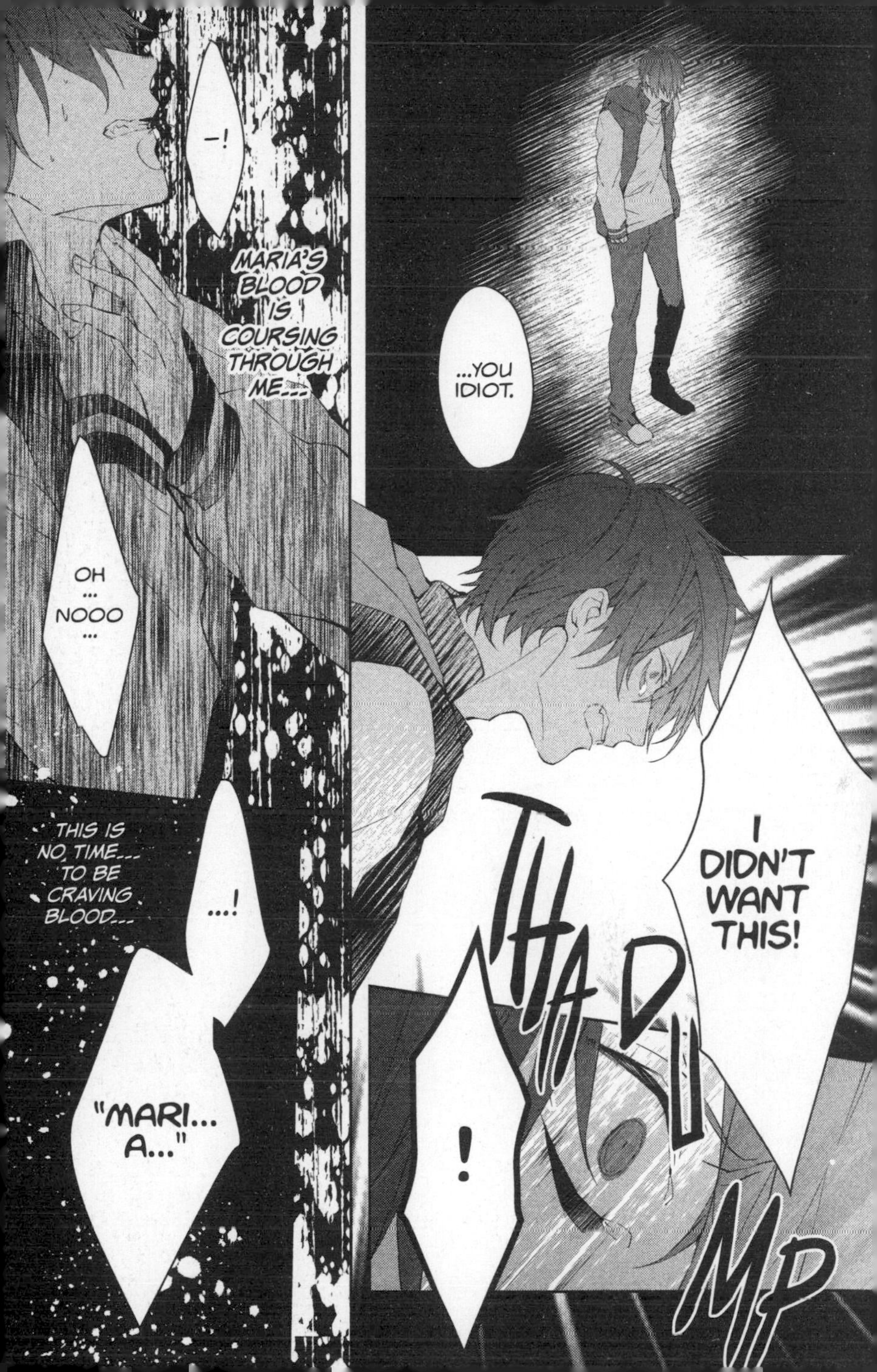
...YOU IDIOT.
I DIDN'T WANT THIS!
THADUMP
!
—!
MARIA'S BLOOD IS COURSING THROUGH ME...
OH... NOOO...
...!
THIS IS NO TIME... TO BE CRAVING BLOOD...
"MARI... A..."

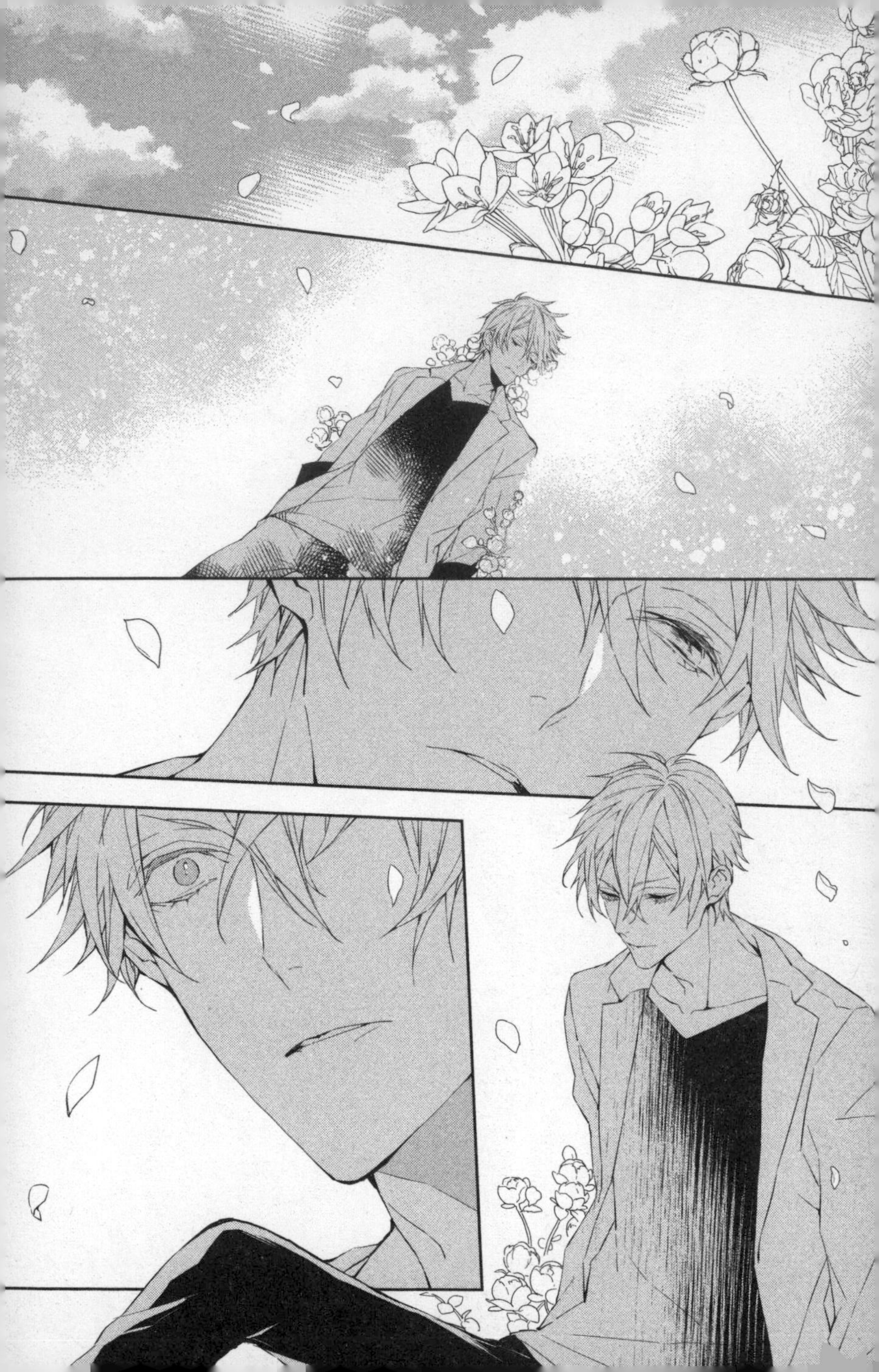

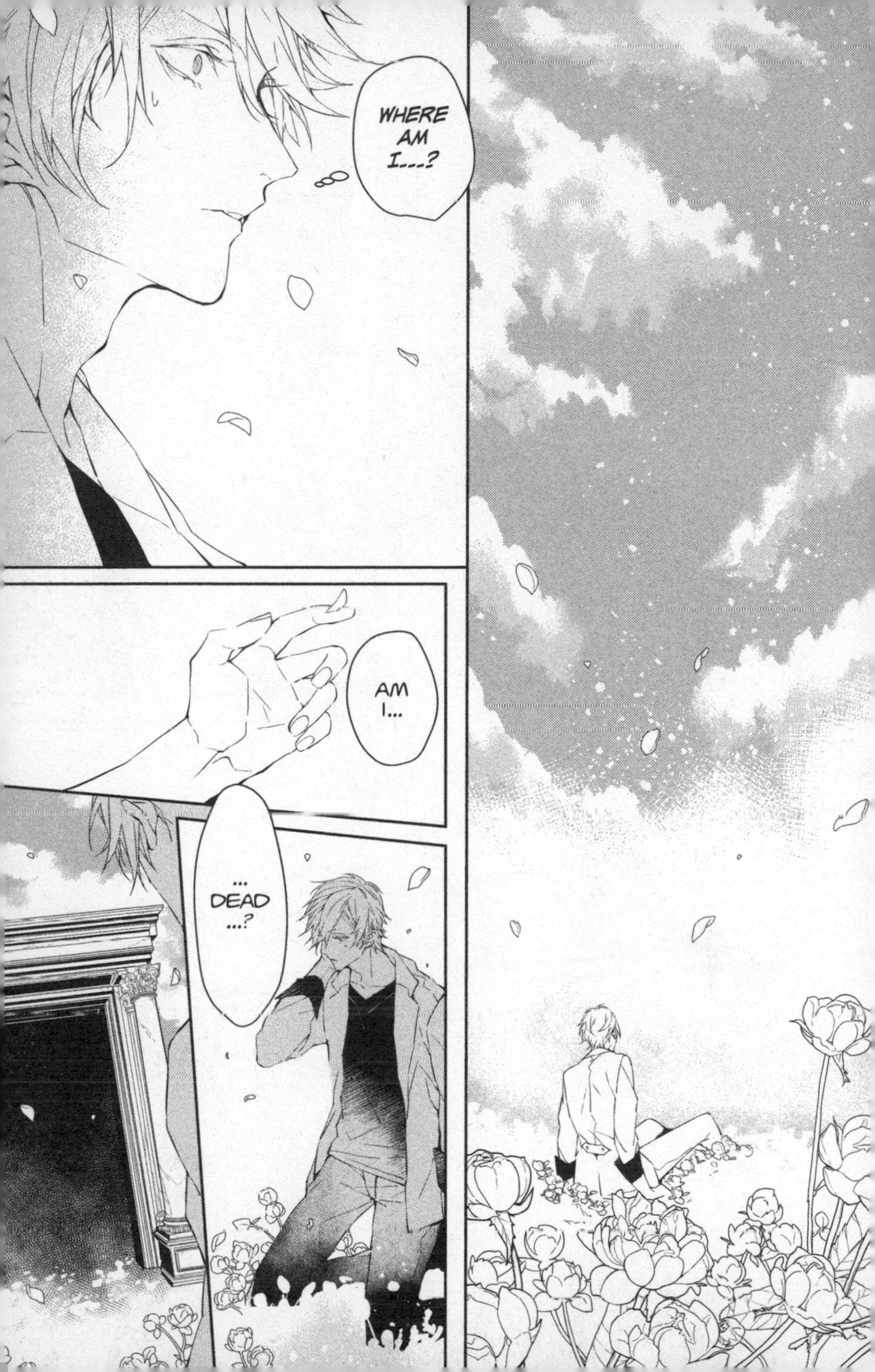
WHERE AM I...?
AM I...
...DEAD...?

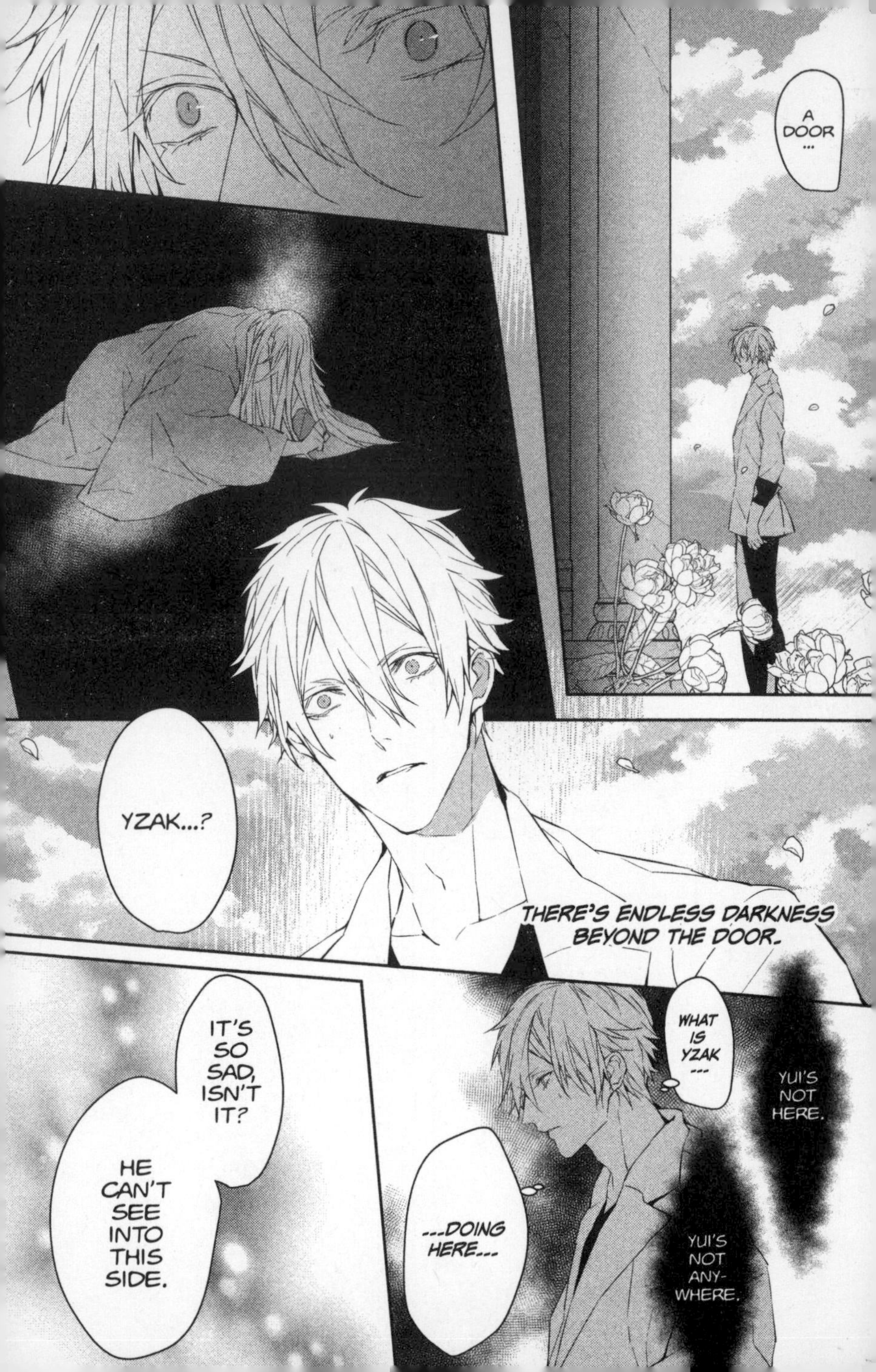
A DOOR ...
YZAK...?
THERE'S ENDLESS DARKNESS BEYOND THE DOOR.
WHAT IS YZAK ---
---DOING HERE...
YUI'S NOT HERE.
YUI'S NOT ANYWHERE.
IT'S SO SAD, ISN'T IT?
HE CAN'T SEE INTO THIS SIDE.

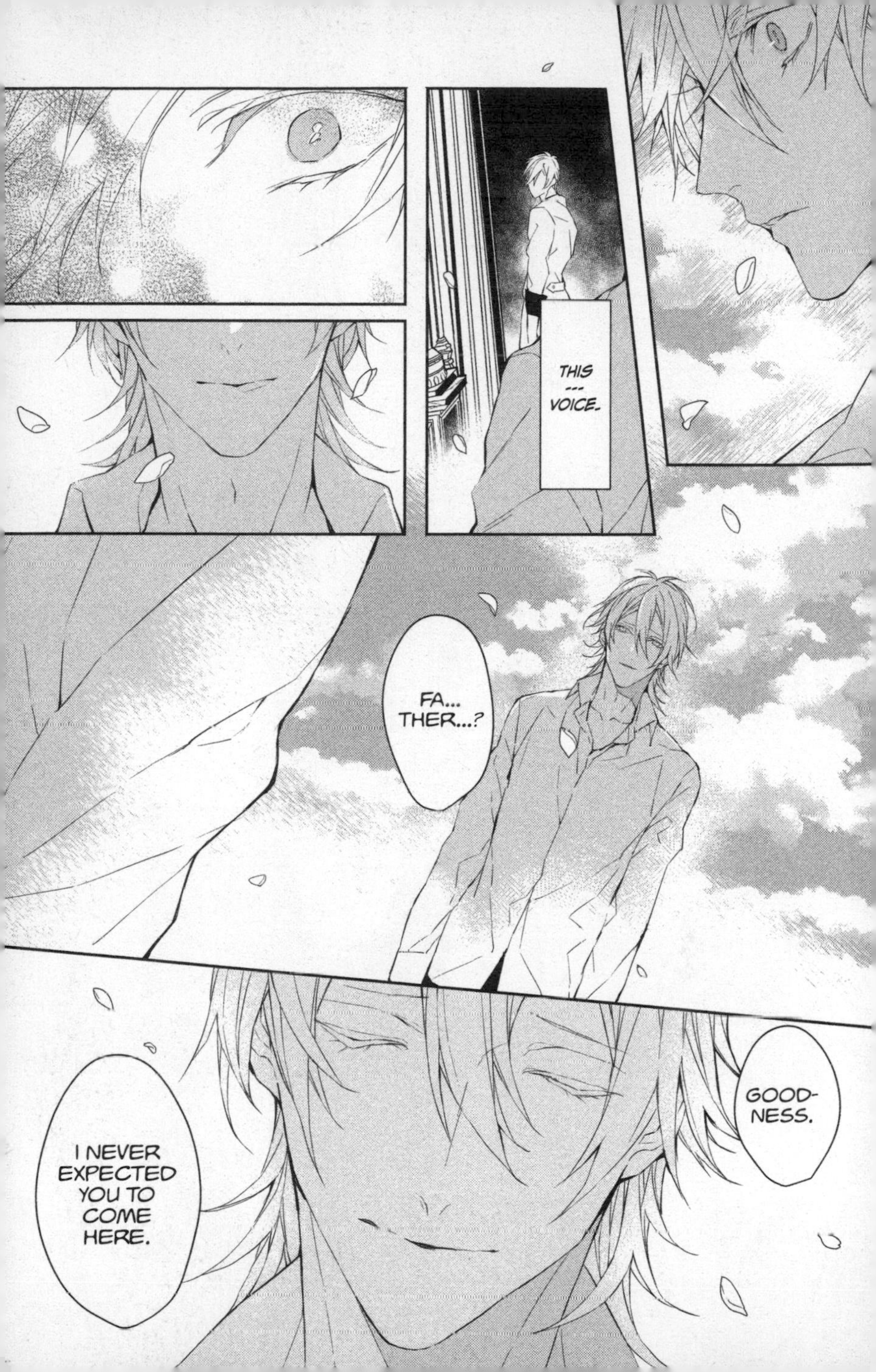
THIS --- VOICE.
FA... THER...?
GOOD-NESS.
I NEVER EXPECTED YOU TO COME HERE.

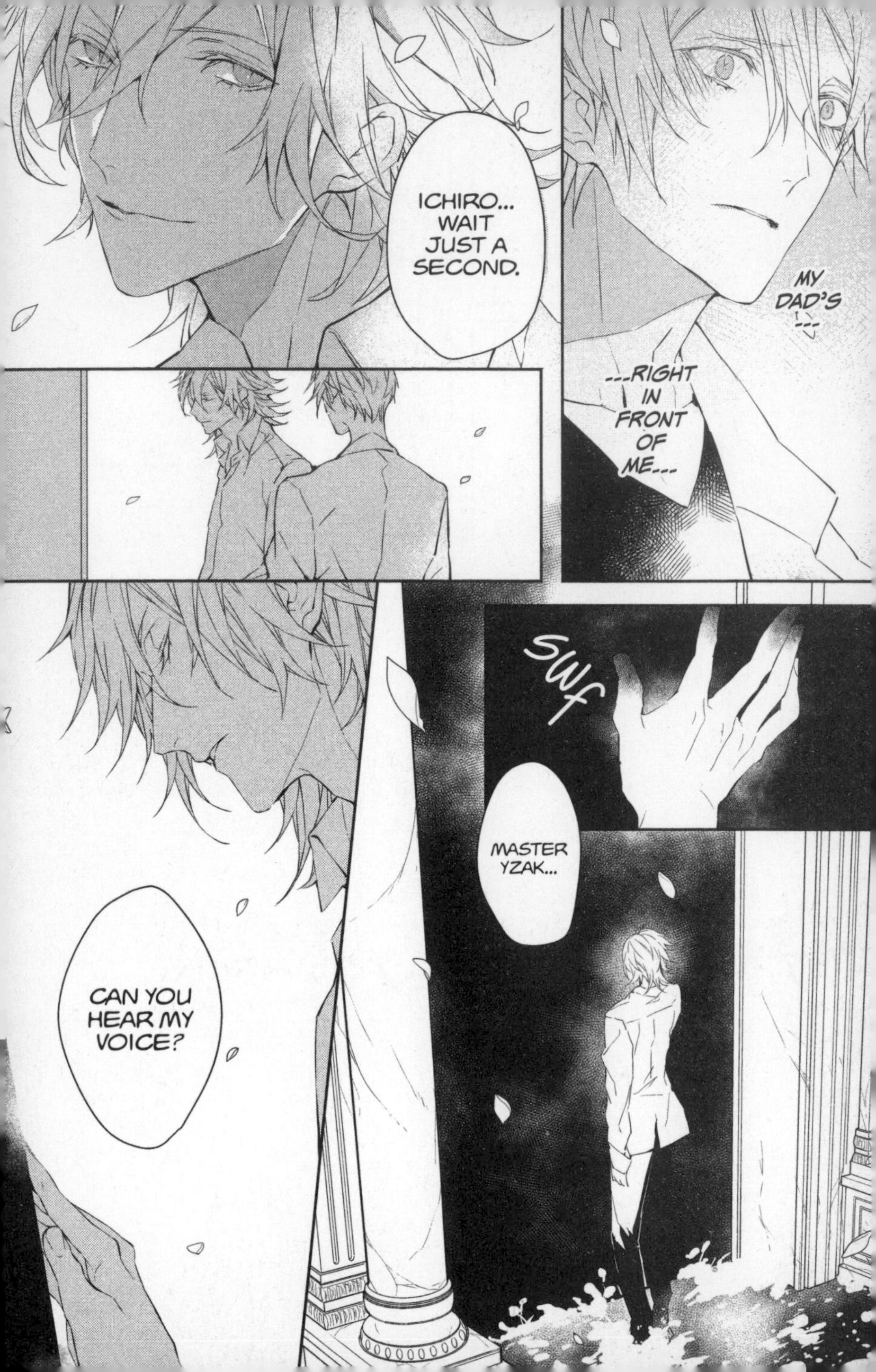
MY DAD'S ---
---RIGHT IN FRONT OF ME...
ICHIRO... WAIT JUST A SECOND.
SWF
MASTER YZAK...
CAN YOU HEAR MY VOICE?

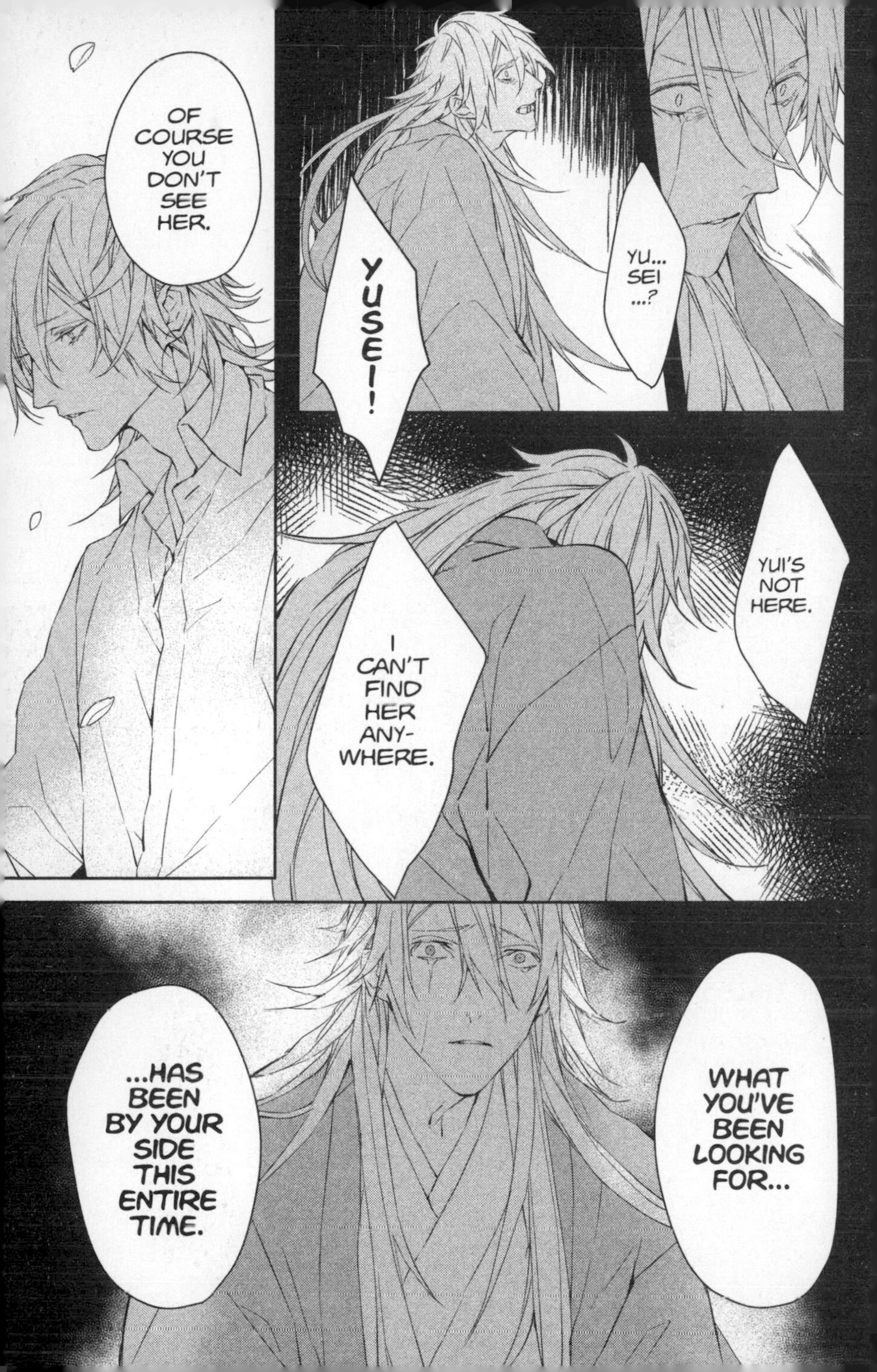
YU... SEI ...?
YUSEI!!
YUI'S NOT HERE.
I CAN'T FIND HER ANY-WHERE.
OF COURSE YOU DON'T SEE HER.
WHAT YOU'VE BEEN LOOKING FOR...
...HAS BEEN BY YOUR SIDE THIS ENTIRE TIME.

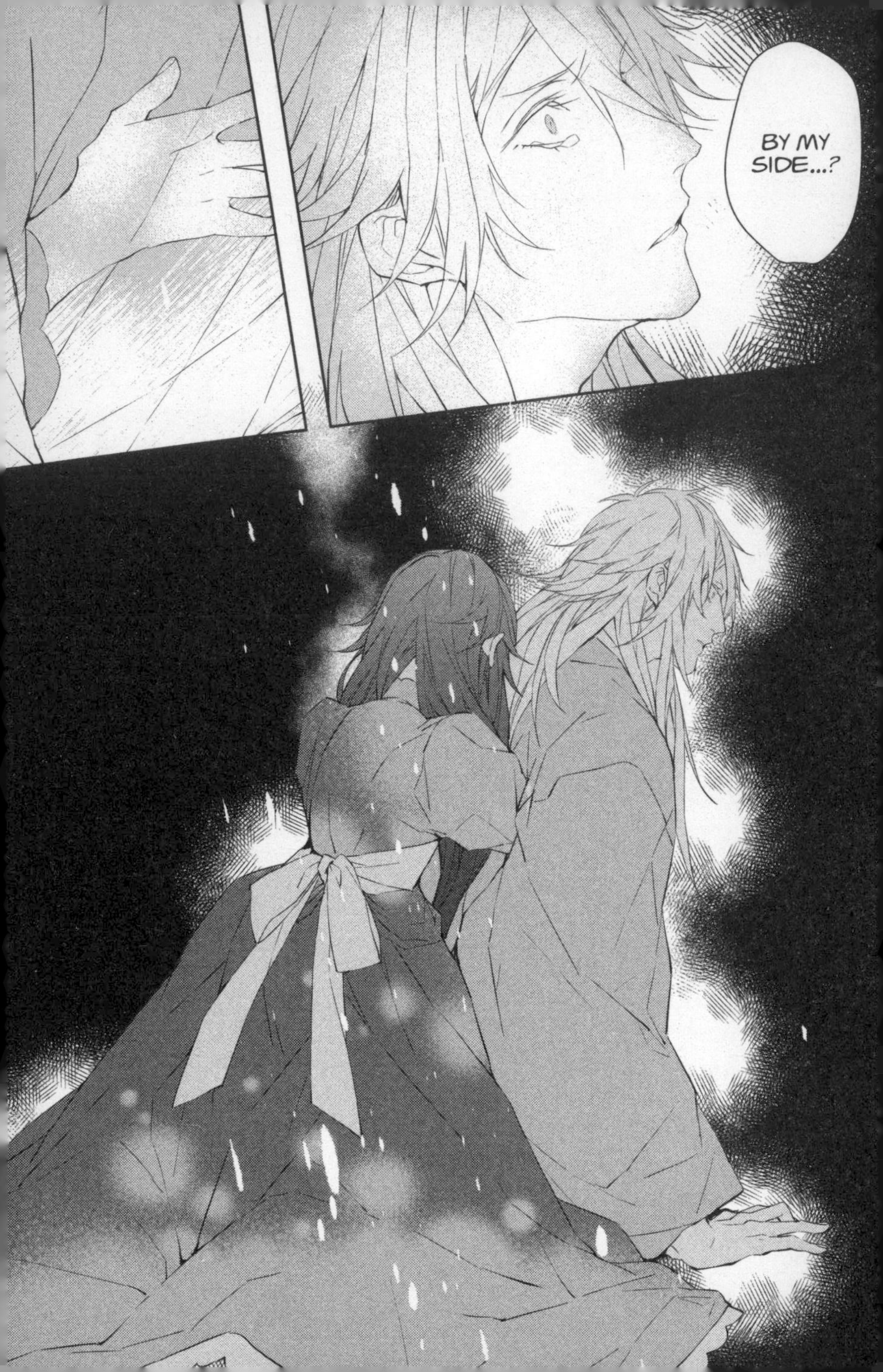
BY MY SIDE...?

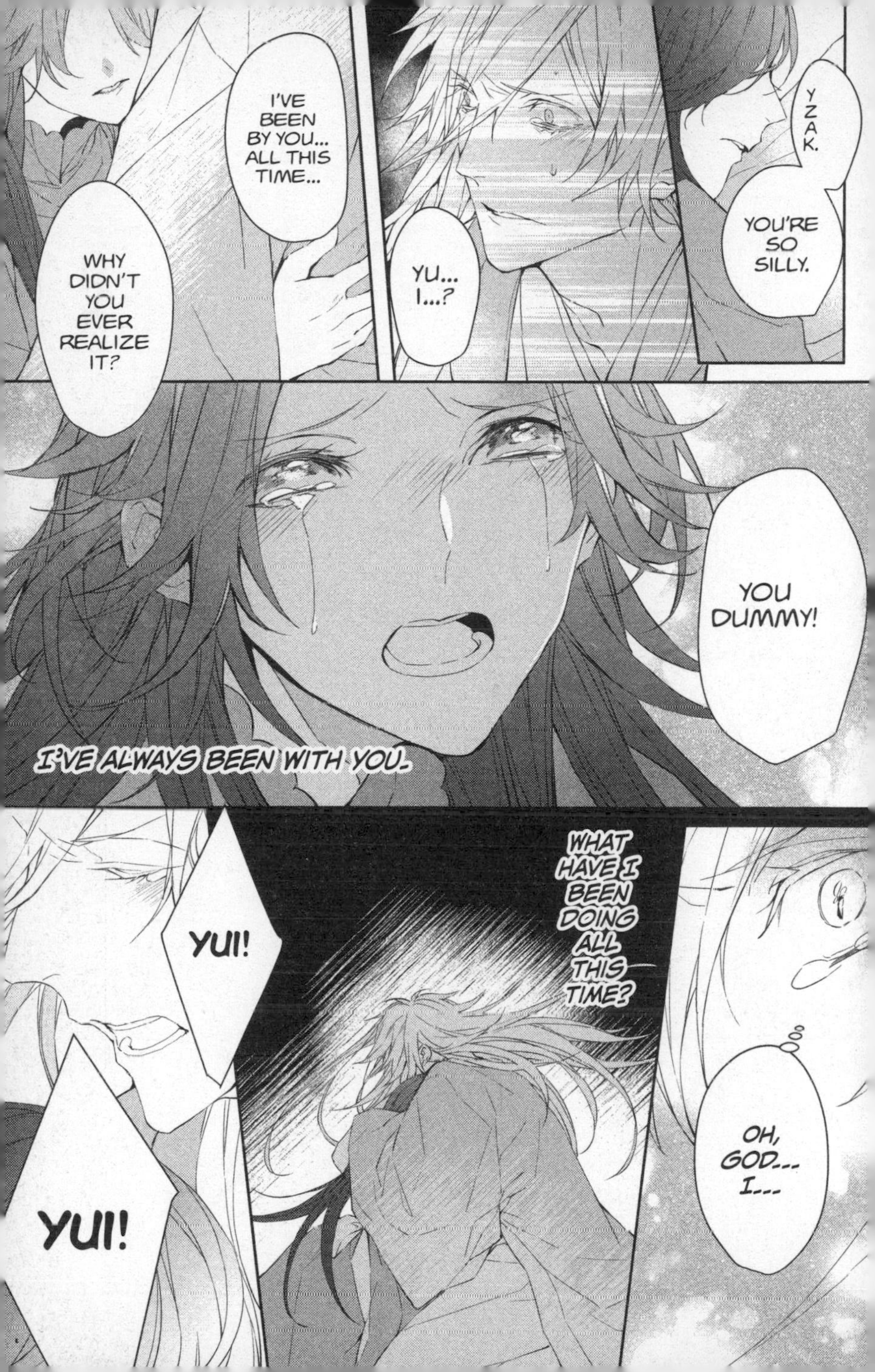
YZAK.
YOU'RE SO SILLY.
YU... I...?
I'VE BEEN BY YOU... ALL THIS TIME...
WHY DIDN'T YOU EVER REALIZE IT?
YOU DUMMY!
I'VE ALWAYS BEEN WITH YOU.
OH, GOD... I...
WHAT HAVE I BEEN DOING ALL THIS TIME?
YUI!
YUI!

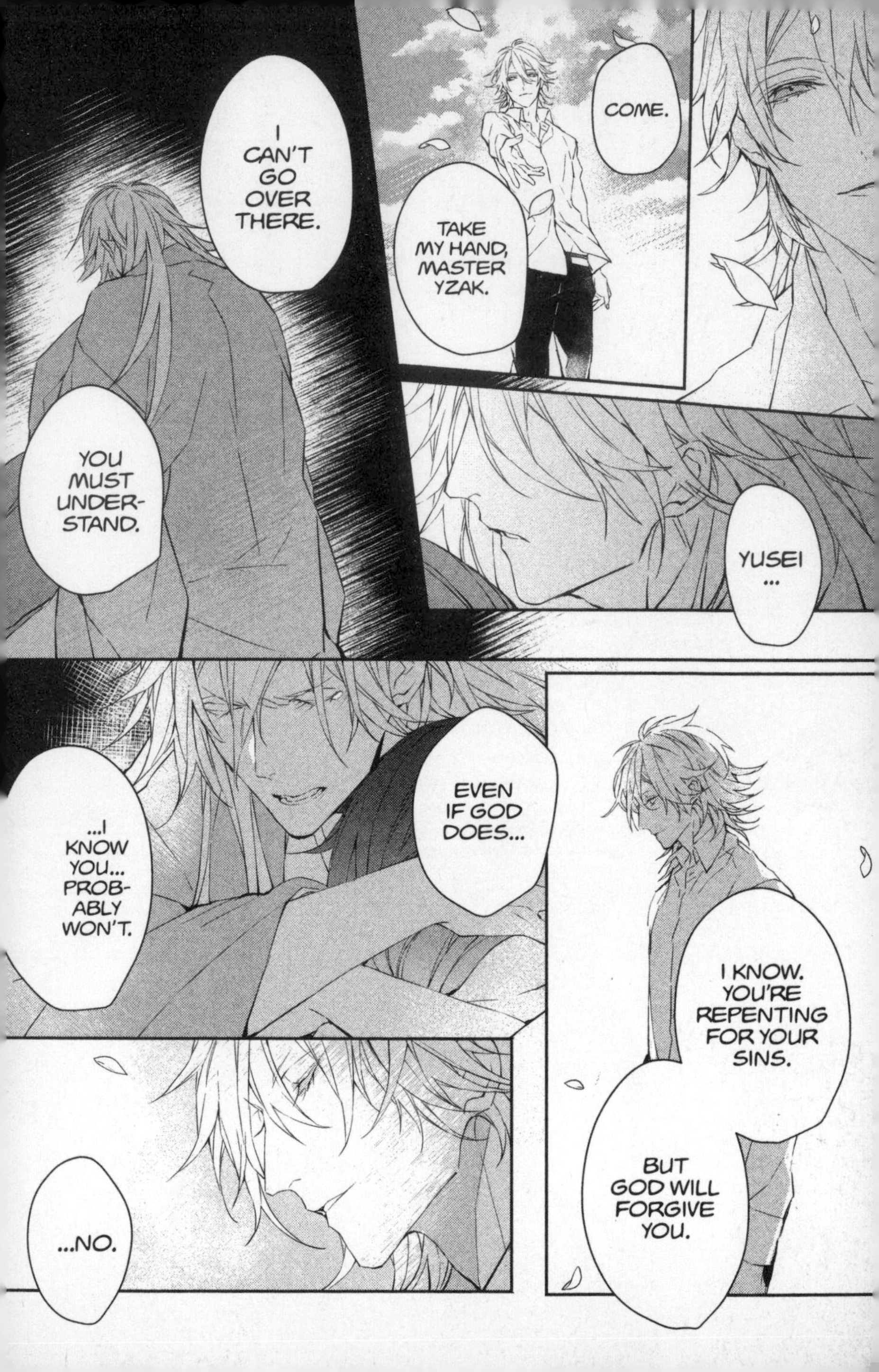
COME.
TAKE MY HAND, MASTER YZAK.
YUSEI...
I CAN'T GO OVER THERE.
YOU MUST UNDERSTAND.
I KNOW. YOU'RE REPENTING FOR YOUR SINS.
BUT GOD WILL FORGIVE YOU.
EVEN IF GOD DOES...
...I KNOW YOU... PROBABLY WON'T.
...NO.

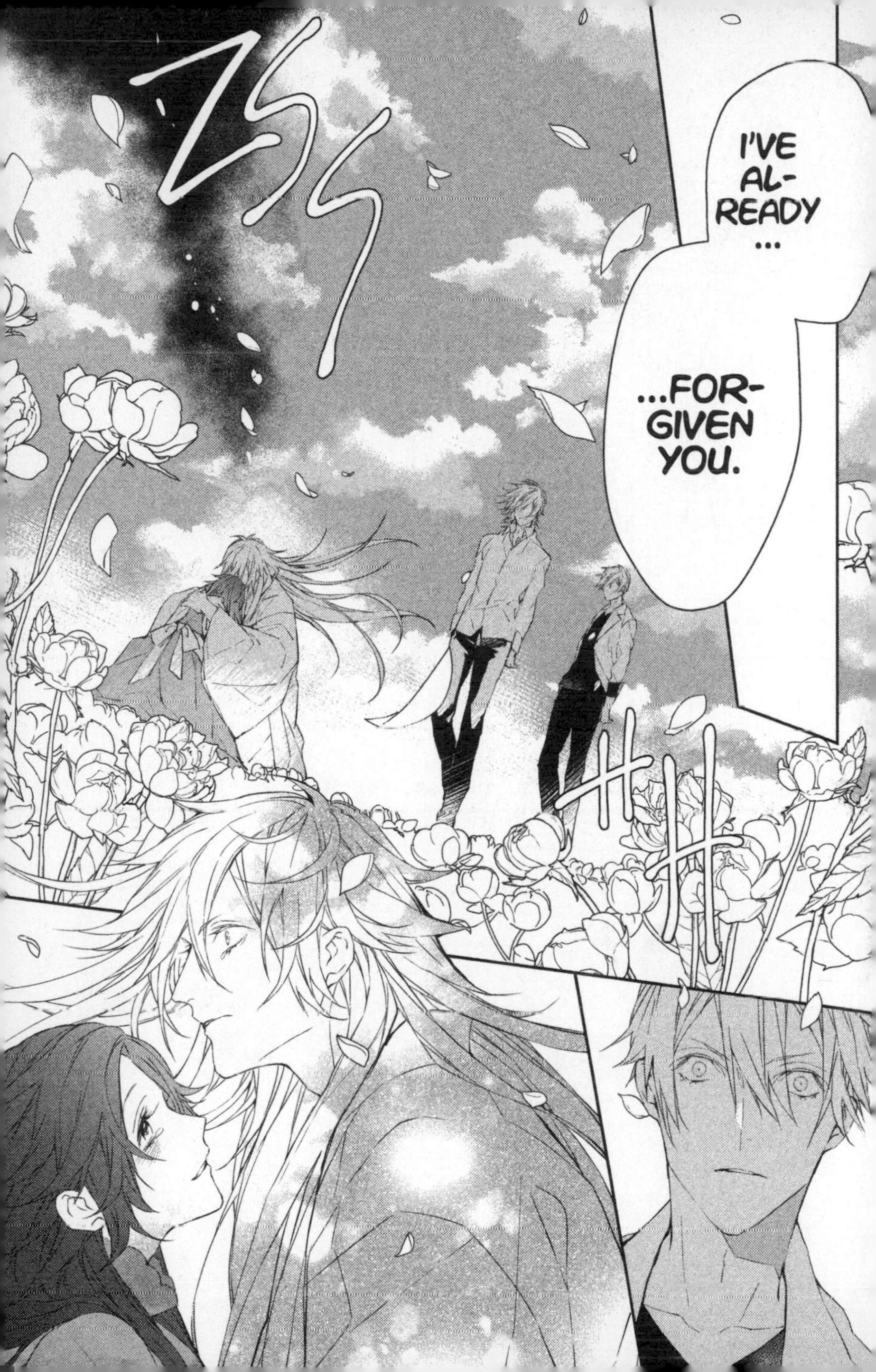
I'VE AL-READY ...
...FOR-GIVEN YOU.

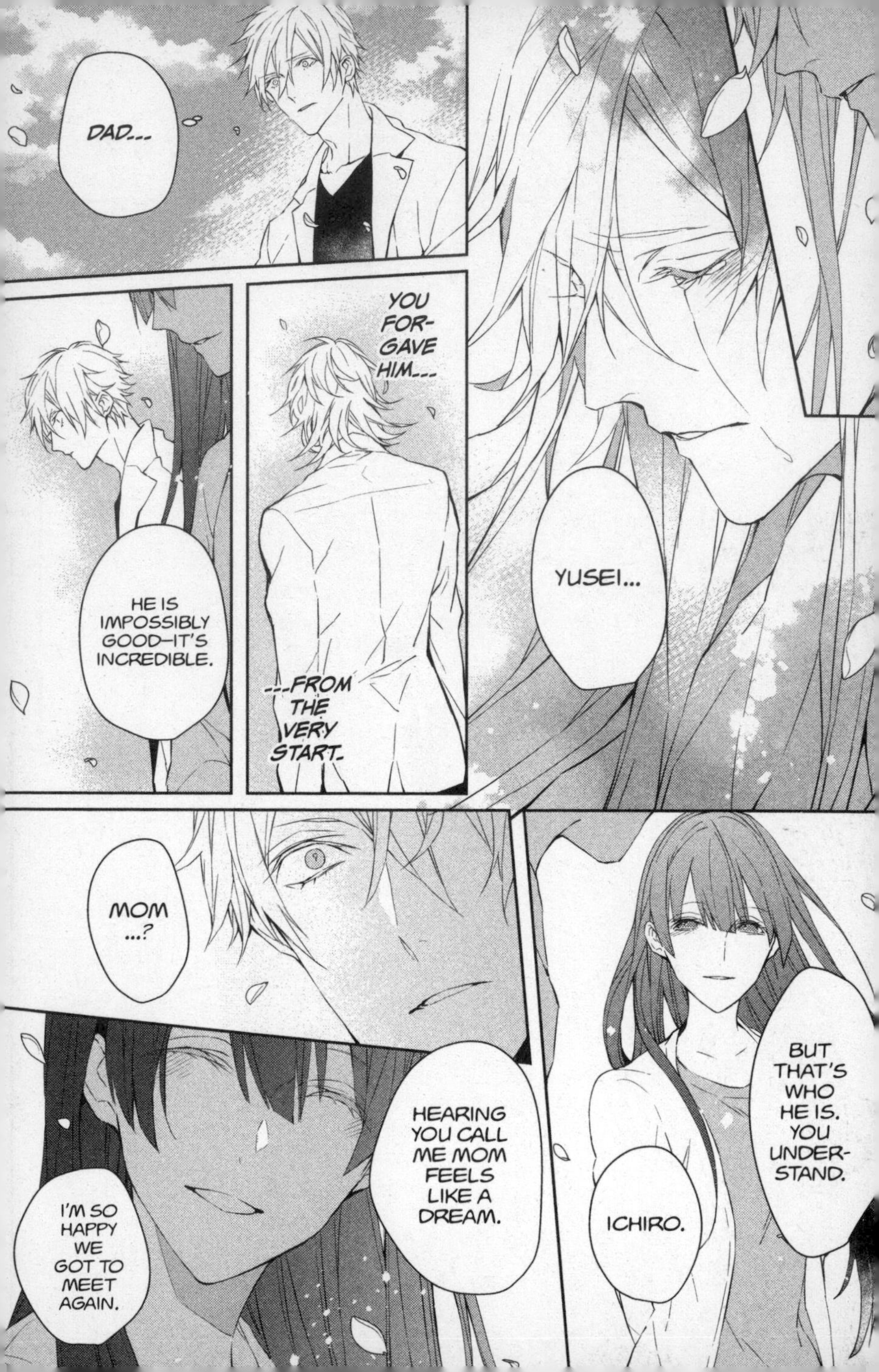
YUSEI...
DAD...
YOU FOR-GAVE HIM...
...FROM THE VERY START.
HE IS IMPOSSIBLY GOOD—IT'S INCREDIBLE.
BUT THAT'S WHO HE IS. YOU UNDER-STAND.
ICHIRO.
MOM ...?
HEARING YOU CALL ME MOM FEELS LIKE A DREAM.
I'M SO HAPPY WE GOT TO MEET AGAIN.

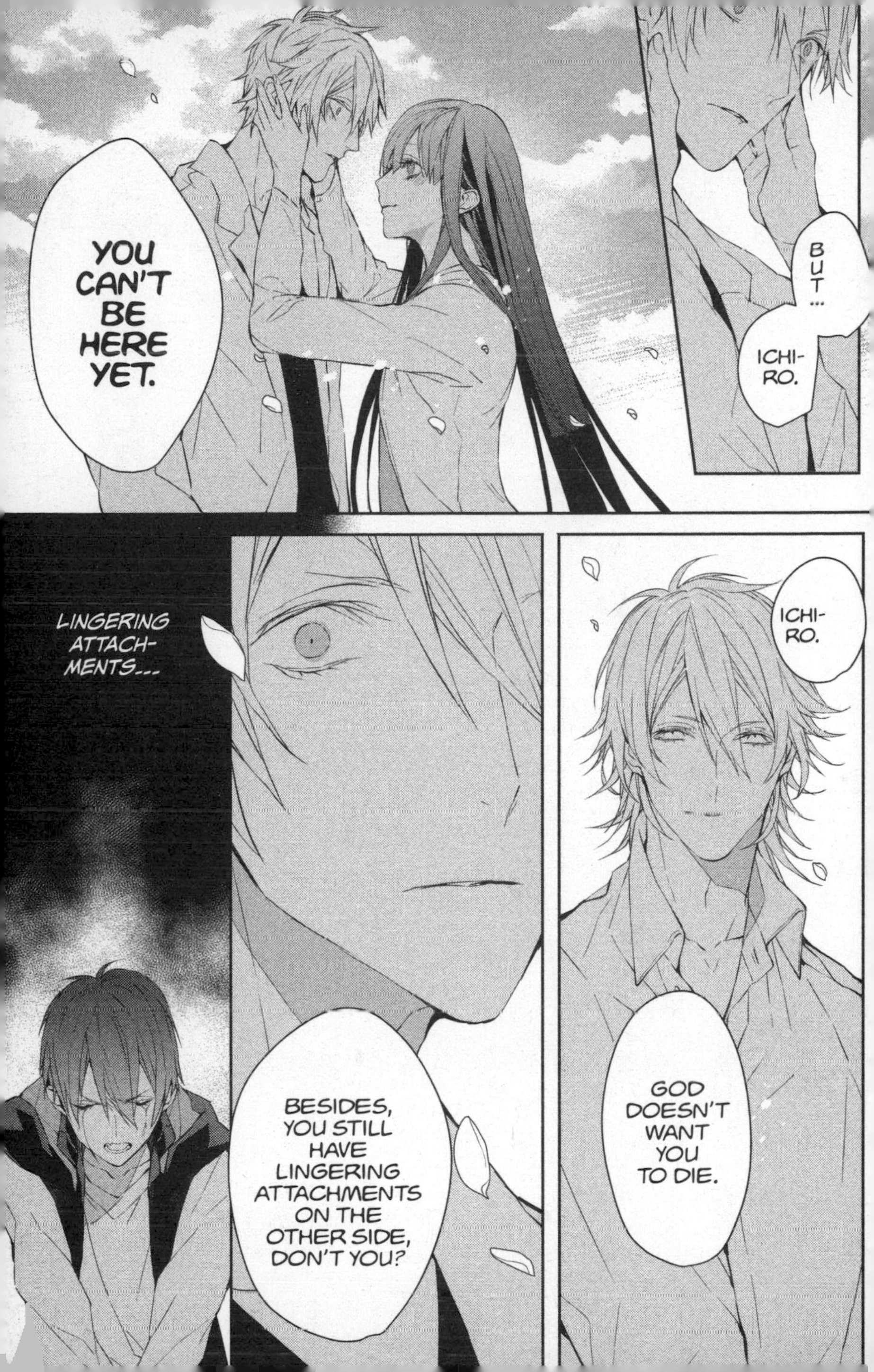
BUT...
ICHIRO.
YOU CAN'T BE HERE YET.
ICHIRO.
GOD DOESN'T WANT YOU TO DIE.
BESIDES, YOU STILL HAVE LINGERING ATTACHMENTS ON THE OTHER SIDE, DON'T YOU?
LINGERING ATTACHMENTS...

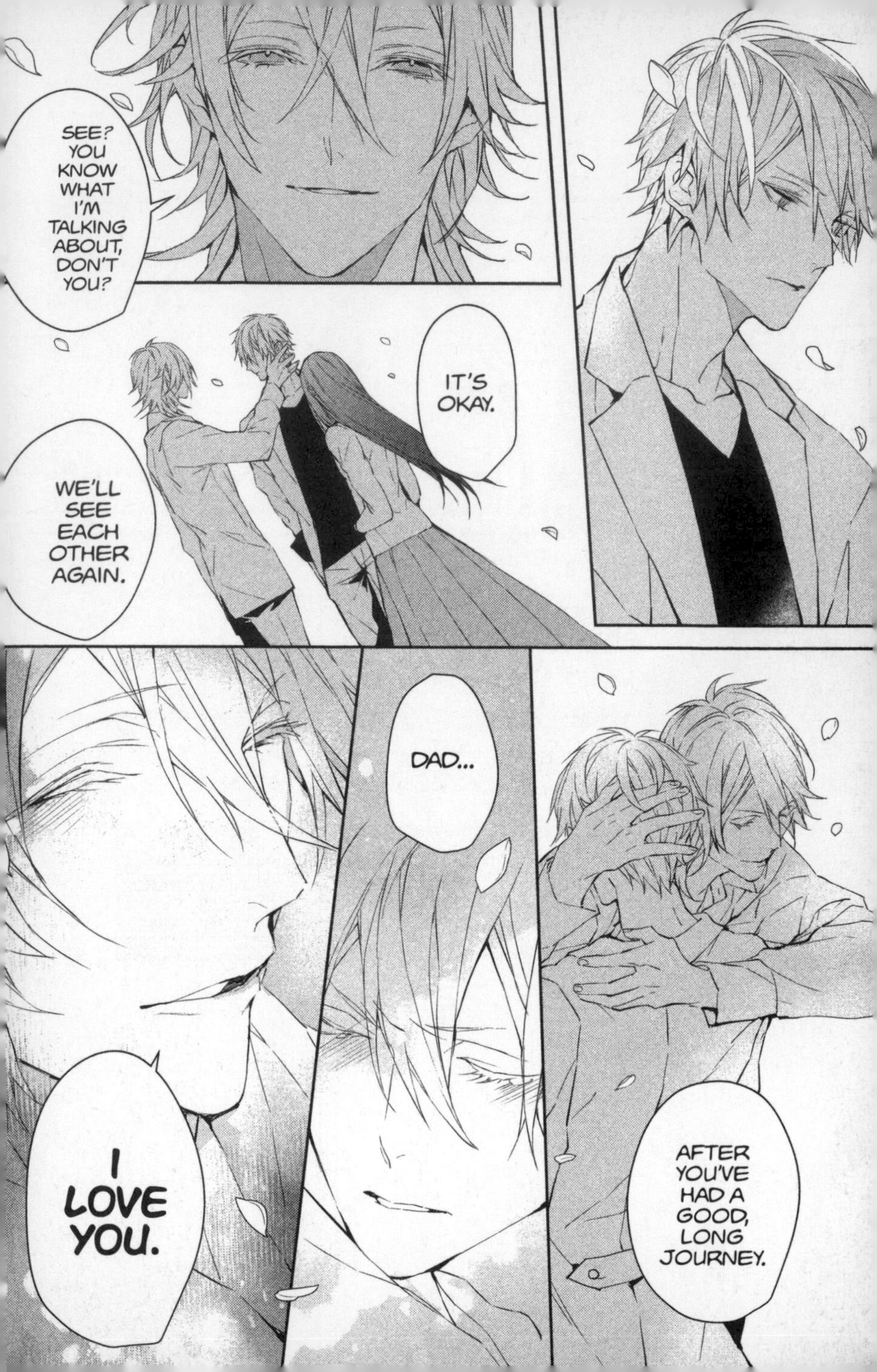
SEE? YOU KNOW WHAT I'M TALKING ABOUT, DON'T YOU?
IT'S OKAY.
WE'LL SEE EACH OTHER AGAIN.
AFTER YOU'VE HAD A GOOD, LONG JOURNEY.
DAD...
I LOVE YOU.

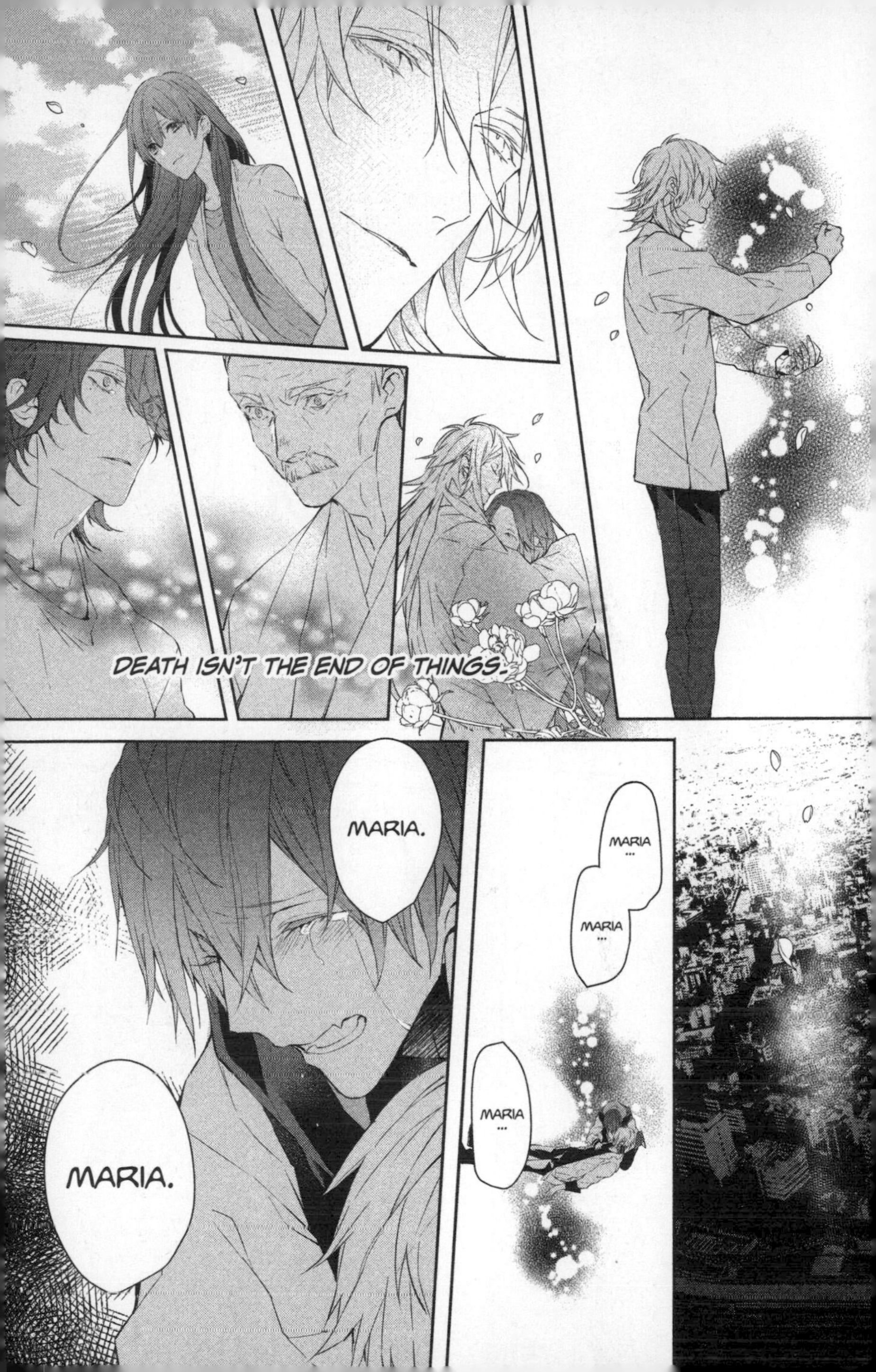
DEATH ISN'T THE END OF THINGS.
MARIA ...
MARIA ...
MARIA ...
MARIA.
MARIA.

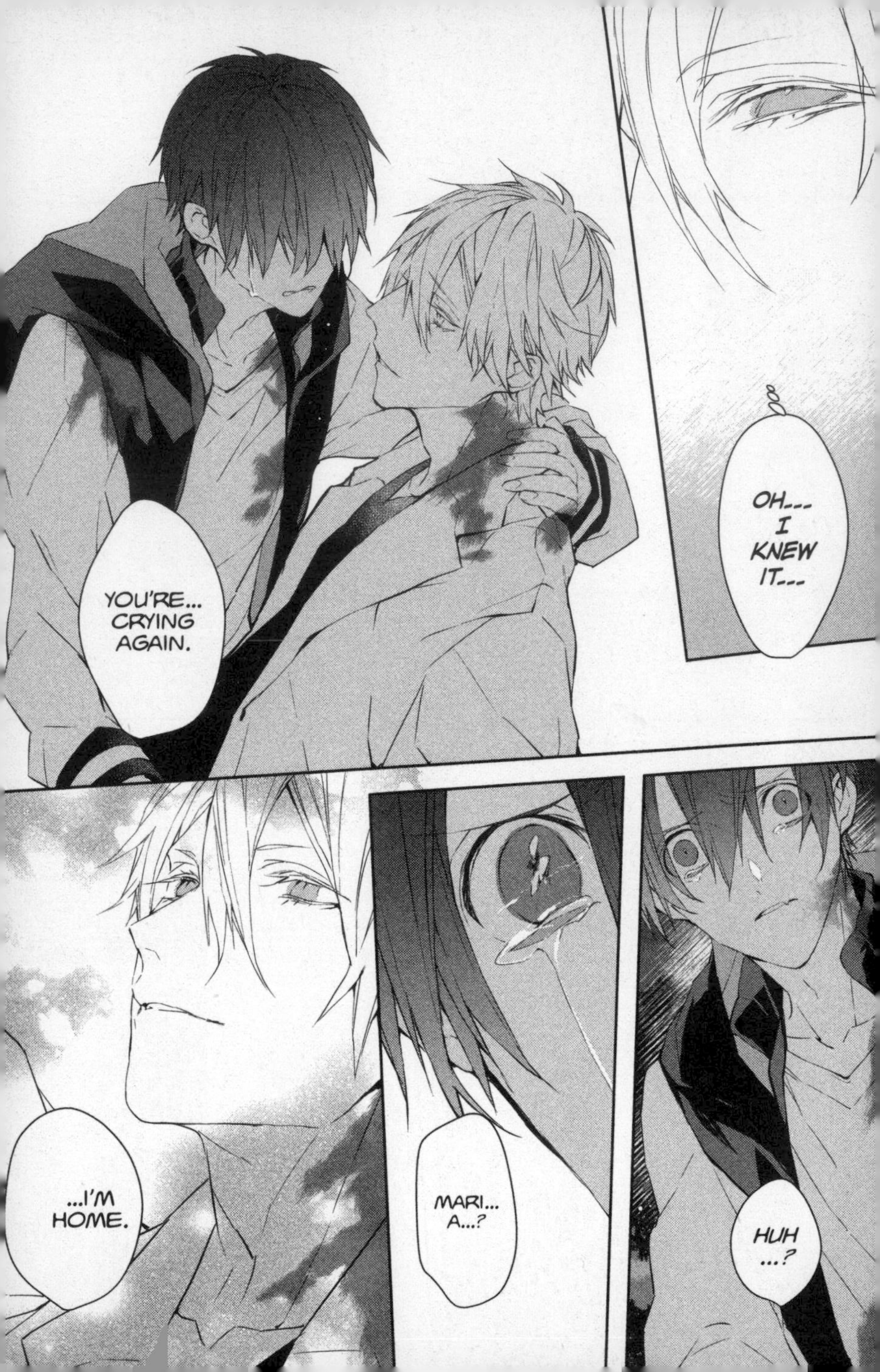
OH... I KNEW IT...
YOU'RE... CRYING AGAIN.
HUH ...?
MARI... A...?
...I'M HOME.

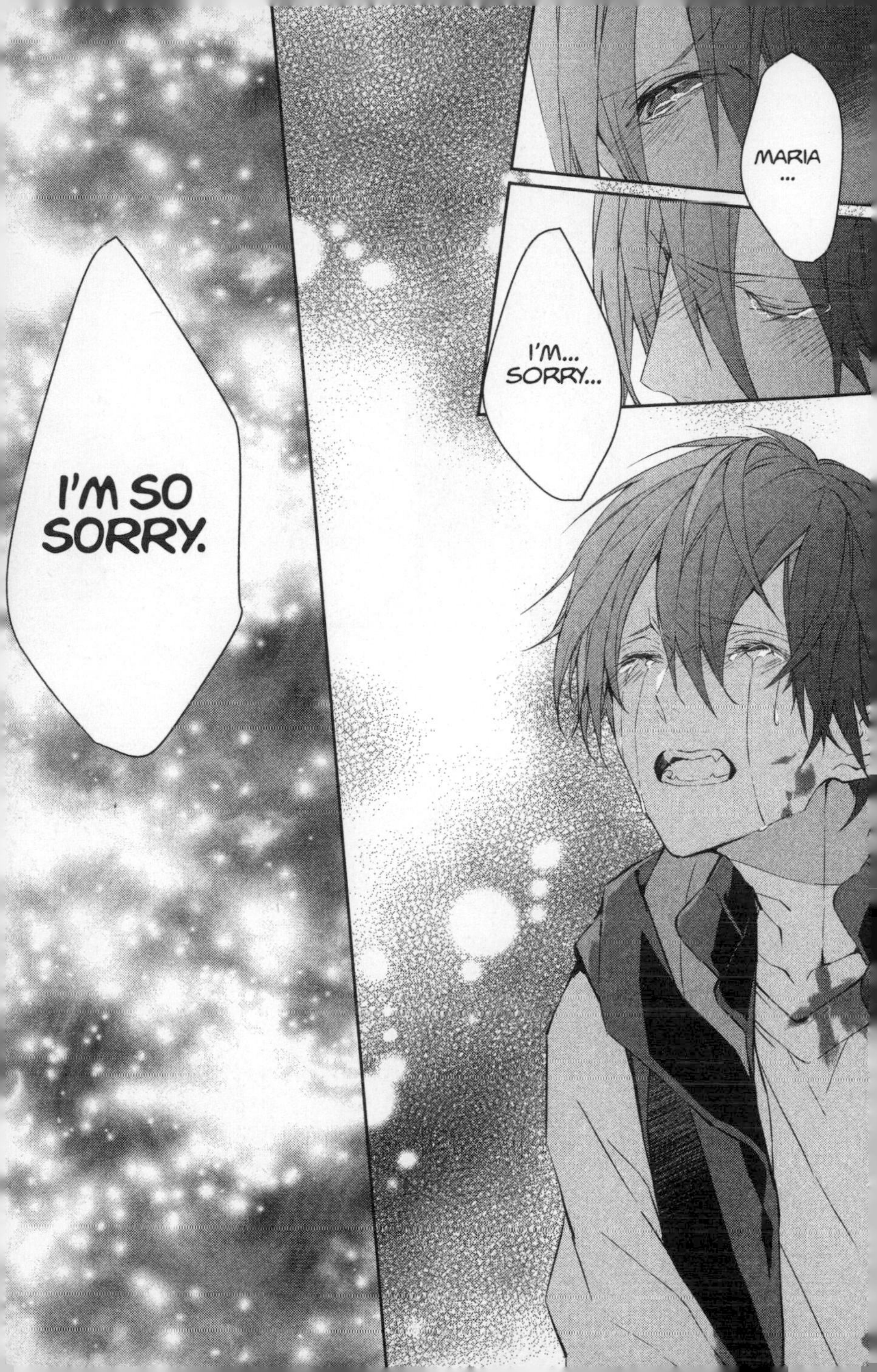
MARIA...
I'M... SORRY...
I'M SO SORRY.

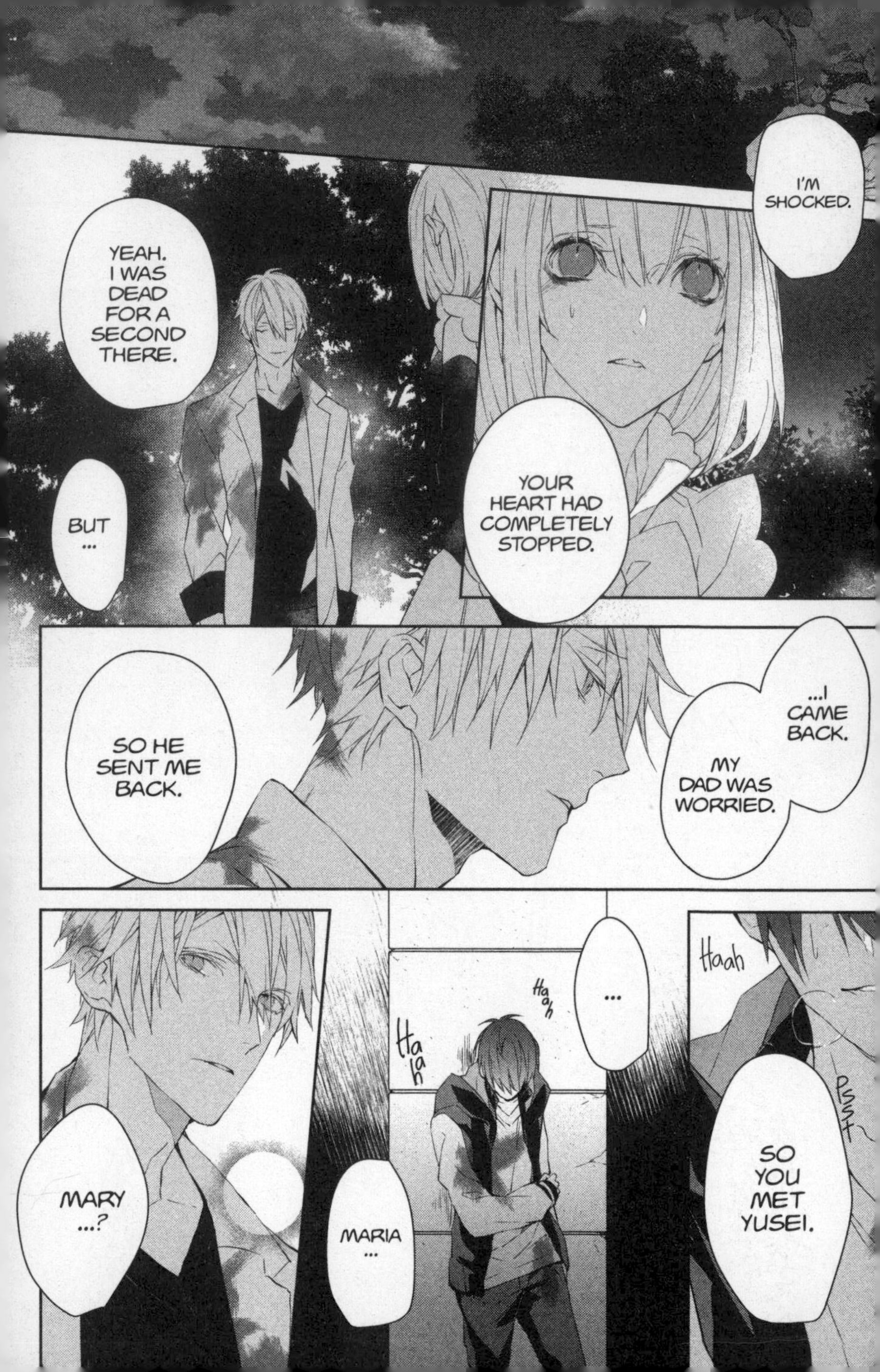
I'M SHOCKED.
YOUR HEART HAD COMPLETELY STOPPED.
YEAH. I WAS DEAD FOR A SECOND THERE.
BUT ...
...I CAME BACK.
MY DAD WAS WORRIED.
SO HE SENT ME BACK.
Haah
PSST
SO YOU MET YUSEI.
...
Haah
Haah
MARIA ...
MARY ...?

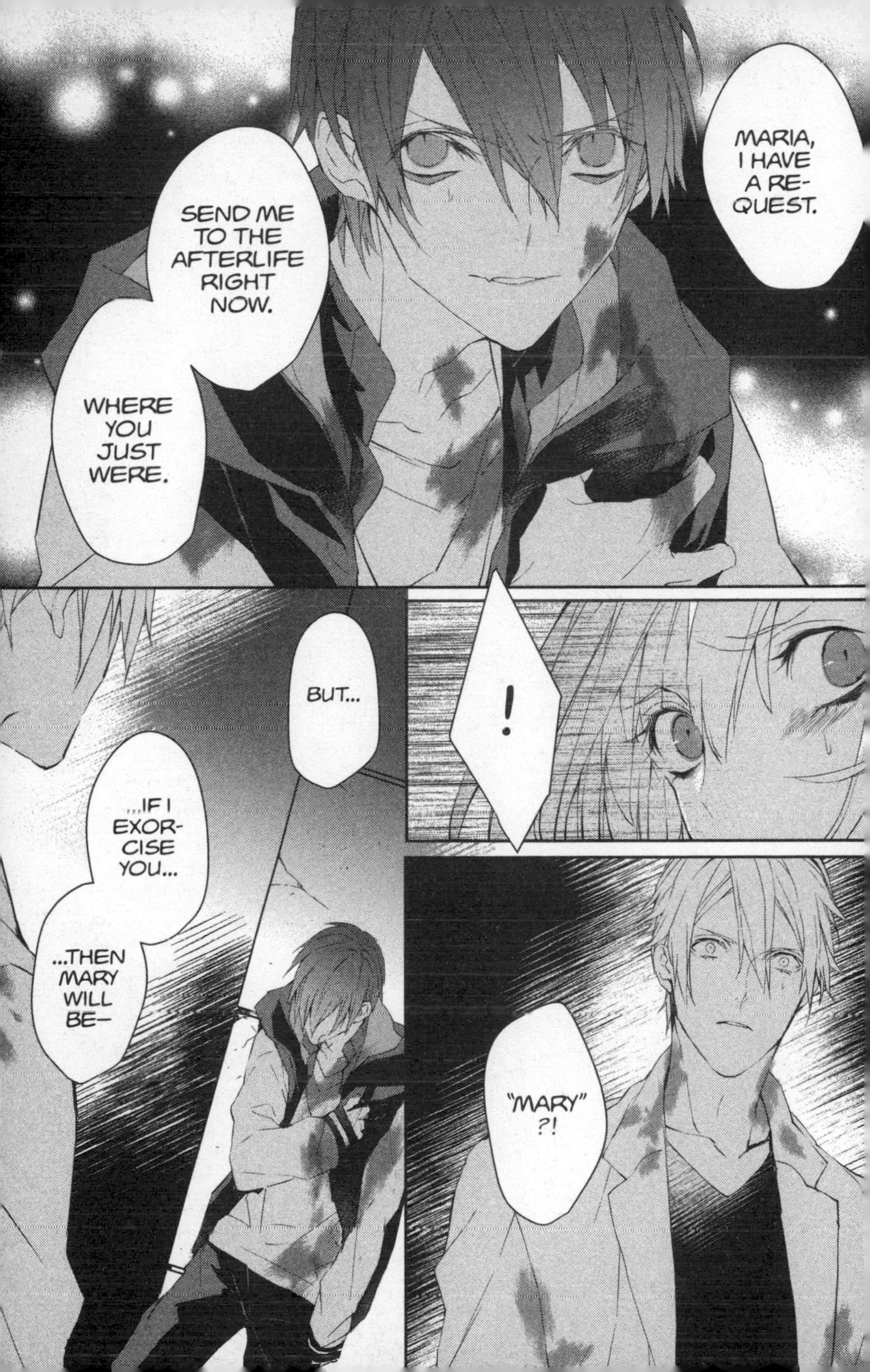
MARIA, I HAVE A RE-QUEST.
SEND ME TO THE AFTERLIFE RIGHT NOW.
WHERE YOU JUST WERE.
!
"MARY" ?!
BUT...
...IF I EXORCISE YOU...
...THEN MARY WILL BE—

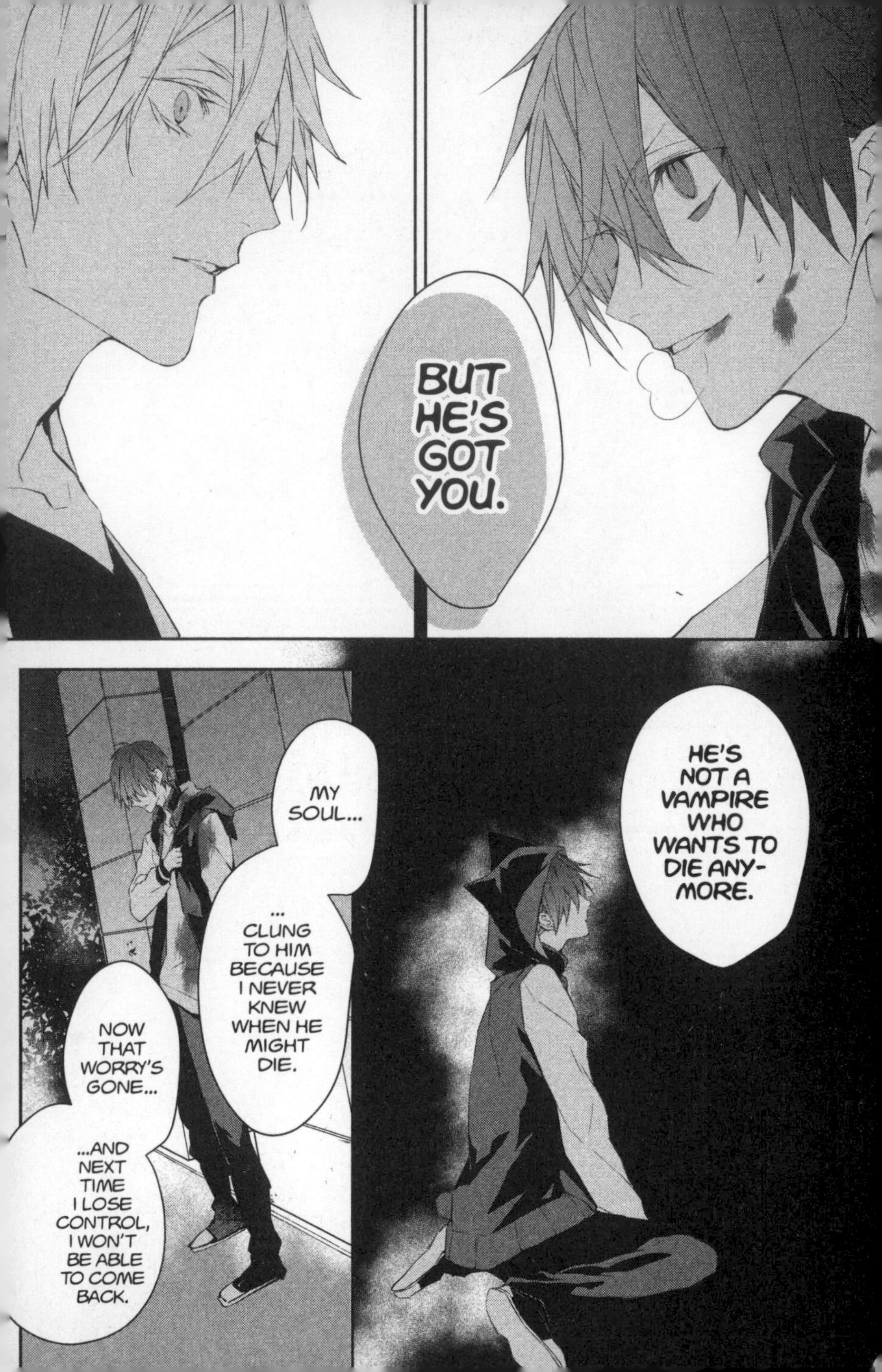
BUT HE'S GOT YOU.
HE'S NOT A VAMPIRE WHO WANTS TO DIE ANY-MORE.
MY SOUL...
...CLUNG TO HIM BECAUSE I NEVER KNEW WHEN HE MIGHT DIE.
NOW THAT WORRY'S GONE...
...AND NEXT TIME I LOSE CONTROL, I WON'T BE ABLE TO COME BACK.

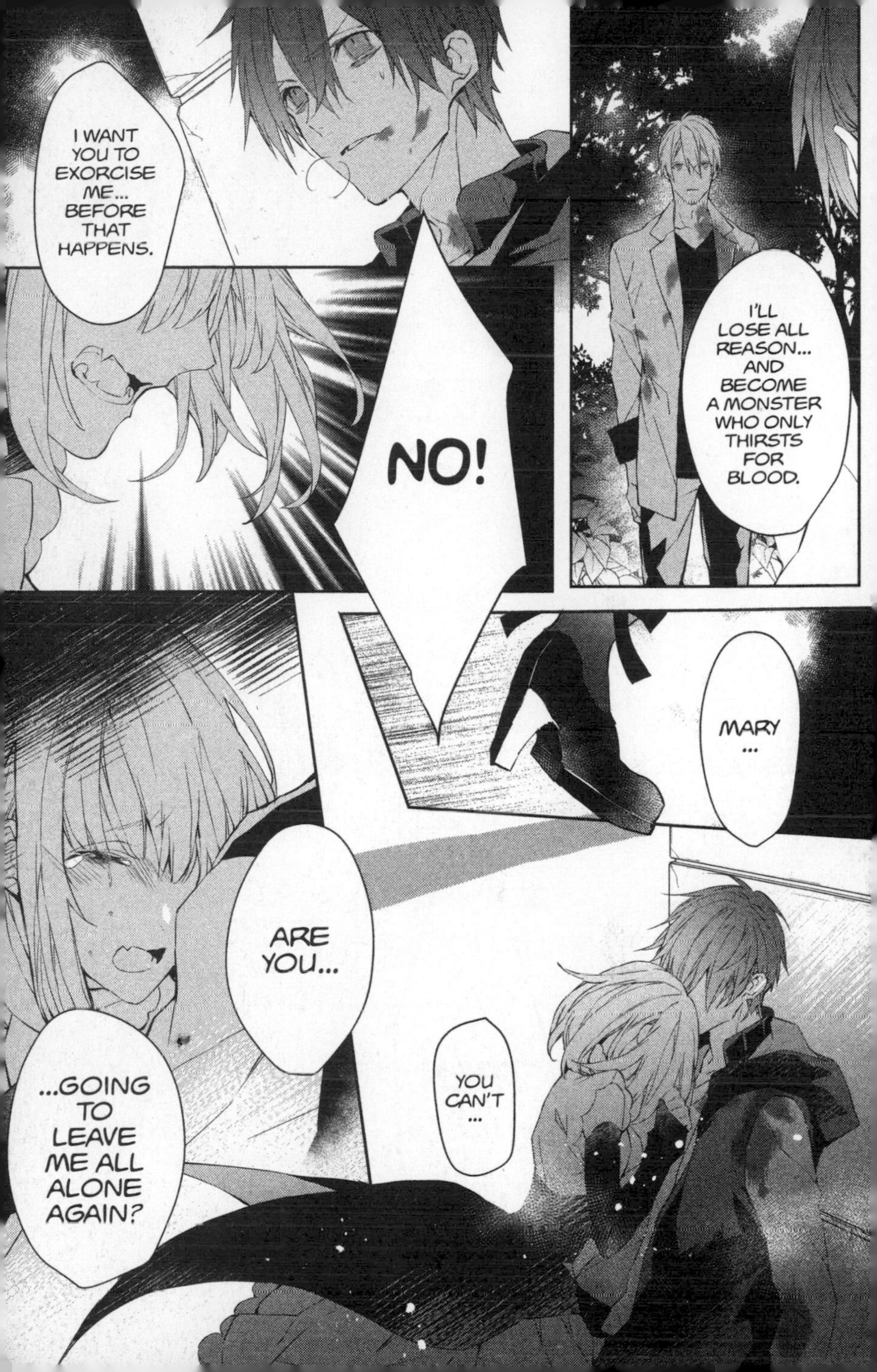
I'LL LOSE ALL REASON... AND BECOME A MONSTER WHO ONLY THIRSTS FOR BLOOD.
I WANT YOU TO EXORCISE ME... BEFORE THAT HAPPENS.
NO!
MARY...
YOU CAN'T...
ARE YOU...
...GOING TO LEAVE ME ALL ALONE AGAIN?

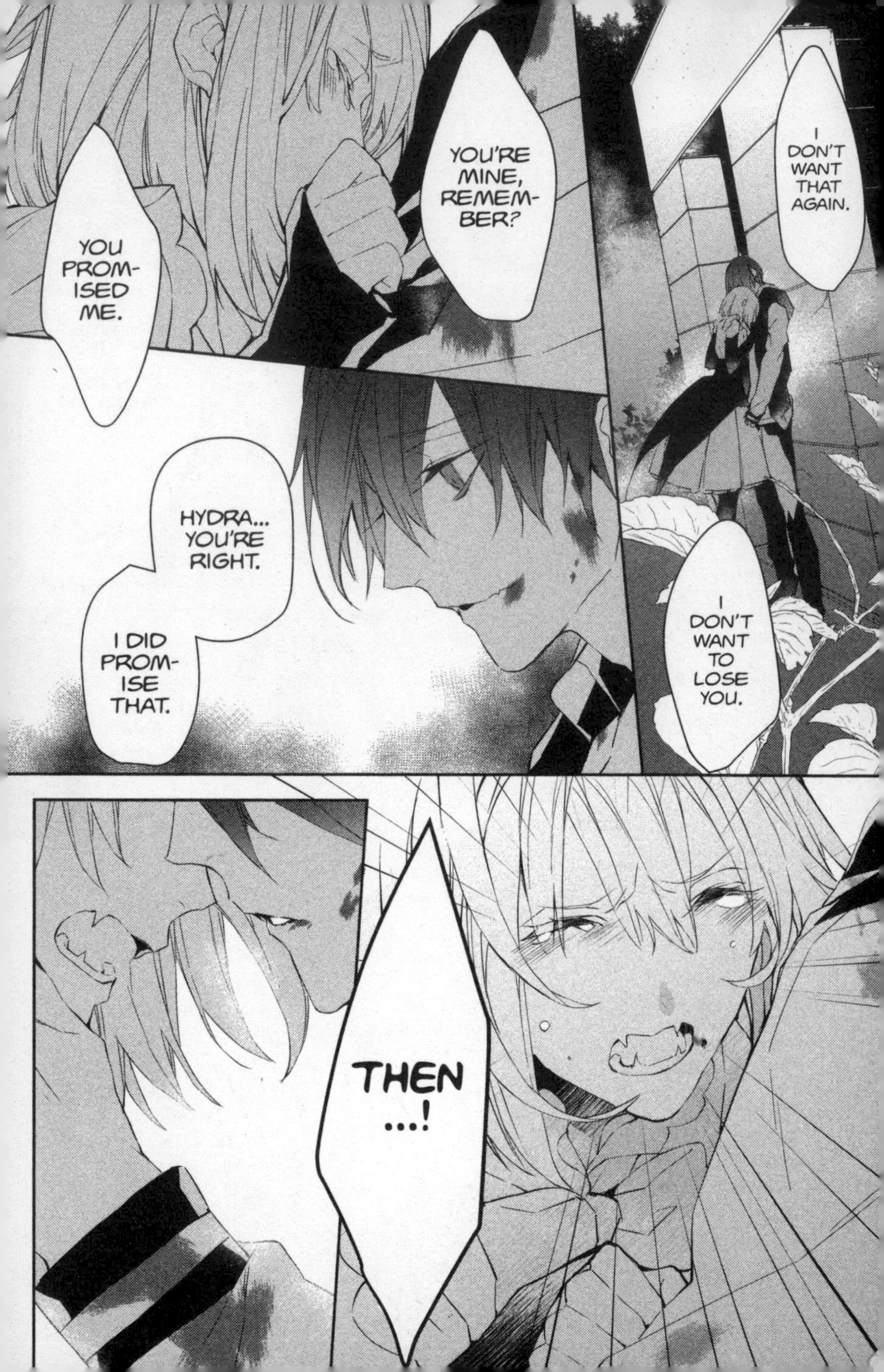
I DON'T WANT THAT AGAIN.
I DON'T WANT TO LOSE YOU.
YOU'RE MINE, REMEMBER?
YOU PROMISED ME.
HYDRA... YOU'RE RIGHT.
I DID PROMISE THAT.
THEN ...!

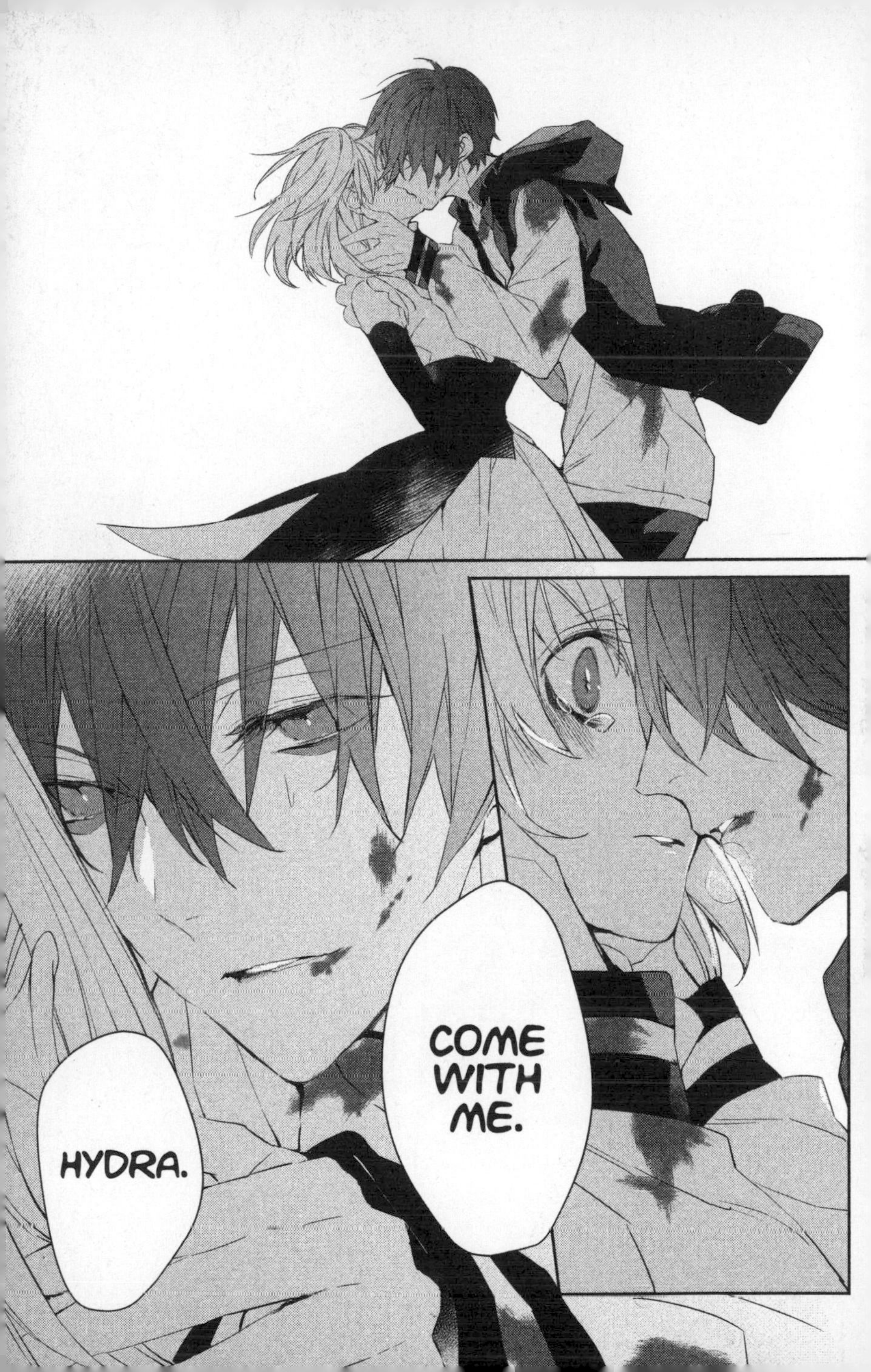
COME WITH ME.
HYDRA.

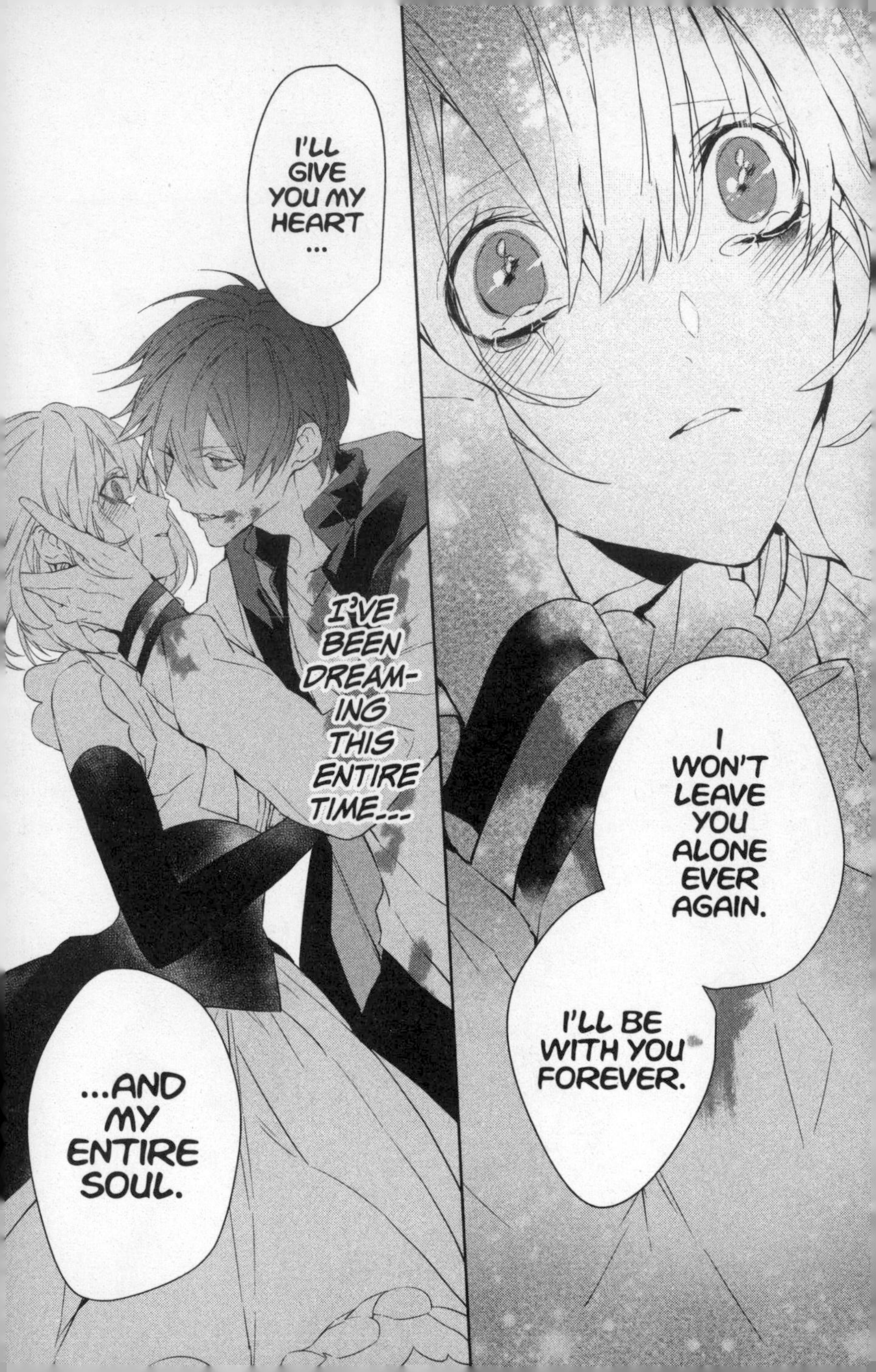
I WON'T LEAVE YOU ALONE EVER AGAIN.
I'LL BE WITH YOU FOREVER.
I'LL GIVE YOU MY HEART ...
I'VE BEEN DREAM-ING THIS ENTIRE TIME...
...AND MY ENTIRE SOUL.

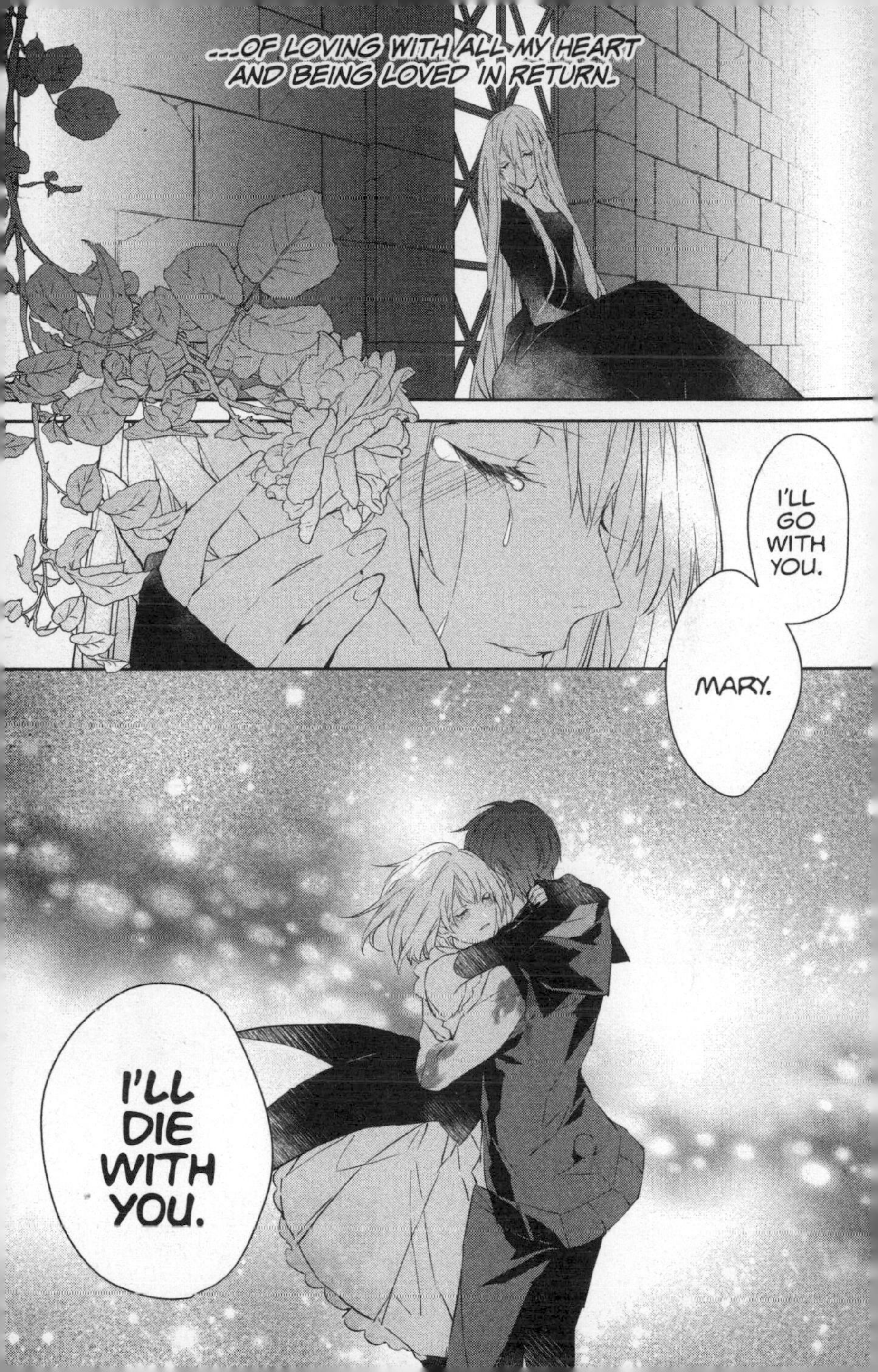
...OF LOVING WITH ALL MY HEART AND BEING LOVED IN RETURN.
I'LL GO WITH YOU.
MARY.
I'LL DIE WITH YOU.

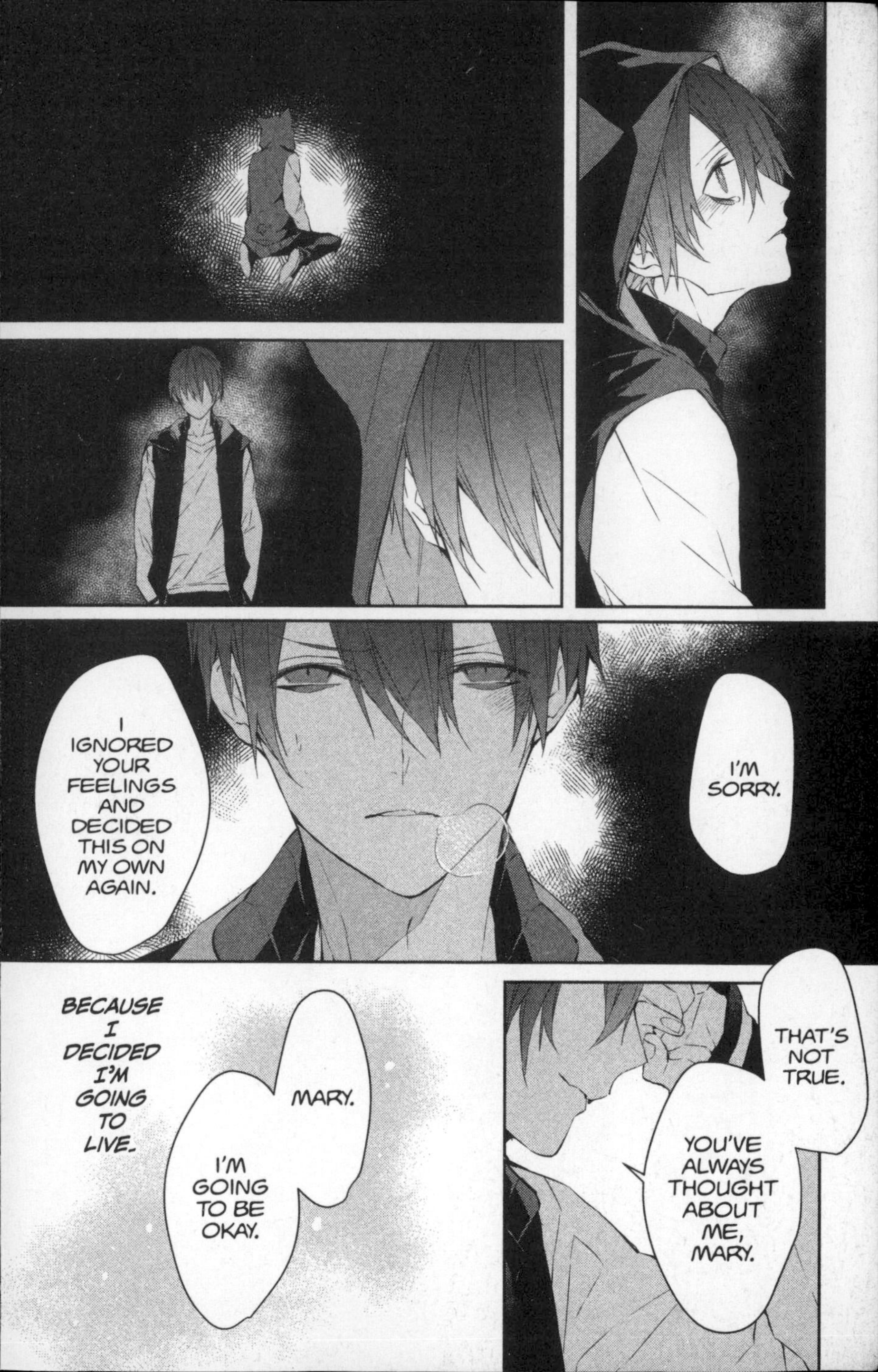
I'M SORRY.
I IGNORED YOUR FEELINGS AND DECIDED THIS ON MY OWN AGAIN.
THAT'S NOT TRUE.
YOU'VE ALWAYS THOUGHT ABOUT ME, MARY.
MARY.
I'M GOING TO BE OKAY.
BECAUSE I DECIDED I'M GOING TO LIVE.

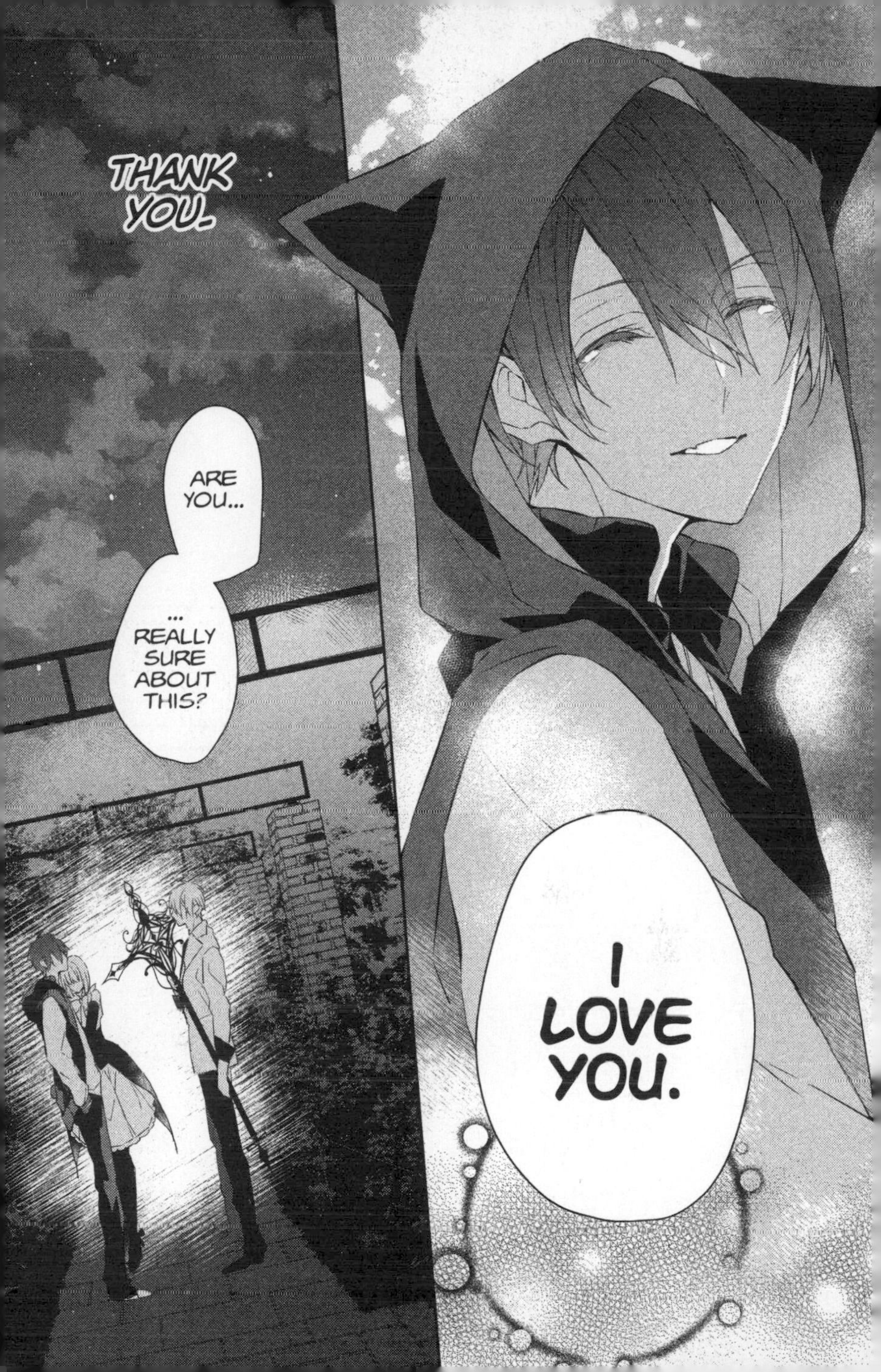
I LOVE YOU.
THANK YOU.
ARE YOU...
...REALLY SURE ABOUT THIS?

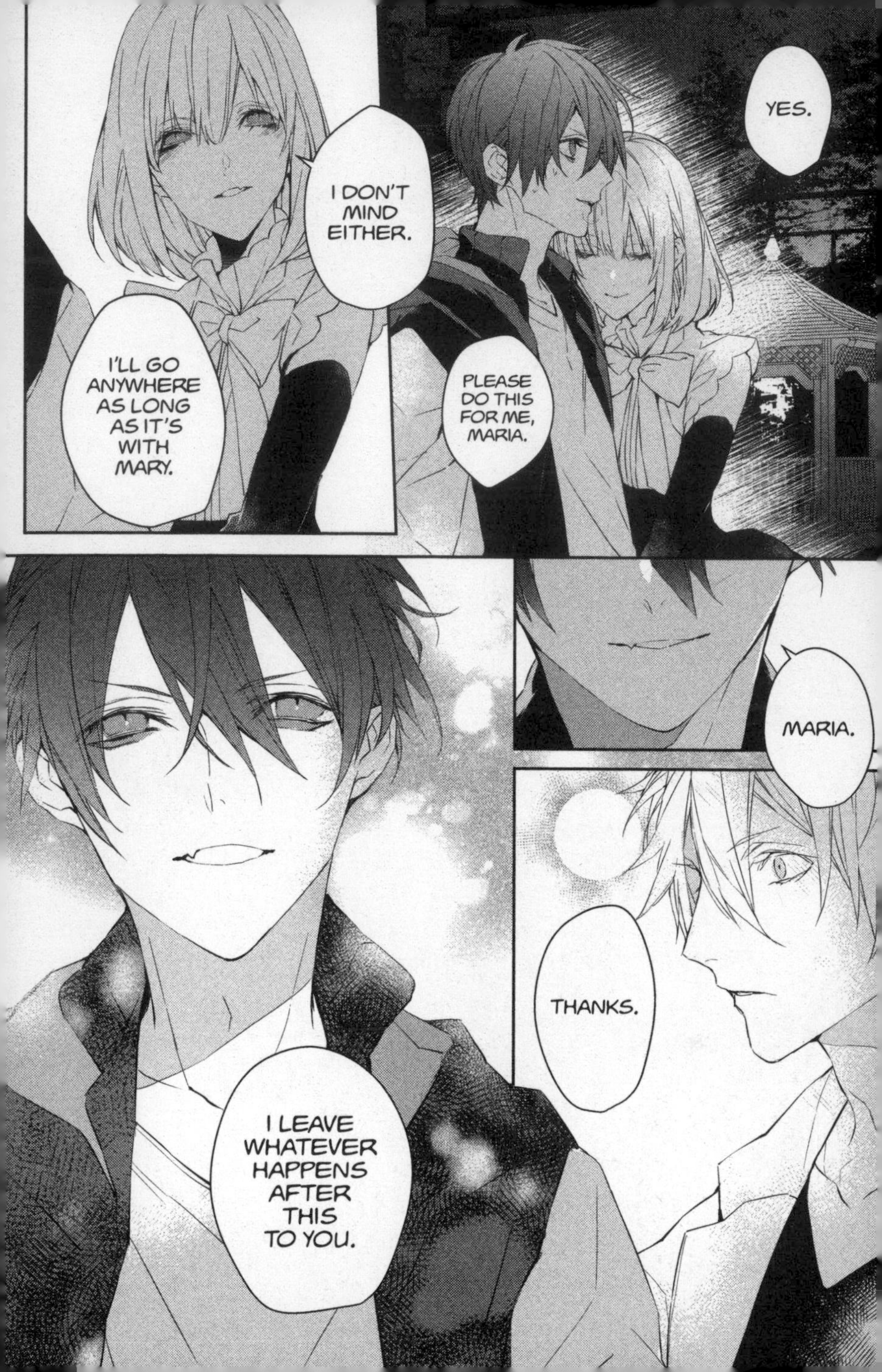
YES.
PLEASE DO THIS FOR ME, MARIA.
I DON'T MIND EITHER.
I'LL GO ANYWHERE AS LONG AS IT'S WITH MARY.
MARIA.
THANKS.
I LEAVE WHATEVER HAPPENS AFTER THIS TO YOU.

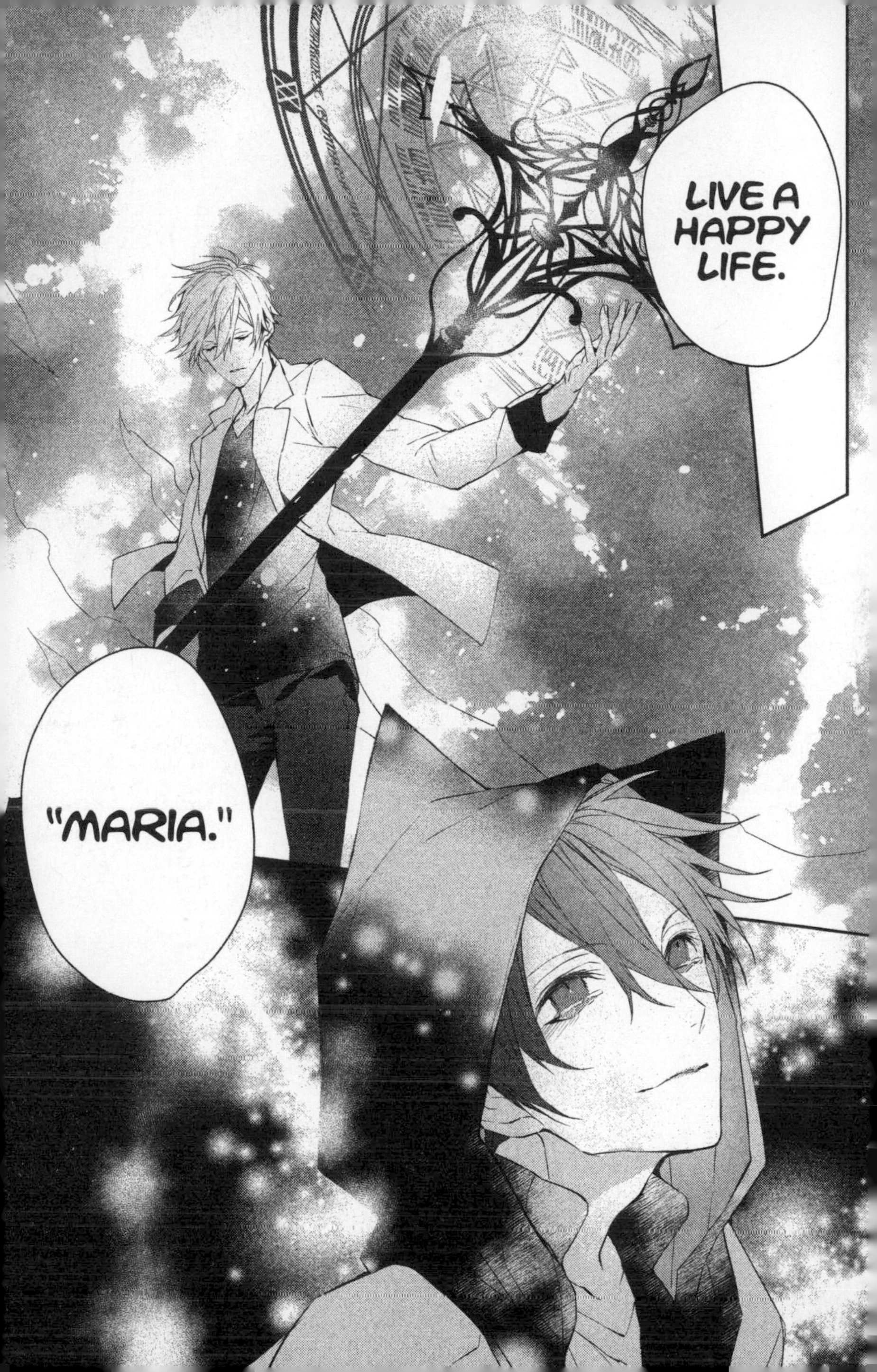
LIVE A HAPPY LIFE.
"MARIA."

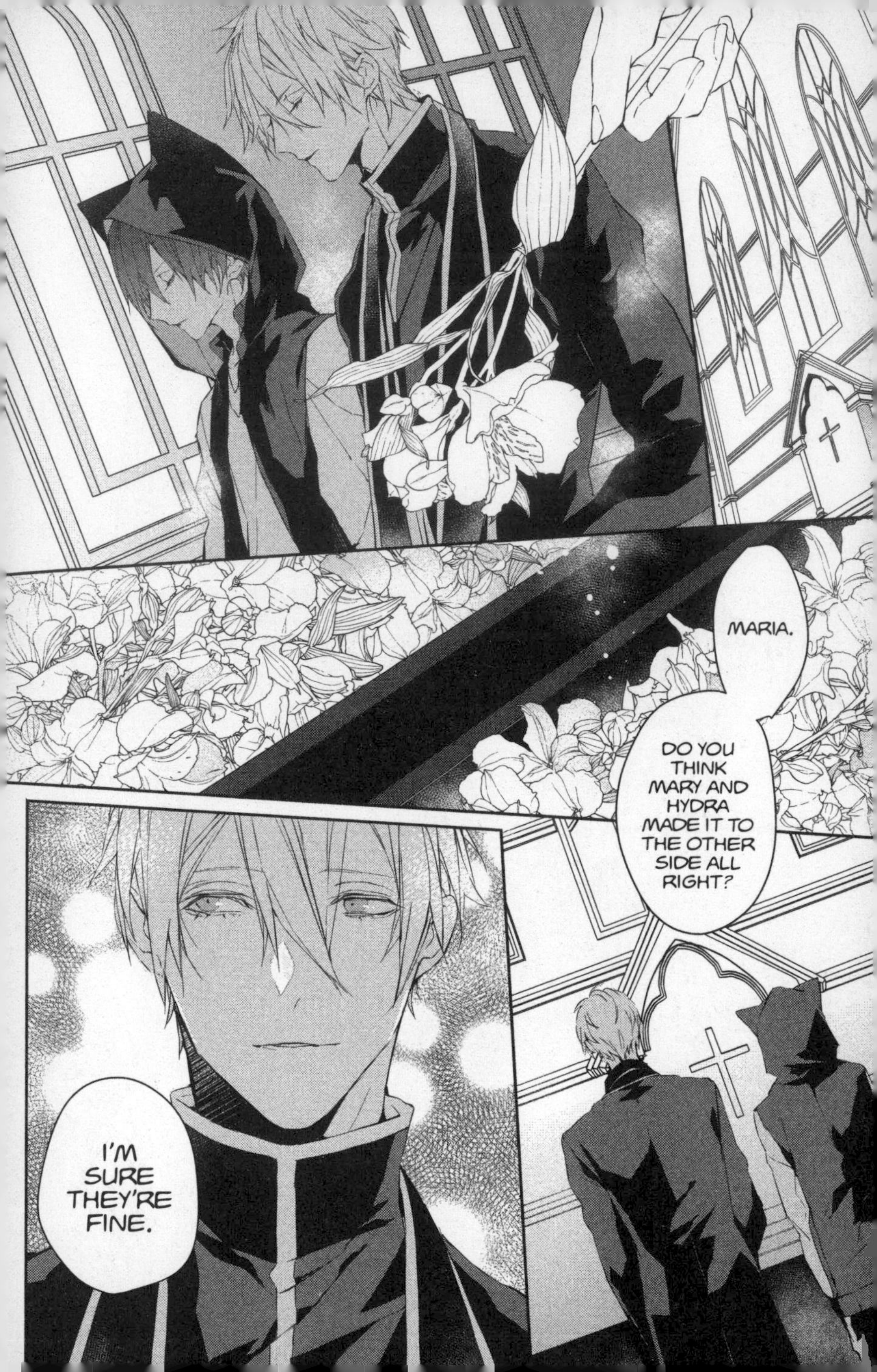
MARIA.
DO YOU THINK MARY AND HYDRA MADE IT TO THE OTHER SIDE ALL RIGHT?
I'M SURE THEY'RE FINE.

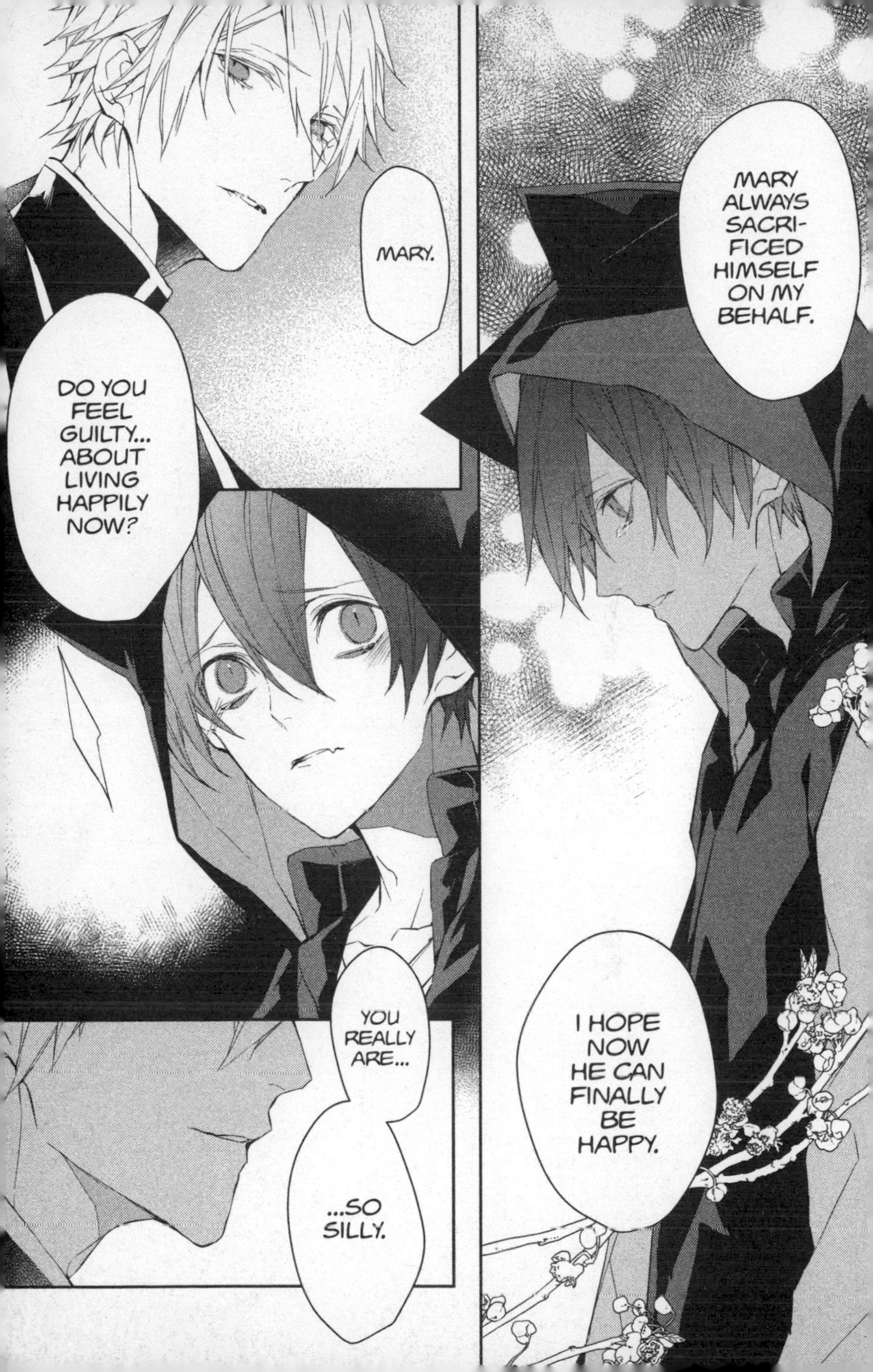
MARY ALWAYS SACRIFICED HIMSELF ON MY BEHALF.
I HOPE NOW HE CAN FINALLY BE HAPPY.
MARY.
DO YOU FEEL GUILTY... ABOUT LIVING HAPPILY NOW?
YOU REALLY ARE...
...SO SILLY.

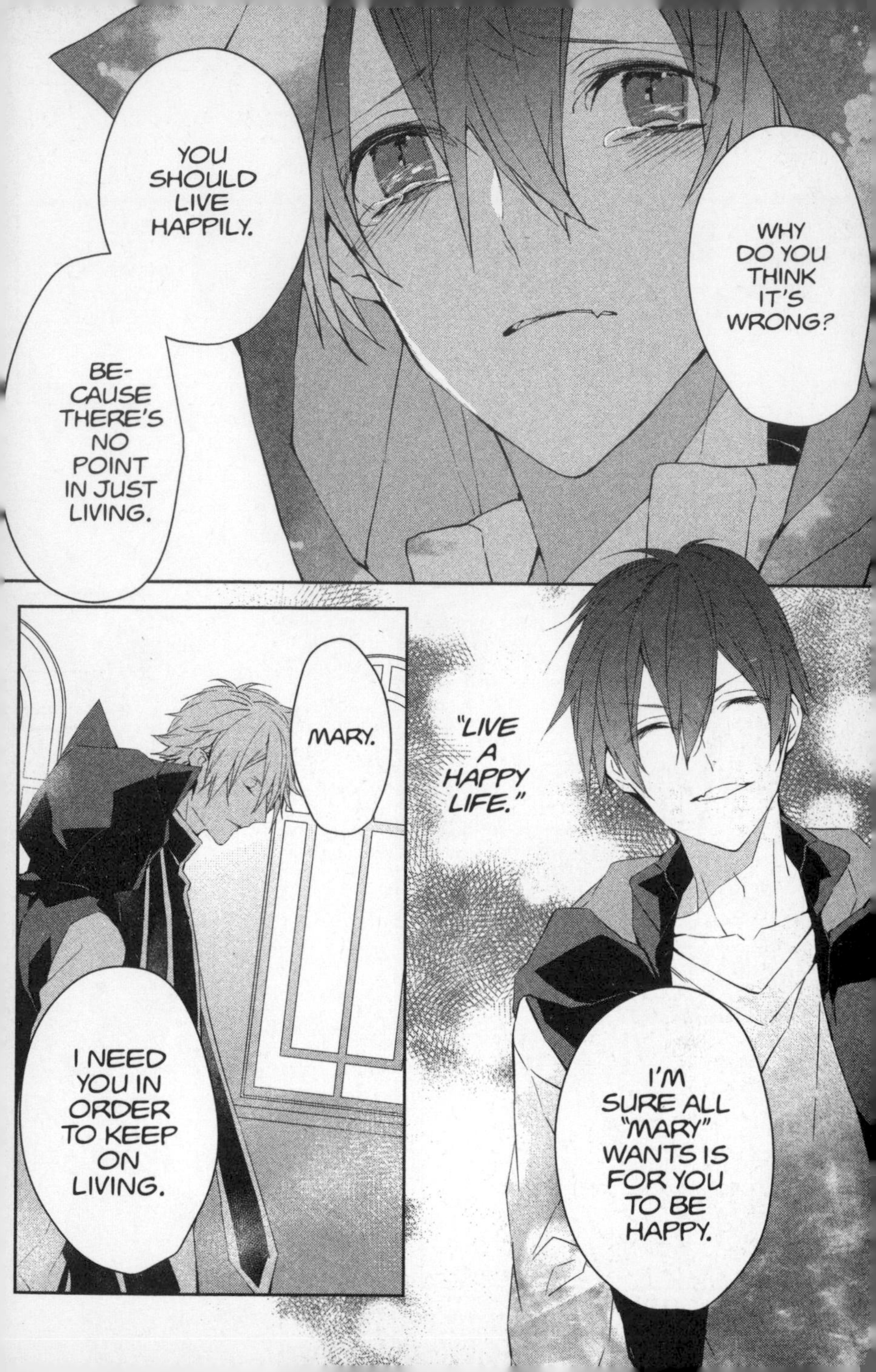
WHY DO YOU THINK IT'S WRONG?
YOU SHOULD LIVE HAPPILY.
BE-CAUSE THERE'S NO POINT IN JUST LIVING.
"LIVE A HAPPY LIFE."
I'M SURE ALL "MARY" WANTS IS FOR YOU TO BE HAPPY.
MARY.
I NEED YOU IN ORDER TO KEEP ON LIVING.

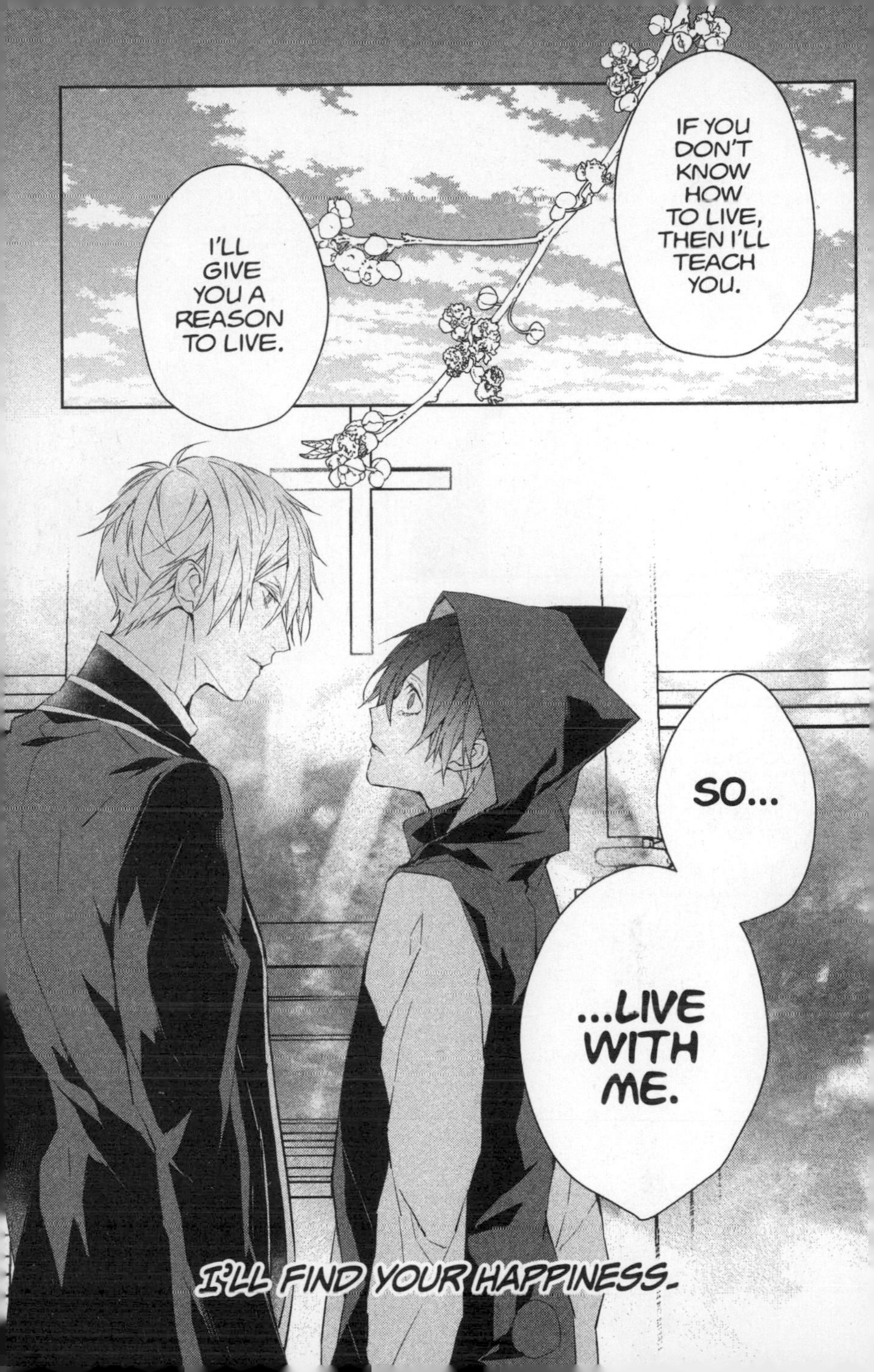
IF YOU DON'T KNOW HOW TO LIVE, THEN I'LL TEACH YOU.
I'LL GIVE YOU A REASON TO LIVE.
SO...
...LIVE WITH ME.
I'LL FIND YOUR HAPPINESS.

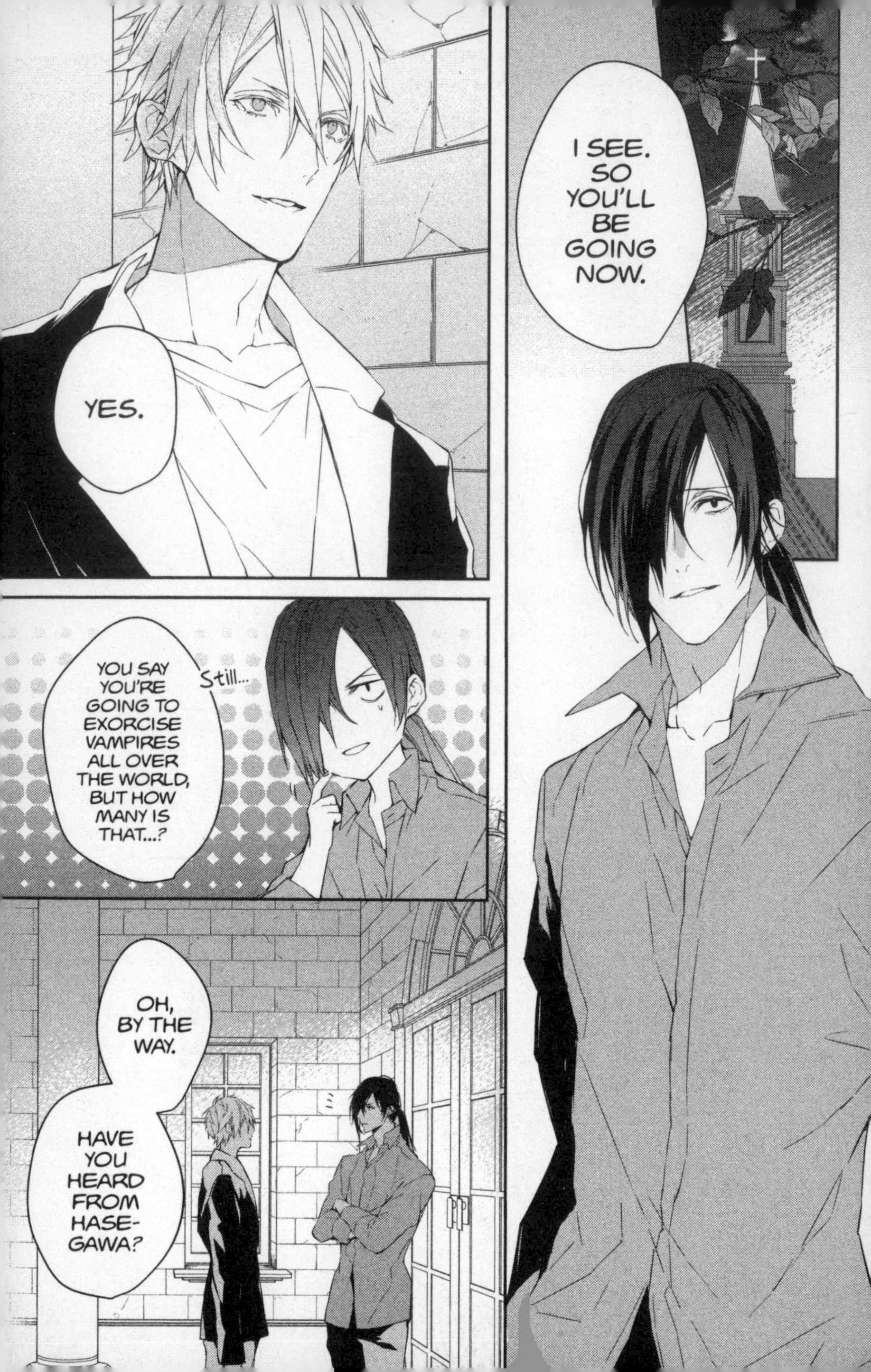
I SEE. SO YOU'LL BE GOING NOW.
YES.
Still...
YOU SAY YOU'RE GOING TO EXORCISE VAMPIRES ALL OVER THE WORLD, BUT HOW MANY IS THAT...?
OH, BY THE WAY.
HAVE YOU HEARD FROM HASE-GAWA?

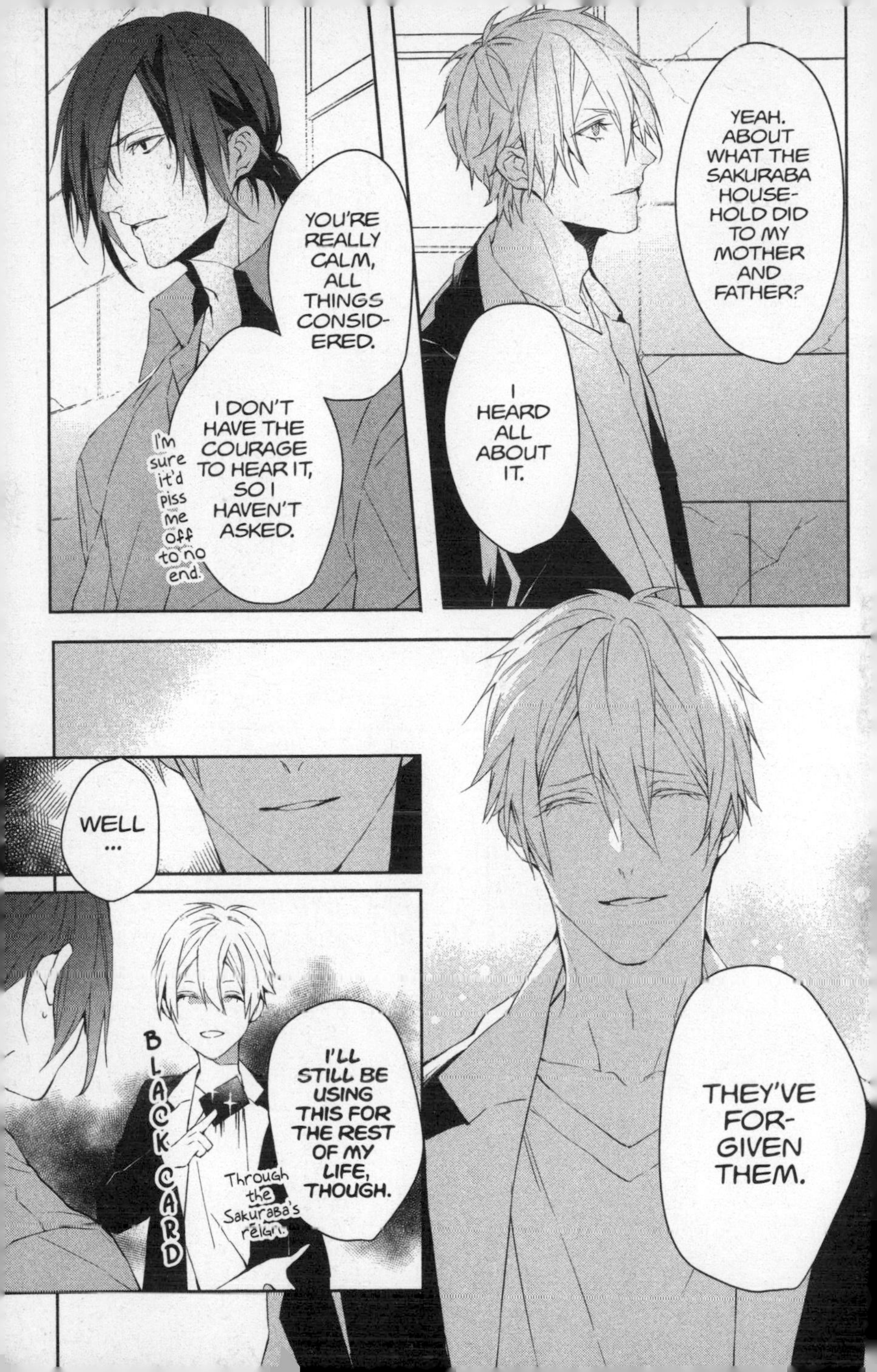
YEAH. ABOUT WHAT THE SAKURABA HOUSEHOLD DID TO MY MOTHER AND FATHER?
I HEARD ALL ABOUT IT.
YOU'RE REALLY CALM, ALL THINGS CONSIDERED.
I DON'T HAVE THE COURAGE TO HEAR IT, SO I HAVEN'T ASKED.
I'm sure it'd piss me off to no end.
THEY'VE FORGIVEN THEM.
WELL ...
I'LL STILL BE USING THIS FOR THE REST OF MY LIFE, THOUGH.
BLACK CARD
Through the Sakuraba's reign.

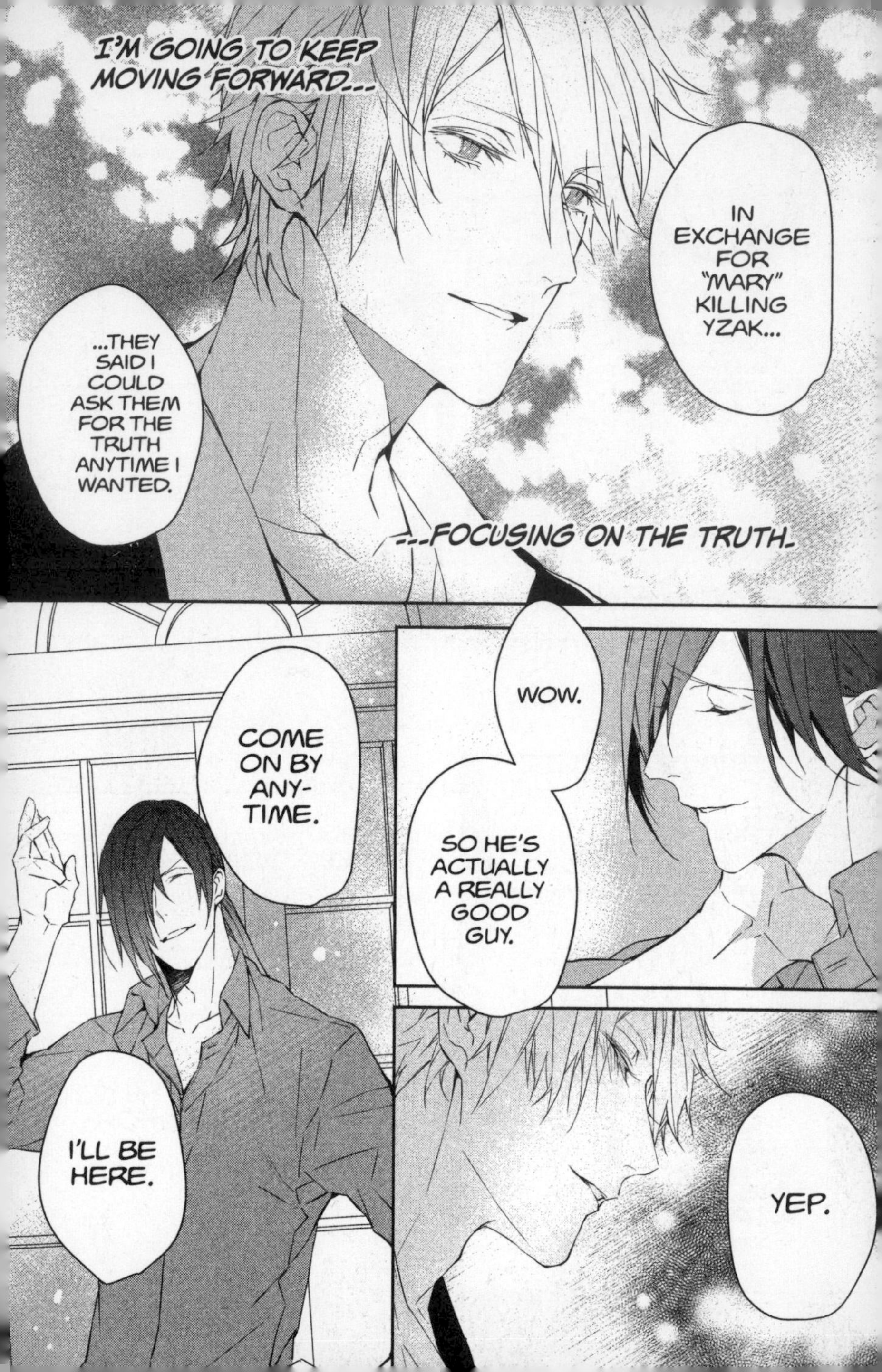
I'M GOING TO KEEP MOVING FORWARD...
IN EXCHANGE FOR "MARY" KILLING YZAK...
...THEY SAID I COULD ASK THEM FOR THE TRUTH ANYTIME I WANTED.
---FOCUSING ON THE TRUTH.
WOW.
SO HE'S ACTUALLY A REALLY GOOD GUY.
YEP.
COME ON BY ANY-TIME.
I'LL BE HERE.

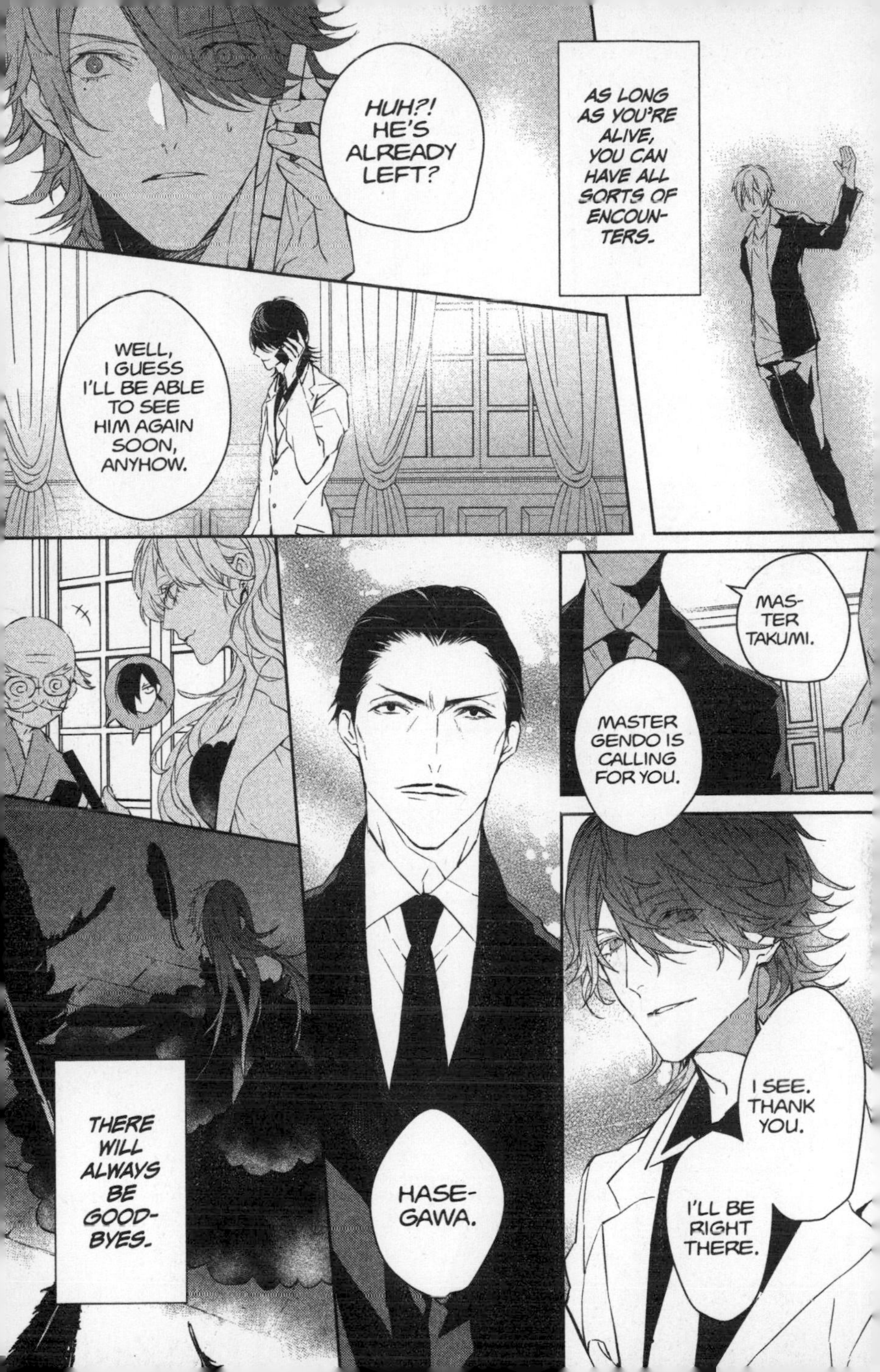
AS LONG AS YOU'RE ALIVE, YOU CAN HAVE ALL SORTS OF ENCOUNTERS.
HUH?! HE'S ALREADY LEFT?
WELL, I GUESS I'LL BE ABLE TO SEE HIM AGAIN SOON, ANYHOW.
MASTER TAKUMI.
MASTER GENDO IS CALLING FOR YOU.
I SEE. THANK YOU.
I'LL BE RIGHT THERE.
HASEGAWA.
THERE WILL ALWAYS BE GOODBYES.

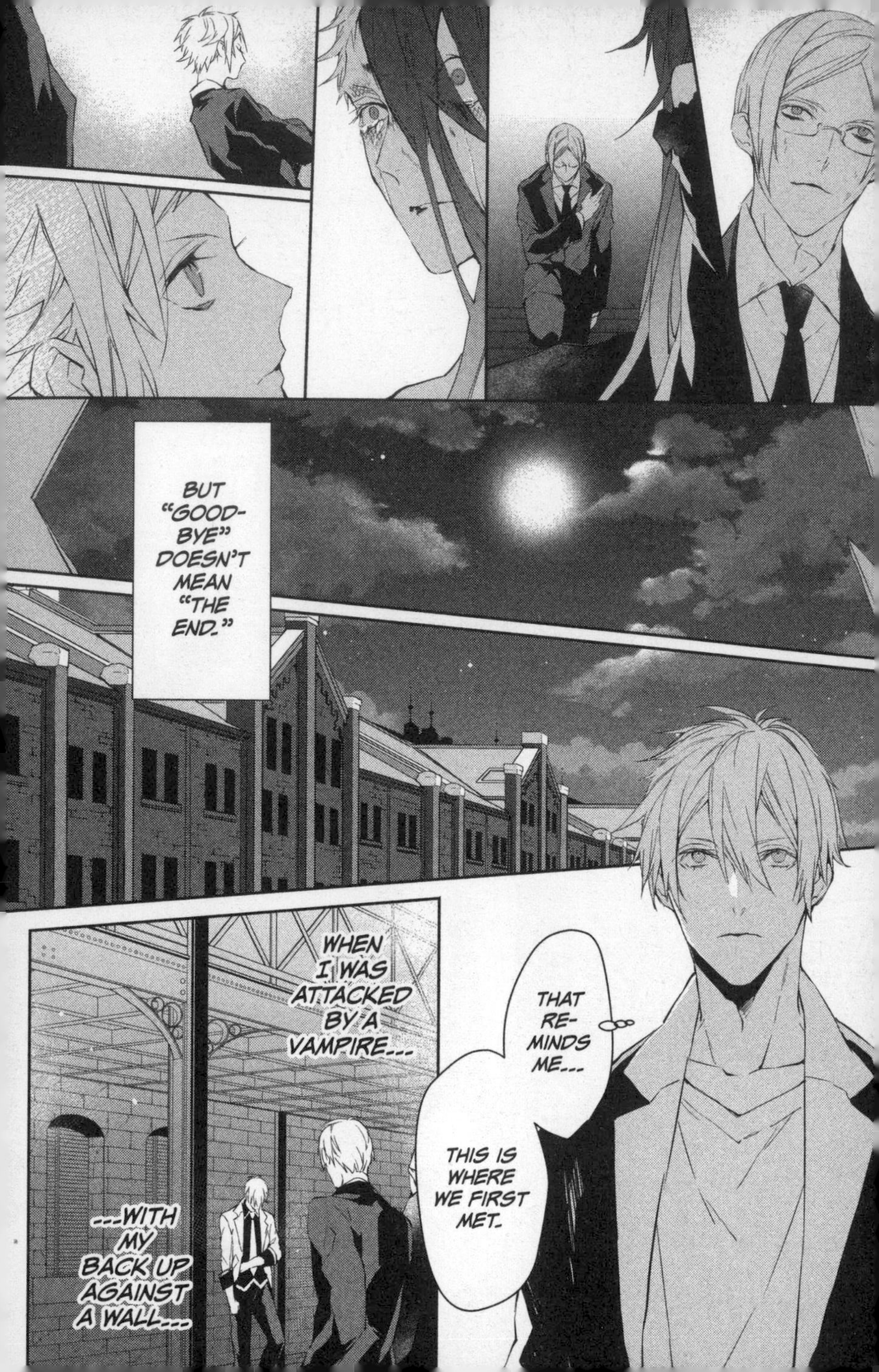
BUT "GOOD-BYE" DOESN'T MEAN "THE END."
THAT RE-MINDS ME...
THIS IS WHERE WE FIRST MET.
WHEN I WAS ATTACKED BY A VAMPIRE...
...WITH MY BACK UP AGAINST A WALL...

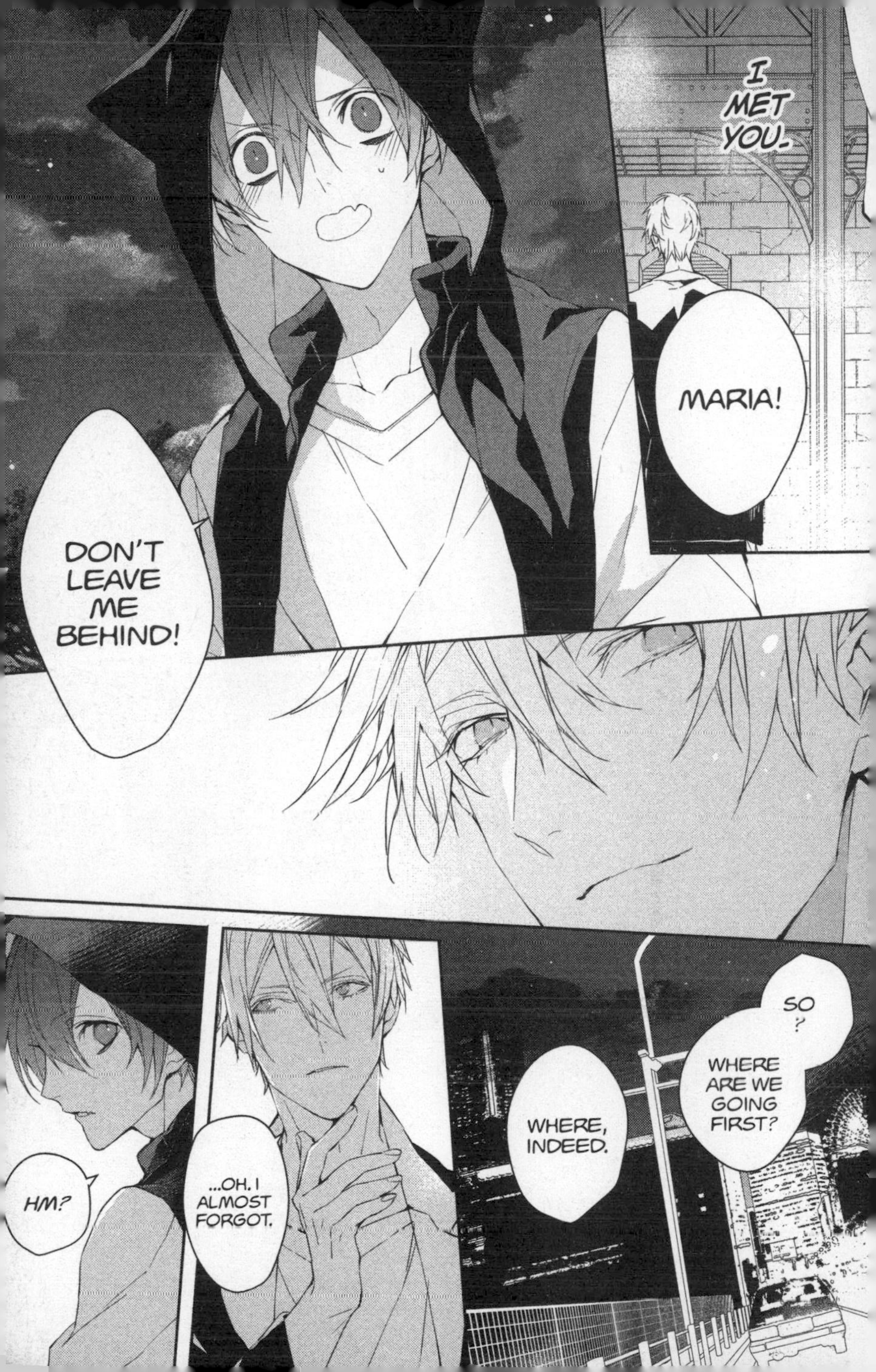
I MET YOU.
MARIA!
DON'T LEAVE ME BEHIND!
SO?
WHERE ARE WE GOING FIRST?
WHERE, INDEED.
...OH. I ALMOST FORGOT.
HM?

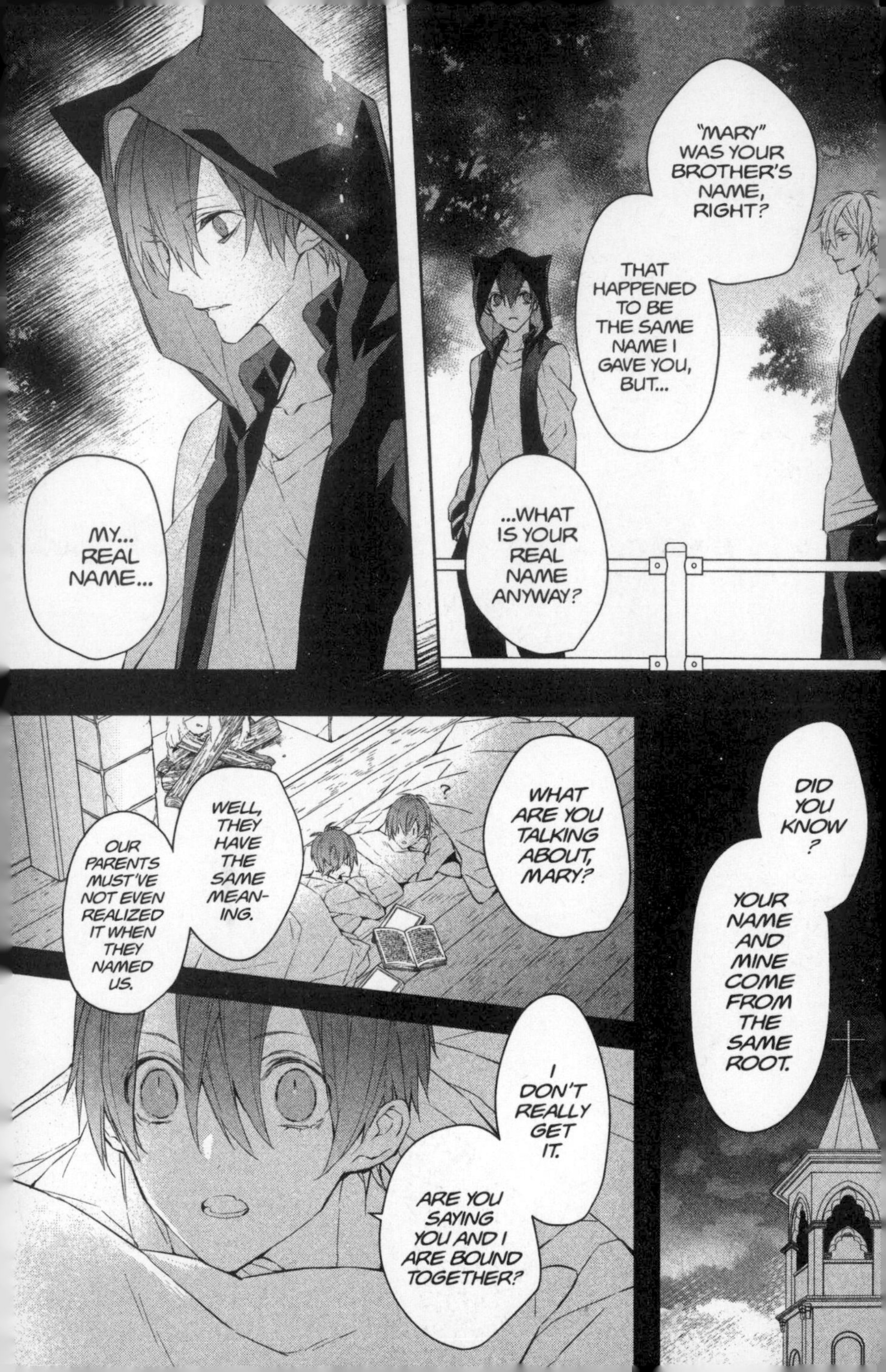
"MARY" WAS YOUR BROTHER'S NAME, RIGHT?
THAT HAPPENED TO BE THE SAME NAME I GAVE YOU, BUT...
...WHAT IS YOUR REAL NAME ANYWAY?
MY... REAL NAME...
DID YOU KNOW?
YOUR NAME AND MINE COME FROM THE SAME ROOT.
WHAT ARE YOU TALKING ABOUT, MARY?
WELL, THEY HAVE THE SAME MEAN-ING.
OUR PARENTS MUST'VE NOT EVEN REALIZED IT WHEN THEY NAMED US.
?
I DON'T REALLY GET IT.
ARE YOU SAYING YOU AND I ARE BOUND TOGETHER?

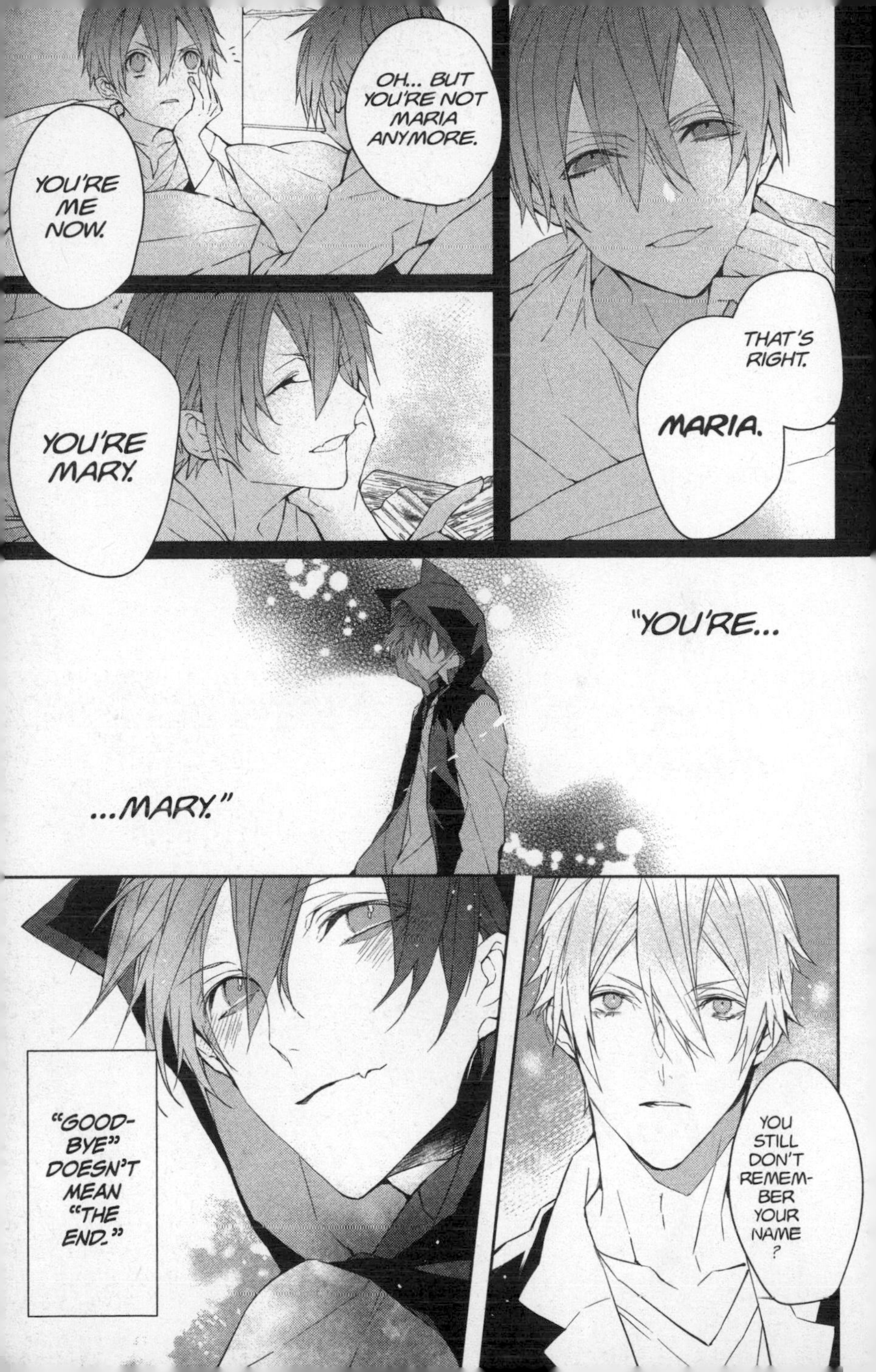
THAT'S RIGHT.
MARIA.
OH... BUT YOU'RE NOT MARIA ANYMORE.
YOU'RE ME NOW.
YOU'RE MARY.
"YOU'RE...
...MARY."
YOU STILL DON'T REMEM-BER YOUR NAME ?
"GOOD-BYE" DOESN'T MEAN "THE END."

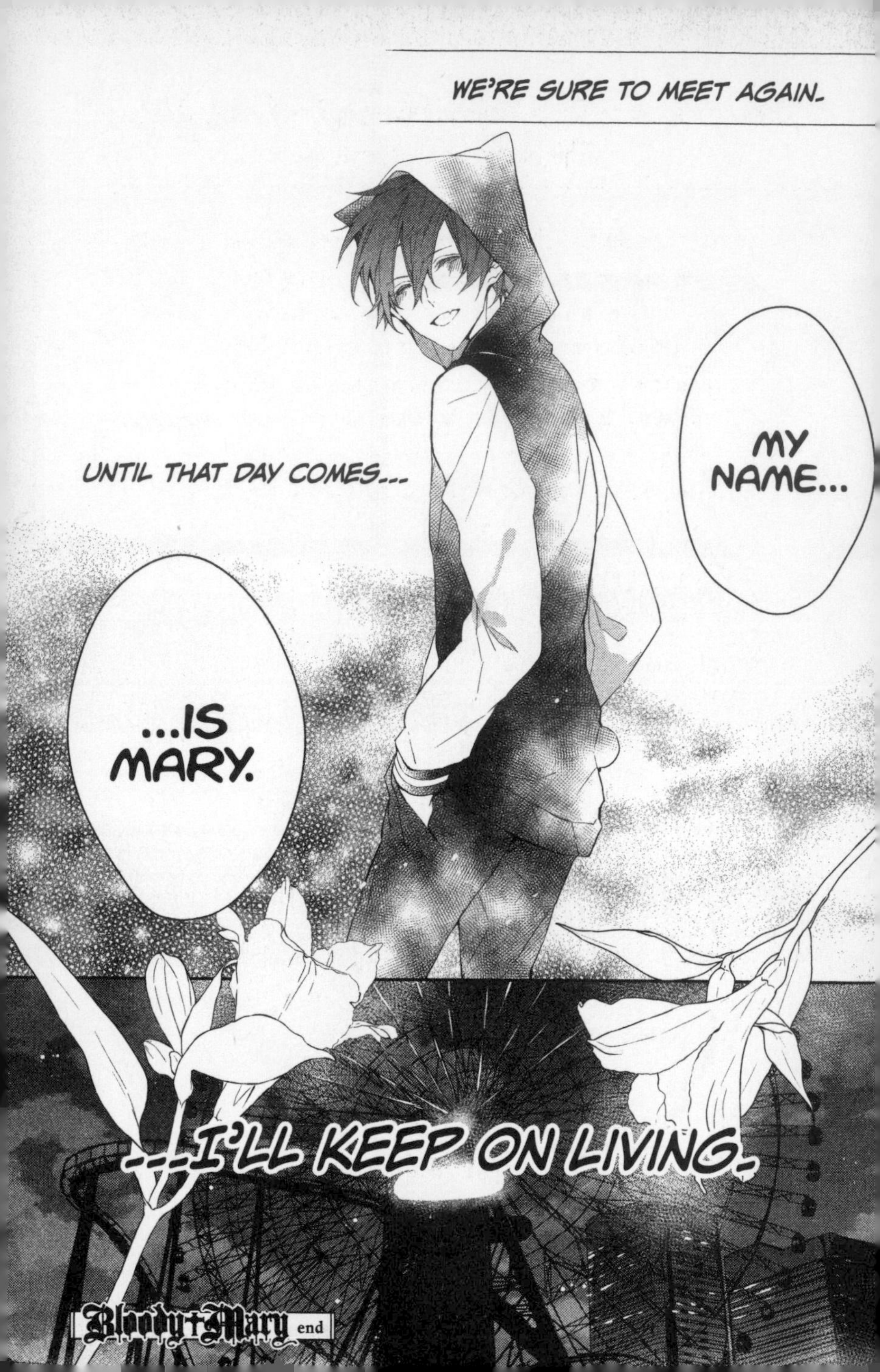
WE'RE SURE TO MEET AGAIN.
MY NAME...
UNTIL THAT DAY COMES...
...IS MARY.
...I'LL KEEP ON LIVING.
Bloody+Mary end

Thank you so much for picking up volume 10 of *Bloody Mary*!
This is the final volume!

With the last chapter running in the magazine and
the characters' missions coming to an end, the reality
of the end of this story is finally settling in.
I feel sad, accomplished and a whole myriad of feelings.
But it was a fun ride! That's probably what I feel most
strongly. To everyone who watched over me and cheered
me on until the very end, thank you so, so much!
My deepest gratitude to all the people involved in the
creation of this work.

# THANK YOU SO MUCH! ♡♡

My new series will be about angels and demons and is called
*Ballad Opera*. It's possible a certain someone from *Bloody Mary*
might make an appearance in it. If you would like to follow along
with that story too, then I hope you will do
your best to find that certain someone!

That        Was        the
                       Post-
                       script

# SPECIAL THANKS

Mihoru / M-fuchi / H-gawa / T-mizu-sama / T-ko-sama

Production Team/Support
Haruo / Sumida / M-ika

Editor S / Designer / Everyone at Kosaido
Comics director Y / Everyone involved

And everyone who read this

◁ After this comes a bonus story. ♡

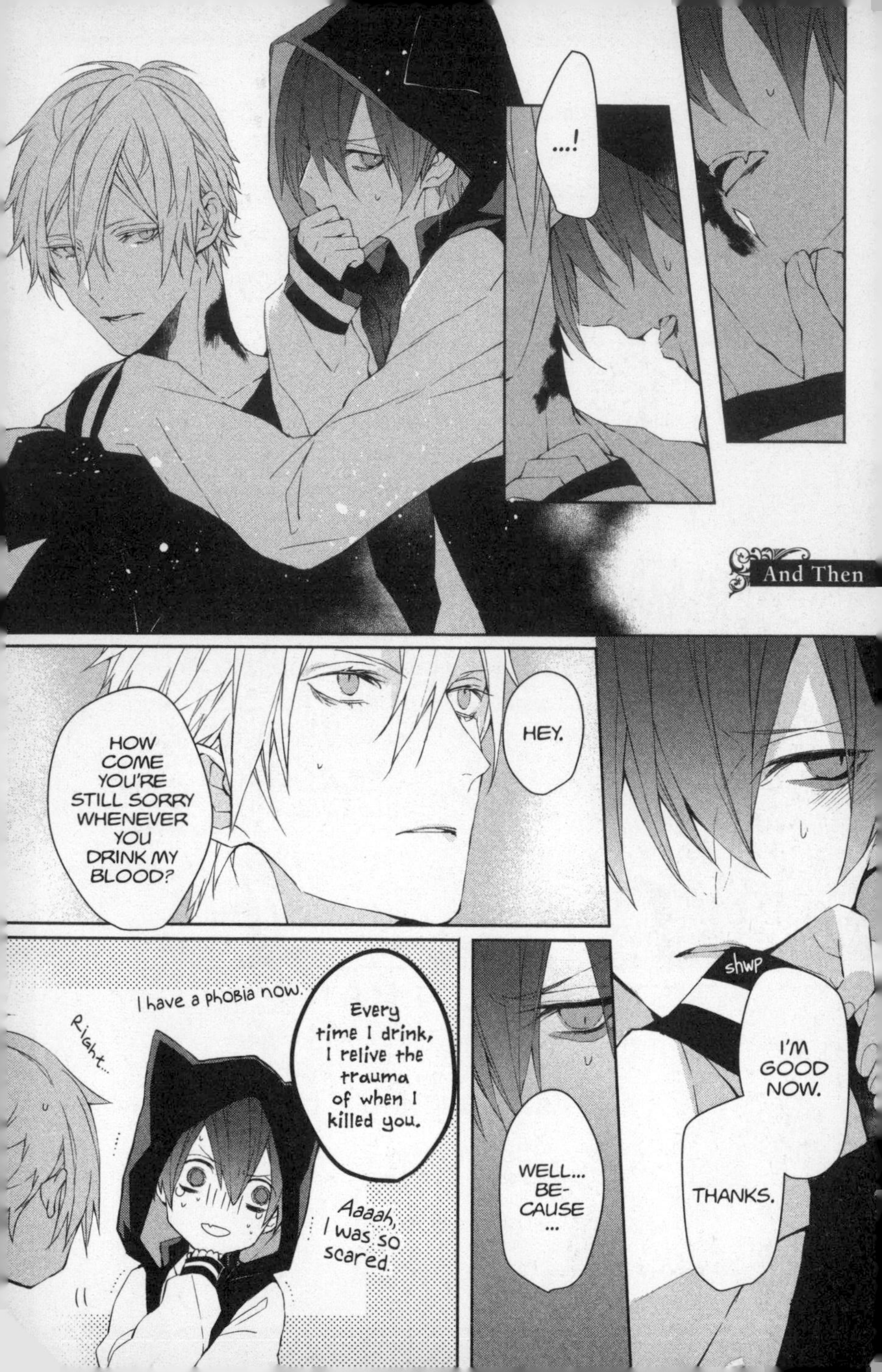
...!
And Then
HEY.
HOW COME YOU'RE STILL SORRY WHENEVER YOU DRINK MY BLOOD?
shwp
I'M GOOD NOW.
THANKS.
WELL... BE-CAUSE ...
Every time I drink, I relive the trauma of when I killed you.
I have a phobia now.
Right...
Aaaah, I was so scared.

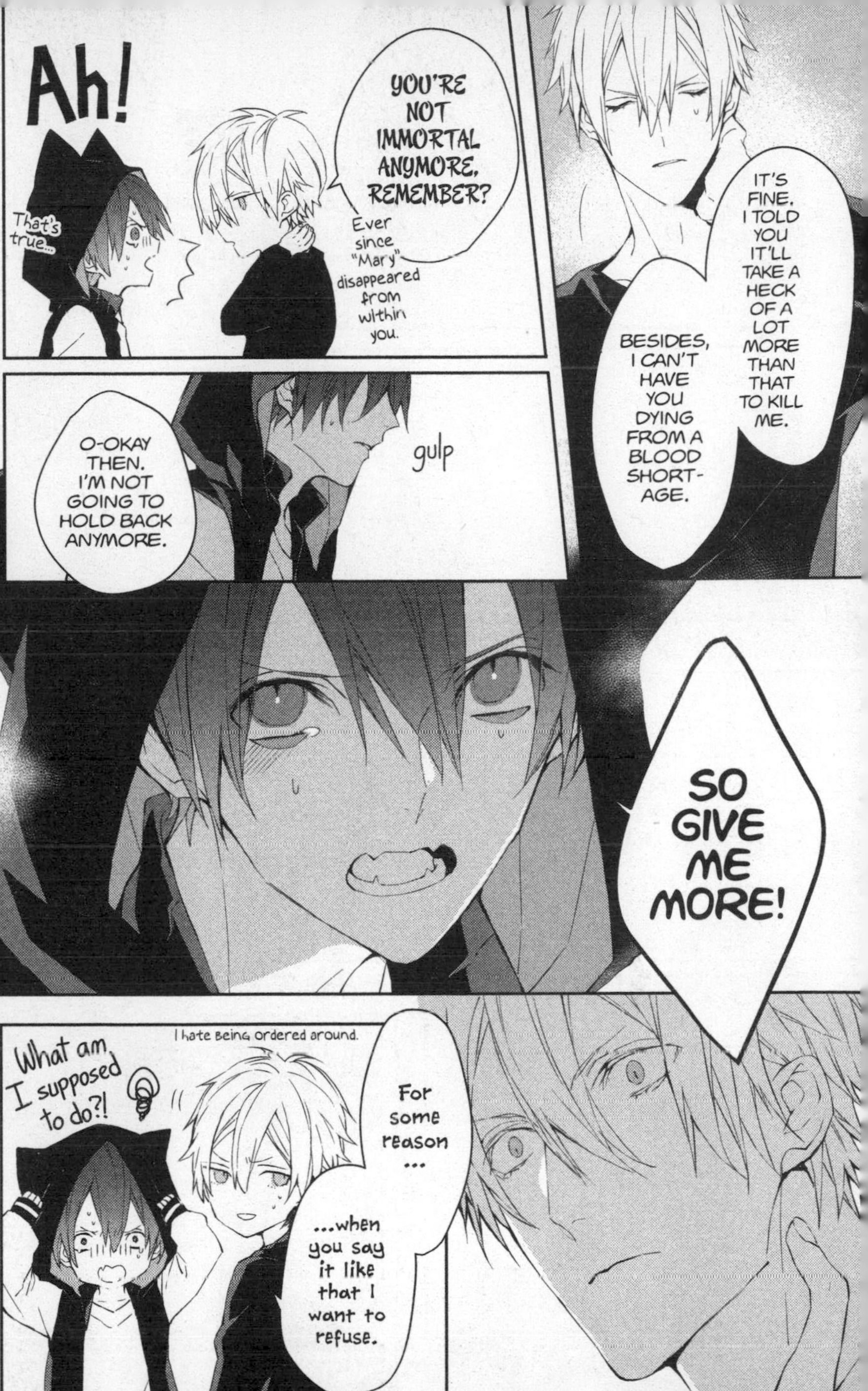
IT'S FINE. I TOLD YOU IT'LL TAKE A HECK OF A LOT MORE THAN THAT TO KILL ME.
BESIDES, I CAN'T HAVE YOU DYING FROM A BLOOD SHORTAGE.
YOU'RE NOT IMMORTAL ANYMORE, REMEMBER?
Ever since "Mary" disappeared from within you.
Ah!
That's true...
gulp
O-OKAY THEN. I'M NOT GOING TO HOLD BACK ANYMORE.
SO GIVE ME MORE!
For some reason...
...when you say it like that I want to refuse.
I hate being ordered around.
What am I supposed to do?!

DEEP DOWN, MARIA HASN'T CHANGED.

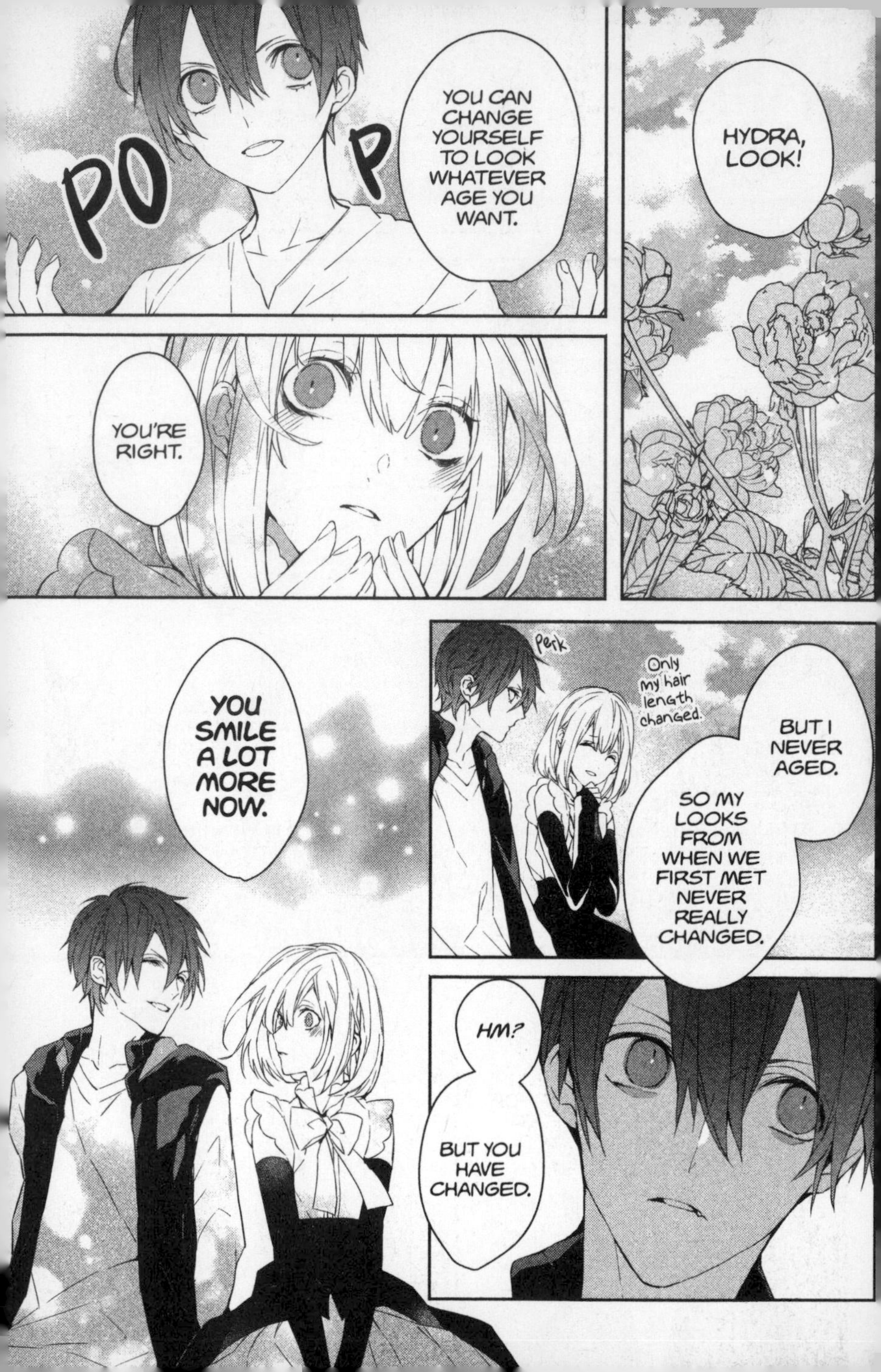
HYDRA, LOOK!
POP
YOU CAN CHANGE YOURSELF TO LOOK WHATEVER AGE YOU WANT.
YOU'RE RIGHT.
BUT I NEVER AGED.
SO MY LOOKS FROM WHEN WE FIRST MET NEVER REALLY CHANGED.
Only my hair length changed.
Perk
HM?
BUT YOU HAVE CHANGED.
YOU SMILE A LOT MORE NOW.

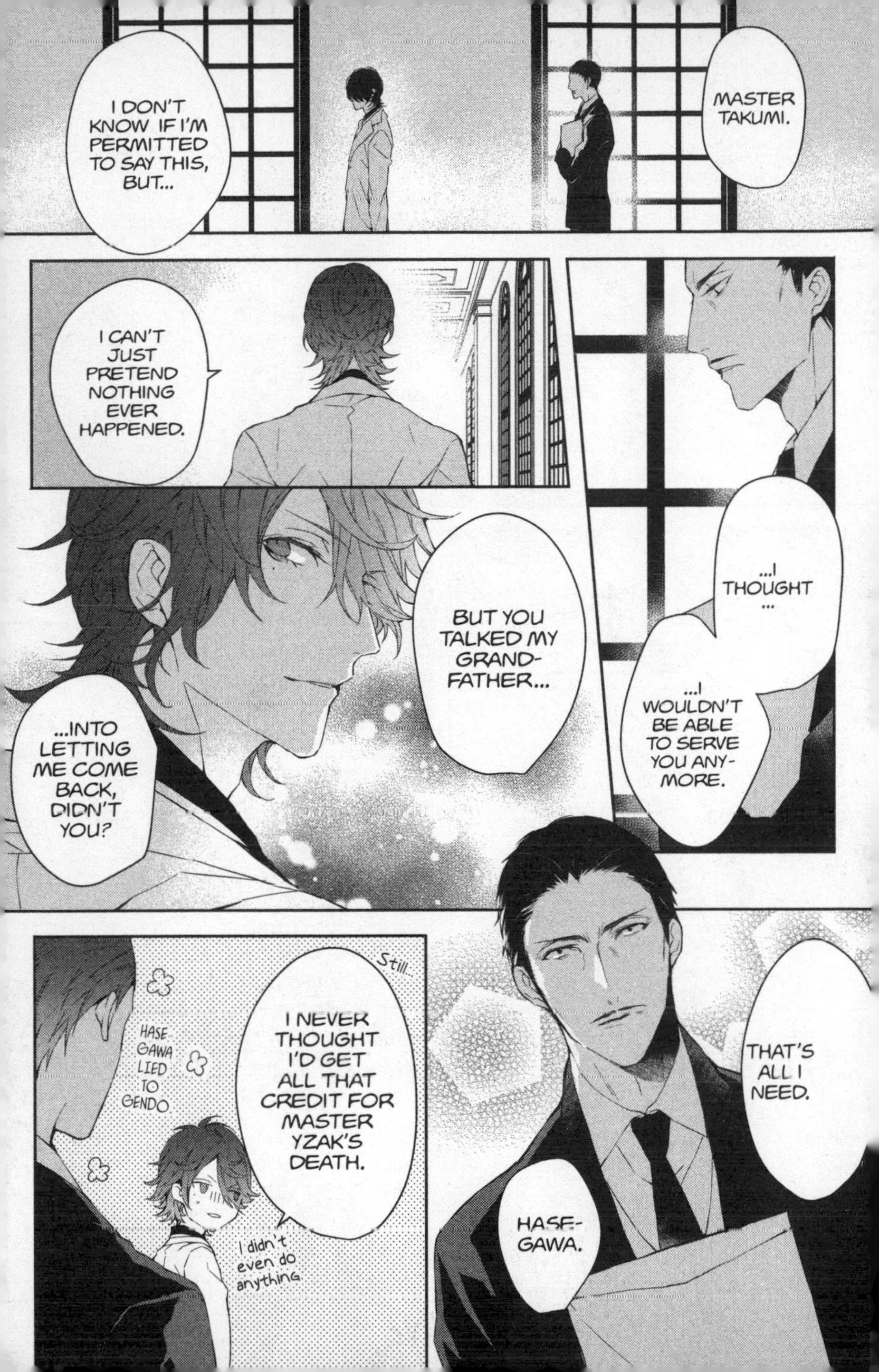
MASTER TAKUMI.
I DON'T KNOW IF I'M PERMITTED TO SAY THIS, BUT...
...I THOUGHT...
...I WOULDN'T BE ABLE TO SERVE YOU ANY-MORE.
I CAN'T JUST PRETEND NOTHING EVER HAPPENED.
BUT YOU TALKED MY GRAND-FATHER...
...INTO LETTING ME COME BACK, DIDN'T YOU?
THAT'S ALL I NEED.
HASE-GAWA.
Still...
I NEVER THOUGHT I'D GET ALL THAT CREDIT FOR MASTER YZAK'S DEATH.
HASE-GAWA LIED TO GENDO
I didn't even do anything.

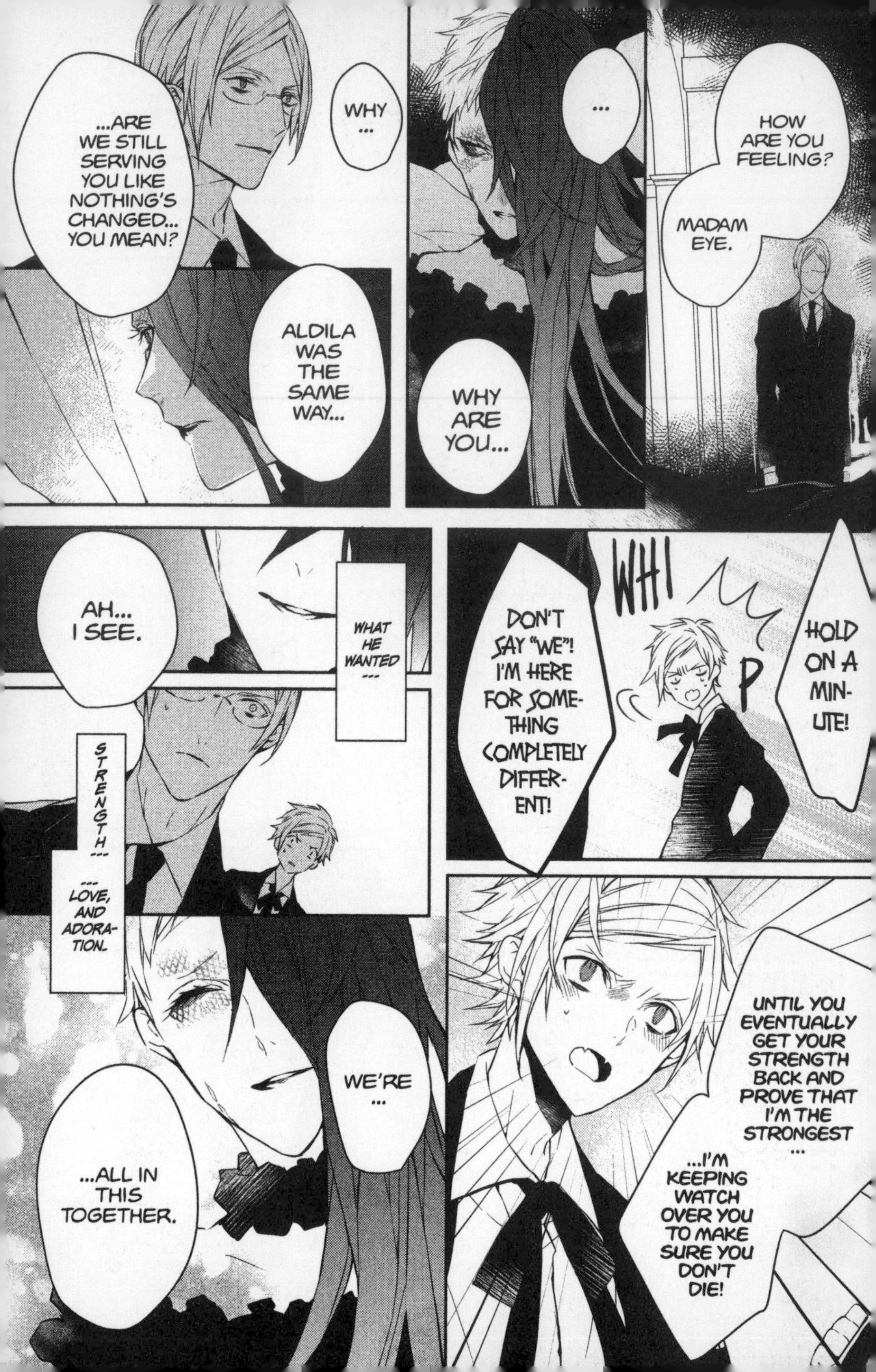
HOW ARE YOU FEELING?
MADAM EYE.
...
WHY ARE YOU...
WHY...
...ARE WE STILL SERVING YOU LIKE NOTHING'S CHANGED... YOU MEAN?
ALDILA WAS THE SAME WAY...
HOLD ON A MIN-UTE!
WHIP
DON'T SAY "WE"! I'M HERE FOR SOME-THING COMPLETELY DIFFER-ENT!
UNTIL YOU EVENTUALLY GET YOUR STRENGTH BACK AND PROVE THAT I'M THE STRONGEST...
...I'M KEEPING WATCH OVER YOU TO MAKE SURE YOU DON'T DIE!
AH... I SEE.
WHAT HE WANTED---
STRENGTH---
---LOVE, AND ADORA-TION.
WE'RE...
...ALL IN THIS TOGETHER.

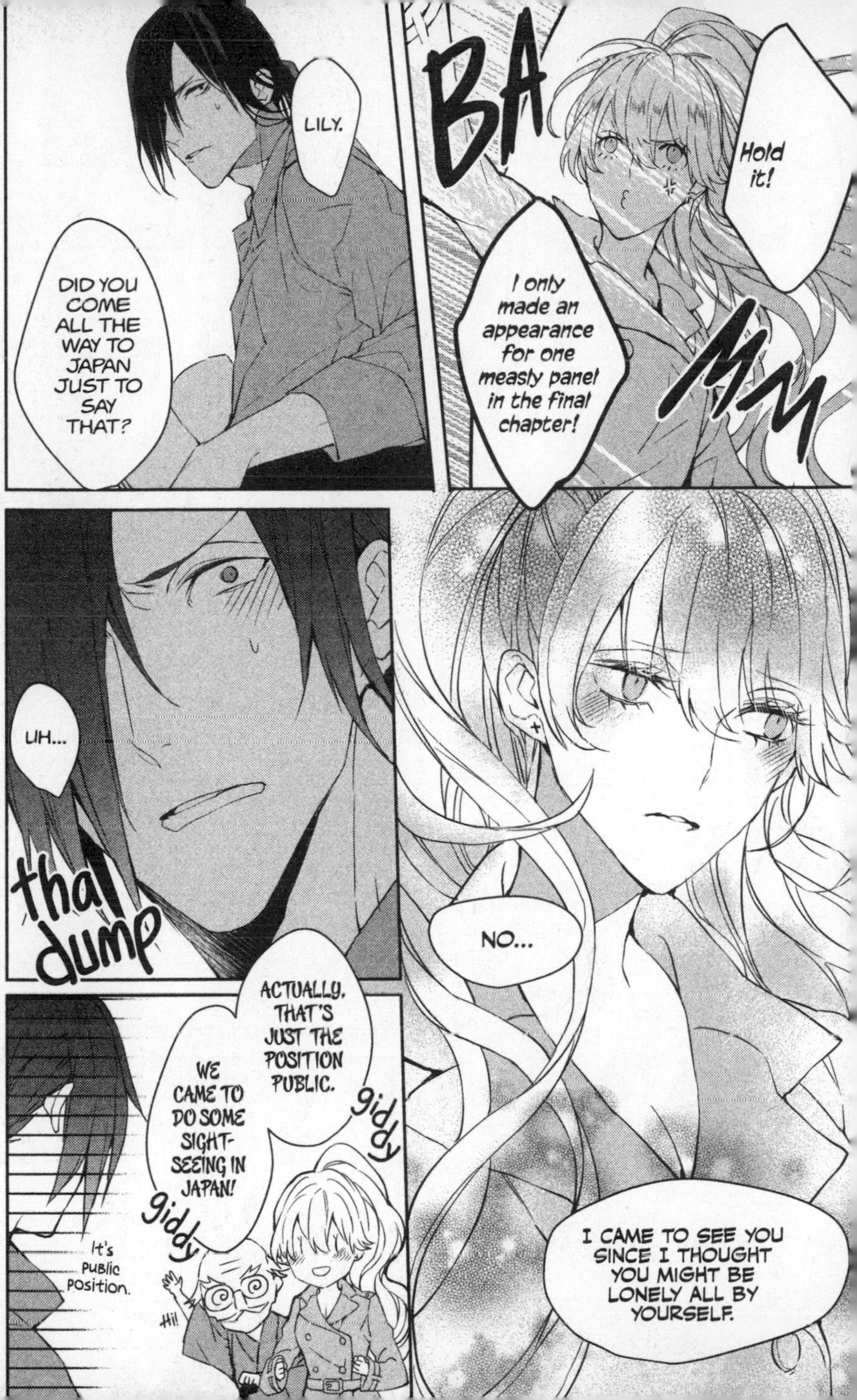
BAMM
Hold it!
I only made an appearance for one measly panel in the final chapter!
LILY.
DID YOU COME ALL THE WAY TO JAPAN JUST TO SAY THAT?
NO...
I CAME TO SEE YOU SINCE I THOUGHT YOU MIGHT BE LONELY ALL BY YOURSELF.
UH...
thadump
ACTUALLY, THAT'S JUST THE POSITION PUBLIC.
WE CAME TO DO SOME SIGHT-SEEING IN JAPAN!
giddy
giddy
It's public position.
Hi!

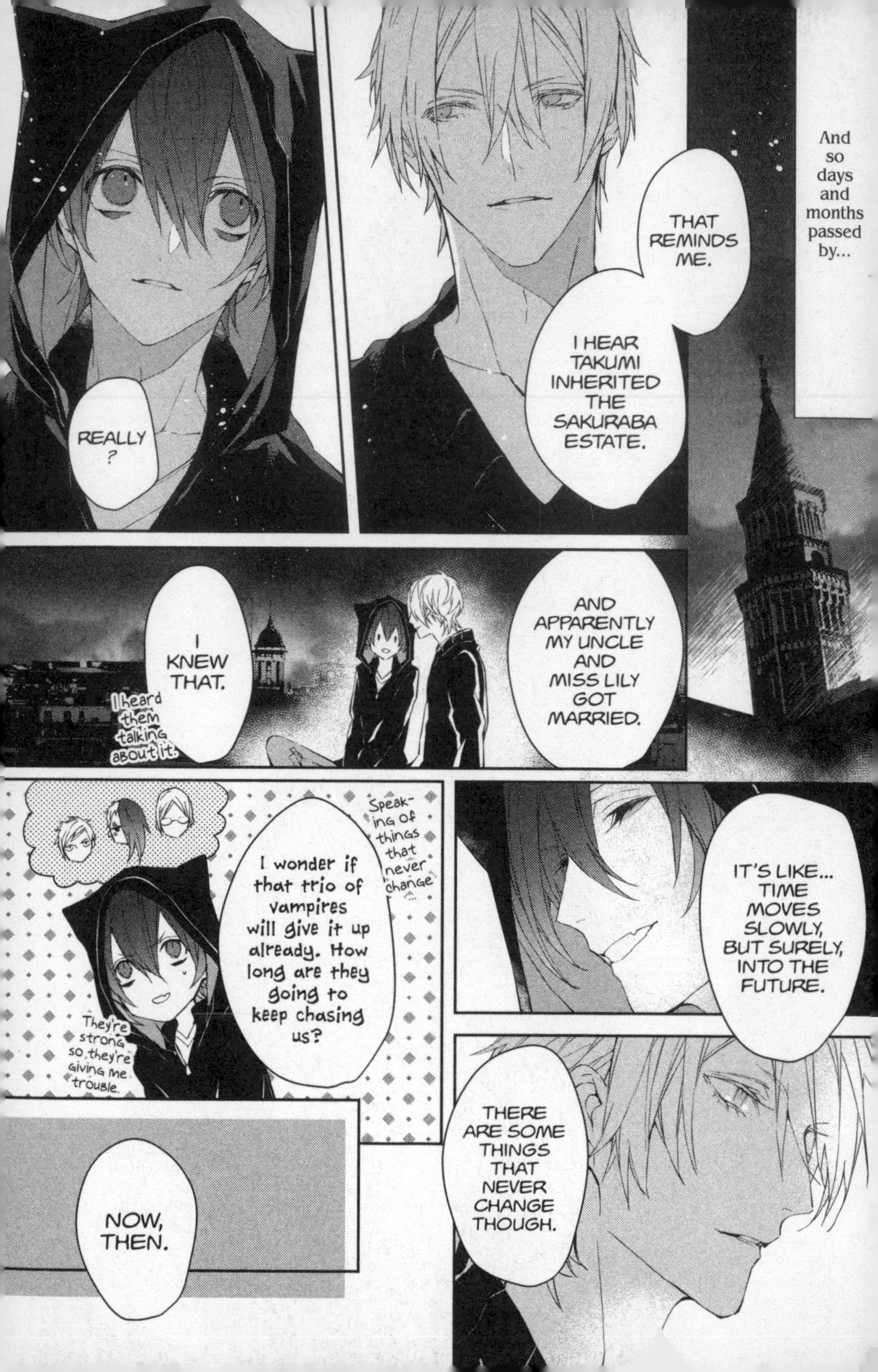

And so days and months passed by...
THAT REMINDS ME.
I HEAR TAKUMI INHERITED THE SAKURABA ESTATE.
REALLY?
AND APPARENTLY MY UNCLE AND MISS LILY GOT MARRIED.
I KNEW THAT.
I heard them talking about it.
IT'S LIKE... TIME MOVES SLOWLY, BUT SURELY, INTO THE FUTURE.
THERE ARE SOME THINGS THAT NEVER CHANGE THOUGH.
Speaking of things that never change...
I wonder if that trio of vampires will give it up already. How long are they going to keep chasing us?
They're strong so they're giving me trouble.
NOW, THEN.

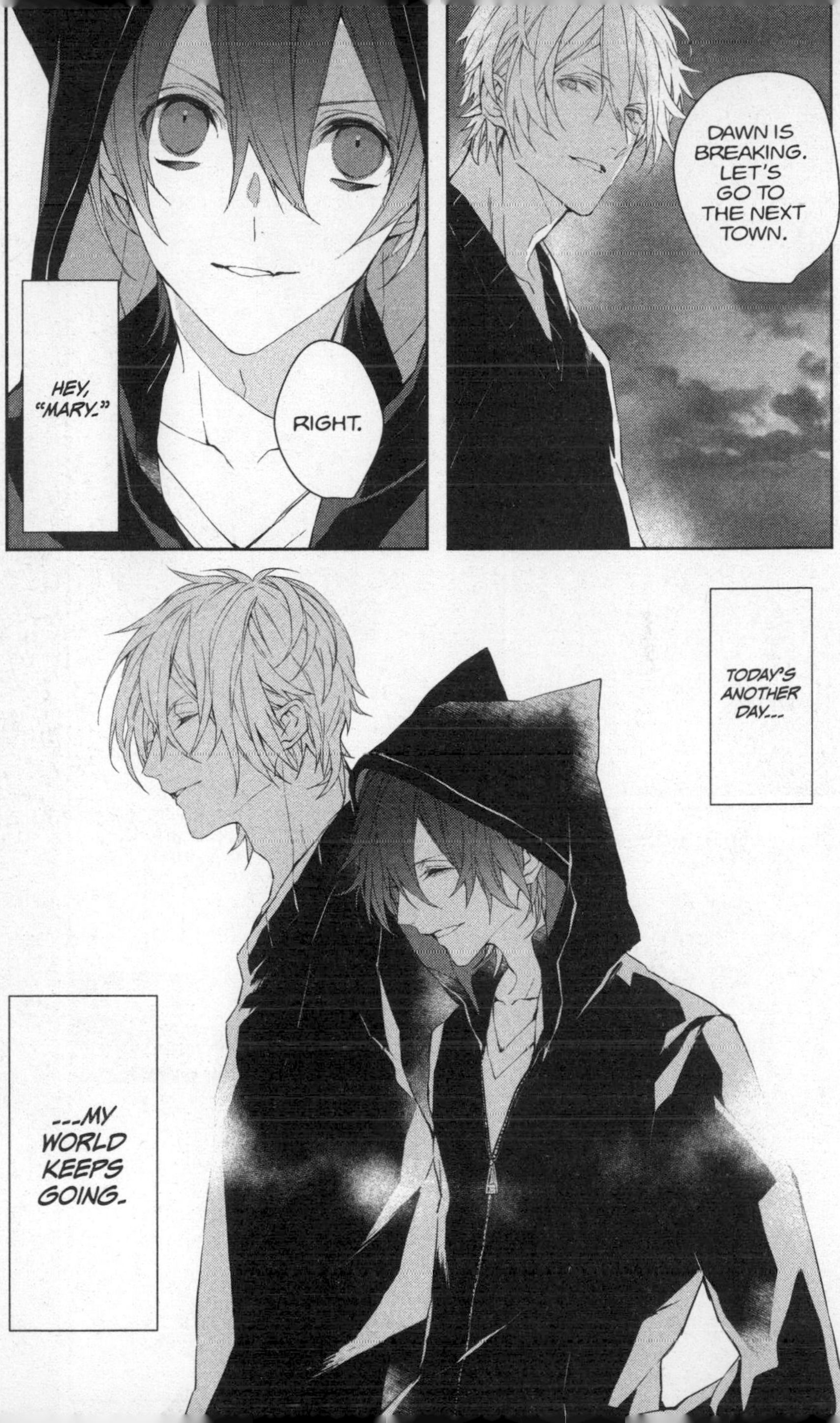
DAWN IS BREAKING. LET'S GO TO THE NEXT TOWN.
RIGHT.
HEY, "MARY."
TODAY'S ANOTHER DAY...
...MY WORLD KEEPS GOING.

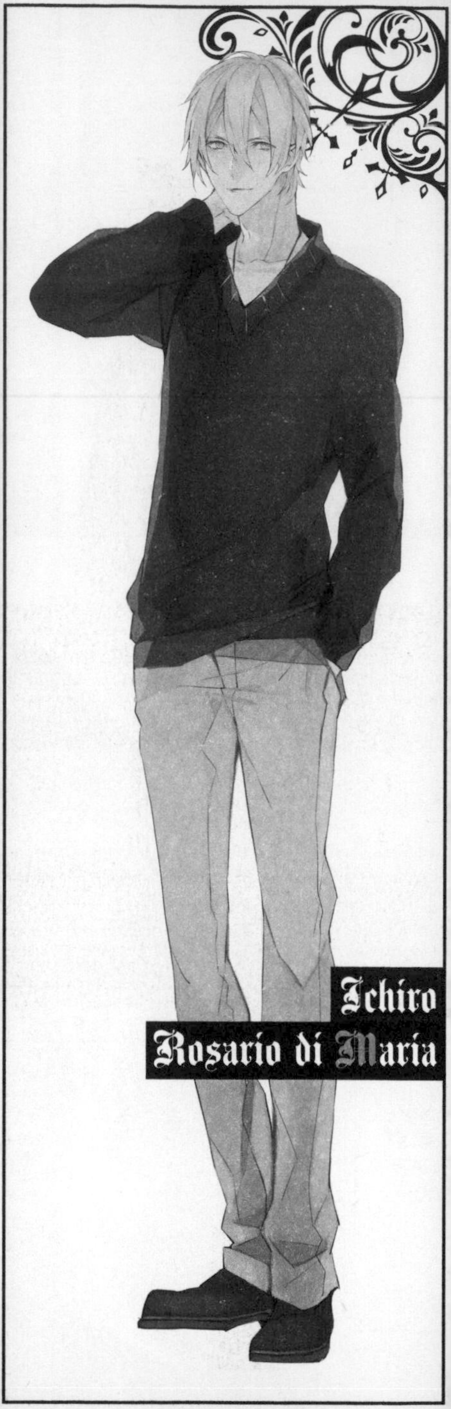
Ichiro
Rosario di Maria

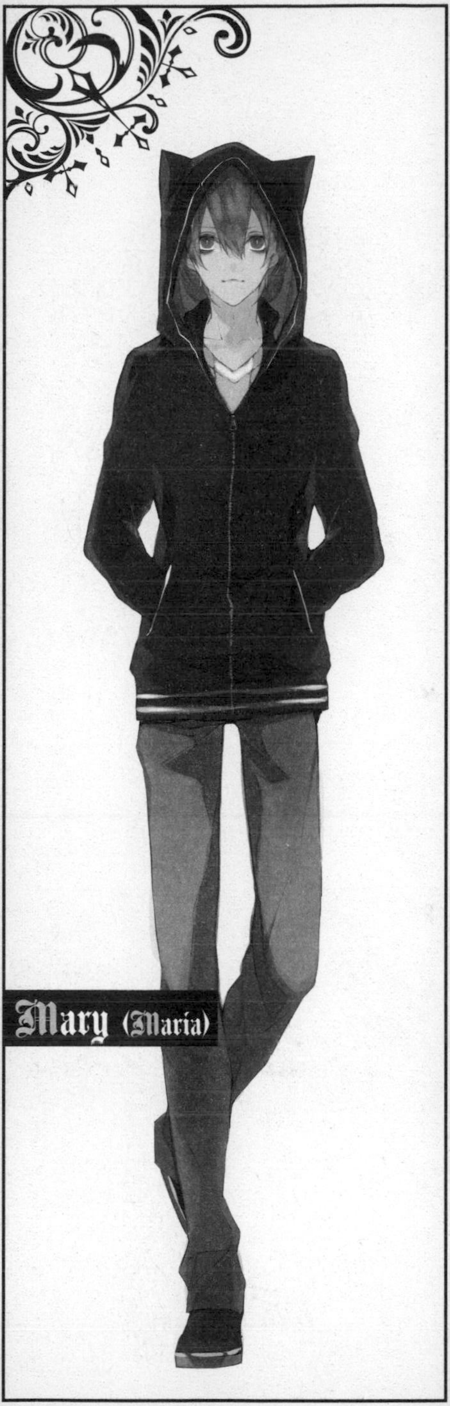
Mary (Maria)

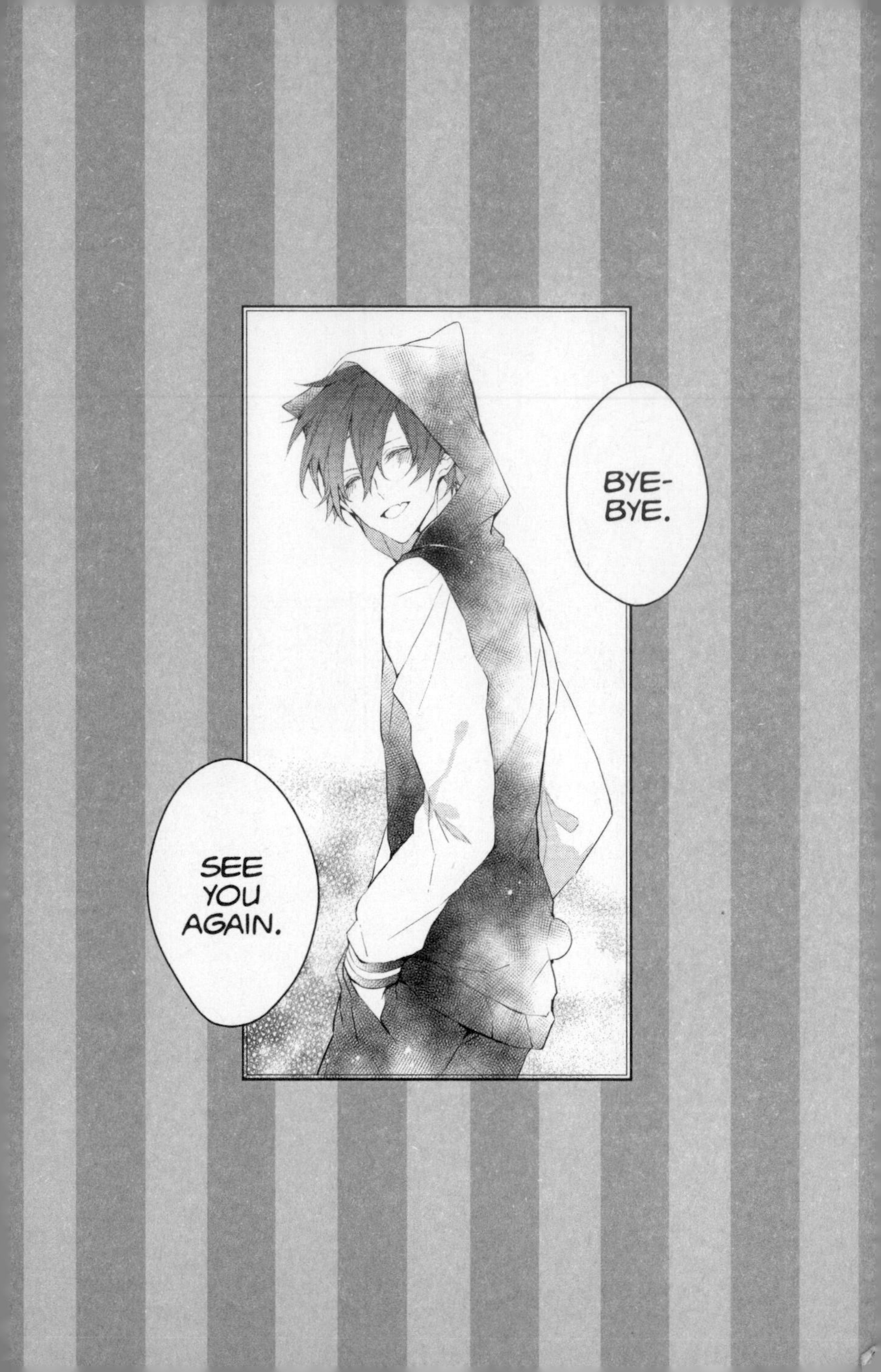
BYE-BYE.
SEE YOU AGAIN.

# Bloody † Mary

Akaza Samamiya

# akaza samamiya

Born November 7, Scorpio, blood type B.
It's the final volume! Thank you so much
for reading all the way to the very end!

# Bloody Mary
Volume 10
Shojo Beat Edition

**story and art by** Akaza Samamiya

**translation** Katherine Schilling
**touch-up art & lettering** Sabrina Heep
**design** Shawn Carrico
**editor** Erica Yee

BLOODY MARY Volume 10
© Akaza SAMAMIYA 2017
First published in Japan in 2017 by KADOKAWA
CORPORATION, Tokyo.
English translation rights arranged with KADOKAWA
CORPORATION, Tokyo.

The stories, characters and incidents mentioned
in this publication are entirely fictional.

Printed in the U.S.A.

Published by VIZ Media, LLC
P.O. Box 77010
San Francisco, CA 94107

10 9 8 7 6 5 4 3 2 1
First printing, March 2018

www.viz.com          www.shojobeat.com

stop

YOU MAY BE READING THE

# wrong way

IT'S TRUE: In keeping with the original Japanese comic format, this book reads from right to left—so action, sound effects and word balloons are completely reversed. This preserves the orientation of the original artwork—plus, it's fun! Check out the diagram shown here to get the hang of things, and then turn to the other side of the book to get started!

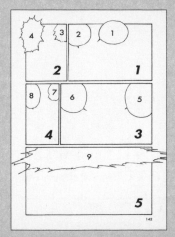